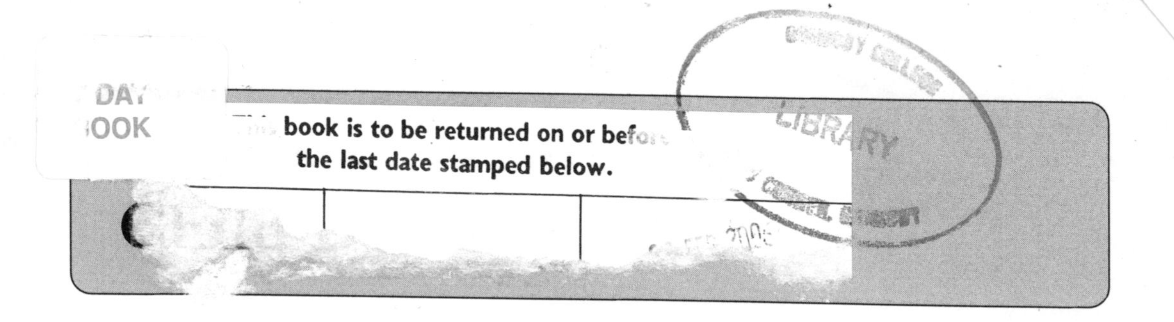

London: Sage, 2002 0761962204

Sage
Foundations
of Psychology
Series

Series editors:
Craig McGarty, Australian National University
Alex Haslam, University of Exeter

Sage Foundations of Psychology is a major new series intended to provide introductory textbooks in all the main areas of psychology. Books in the series are scholarly but written in a lively and readable style, assuming little or no background knowledge. They are suitable for all university students beginning psychology courses, for those studying psychology as a supplement to other courses, and for readers who require a general and up-to-date overview of the major concerns and issues in contemporary psychology.

Already published:

Doing Psychology: an introduction to research methodology and statistics
S. Alexander Haslam and Craig McGarty

Statistics with Confidence: an introduction for psychologists
Michael J. Smithson

An Introduction to Child Development
Thomas Keenan

Forthcoming:

An Introduction to Personality
Nick Haslam

An Introduction to Social Psychology
John Turner

An Introduction to Child Development

Thomas Keenan

SAGE Publications London • Thousand Oaks • New Delhi

First published 2002

Reprinted 2002

SAGE Publications Ltd
6 Bonhill Street
London EC2A 4PU

SAGE Publications Inc
2455 Teller Road
Thousand Oaks, California 91320

SAGE Publications India Pvt Ltd
32, M-Block Market
Greater Kailash – I
New Delhi 110 048

British Library Cataloguing in Publication data

A catalogue record for this book is available
from the British Library

ISBN 0 7619 6219 0
ISBN 0 7619 6220 4 (pbk)

Library of Congress Control Number: 2001131865

Typeset by Mayhew Typesetting, Rhayader, Powys
Printed in Great Britain by The Alden Press, Oxford

This book is dedicated to Kathy, without whom this work would not have come into being

Contents

List of Figures and Tables

Figures

Tables

Foreword

Child development was not originally the field in which I envisioned myself working. My original goal was to become a clinical psychologist. I imagined myself working one on one with intriguing clients who presented with interesting cases – a sort of modern day Sigmund Freud, complete with a well-appointed office and Wednesdays off. As I became more and more aware that this was not an accurate depiction of the life of your average clinical psychologist, my interests (not surprisingly) changed. I came across an opportunity to study at the Ontario Institute for Studies in Education, in Toronto (Canada), where I was first exposed to the idea of working with young children by my supervisor, Professor David Olson. I quickly came to appreciate the intriguing nature of the research that he presented me with an opportunity to conduct, while at the same time, I learned how much fun working with preschoolers could be.

Since that time, I haven't looked back. Conducting research on children's understanding of the world has provided me with a rewarding set of experiences. My studies have looked at topics such as *deception*, *knowledge acquisition*, *surprise*, *language comprehension* and more, with the promise of further interesting work in the wings. Better yet, I still enjoy what I do. In this book, I hope to share with you some of what I think makes the study of child development such an engaging area.

A book such as this requires the support of many people in order to come together. First and foremost, I would like to thank my wife, Kathy, for all of her efforts on my behalf. It is difficult to express how much her support has meant to me through this process. I would also like to thank those from whom I learned about many of the issues which I cover in this book. While the list is a long one, I would like to offer a special note of thanks to John Benjafield who helped me from my undergraduate years through to my Ph.D., and who provided three excellent examples of what a textbook should be. To David Olson, I am extremely grateful for supervising my Ph.D. thesis, exposing me to the study of the child's theory of mind, and helping shape my thinking and writing. To Janet Astington, Robbie Case, and Daniel Keating at the University of Toronto, I offer my thanks for providing such a stimulating graduate environment. During my time as a sessional instructor at Brock University, I had the opportunity to work with many good people but I particularly offer my thanks to Darla MacLean, for allowing me to venture into her research on cognitive development in infancy. Finally, as anyone who has taken on such a project well knows, a good research assistant is invaluable. My own RA was no exception, and thus I offer my gratitude to Subhadra White for her diligence and hard work over the past year.

Tom Keenan

The Principles of Developmental Psychology

1

LEARNING AIMS

At the end of this chapter you should:

- **be able to articulate the principles of a life-span developmental approach**
- **be able to explain the different meanings of *development***
- **be familiar with and able to describe the key issues in the study of child development**
- **be aware of the evidence relevant to both sides of these issues**

Introduction

Life-span developmental psychology is the field of psychology which involves the examination of both constancy and change in human behaviour across the entire life span, that is, from conception to death (Baltes, 1987). Developmental psychologists are concerned with diverse issues ranging from the growth of motor skills in the infant, to the gains and losses observed in the intellectual functioning of the elderly. The goal of study in developmental psychology is to further our knowledge about how development evolves over the entire life span, developing a knowledge of the general principles of development and the differences and similarities in development across individuals. The range of topics comprising the study of modern psychology is vast, and encompasses sub-areas as diverse as social psychology, comparative psychology, the study of learning, neuropsychology, abnormal psychology, and cognitive psychology. However, the study of development is possible *within* each of these areas. Thus, in one sense, developmental psychology can be thought of as an *approach* that one takes to the broader study of psychology (Buss, 1995).

This text focuses on a narrower portion of the life span, specifically, on the time development between conception and adolescence. This area of study is known as the study of **child development**. The study of children is obviously important in its own right but it also has the potential to significantly inform us about the nature of human development. By studying the earlier forms of a behaviour and the changes which behaviour undergoes, we can gain a better understanding of the 'end product', that is, adult behaviour. While this text does focus specifically on children's development, the wider principles of life-span developmental psychology (which we discuss shortly) apply equally to this area as they do to the study of development across the life span.

What is 'development'?

When we speak of **development**, to what, in fact are we referring? One frequently used definition refers to development as *patterns of change over time which begin at conception and continue throughout the life span.* Development occurs in different domains, such as the *biological* (changes in our physical being), *social* (changes in our social relationships), *emotional* (changes in our emotional understanding and experiences), and *cognitive* (changes in our thought processes). Some developmental psychologists prefer to restrict the notion of development only to changes which lead to qualitative reorganizations in the structure of a behaviour, skill or ability (Crain, 2000). For example, Heinz Werner (1957) argued that development refers only to changes which increase the organization of functioning within a domain. Werner believed that development consisted of two processes: **integration** and **differentiation**. Integration refers to the idea that development consists of the integration of more basic, previously acquired behaviours into new, higher level structures. For example, according to Piaget (1952), the baby who learns to successfully reach for objects has learned to coordinate a variety of skills such as maintaining an upright posture, moving the arm, visually coordinating the position of the hand and the object, and grasping the object under an integrated structure called a *scheme*. New developments build on and incorporate what has come before.

Differentiation refers to the idea that development also involves the progressive ability to make more distinctions among things, for example, learning to adjust one's grasp to pick up small objects (which requires the use of the fingers and fine motor control) versus larger objects (which only require closing the hand around the object and less fine motor control). Werner defined development as a combination of these two processes of integration and differentiation; he saw development as a process of increasing hierarchical integration and increasing differentiation. Of course, Werner's view of development is by no means universally accepted within developmental psychology. Many developmentalists argue that anything which evidences change over time is relevant to the study of development (Crain, 2000). Thus, this debate remains a tension within the study of human development.

Principles of life-span development

Paul Baltes (1987) has articulated a set of principles which guide the study of human development within a life-span framework. Baltes argues that these principles form a family of beliefs which specify a coherent view of the nature of development. It is the application of these beliefs as a coordinated whole which characterizes the life-span approach. In this book, although we focus on development in children, we will take a life-span approach to the study of development.

The first of the principles which Baltes (1987) discussed is the belief that *development is lifelong*. This belief has two separate aspects. First, the potential for development extends across the entire life span: there is no assumption that the life course must reach a plateau or decline during adulthood and old age. Second, development may involve processes which are not present at birth but emerge throughout the life span. Development is also *multidimensional* and *multidirectional*. Multidimensionality refers to the fact that development cannot be described by a single criterion such as increases or decreases in a behaviour. The principle of multidirectionality maintains that there is no single, normal path that development must or should take. In other words, healthy developmental outcomes are achieved in a wide variety of ways. Development is often comprised of multiple abilities which take different directions, showing different types of change or constancy. Another principle of development is the belief that development involves both *gains and losses*. According to Baltes, any developmental process involves aspects of growth and decline. For example, formal schooling increases a child's knowledge base and develops their cognitive abilities but also restricts their creativity as they learn to follow rules defined by others. These two aspects of growth and decline need not occur in equal strength, and, moreover, the balance between gains and losses can change with time.

A fifth principle articulated by Baltes (1987) is that development is *plastic*. Plasticity refers to the within-person variability which is possible for a particular behaviour or development. For example, infants who have a hemisphere of the brain removed shortly after birth (as a treatment for epilepsy) can recover the functions associated with that hemisphere as the brain reorganizes itself and the remaining hemisphere takes over those functions. A key part of the research agendas in developmental psychology is to understand the nature and the limits of plasticity in various domains of functioning. The sixth principle states that development is also situated in *contexts* and in *history*. Development varies across the different contexts in which we live our lives. For example, social and rural environments are associated with different sets of factors which have the potential to impact on development; understanding how development differs for individuals within these two settings requires an understanding of the differing contexts. Development is also historically situated; that is, the historical time period in which we grow up affects our development. Finally, Baltes suggests that the study of developmental psychology is *multidisciplinary*. That is, the sources of age-related changes do not lie within the province of any one discipline. For example, psychological methodologies may not be appropriate for understanding factors that are sociological in nature. Rather, an understanding of human development will be achieved only by research conducted from the perspective of disciplines such as sociology, linguistics, anthropology, and computer science.

Contextualism in developmental psychology

As we have seen, Baltes (1987) stressed the importance of contextualism to the study of life-span development. In order to create a coherent framework for understanding contextual influences, Baltes proposed a three-factor model of contextual influences on development (Baltes, Reese, & Lipsitt, 1980). The first factor is **normative age-graded influences**. These are the biological and environmental influences that are similar for individuals in a particular age group. Examples of normative age-graded influences are events such as puberty or the entry into formal schooling. A second type of influences is what Baltes referred to as **normative history-graded influences**. These are biological and environmental influences associated with historical periods in time which influence people of a particular generation. For example, the effects of World War II on much of the world's population or the changes in the structure of government experienced by the people of the Soviet Union during the 1980s would constitute examples of normative history-graded influences.

Nonnormative life events are unusual occurrences that have a major impact on a individual's life. The occurrence of these events is relatively unique to an individual and is not tied to a historical time period. Moreover, the influence of these events often does not follow a typical developmental course. Being struck with a major illness or losing a parent in childhood are examples of this kind of contextual influence. It is important for developmentalists to recognize that explanations of behavioural development are likely to be complex and require consideration of the wide variety of possible influences on a given individual's development.

Chronological age in developmental psychology

The variable which is most often studied in developmental psychology is *age*. **Chronological age**, the time that has elapsed since a person's birth, is found in many developmental studies. Chronological age is commonly examined in developmental research because performance on any given task strongly covaries with age. For example, in the study of child development, we find more often than not that older children perform at a higher level than younger children on a given task or that older children use immature strategies less often than do younger children. However, what do age effects mean to us? Are we any better off for knowing that older children score better on a test than younger children?

It is very important to recognize that chronological age does not *cause* development, but simply reflects the fact that we have existed for a certain amount of time. In other words, age is a *proxy variable* (Hartmann & George, 1999). By proxy variable, we mean that chronological age stands in for other developmental processes we have not measured. When we find a difference between age groups on some variable, all we can say is that there is a performance difference between age groups; what causes the difference is not known unless specific measures are included. Age differences are only a small part of what developmental psychologists examine. The real interest lies in examining what mechanisms cause developmental change and, thus, performance differences between age groups.

Themes and issues in developmental psychology

A number of major themes have emerged in the study of child development, themes which are recurrent across the various domains of study. For example, the debate over whether development is best characterized as driven by biological or environmental factors has guided study within areas as diverse as emotional, social and cognitive development. The same is true for each of the other major themes which we will examine. After you become familiar with each of the issues described here, you should think about these themes as you read Chapters 4 through 10. You should be able to identify where these themes occur when studying the areas of development discussed in the last seven chapters.

Continuity and discontinuity

An important question which continually confronts the researcher in the study of child development is how to best characterize the nature of developmental change. There are two contrasting positions on developmental change. According to those who hold to the first position, development is best viewed as a **continuous** process. That is, development is conceived of as a process of the gradual accumulation of a behaviour, skill, or knowledge. On this model, development proceeds in a smooth and orderly fashion, with each change building on previous abilities. In contrast, those who hold to the second view would suggest that developmental change is best characterized as

discontinuous in nature. These theorists suggest that behaviours or skills often change qualitatively across time, and that new organizations of behaviours, skills, or knowledge emerge in a rather abrupt or discrete fashion. The notion of a **stage** of development is central to discontinuous views of development. A stage of development can be thought of as a particular organization of the child's knowledge and behaviour that characterizes their development at a particular point in time. The movement to a new stage of development means that a qualitative reorganization of previous knowledge or behaviour has taken place. For example, Piaget (1952) believed that between 7 to 11 years of age, children's thinking could be described as concrete, in that it is closely tied to the nature of the objects with which they interact. In contrast, during adolescence, thinking becomes more abstract; it is less bound to particular objects and takes into account the possible or hypothetical. It should be clear that these two positions – development viewed as a continuous process or as a discontinuous process – describe development in quite different ways; ways that on the surface are seemingly difficult to reconcile with one another.

Siegler (1998) has argued that whether a particular aspect of development appears to be continuous or discontinuous in nature depends largely on how we choose to examine development. When we examine the change in a given behaviour at large intervals (e.g., yearly) or in different age groups such as 4-year-olds and 8-year-olds, development will tend to look very discontinuous or stage-like. If we plotted the level of development of some skill over time, the developmental function might look like a staircase, with periods of little change followed by abrupt shifts in the level of performance. In contrast, if we were to examine the behaviour more closely, at smaller intervals, we might find that development took on a much more continuous character. That is, increases in the level of performance would be seen to occur gradually, with no abrupt shifts. We would also find that there is great variability in the methods or strategies that children use to solve problems. Siegler's (1998) own work on children's learning in the domain of mathematics shows that children often use a variety of strategies in their attempts to learn how to add together two numbers. Because learning to decide which strategies work best takes some time, the shifts between the use of different strategies is a gradual process. If we plotted the development of strategy use for addition problems, Siegler claims we would obtain a picture quite different from the staircase model just described. Instead, we would see what he calls 'overlapping waves' of development. The waves occur as the variability in strategy use gradually peaks and declines while the overlap between the waves reflects the fact that children use multiple strategies at the same time. Thus, how we look at development in time has a great deal to do with the picture we obtain. (See Figure 1.1 for an overview of these three models.)

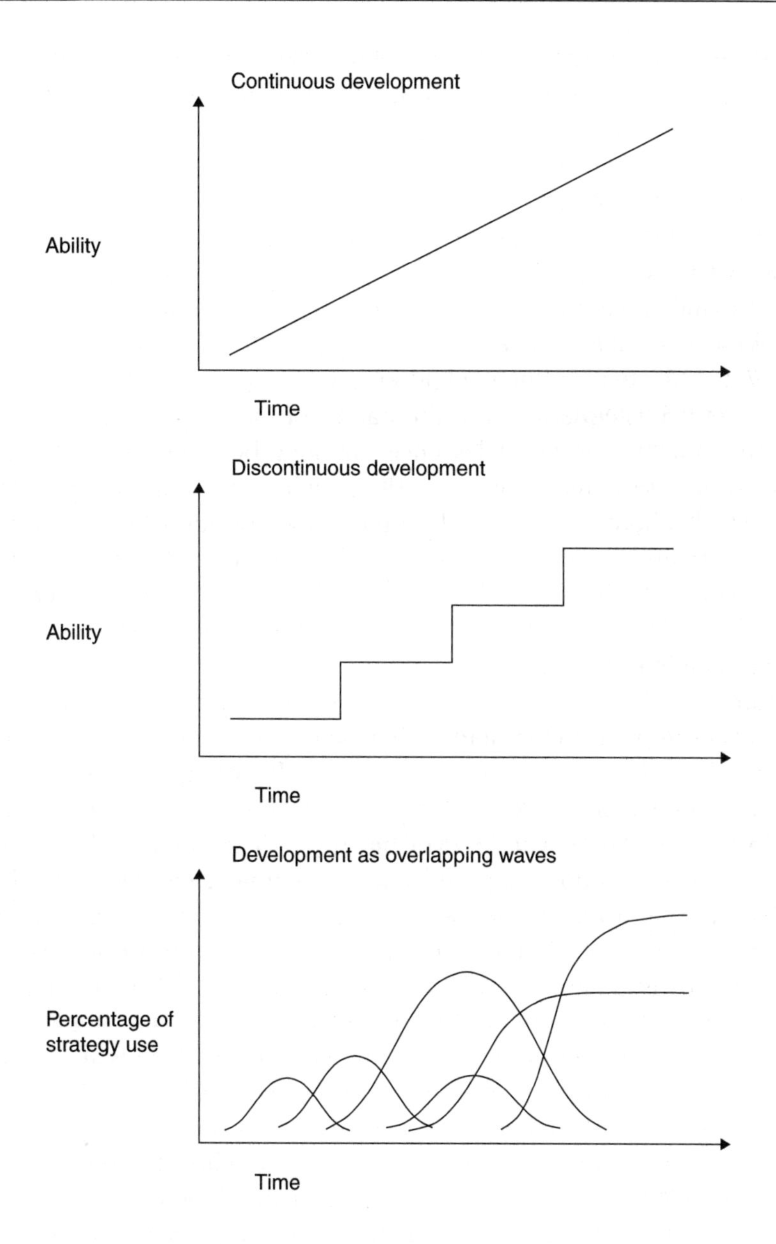

FIGURE 1.1 Models of developmental change

Sternberg and Okagaki (1989) have suggested that the attempt to characterize development as uniformly continuous or discontinuous has the appearance of an unanswerable question, being based on a false presupposition. Instead, Sternberg and Okagaki suggest that a better question to ask is: 'What are the sources of continuity and discontinuity in development?' In their view, 'either–or' debates are misleading: development has both discontinuous and continuous aspects and the real question for developmental psychologists is to find out how these differing aspects arise in the course of development.

Stability and change

Another issue which is of importance to developmental psychologists is the issue of **stability versus change**. Simply put, we can ask whether development is best characterized by stability (for example, does a behaviour or trait such as *shyness* stay stable in its expression over time?) or change (could a person's degree of shyness fluctuate across the life span?). Studies of children have often revealed impressive stability over time in aspects of development such as the attachment bond to their parents (e.g., Sroufe, Egeland, & Kreutzer, 1990) or in personality (Caspi & Silva, 1995). Of course, there is evidence which suggests a contrary view, that change is both possible and indeed, is likely under the appropriate conditions. For example, research on children's temperament (e.g., Thomas & Chess, 1977) raises the possibility that our inherited predispositions to react emotionally in certain ways can be altered by our environment, particularly by the attitudes and behaviours of their caregivers.

An important aspect of the debate on stability versus change has to do with the degree to which early experiences play a formative role in our later development. Freud was one of the first psychologists to emphasize the critical nature of our early experiences for our later development. In Freud's view, how we resolve our sexual and aggressive urges is strongly tied to the nature of our personality as adults. Similarly, Erik Erikson (1963) believed that how we dealt with key issues such as the development of a warm, caring relationship with our parents or the ability to think and act autonomously were important determinants of later developments (although unlike Freud, Erikson made a greater allowance for the different contexts in which children develop). These early theories of human development as well as a great deal of later research suggest that there is a highly stable quality to our development and that early experience is crucial to this stability. In contrast to this position, researchers who have focused on adult development such as Baltes (1987) have emphasized that we are malleable throughout the life span and that later experiences are very important to whether development shows stability or plasticity. Baltes has argued that too little attention has been focused on the aspects of development that support change, and has proposed a methodology for the study of behaviour across the life span which tests the potential for change in behaviour.

One study that has examined the effects of early experience on children's social, physical and cognitive development was conducted by British psychiatrist Sir Michael Rutter and his colleagues. Rutter (Rutter, and the

English and Romanian Adopteer Study Team, 1998) examined the psychological and physical development of Romanian orphans who were adopted into British families after the fall of the Ceaucescu regime in Romania. These Romanian orphans were reared in extremely poor conditions in their native country. As a result, a large proportion of these children showed severe problems including mental retardation, growth deficiencies, and major health problems. The records of the institutions provided data on how long and at what age they had been placed into the institution. As a result, Rutter et al. were able to examine whether the degree of children's recovery from these early experiences was affected by how long they had been institutionalized.

The infants were assessed on their arrival into the United Kingdom (UK) and again, a few years after their arrival. A control group of children adopted within the UK was also included for comparison purposes. At the time of their entry into the UK, the Romanian adoptees were very poorly off when compared to developmental norms for children in the UK. The Romanian adoptees showed deficits on height and weight (more than two standard deviations below the mean) and their cognitive scores indicated that they scored in the mildly retarded range. When the adoptees were compared among themselves in regard to the length of their institutionalization, a number of important differences emerged. The few adopted children who were raised mainly in a family environment (experiencing less than two weeks of institutional care) were markedly better off in terms of their physical and cognitive development scores than their peers who spent much longer periods in institutional care. Given the significant deficits in both physical and cognitive development observed in this group, you might reasonably infer that their future prospects were poor.

However, the long-term follow up of these children revealed a rather different picture. When the Romanian adoptees were compared to the control group of children adopted within the UK, a high level of **catch-up growth** was observed. Catch-up growth refers to the tendency to rapid recovery with the establishment of normal environmental conditions (as opposed to the privation which caused the initial deficit). In comparison to the control group, the Romanian adoptees showed substantial catch-up growth, attaining similar levels of height, weight and head circumference (although the Romanian adoptees were still on average slightly smaller than the control group). The findings in regard to cognitive growth were similarly impressive. Infants who were placed in adoptive families before the age of 6 months scored no differently on the cognitive measures than the control group. For those infants placed in families after having between 6 to 24 months of institutional care, there were significant differences in comparison to the control group: the Romanian adoptees scored significantly lower on the cognitive measure, although the mean score was well within the normal range for children of their age. Rutter et al. highlight the possibility that catch-up growth is not yet complete in this group of children.

The authors also note that, although the degree of recovery of the adopted children was very high, it is too early to tell whether there will be other long-term effects associated with their early environment. Further follow-up research is required. In short, the findings of this study suggest that, while early experiences are clearly associated with negative child outcomes, recovery of functioning is very possible. Thus, children's early experiences are not necessarily associated with long-term consequences as some researchers have suggested.

Maturation versus experience in development: the nature–nurture debate

Of all of the issues which have aroused debate within the study of child development and developmental psychology, the **nature versus nurture issue** has generated the most controversy by far. This may be due to the fact that unlike the other debates we have discussed, the nature–nurture question (as it is often called) focuses on the question of the best explanation for how development takes place. The issue is usually posed as a debate between two positions regarding the relative roles of biological and environmental factors in development. **Nature** refers to the position that our genetic inheritance, through the process of heredity, is the primary influence on development. In contrast, **nurture** refers to the position that the environment (broadly construed as children's experiences, including parenting, education, learning, cultural influences) is primarily responsible for development.

In developmental psychology's past, extreme positions have been taken on the nature–nurture debate. Arnold Gesell (1928) was a strong advocate of the position that the course of our development was largely dictated by genetic factors. Our genetic heritage specifies the set of biological processes which determine the patterns of growth that we observe, which Gesell referred to as **maturation**. Simply put, maturation is the sequence of growth which is specified and controlled by our genes. Gesell used studies of identical twins to study how experience and maturation lead to development (see Chapter 4). His studies compared twins given special experience learning a particular skill to the other twin who was given no such experience. Gesell's findings consistently showed that the acquisition of the behaviours was relatively unaffected by the special training; that is, the untrained twin tended to acquire the behaviour as quickly as the trained twin.

In contrast to Gesell's maturationist position, John B. Watson (1928) argued for the dominance of the environment on children's development. Watson believed that genetic factors placed no limits on how environments could shape the course of children's development. Watson was famous for his boast that, given the ability to manipulate the environment to his own standards, he could shape the development of any child:

> Give me a dozen healthy infants, well-formed, and my own specified world to bring them up in, and I'll guarantee to take any one at random and train him to become any type of specialist I might select – doctor, lawyer, artist, merchant-chief, and yes, even beggar-man and thief, regardless of his talents, penchants, tendencies, abilities, vocations, and race of his ancestors. (Watson, 1930: 104)

While Watson was never able to make good on his boast, he did show how environmental experiences played a role in shaping children's behaviour through the processes of **classical conditioning**, a type of learning in which a stimulus can come to evoke a response after the repeated pairing of the two stimuli (Watson, 1928).

The positions held by Gesell and Watson regarding the relative roles of maturation and environment on development are essentially extremist positions which are no longer supported in light of current research on child development. Today, most developmental psychologists recognize that nature and nurture both play an important role in development. Rather than discussing nature *versus* nurture, we commonly talk about the interaction between nature *and* nurture. Given the widespread recognition that both nature and nurture play crucial roles in shaping development, the challenge which lies before us now is to examine the interplay between biological and environmental factors, figuring out how they interact to produce developmental change. The interaction between nature and nurture, referred to as **epigenesis**, has been characterized as being less of an answer to the nature–nurture debate than as a starting point for the study of development (Elman, Bates, Johnson, Karmiloff-Smith, Parisi & Plunkett, 1996). Elman et al. (1996) point out that the interactionist position is certainly the correct position to take on the nature–nurture debate. However, they argue that future research needs to specify exactly how nature and nurture interact to produce development if an interactionist position is to be anything other than 'lip service' to the debate.

One way we can approach the interaction between nature and nurture is through an examination of the extent to which our biological programming can be altered by environmental influences (Dellarosa Cummins & Cummins, 1999; Elman et al., 1996). The biologist C.H. Waddington (1975) used the term **canalization** to refer to this phenomenon. In other words, is the genetic influence on a particular development robust across varied environments or does it show susceptibility to change? Highly canalized behaviours are relatively unaltered by changes in the environment. For example, the tendency to acquire a language is a highly canalized development in that it occurs across a wide degree of environmental variation. In contrast, some behaviours are easily modified by environmental factors and are less canalized. Intelligence is a trait which is dramatically altered by environmental variations (e.g., Bronfenbrenner & Crouter, 1983). For example, it is well documented that children who grow up in enriched environments tend to show higher levels of achievement than children growing up in impoverished environments. Studying the relative canalization of different developments has the potential to shed light on the nature of epigenesis.

Our biology is continuously influenced by our environment, our behaviour, and our activity. At the same time, our experience of our environment is continuously influenced by our biological inheritance. Trying to divide the causes of behaviour into parts assignable to nature and parts assignable to nurture is futile; nature and nurture are engaged in a continuous and reciprocal interaction. The attempt to separate their influences as has been done in the past leads to an oversimplified and incomplete picture of human development.

The structure of the book

One of the goals in writing this book is to provide you with a brief but reasonably comprehensive survey of some of the key issues in the field of child development. This first chapter was intended to provide you with a background to the study of child development by locating the field as a branch within the study of developmental psychology, highlighting the principles which guide the study of development from a life span approach, and introducing you to some important concepts and key issues within the contemporary study of child development. Hopefully by this point, you will understand what you are getting yourself into by pursuing this text. Thus, this would seem a good time to discuss what topics are covered in the remaining chapters.

In Chapter 2, we will survey a number of theories that are relevant to the study of child development. Some of these theories are more important from a historical perspective, whereas others are theories that are relatively recent statements which are gaining increasing attention from developmental psychologists as important ways for conceptualizing developmental issues. Chapter 2 also takes up the question of what theories are and what role they play in the study of psychology. Chapter 3 follows up on Chapter 2 by addressing the issues surrounding how developmental psychologists actually go about the business of conducting research on children's development. In Chapter 3, we take up issues involving ways of obtaining information from children, the various types of research designs employed by developmental psychologists, and specific methods for examining change over time.

In the remaining chapters, we survey a number of the most important areas in child development. This survey is by no means a complete one; there are a great many other topics which could have been addressed. Recall our discussion of developmental psychology as an *approach* one takes to a particular area. Based on this, you'll recognize that this text could be as broad as the field of psychology itself. However, the decision regarding which areas to include was not made lightly, and it is safe to say that most of the critical areas in child development are discussed in this text. While you may find some area in which you are particularly interested was missed entirely or touched on only briefly, this book should hopefully provide you with a solid foundation on which to build a more in-depth understanding of the issues which capture your imagination as a student of psychology.

In Chapter 4 we examine the biological foundations of development, that is, the patterns of physical growth, motor development, and the structure of the human brain. In many areas of child development, knowledge of these biological structures and the patterns of change they undergo is critical to developing a deeper understanding of seemingly unrelated topics, from children's memory development to their sexual identity. We finish Chapter 4 by dealing with the influence of hereditary influences on child development through the study of genes and their effects on behaviour.

Chapter 5 covers the development of perceptual abilities by looking at change in each of the five senses from birth through to early childhood and sometimes beyond. In contrast to early conceptualizations of the infant's experience of the world as a 'blooming, buzzing confusion' we see that infants are born with a remarkable ability to make sense of their world which develops extremely rapidly over the first few months of life. Chapter 6 takes up the study of cognitive development, that is, the child's ability to think and reason about the world. Instead of covering specific topics such as the growth of memory or problem-solving ability, we look at three very different and critically important theoretical frameworks for the study of cognitive development. A solid understanding of the theories covered in Chapter 6 will provide you with a strong foundation on which to build a further understanding of human cognition, whether in children or adults. Given the centrality of the study of cognition to an understanding of human behaviour, the hope is that this approach will prove helpful to you in your study of psychology or of the many other disciplines where an understanding of human cognition is important (e.g., economics, consumer behaviour, or linguistics).

Chapter 7 provides an introduction to the study of language development. Language is a behaviour which children acquire very rapidly, as you will undoubtedly have observed for yourself or heard about from your own parents. As we will see, the process of language acquisition begins early in infancy and is well underway before children use their first words.

Chapter 8 takes up the study of emotional development. After a brief consideration of the seemingly simple question 'what are emotions?', we look at some of the most important issues in this area including the course of emotional development (e.g., from the first facial expressions to the ability to experience simultaneous and conflicting emotions), how we learn to control our emotions, the emotional bond between caregivers and children, and finally, the concept of *temperament*, what many psychologists think of as our 'emotional nature'.

In Chapter 9, the concept of social development is introduced. As you will learn, the study of social development includes elements of cognition, language, and emotional development, which explains why this chapter follows these others. Chapter 9 introduces you to diverse topics such as the growth of social relations, the nature and functions of play, how conceptions of friendship change with age, the importance of being accepted by one's peers, and the development of an understanding of the important role of *minds* in social behaviour.

Finally, we address the issue of psychopathology from a developmental perspective. In Chapter 10, we examine the tenets of the *developmental psychopathology* approach, discuss the measurement of psychopathology, look at some common disorders of childhood (e.g., depression, anxiety, autism, and conduct disorder), the issues of *risk* and *resiliency*, and finally, issues surrounding the prevention and treatment of psychopathology in childhood.

How to use this book

By this point, you will likely have noticed that throughout this chapter, some words have appeared in **bold** type. Words that appear in bold indicate key concepts that you should understand, remember, and be able to describe. A useful method to enhance your ability to remember the meaning of these terms is to think the definition through carefully and recast it in your own words. It is also very helpful to associate new terms with examples from the text so that you can illustrate the meaning in a more concrete fashion. Finally, each chapter contains a glossary – a list of these important concepts which should allow you to look up terms quickly and easily.

I have purposefully tried to make this a readable text. Hopefully you will find it easy to read and pitched at the right level for a student being introduced to the topic for the first time. Unlike many other texts, this book does not use many illustrations to make the points that I feel are important to get across to the student of child development. Instead, my hope is that you will feel as excited about this field as I do, and that, as a result, you will be motivated to read, reflect on, and think through the material contained in these chapters and use it as the foundation for developing a greater knowledge of theory and research in the contemporary study of child development.

Glossary

Canalization refer to the extent to which our biological programming can be altered by environmental influences.

Catch-up growth refers to the tendency to the rapid recovery of physical growth (after a period of deprivation) with the establishment of normal environmental conditions.

Child development is the study of development between conception and adolescence.

Chronological age is the time which has elapsed since an individual's birth.

Classical conditioning is a type of learning in which a new stimulus can come to evoke a familiar response after the repeated pairing of the new stimulus with a stimulus which already evokes the response.

Continuous refers to the idea that developmental change can be characterized as a process of gradual change, progressing in a smooth and orderly fashion.

Development refers to patterns of change over time which begin at conception and continue throughout the life span.

Differentiation refers to the idea that development involves the progressive ability to make more distinctions among stimuli, concepts or behaviours.

Discontinuous refers to the idea that developmental change is best characterized as occurring in an abrupt and discrete fashion, rather than in a gradual, orderly fashion. The idea that development occurs in stages is central to the discontinuous view.

Epigenesis refers to the interaction between nature and nurture.

Integration refers to the idea that development consists of the integration of more basic, previously acquired behaviours into new, higher level structures.

Life-span developmental psychology is the field of psychology which involves the examination of both constancy and change in human behaviour across the entire life span.

Maturation is a sequence of growth which is specified and controlled by our genes.

Nature refers to the position on the *nature–nurture issue* that our genetic inheritance is the primary influence on development.

Nature versus nurture refers to the debate regarding the relative roles of biology and experience in human development. 'Nature' refers to the biological factors and 'nurture' to environmental factors.

Normative age-graded influences are the biological and environmental influences that are similar for individuals in a particular age group.

Normative history-graded influences are the biological and environmental influences associated with historical periods in time and which influence people of a particular generation.

Nonnormative life events are unusual occurrences that have a major impact on a individual's life. The occurrence of these events is relatively unique to an individual and is not tied to a particular historical time period.

Nurture refers to the position on the *nature–nurture issue* that the environment is primarily responsible for developmental outcomes.

Stability versus change is the debate over whether a particular trait or behaviour is best characterized by stability over time or by change.

Stage is a particular organization of knowledge and behaviour that can be used to characterize a child's level of development at a particular point in time.

Theories of Development

2

LEARNING AIMS

At the end of this chapter you should:

- **be able to explain the importance and function of theories**
- **be aware of and able to explain the essence of each of the theoretical positions covered**
- **be able to define and give examples of the key concepts associated with each of the theoretical positions covered**

What is a theory?

A theory is an interconnected, logical system of concepts that provides a framework for organizing and understanding observations. The function of a theory is to allow us to understand and predict the behaviour of some aspect of the world (e.g., the tendency of an object to slide down an inclined plane or the ability to infer the feelings of a friend from their behaviour). Theories can be either **formal** or **informal**; what differentiates formal from informal theories is how explicit the concepts which make up the theory are made. Formal theories take the form of an interconnected set of hypotheses, definitions, axioms, and laws, each of which is an explicit concept which fits with or can be deducted from the overall theory (Miller, 1993). Formal theories can be expressed in a variety of ways: using ordinary language; in mathematical form; or sometimes in the form of logical principles. Ideally, a formal theory should be logically consistent and contain no contradictions, fit well with empirical observations (rather than be contradicted by them), be testable, be as simple as possible, and should cover a reasonable range of phenomena (Miller, 1993). In contrast, informal theories take a less rigorous form than formal theories; they are often little more than organized sets of intuitions or expectations about our world (these informal theories are often referred to as *implicit theories*). In developmental psychology, we have no formal theories of human development (Miller, 1993), although most theories of child development are somewhat more developed than the intuitive expectations about human behaviour that we all hold. However, we can evaluate developmental theories in terms of how likely they are to develop into formal theories using the criteria for a formal theory.

A good theory must state the range of phenomena it is trying to explain. For example, a theory of intellectual development may include hypotheses about the evolution of the brain, or the growth of symbolic abilities, but we would not expect the theory to explain changes in motor ability. Understanding the focus of a theory helps us identify its **range of applicability**, that is, the range of phenomena to which it properly applies. We must also know what **assumptions** a theory is based on. Assumptions are the guiding premises underlying the logic of a theory. For example, evolutionary psychologists take for granted the assumption that natural selection is the only process which can produce changes in physical structures of an organism over time. In order to properly evaluate a theory, you must first understand what its assumptions are. This is because the assumptions of a theory may be questionable or even incorrect. Assumptions may be influenced by cultural contexts and belief systems, by the sample the researcher was observing, or by the current knowledge base of the field.

Now that we know what a theory is, we can ask 'what do theories do?' First, theories are constructed to organize and interpret our observations of the world and to help us identify orderly relationships among many diverse events. They help us to distinguish factors which are central to understanding a behaviour from factors which are only related in a peripheral way. Our theories give meaning to the facts we discover about the world, serving as a framework within which to interpret facts and integrate new information with previously acquired knowledge. Second, theories guide the acquisition of new knowledge. The statement of a theory should make specific predictions which can be tested. Theories can also cause us to reinterpret knowledge which we have previously acquired; that is, the formulation of a theory may require us to look more carefully at factors we had previously taken for granted or ignored. For more on the role of theories in the study of psychology, see Haslam and McGarty (1998).

According to Miller (1993), theories of human development differ from other theories in a particular way. The critical aspect of developmental theories is a focus on change over time in some particular behaviour or domain of functioning. Miller further argues that any developmental theory should manage three tasks. First, it needs to describe change within a given domain or domains. For example, if one is proposing a theory of emotional development, a good theory would describe what the development of emotion looks like: are there particular emotional states which proceed or follow others? Do we come endowed with any emotional expressions and, if so, how do these change or remain stable with development? Second, it needs to describe changes in the relationships between domains. For example, do changes in cognitive functioning give rise to changes in social or emotional functioning? Third, it should explain how the changes in behaviour that have been described take place; that is, what accounts for the transitions between different states of development? Are the observed changes a function of maturation, learning, or an interaction of both? A developmental theory needs a clear description of the mechanisms which guide change.

Now that we have considered what a theory is and what it should provide, let us next examine a selection of theories which are currently used or have previously been important to the study of child development.

Theories of human development

In this section, we review a number of the most important theories of child development. Some theories such as Freud's psychosexual theory of development are discussed not because they are currently important to the field of child development, but for their historical value to the discipline. Other theories are discussed because of their current importance to the field.

While there are a large number of theories of human development, the search for underlying commonalities across these theories has revealed that all developmental theories can be classified as based on at least one of two philosophical models (Dixon & Lerner, 1999): **organicism** and **mechanism**. These models detail the assumptions about the nature of human development that underlie the various theories which we will review here. Models based on organicism stress the qualitative features of developmental change and emphasize the organism's role in bringing about these changes; that is, organicism focuses on developmental change which is a reorganization based on previous forms and is not simply a change in the quantity of a given behaviour. In contrast, mechanistic theories stress quantitative changes in behaviour and emphasize that factors outside the control of the organism play the major role in developmental change. Of course, not all theories of development are based exclusively on one model; some theories have adopted elements of both mechanism and organicism to explain human development. As we review each of the theories, see if you can classify the theories discussed in terms of whether they subscribe to organicism, mechanism, or some combination of the two positions.

Psychodynamic theory

Modern **psychodynamic** theories of human behaviour and development have their roots in the thinking of Sigmund Freud (1856–1939). While there are few psychologists who are strict adherents to Freudian theory (which we discuss later), psychodynamic theories continue to influence many theorists.

At their heart, psychodynamic theories emphasize the belief that forces or dynamics within the individual are responsible for our behaviour. In general, psychodynamic theories (although Erikson's work is an exception) are more influential in therapeutic contexts than they are in developmental theory. However, as Dixon and Lerner (1999) suggest, psychodynamic theories have exerted an influence on developmental theory, thus it would be unwise to ignore them.

In his theory of human personality, Freud stressed the formative nature of early experience and of biologically based drives; his belief was that development is the result of a balance being struck between unconscious drives and a conscious need to adapt one's self to the reality in which we find ourselves. Freud (1917) believed that our personality is made up of three structures: the **id**, the **ego**, and the **superego**. The id is the part of our personality which is made up of instinctual drives. The id operates according to what Freud termed the **pleasure principle**; that is, the id is directed towards maximizing its pleasure in an immediate fashion. Freud believed that the id dominated an infant's behaviour. As we develop and our instincts come into conflict with reality, the ego emerges. The ego works to satisfy our drives but does so in a socially acceptable manner; it attempts to gratify our needs through constructive and socially appropriate methods. For example, the ego redirects aggressive urges such as a desire to lash out physically at another into more socially acceptable forms such as verbal aggression or vigorous physical play. As the ego operates in this fashion, we begin to internalize the values of our parents and the wider society around us, forming the structure that Freud called the superego. During the preschool years, children accept their parents' values and take these on in the form of their conscience as they apply these standards to their own behaviour. The ego now takes on the role of arbitrating between the id and the superego in an attempt to satisfy both sets of demands. According to Freud, the dynamics of this struggle, occurring during early childhood, sets the stage for our adult personality.

In Freud's view, development is a discontinuous process. Freud postulated five stages of development in his theory of psychosexual development: the *oral*, *anal*, *phallic*, *latency*, and *genital* stages. Each stage revolves around the movement of sexual impulses from one **erogenous zone** to the next. In the first year and a half of life, during the oral stage of development, the infant's pleasure is centred around the mouth and involves behaviours such as biting, chewing, and sucking as the sources of pleasure. The behaviours infants engage in change during the second year as they enter the anal stage and their pleasure becomes centred around the eliminative function. A potential source of conflict during this stage is the child's desire to immediately expel faeces coming up against their parents' attempts to train the child into waiting to use the toilet. The phallic stage, which occurs from about the ages of three to six years is centred around the genitals and the discovery that their own genitalia provide them with a sense of pleasure. During the phallic stage, Freud believed that children must cope with a sexual attraction to the opposite sex parent which must eventually be relinquished and replaced by an identification with the same sex parent. This process of identification leads to the latency stage, which lasts until puberty, during which the child suppresses sexual drives and instead focuses on developing social and intellectual skills. Finally, during the genital stage which occurs during puberty, the sexual desires reawaken and the adolescent looks for appropriate peers (instead of family) to which to direct their sexual drives.

Freud's theory was influential in that it focused developmentalists' attention on the role of early experiences in personality formation. It also emphasized a view of development as shaped by the dynamics of the conflict between the individual's biological drives and society's restrictions on the expression of these drives, which many subsequent theorists (such as Erik Erikson) found inspiring. Finally, Freud's theory, notwithstanding the many negative assessments it has faced, has been a rich source of hypotheses about development (Miller, 1993). Despite all of these benefits, Freud's theory has been heavily criticized. Freud focused largely on males (as exemplified by his labelling the second phase of development 'phallic'), and neglected to examine issues which might be important to the development of females. In addition, Freud's theory relied mainly on the use of methods such as free association, and the use of dream analysis, which make scientific tests of his theory difficult, if not impossible. Most tellingly, when Freud's claims have been put to the test, many of the most significant claims have not been supported by empirical tests. Thus, Freud's views do not stand up well to modern psychology's demand for scientific validation.

Psychoanalytic theory has been revised significantly and has spawned many offshoots or schools of thought such as *object relations theory*. Modern psychoanalysts emphasize the role of unconscious processes in our behaviour, but place less emphasis on sexual and aggressive instincts and spend more effort highlighting the importance of experience and an understanding of one's life history.

Psychosocial theory

In contrast to Freud's emphasis on sexual and aggressive drives, Erik Erikson (1902–1990) proposed a theory of development which emphasized the role of social and cultural factors in development. In addition, Erikson's theory did not characterize development as ending with adolescence but proposed a true life-span developmental theory which suggests development continues through to old age.

Erikson (1963) believed that human development is best understood as the interaction of three different systems: the *somatic* system, the **ego** system, and the *societal* system. The somatic system is all of those biological processes necessary for the functioning of the individual. The ego system includes those processes central to thinking and reasoning. Finally, the societal system is those processes by which a person becomes integrated into their society. Thus, Erikson's psychosocial approach focuses the study of development on the interaction between changes in these three systems.

Erikson (1963) took a discontinuous view to development, believing that each of us progresses through eight stages of development. Erikson viewed these stages as occurring in an orderly sequence and he believed that each individual must pass through the stages in this order. At each stage, the individual is confronted with a unique **crisis**, an age-related task, which must be faced and resolved by the individual. How successfully an individual resolves each crisis determines the nature of further development: successful resolutions lead to healthier developmental outcomes while unsuccessful or incomplete resolutions lead to less optimal outcomes. In addition, at each stage of development, the accomplishments from the previous stage serve as resources to be applied towards mastering the present crisis or challenge. Each stage is unique and leads to the acquisition of new skills and capabilities.

As noted, Erikson proposed eight stages of psychosocial development: (1) basic trust versus mistrust (birth to 1 year); (2) autonomy versus shame and doubt (1 to 3 years); (3) initiative versus guilt (3 to 6 years); (4) industry versus inferiority (6 to 11 years); (5) identity versus identity diffusion (adolescence); (6) intimacy versus isolation (young adulthood); (7) generativity versus stagnation (middle adulthood); (8) ego integrity versus despair (old age) (see Table 2.1). In what follows, we briefly consider the task of development at each of the eight stages of life proposed by Erikson.

During infancy (*trust/mistrust*), the infant's first task is to develop a sense of trust and a sense of comfort in their caregivers, and eventually, in their environment and in themselves; infants who fail to resolve this crisis in a positive manner may end up mistrusting both themselves and others. During the second stage (*autonomy/shame and doubt*), the infant develops a sense of their independence and autonomy. However, shame and doubt in one's self may arise if the child is forced into activities which they do not choose. In the third stage (*initiative/guilt*), the young child develops a sense of initiative, a desire to master their environment. However, guilt can arise if the child shows too much aggression or is irresponsible. During middle childhood (*industry/inferiority*), children are keen to master intellectual and social challenges but failures may lead to feelings of inferiority and incompetence. During adolescence (*identity/identity diffusion*), individuals strive to discover who they are, that is, to develop a self-identity. Adolescents who fail to adequately explore alternative pathways

TABLE 2.1 Erikson's eight stages of development

Stage of development	Age	Crisis
Trust vs. mistrust	Birth to 1 year	Developing a sense of trust in caregivers, the environment, and one's self
Autonomy vs. shame and doubt	1 to 3 years	Developing a sense of one's autonomy and independence from the caregiver
Initiative vs. guilt	3 to 6 years	Developing a sense of mastery over aspects of one's environment, coping with challenges and assumption of increasing responsibility
Industry vs. inferiority	6 years to adolescence	Mastering intellectual and social challenges
Identity vs. identity diffusion	Adolescence (12 to 20 years)	Developing a self-identity, that is, a knowledge of what kind of a person one is
Intimacy vs. isolation	Young adulthood (20 to 40 years)	Developing stable and intimate relationships with another person
Generativity vs. stagnation	Middle adulthood (40 to 60 years)	Creating something so that one can avoid feelings of stagnation
Integrity vs. despair	Old age (60 years +)	Evaluating one's life by looking back; developing a sense of integrity through this evaluative process

for themselves or who allow their identity to be determined by parents and others may experience confusion about who they are. During young adulthood (*intimacy/isolation*), the task is to achieve a stable and intimate sexual relationship with another person. How well the individual has resolved previous crises (e.g., learning to trust others; making friends and developing social skills) will determine how successful the individual is in achieving intimacy with others; individuals who cannot achieve intimacy are vulnerable to isolation. In middle adulthood (*generativity/stagnation*), the creation of something, whether it is children or something more abstract like ideas or art becomes the central task. The failure to express one's self in this way can lead to feelings of stagnation and the feeling that one has no meaningful accomplishments. Finally, in old age (*ego integrity/despair*) we look back and assess our lives. The individual who has resolved previous stages in a negative fashion will tend to look back on their lives with a feeling of despair and gloom while the individual who has been successful will look back on a life well spent and can derive a sense of integrity.

Erikson's theory of development has been criticized as taking the form of a loosely connected set of ideas which lacks a systematic quality, rather than as a coherent theory of development (Miller, 1993). Concepts such as *generativity* are used in a way that is different from their normal meaning and thus they are somewhat difficult to understand. More problematic is the fact that his theory is difficult to test empirically. Finally, Erikson's theory proposes no specific mechanisms for how development occurs, that is, how a person moves from one stage to the next. It *describes* the roles of factors such as maturation and social forces but fails to clearly state *how* these factors create movement between stages. Despite its weaknesses, Erikson's theory has a number of strengths. One of these was Erikson's push to widen the scope of psychoanalytic theory through the integration of social and cultural factors in development. Erikson also stimulated a renewed interest in topics such as the development of a sense of identity in adolescence (e.g., Waterman, 1985) and generativity in adulthood (Hawkins & Dollahite, 1997).

Behaviourism and social learning theory

Modern behaviourist theory began with the work of John B. Watson (1878–1958). Watson wanted to create an objective science of psychology and he believed that directly observable events should be the focus of the study, not hypothetical internal constructs like Freud's *id,* and *ego* or the cognitive psychologist's appeal to constructs such as *mind.* Watson (Watson & Raynor, 1920) applied Pavlov's principles of classical conditioning to children's behaviour. In one of his most famous research programmes Watson trained Albert, a 9-month-old baby, to fear a neutral stimulus (a white rat) after presenting it several times in the company of a loud sound (clanging an iron bar behind the infant's head). While initially Albert reached out to touch the rat, he soon learned to fear the rat, crying and turning his head away from the sight of the animal. On the basis of findings like these, Watson concluded that the environment was the most important factor in child development. Watson believed that children could be moulded in any direction adults desired if they carefully controlled stimulus–response associations. Watson and his fellow behaviourists eschewed all notions that cognitive processes intervened in the shaping of the individual. In Watson's behaviourism, learning became the key element in explaining development, whereas biological factors were relegated to the sidelines and believed to be important only in providing a basic foundation for learned responses.

Another variant of behaviourism was B.F. Skinner's **operant conditioning** theory. According to this theory, the likelihood of a child's behaviour reoccurring can be increased by following it with a wide variety of rewards or **reinforcers**, things such as praise or a friendly smile. Furthermore, Skinner believed that the likelihood of behaviour can be decreased with the use of **punishments** such as the withdrawal of privileges, parental disapproval, or being sent alone to one's room. In other words, reward increases the likelihood of a behaviour reoccurring while punishment decreases the likelihood of its reoccurring. The result of Skinner's work was that operant conditioning became broadly applied to the study of child development.

A variant of traditional behaviourist views on development comes from the work of Albert Bandura (1977, 1989) on **social learning theory**. Bandura believed that the principles of conditioning and reinforcement elaborated by Skinner and others were important mechanisms of development, but he expanded on how children and adults acquired new responses. Bandura is responsible for an extensive line of laboratory research demonstrating that **observational learning** (often referred to as **modelling**), is the basis of the development of a wide variety of behaviours, such as *aggression*, *helping*, *sharing*, and even *sex-typed responses*. Bandura recognized that, from an early age, children acquire many skills in the absence of rewards and punishments, simply by watching and listening to others around them. However, children do not imitate everyone around them; children are more selective, being drawn towards models who are warm and powerful and who possess desirable objects and characteristics.

Bandura continues to influence much of the work in the area of children's and adult's social development (Rubin, Coplan, Nelson, Cheah & Lagace-Seguin, 1999). Over time, Bandura's theory has become increasingly cognitive (e.g., Bandura, 1989, 1992), acknowledging that children's ability to listen, remember, and abstract general rules from complex sets of observed behaviour affects their imitation and their learning. In Bandura's more recent work, his emphasis has been on the development of a sense of **self-efficacy**, beliefs about one's own effectiveness and competence that guide one's ability to cope with particular situations such as difficult academic problems at school. According to Bandura, children develop a sense of self-efficacy through observation, watching others comment on their own behaviour and developing standards based on these experiences. Thus, children who are exposed to positive models who demonstrate qualities such as persistence are likely to develop a stronger sense of self-efficacy than children exposed to models that demonstrate less positive qualities such as giving up in response to frustration.

A strength of Bandura's social learning theory is its emphasis on particular aspects of the environment, such as the nature of the role models available to children, which can impact on their development. In addition, social learning theory is easily testable (Miller, 1993): the variables of interest are clearly defined and its hypotheses are stated in a precise fashion. The resultant testing of the theory has led to substantial revisions such as its increased emphasis on cognitive factors. At the same time, the cognitive model which underlies the theory has been criticized for being poorly worked out in comparison to information processing theories which present detailed models of cognitive processes. Finally, social learning theory has been criticized for not paying enough attention to a wide range of contextual variables which may impact on children's observational learning. While the theory has addressed some contextual variables like the characteristics of models which effect development, other context effects such as socioeconomic factors, race, sex and education remain relatively unexplored (Miller, 1993).

The ethological perspective

Ethology is a perspective on the study of animal behaviour which began to be applied to research on children during the 1960s and continues to be influential today. Ethology is concerned with understanding the adaptive value of behaviour and its evolutionary history. The origins of ethology can be traced to Charles Darwin and his work on evolution, however, the modern theory owes its origins to the work of two European zoologists, Konrad Lorenz, and Niko Tinbergen. In his theory of evolution, Darwin proposed that we evolved from more simple forms of life through a process called **natural selection**. Natural selection works through the effects of a trait on survival; if a change to our physical structure or behaviour leads to a survival advantage, the change is more likely to be passed on through the genes to the organism's offspring during mating. If the change leads to no advantages, it is less likely to be passed on, and the trait will tend to disappear. Thus, only traits which lead to a survival advantage for the organism are passed on. Natural selection is so called because nature weeds out those individuals who are unfit; in other words, natural selection is the 'survival of the fittest'.

Based on the careful observation of animals in their natural habitats, researchers like Lorenz and Tinbergen noted that many animal species come equipped with a number of behaviour patterns that promote their survival. One of these behaviour patterns studied by Lorenz is known as **imprinting**. Imprinting refers to the 'following behaviour' of many species of birds. Imprinting is a behaviour which is acquired extremely rapidly and serves to ensure that the offspring will stay close to the mother so as to be fed and protected from predators. While nothing like imprinting seems to occur in human beings, a related concept from ethology has been very usefully applied to the study of child development. In birds such as geese, imprinting occurs during a restricted time period of development known as a **critical period**. A critical period is a time when an organism is biologically prepared to acquire a particular behaviour. For example, using geese, Lorenz found that if the mother goose was not present during the critical period, her goslings would imprint on a moving object which resembled her important features, such as Lorenz himself. Lorenz (1963) showed that the gosling's instinct to follow its mother was not preprogrammed. Instead, the *tendency* to acquire a particular behaviour is programmed but the support of the environment is critical to the acquisition of this behaviour.

Ethologists' observations of a wide variety of animal behaviours have sparked investigations with humans regarding the development of such social behaviours as attachment, dominance hierarchies, aggression, and cooperation. For example, Strayer and Strayer (1976) recorded naturally occurring conflicts among preschoolers and found evidence of a stable dominance hierarchy (see Chapter 9), with some children being more dominant and less likely to be aggressed against by other children. John Bowlby's work on the attachment bond between caregivers and their children was also inspired by attachment theory (see Chapter 8). Bowlby argued that infants have a built-in signalling system to which mothers are geared to respond, a system which is designed to promote nurturance and protective behaviours by the parent.

Are there critical periods in human development? Bornstein (1989) suggested that the term **sensitive period** is a better descriptor of human development than the term critical period. According to Bornstein, a sensitive period is a window of time in a child's development during which they are particularly responsive to environmental influences. For example, there is a sensitive period for the acquisition of human language which lasts from shortly after birth to early adolescence (see Chapter 7). Learning language is particularly easy for children during this period, but extremely difficult after it. Given the length of time involved for language acquisition, it seems that the notion of a critical period is an inaccurate descriptor of how language learning takes place. Clearly, the notion of a sensitive period for language provides a more accurate picture of language acquisition.

Ethological theory has been extremely important to the study of child development in regard to its methodological contributions to the field (Rubin et al., 1999). Behavioural observations using techniques developed by ethologists are widely employed by researchers studying children. In addition, the emphasis on the evolutionary roots of behaviours has proven to be an important theoretical development within the study of child development. Asking how environmental pressures may have operated to select for a particular behaviour such that, over time, it becomes widely distributed in the species helps us to understand the cause of many important behaviours such as attachment behaviour. In addition, concepts such as sensitive periods have been criticized in that they only put off the question of an ultimate explanation for a particular behaviour; more work needs to go into discovering how sensitive periods operate. Finally, looking for the causes of a particular behaviour in our evolutionary history is difficult because we cannot go back in time. The sources of information that are available are not always reliable and are often extremely ambiguous.

Evolutionary developmental theory

According to a recent review of the history of developmental psychology (Dixon & Lerner, 1999), Charles Darwin's theory of evolution has had a profound influence on theories of human development. As we have just seen, evolutionary theory influenced the development of ethological theories of human development. Evolutionary theory has also influenced theories of development as diverse as Freud's psychosexual theory, to information processing theories of cognitive development (Siegler, 1996). Perhaps not surprisingly, evolutionary theory has come into its own as a theory of human behaviour (e.g., Barkow, Cosmides, & Tooby, 1992). As David Buss argues: 'Any reasonably comprehensive theory of human development must include an account of where people come from, where they are going, and how long they live' (1995: 24). In Buss' view, an evolutionary psychological approach to human development has much to offer in the attempt to address these issues.

Geary and Bjorkland (2000) have recently applied the evolutionary psychology framework to generating an increased understanding of human development. In their view, **evolutionary developmental psychology** is the 'study of the genetic and ecological mechanisms that govern the development of social and cognitive competencies common to all human beings and the epigenetic processes that adapt these competencies to local conditions' (Geary & Bjorkland, 2000: 57). Let's examine this definition more closely.

Perhaps the first point of interest is that the consideration of development from an evolutionary framework involves the study of *both* biological factors such as the hereditary transmission of traits from parents to their children, *and* the ecology in which development occurs (i.e., environmental effects on behaviour). The second point is that Geary and Bjorkland do not advocate a simplistic division between biological and environmental factors (or nature versus nurture); rather, they suggest that development is governed by **epigenetic** processes, that is to say, *interactions* of genes and environments. In their view, genes provide the instructions for guiding the development of observable traits such as height or personality, but that these genetic blueprints are highly sensitive to 'local conditions' – that is, aspects of the environment that may require changes to the genetic blueprints in order for a trait to lead to optimal outcomes.

What has an evolutionary developmental psychology contributed to our understanding? To date, relatively little research has been conducted from this perspective, in large part, because the theory is a relatively recent arrival on the scene. Buss (1995) cites a number of instances where an evolutionary developmental framework has contributed to a greater understanding of developmental phenomena. For example, research on children's relationships with their parents and the warmth of the parent–child bond has been viewed as an evolved system which facilitates parental investment in the child, promoting their survival and ensuring cohesive family relations. The timing of puberty and the effects of early environments on physical maturation is another area which Buss suggests has been aided by an evolutionary analysis. As we discuss in Chapter 4, recent research (Moffit, Caspi, Belsky, and Silva, 1992) demonstrated that ecological factors such as family conflict and the absence of fathers in the household predicted the earlier onset of menstruation in females. Belsky, Steinberg, and Draper (1991) explained these findings by suggesting that particular events during childhood predispose the child towards different developmental pathways. The presence of the father during childhood may push the child towards a later mating strategy which will be characterized by long-term relationships and high levels of parental investment. In contrast, early father absence may push the child towards an earlier mating strategy marked by early sexual maturation and more short-term relationships. These are just a few examples of the sort of contributions that evolutionary developmental psychology has made to the study of child development. However, much more work remains to be done in elaborating the theory and assessing how useful it will be to generating a better understanding of child development.

The bioecological model of development

A view which has received an increasing amount of attention from developmental psychologists is Urie Bronfenbrenner's **bioecological model** of human development (Bronfenbrenner & Morris, 1998) (see Figure 2.1). Bronfenbrenner (1974) is famous for his suggestion that an overemphasis on lab research had caused developmental psychology to become 'the study of the strange behaviour of children in strange situations for the briefest possible period of time'. In contrast to the bulk of developmental research which is conducted in laboratory settings, Bronfenbrenner argued that the proper study of development required one to observe children and adults in their actual environment; most laboratory research misses out on critical information which can only be gained by studying children in natural contexts. In addition, a great deal of laboratory-based research is not generalizable to the everyday contexts in which humans live and grow (Bronfenbrenner, 1979).

When psychologists examine the effects of the environment on children, the environment is typically construed in a very static and narrow fashion – often as the child's immediate surroundings. In contrast, Bronfenbrenner (1989) views the environment as a dynamic entity which is constantly changing. In addition, in Bronfenbrenner's (1979) bioecological model of human development, the environment is conceived of in a very wide sense, as a series of nested structures that extends beyond the child's immediate

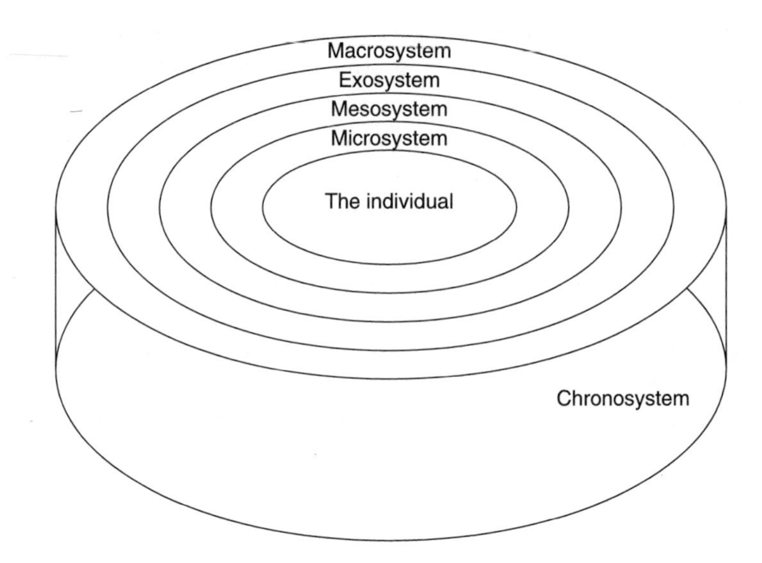

FIGURE 2.1 Bronfenbrenner's bioecological model of development

environment (e.g., their home or neighbourhood) to include their school, community, and the social and cultural institutions that impact on their lives. In Bronfenbrenner's model, the individual is the centre of a system which includes four layers, each representing different aspects of the environment. Each of the four layers is regarded as having a powerful impact on the child's development.

The innermost level is called the **microsystem**. The microsystem is the immediate setting in which a child lives; it refers to family, peers, school as well as the activities, roles, and relationships in their immediate surroundings. In Bronfenbrenner's view, the individual is viewed as an active force, exerting an influence on the people around her and on the relationships she has with others. The child is not a passive recipient of others' attention and actions. Thus, within the microsystem, development is often understood in terms of complex, interacting relationships.

The second level of Bronfenbrenner's model is called the **mesosystem**. It refers to relationships among microsystems, such as home, school, neighbourhood, and childcare centre. One could think about the mesosystem as the connections which bring together the different contexts in which a child develops. For example, a child's ability to learn to read may depend not just on learning activities that take place in school, but also on the extent to which those activities carry over to the home environment, such as the presence of books in the home or how much time parents spend reading with their children. The view that 'it takes a village to raise a child' is a recognition of the importance of the mesosystem in development. Bronfenbrenner and

Morris (1998) suggested that the best and most complete picture of a child's development will be obtained when they are examined in multiple contexts rather than just in the home or the school.

Exosystems are broad social settings that provide support for the development of children and adults. These are social settings and institutions that do not directly involve children yet which can have a profound impact on their development. Exosystems include formal settings such as community health services, parks, recreation centres, city government, and informal groups such as one's extended family, social support networks, and the workplace. These groups can provide important support for the family – such as flexible work schedules, paid maternity and paternity leave, or low-cost childcare – support that can enhance the development of children. Negative impacts on development can also result when the exosystem breaks down. For example, families who are affected by unemployment show an increased incidence of child abuse and neglect.

At the outermost level of Bronfenbrenner's model is the **macrosystem**. The macrosystem is not a specific environmental context but, rather, the overarching ideology, values, laws, regulations, and customs of a given culture. Cultural influences can have a powerful effect on children's development. Comparisons made across cultures have the potential to provide very important information about the effects of culture on development.

Bronfenbrenner also included in his model the notion that development occurs in historical time within his model. He called this temporal aspect the **chronosystem**. The chronosystem involves all aspects of time, and how they impact on development. For example, research on the timing of puberty has shown that the age at which puberty begins can have a profound impact on later development (Jones & Bayley, 1950). Historical events which occur in time also have important effects on development. For example, the work of Elder (1974) showed that the economic depression of the 1930s had significant impact on the lives of children growing up during that period. In these ways and many others, the chronosystem has a powerful influence on development.

Life-course theory

In a recent review of his bioecological theory of development, Bronfenbrenner (Bronfenbrenner & Morris, 1998) emphasized the importance of time as a variable which demands the attention of developmental psychologists. Another theoretical orientation which emphasizes the role of time in human development is **life-course theory** (Elder, 1995, 1998). The **life course**, refers to a 'sequence of socially defined, age-graded events and roles that the individual enacts over time' (Elder, 1998: 941). According to Elder, our lives are defined in large part by the social context in which we develop. For example, in many Western societies, parents' conceptions of when it is appropriate for their children to begin dating are changing, partly as our societal expectations for what constitutes normal, age-appropriate experiences evolves.

Life-course theory emphasizes the view that human development must be understood in terms of four interdependent principles. First, human lives are situated in historical time and place. The timing of an individual's birth is an important determinant of the development trajectories they will likely follow. Historical influences can impact on us in different ways. One way in which historical forces impact on us is through **cohort effects**. A cohort is a group of people born at a particular point in time (e.g., 'baby boomers' or 'generation X'). A cohort effect occurs when people from different birth cohorts are differentially impacted upon by some historical event. For example, in his work on the effects of the US economic depression in the 1930s, Elder (1974) showed that younger children were more adversely effected by the impact of the depression than were older children. Another type of historical effect is called a **period effect**. This occurs when a historical event exerts a relatively uniform influence across different birth cohorts. For example, Elder notes that whatever cause is responsible for the increase in divorce rates over the past four decades, it has affected most birth cohorts in a similar fashion. Finally, in regard to historical time and place, Elder notes that geographical settings are often an extremely important factor neglected in developmental studies, and furthermore, that time and place are often inextricably linked.

A second key element of life-course theory is the idea that developmental studies must pay attention to the timing of lives. Our lives are socially timed in that the way social roles and events are organized has much to do with what is considered normative for a particular age group by the society in which an individual develops. We often ask of ourselves or others, whether we are 'on course' or 'on time' in regard to specific aspects of our development. For example, it is highly likely that our parents worried about whether our academic performance as adolescents was 'normal' relative to other adolescents. The social timing of lives can have profound effects on development: consider the woman who puts off having a child until her career is established versus the teenage girl who becomes pregnant. Clearly, this choice entails different developmental pathways for the two women, with each pathway offering opportunities for personal growth, albeit of different kinds.

Third, life-course theory emphasizes that human lives are interdependent or linked with each other. Our lives are embedded in family relationships, peer relationships, romantic relationships and in various other relationships such as those we have with our coworkers or classmates. Attachment theory suggests that the quality of the relationship that we form with our primary caregiver in infancy has an impact on later relationships we form with friends and, eventually, with our romantic partners. In turn, our attachment relationship with our own children is affected by the relationship we had with our caregivers. Attachment theory is built on the premise that human lives are linked with each other. Throughout this text we will continue to examine how relationships affect children's development.

Finally, the fourth principle of life-course theory is that within certain social constraints, human beings have *agency*, that is, the power to make decisions and change our lives. The social environment places constraints on the kinds of actions that people can take to change their lives. For example, one cannot pursue a career in engineering without the appropriate education, thus, a person's choice of career is necessarily limited by the education they have chosen to pursue. However, although there are constraints, our choices have a high degree of impact on our lives. For example, Rutter and Rutter (1993) note that how we choose to behave with and relate to other people serves to shape and select the environment that we actually experience. In addition, Rutter and Rutter note that planning one's decisions proves to be a protective process in the long term whereas the lack of planning is considered to be a risk factor for poor outcomes. Going back to an earlier example, the adolescent who anticipates engaging in sexual activity, and takes steps to obtain contraception reduces not only the risk of an unwanted pregnancy or sexually transmitted disease, but also the risk of embarking on a developmental pathway which may lead to unhappiness.

In summary, life-course theory has much in common with theories such as Bronfenbrenner's bioecological theory with its emphasis on the importance of the various types of environments which impact on development and with the principles of Baltes' (1987) life-span developmental psychology which emphasizes the importance of contexts and timing. However, in Elder's view, social environments should be the major emphasis of developmental studies. This differs from the views of Bronfenbrenner and Baltes, who both place the individual at the centre of their models of development.

Dynamic systems theory

Dynamic system theories of development emerge out of a growing disenchantment with the traditional theories' focus on environmental causes, biological causes, and interactions of biology and environment as explanations of development. A growing number of researchers have put forward theories which emphasize systems thinking (e.g., Bertalanffy, 1968; Sameroff, 1983; Thelen & Smith, 1994). These researchers have suggested that human beings and their environments can be thought of as a collection of systems, where a system is defined as being composed of a number of elements which are organized in some fashion. A family is a good example of a system. Families consist of a number of clements such as father, mother, children. Moreover, the relations of the elements to one another can be described; for example, children normally obey mother's and father's rules. However, the behaviour of the family can only be truly understood in systems terms, that is, by considering the interrelations among all the parts, the family's history, and external influences which may operate to stabilize or destabilize its functioning. In other words, the family's behaviour is more than just the sum of its individual parts.

So then, what is dynamic systems theory? According to a review by Thelen and Smith (1998), dynamic systems theory is a *metatheory*; that is, it is an approach to studying development that can be widely applied to many domains, for example, from areas as diverse as **embryology** (the study of how a fertilized egg becomes an infant), family functioning, and the development of motor skills (Thelen & Ulrich, 1991). However, Thelen and Smith also argue that dynamic systems theory can be employed as a specific theory of how humans gain knowledge via action, perhaps best exemplified in Thelen's work on the development of motor skills.

Thelen and Smith (1998) suggest a metaphor which is useful in understanding the way in which dynamic systems theorists view development. They ask us to consider a fast-moving mountain stream. The stream shows stable patterns in its flow, for example, whirlpools, eddies, and ripples which occur because of rocks in the stream bed, or waves and spray where the stream bed is shallow and steep. Thelen and Smith argue that no one would explain the regularities in the flow of the stream by invoking a 'grand plan'. Instead, we recognize that the stream shows the patterns it does because of the constraints under which it operates. The regularities in the patterns we observe occur because of multiple factors operating simultaneously: the configuration of the stream bed and the placement of rocks; the rate of flow of water; the erosion of the stream bed. Thelen and Smith suggest that this metaphor of a mountain stream depicts development as truly epigenetic, that is, as constructed by the system's own history, by its current activity, and by the constraints under which the system operates.

How can a dynamic systems perspective be applied to the study of child development? Thelen has led the way in her own research, illustrating how a dynamic systems approach can help us to better understand behaviour. For example, it is well known that newborns, when held upright in a standing position, show a stepping reflex. After some time, this reflex disappears and later re-emerges. In contrast to theories which postulated that this process was under the control of genetic factors, Thelen and Fisher (1982) showed that the reflex 'disappears' because of changes in other aspects of the infant's physiology. In the case of the stepping reflex, body fat begins to accumulate on the infant's leg, making the leg heavier. However, muscle mass is not added at the same rate, meaning the infant is no longer able to physically lift their leg, thus the stepping reflex 'disappears'. However, the stepping reflex can be made to reappear by immersing the infant in water from the waist down. The effects of buoyancy act to reduce the weight of the infant's legs and the stepping reflex reappears. In Thelen's view, the best way in which to understand this finding is from a dynamic systems perspective: as changes are made to the system, behaviours are reorganized in a dynamic fashion. The stable patterns previously observed can be brought back by changing the effects of the constraints which altered the behaviour.

Consider another example from the study of infant motor development. Previous theories of motor development have suggested that behaviours such as the development of 'creeping' or 'crawling' are programmed to emerge prior to walking. Thelen and Smith (1998) suggest it is unnecessary to invoke a genetic programme to explain this fact, rather, they suggest that we can think of the development of crawling as a behaviour which is **softly assembled** from previously existing competencies. In other words, a genetic blueprint for crawling does not suddenly emerge and guide the baby towards this behaviour; instead, the infant creates the behaviour based on the constraints under which they operate, plus their goals and desires. The infant may desire a toy which is across the room and intends to move towards it. The state of their neuromuscular system is such that they cannot yet maintain enough balance to walk upright so the infant employs another solution, crawling, which allows them to make use of the skills they have already acquired. The development of crawling behaviour is a predictable outcome of the infant's desires and its current range of abilities. However, it is not an inevitable solution: some infants develop alternative methods such as crawling on their bellies or scooting along on their bottoms by using their arms. The development of such alternative strategies depends on the infant's previous history of motor skills and the current state of maturation of their musculature and suggests that crawling is not simply the outcome of a genetic blueprint which dictates development.

Cognitive developmental theories

In regard to the study of cognitive development, there are three theories which have had a dramatic impact on the field. These are Piaget's **cognitive-developmental** theory (e.g., Piaget, 1983), Vygotsky's **sociocultural theory** development (Vygotsky, 1978, 1986), and the **information processing approach** to cognitive development (Klahr & MacWhinney, 1998; Siegler, 1996). Given that these three theories are primarily to do with cognitive development, we will cover them in more detail in Chapter 6. What follows here is a brief summary of each one.

Jean Piaget's theory of cognitive development

Jean Piaget (1896–1980) is widely acknowledged as the theorist who has had the greatest impact on research and theory in the field of child development (e.g., Siegler, 1998). Piaget began working in developmental psychology in the 1920s but it was not until the 1960s that his work garnered much attention as it became increasingly available. Piaget's work was largely at odds with the behaviourist tradition which was dominant in North America until the 1960s. Unlike the behaviourists of the day, Piaget did not view the child as a passive recipient of knowledge whose development is the product of reinforcement or punishment, but, rather, as an active participant in the creation of their own understanding.

Piaget's (1971) theory of development borrowed heavily from the field of evolutionary biology. A central concept in Piagetian theory is the idea that our cognitive structures (i.e., our minds) are *adaptations* which help ensure that our knowledge provides a good 'fit' to the world. Piaget viewed human intelligence as an adaptation which ultimately enhanced our chances of survival. Of course, we know from experience (often, painfully so) that our knowledge does not always match reality perfectly. For example, we often act on the basis of false assumptions, incorrect knowledge or a partial understanding. Young children's thinking is also rife with misunderstandings about the nature of the world. For example, Piaget noted that preschool children's thinking is often strongly tied to the child's own point of view and fails to consider the fact that another person might have a very different perspective on a situation. According to Piaget, cognitive development is a process of revision: children revise their knowledge to provide an increasingly better fit to reality. Piaget referred to this process as the establishment of *equilibrium* between the child's cognitive structures and the nature of the physical and social world.

Piaget viewed children's cognitive development as progressing through four stages. By *stage*, Piaget meant a period of development which is characterized by knowledge structures which are *qualitatively* similar and lead to distinctive modes of thought. In the *sensorimotor stage* of development, lasting from birth to about 2 years of age, the infant thinks about the world through their actions on it. Piaget believed that the basis of our ability to think abstractly is rooted in our ability to act on the world. Eventually, the infant's actions become increasingly organized, leading to the next stage of development which Piaget termed the *preoperational stage*. The major feature of this stage (which characterizes development from the ages of 2 to 7) is the ability to think using symbolic representations, that is, the child no longer has to act on the world to think but can use symbols and carry out operations mentally. The third stage of development, lasting from 7 to 12 years of age, is the *concrete operational stage*, characterized by the increasingly logical character of a child's thinking.

Finally, at the *formal operational stage*, the adolescent gains the ability to think abstractly. Unlike the concrete operational child, the adolescent's thinking is no longer tied to concrete reality but can move into the possible or hypothetical.

As mentioned earlier, Piaget's theory has proven extremely influential to the study of children's cognitive development; however, in recent years, the theory has come under an increasing level of criticism. For example, many developmental psychologists are dissatisfied with Piaget's portrayal of the child as a solitary learner and feel that he did not give enough attention to the role of social and cultural factors in children's cognitive development (e.g., Rogoff, 1998). In Chapter 6, we examine Piaget's theory in detail, and consider both the strengths and weaknesses of the theory.

Vygotsky's sociocultural theory of development

Like Piaget, Lev Vygotsky (1896–1934) was a firm believer that children actively explored their environment and were influential in shaping their own knowledge. Unlike Piaget, however, Vygotsky emphasized that the child's social environment was an extremely important force in their development. Vygotsky (1935/1978) believed that it was through social interactions with more experienced and more knowledgeable members of their society – parents, relatives, teachers, peers – that children are able to acquire the knowledge and skills that a culture deems to be important. Thus, according to Vygotsky, development is a social process: social interactions are a necessary aspect of cognitive development.

Vygotsky also believed that children's development follows a particular pattern. Any development occurs at two different levels: children first evidence development in *interpersonal* interactions which occur between themselves and other people. Only later do children show evidence of development on an individual or *intrapersonal* level. Vygotsky labelled this shift from development being evidenced on the interpersonal to an intrapersonal level as *internalization*. An example of internalization can be seen in children's self-talk while problem solving. Children take the kinds of dialogues they engage in with parents or teachers (e.g., '*take your time*' or '*be careful*') while solving problems and talk to themselves while working on problems alone. Eventually, this self-talk is internalized and the child no longer needs to talk out loud.

Finally, Vygotsky noted that parents and teachers tend to interact with children in the context of a teaching task in a particular fashion. Parents tend to adjust their level of interaction dynamically, responding to the child's level of ability, and trying to pitch their teaching at a level which is just outside what the child can do on their own but at a level which is within the child's ability to do with help. Vygotsky believed that parents and teachers worked at a level that is optimal for stimulating children's development. This example highlights Vygotsky's belief that social interactions are critical to children's cognitive development.

Information processing accounts of development

In recent years, an account of cognitive development has emerged which is founded on the analogy between the digital computer and the human mind. Computers are rule-based systems which process information according to a limited and concretely specified set of rules. Information is input into the system and is encoded into a form that the computer can manipulate. This information is then transformed via a series of operations into useful output, for example, the solution to an equation. Similarly, the human mind is believed to operate in the same fashion, by encoding information input via our senses and transforming it into useful output. For example, we take in sound waves from the environment and transform this information via a specified set of operations into meaningful sentences. Human beings and computers share other similar features which enhance the strength of this analogy, such as the ability to manipulate symbols or the constraints on information processing caused by memory limitations. According to information processing theorists, the digital computer provides a useful tool for testing theories of cognitive development via the modelling of cognitive processes (Klahr & MacWhinney, 1998).

Information processing theories are useful to the study of cognitive development in that they require the researcher to map out the series of steps which they believe best describes the flow of information through the human mind. This process of mapping information flow adds a degree of precision to these accounts of cognitive development which is generally open to empirical tests. Thus, information processing models are often readily tested and updated on the basis of experimentation. Information processing theories also stress the importance of identifying the mechanisms which underlie developmental change; they do not simply provide a description of change but also model how change occurs. Finally, information processing theories often force us to address factors that affect development but which previously may not have been considered.

There are a wide variety of information processing models of children's cognition, ranging from models of children's developing ability to perform addition problems to models of children's learning of the rule for making verbs indicate the past tense in English (Klahr & MacWhinney, 1998). Whereas in the past, information processing theories have been criticized for their lack of attention to cognition in real world tasks, this trend is changing as newer information processing models begin to address this issue via the

TABLE 2.2 Theories of human development

Theory	Organicism vs. mechanism	Discontinuity vs. continuity	Nature vs. nurture
Psychoanalytic theory	Organismic	Discontinuous: Emphasizes stages of development that are qualitatively different	Nature (biological drives) and nurture (role of early experience) both play a role
Psychosocial theory	Organismic	Discontinuous: Emphasizes stages of development that are qualitatively different	Nurture: Age-related social demands are the primary determinants of development
Behaviourism and social learning theory	Mechanistic	Continuous: Increase in learned behaviours is continuous	Nurture: Principles of learning are based on environmental contingencies
Ethological theory	Organismic	Continuous and discontinuous elements: Learned behaviours increase continuously but critical/ sensitive periods may lead to qualitative changes	Nature (biologically based, instinctive behaviours, genetic factors) and nurture (experience plays an important role in learning) interact
Evolutionary developmental theory	Organismic	Not clearly specified	Nature (genetic factors canalize behaviour) and nurture (experiences play an important role in shaping behaviour)
Bioecological theory	Organismic	Not clearly specified	Nature (individual characteristics) and nurture (a variety of environmental influences act on the individual)
Life course theory	Organismic	Discontinuous: Age-related demands lead to qualitative developmental change	Nurture: Social demands and environmental influences play an important role in determining development
Dynamic systems theory	Mechanistic	Continuous and discontinuous elements: Learned behaviours increase continuously with the possibility for qualitative reorganizations	Nature (biological constraints) interacts with nurture (experience in context) to produce developmental change
Cognitive developmental theories			
Piagetian theory	Organismic	Discontinuous: Emphasizes emergence of stages of development that are qualitatively distinct	Nature (reflexive behaviours and drive for organization) and nurture (experience with the environment) interacts to produce development
Vygotsky's sociocultural theory	Organismic	Continuous: Interactions with more competent members of one's culture leads to developmental change in a continuous fashion	Nurture: Social interactions with others are the primary influence on development
Information processing theory	Mechanistic and organismic elements	Continuous: The development of skills and strategies increases in a continuous fashion	Not clearly specified

modelling of performance on everyday tasks such as reading comprehension. A more recent trend in the study of information processing is the use of *connectionist* models, which are models of information processing based on the structure of the human brain and its ability to carry out processing in parallel (that is, to perform multiple operations simultaneously). (See Table 2.2 for an overview of the theories of human development.)

SUMMARY

It should be apparent from our brief survey in Chapter 2 that there are a rather large number of theories of human development. Importantly, the theories we cover here are not mutually exclusive: quite often, the theories focus on distinct parts of the life span (e.g., infancy or adolescence) or different domains of development (e.g., emotion or cognition). Our coverage of theories was not exhaustive but is, in fact, representative of the types of theories which are currently invoked to understand children's development. Developing a knowledge of the different theoretical positions is an important task, as it will help you to better understand the research literature which we will cover throughout this text.

Glossary

Assumptions are the guiding premises underlying the logic of a theory.

Bioecological model is a model in which development is viewed as the product of interactions between an individual's capabilities and a dynamic environment.

Chronosystem In Bronfenbrenner's theory, the notion that development occurs in historical time.

Classical conditioning is a form of learning in which the pairing of a response with a stimulus leads to the ability of the stimulus to evoke the response.

Cognitive developmental theory refers to theories regarding the development of cognition, the most famous of which is Piaget's theory of cognitive development.

Cohort effects A cohort is a group of people born at a particular point in time. Cohort effect events have differential impacts on different birth cohorts.

Crisis refers to Erikson's belief that individuals must resolve a series of age-related tasks. How successfully an individual resolves each crisis determines the course of later development.

Critical period is a time when an organism is biologically prepared to acquire a particular behaviour.

Dynamic system theory is a theory of development which suggests that individuals develop within systems. The proper study of development includes a focus on these systems.

Ego In Freud's theory, the part of the personality that works to satisfy instinctive drives in a socially acceptable manner.

Embryology is the study of how a fertilized egg becomes an infant.

Epigenetic processes refer to the interactions of genes and environments.

Erogenous zones Parts of the body which afford pleasure through their stimulation. In Freud's theory, the erogenous zones change with development.

Ethology is a theory of behaviour concerned with understanding the adaptive value of behaviour and its evolutionary history.

Evolutionary developmental psychology is the study of the genetic and environmental mechanisms that govern the development of competencies common to all human beings and the epigenetic processes that adapt these competencies to local conditions.

Exosystems In Bronfenbrenner's theory, the broad social settings that provide support for the development of children and adults but which do not directly involve children (e.g., community health services, parks, recreation centres).

Id The part of our personality which, according to Freud, is made up of instinctual drives.

Imprinting refers to the extremely rapid acquisition of 'following behaviour' in geese.

Information processing theories Theories of development which focus on documenting how information flows through the cognitive system and the cognitive operations which transform that information.

Life course refers to a sequence of socially defined and age-graded events and roles that the individual enacts over time.

Macrosystem In Bronfenbrenner's theory, the overarching ideology, values, laws, regulations, and customs of a given culture.

Mechanism refers to a class of developmental theories that stress quantitative changes in behaviour and emphasize that factors outside the control of the organism play the major role in developmental change.

Mesosystem In Bronfenbrenner's theory, the relationships among microsystems.

Microsystem In Bronfenbrenner's theory, the immediate setting in which a child lives (e.g., neighbourhood, school, family).

Natural selection works through the effects of a trait on survival; if a change to our physical structure or behaviour leads to a survival advantage, the change will be passed on through the genes to the organism's offspring during mating. If the change leads to no advantages, it will not be passed on and the trait will disappear. Thus, only traits which lead to a survival advantage for the organism are passed on.

Observational learning (often referred to as **modelling**) is the acquisition of a behaviour through the observation or imitation of others around one.

Operant conditioning refers to a type of learning where the likelihood of a behaviour reoccurring can be increased by reinforcements and decreased by punishments.

Organicism refers to a class of developmental theories that stress the qualitative features of developmental change and which emphasize the organism's role in bringing about these changes.

Period effects occur when a historical event exerts a relatively uniform influence across different birth cohorts.

Pleasure principle Freud's belief that the id attempts to maximize its pleasure in an immediate fashion.

Psychodynamic theories emphasize the belief that forces or dynamics within the individual are responsible for our behaviour.

Punishments are the consequences of a behaviour that decrease the likelihood of the behaviour reoccurring.

Range of applicability is the range of phenomena to which a theory properly applies.

Reinforcers are the consequences of a behaviour that increase the likelihood of the behaviour reoccurring.

Self-efficacy refers to beliefs about one's own effectiveness and competence to cope with a situation.

Sensitive period is a window of time in development during which an organism is particularly responsive to environmental influences.

Social learning theory Bandura's theory that the principles of operant conditioning and observational learning are important mechanisms of development.

Sociocultural theory refers to Vygotsky's theory which views development as dependent on the child's interactions with other, more skilled members of the culture.

Softly-assembled the idea, from dynamic systems theory, that a given behaviour does not depend on a genetic blueprint but occurs as a result of changing constraints and supports from the context in which the behaviour occurs.

Superego In Freud's theory, the part of the personality which is the internalized values and standards of the child's parents and culture.

Theories take the form of an interconnected set of concepts used to integrate and to interpret empirical observations. **Formal theories** should be logically consistent and contain no contradictions, fit well with empirical observations, be testable, remain as simple as possible, and cover a defined range of phenomena. **Informal theories** are organized sets of intuitions or expectations about the world, often referred to as *implicit theories*.

3 Research Methodology in Developmental Psychology

LEARNING AIMS

At the end of this chapter you should:

- **understand the importance of research design and methodology to research on child development**
- **be familiar with the various measurement techniques used in developmental research**
- **be able to articulate the strengths and weaknesses of different measurement techniques**
- **understand the relative strengths and weaknesses of the controlled experiments, quasi-experiments, and nonexperiments, and be familiar with the conclusions than can be drawn from each type of study**
- **recognize research designs specifically geared towards understanding developmental questions and the sort of information provided by each type of study**
- **be aware of the ethical issues involved in research with children**

Introduction

In this chapter we examine how researchers who study child development actually go about testing the hypotheses they have formed on the basis of their theories. The study of child development is grounded in the scientific method; that is, developmental psychologists create testable hypotheses on the basis of theory and then develop methods for empirically evaluating whether these hypotheses provide a good fit to the data they have gathered. An important aspect of this method is that observations must be replicable, or able to be duplicated by other researchers. Moreover, research questions should be examined in multiple ways, using different samples of children and different methodologies. When a research question has been thoroughly assessed, researchers can be more confident that they have obtained a valid finding.

Obviously there is no space in this book for a full and detailed treatment of research methods. For a more thorough treatment the reader is referred to the book by Haslam and McGarty (1998) in this series. In this chapter, our focus is on methodological issues of particular importance to developmental psychology.

The issues involved in testing research questions in developmental psychology include: the ways in which information about children can be gathered, that is, issues of measurement; different types of investigations such as case studies, experiments, and quasi-experiments; research designs developed specifically to assess developmental questions; issues regarding the reliability and the validity of data; and ethical issues regarding research with young children.

Measurement techniques: how to gather data about children

Survey methods

One powerful method of gathering information about children is through large-scale surveys. In survey research, a researcher sends out questionnaires or conducts interviews with a **representative sample** of the population of interest (quite often, surveys are conducted at the national level, to assess issues of importance to a particular country). A representative sample is one in which the population surveyed resembles the larger population about which data are being gathered. Researchers need to be extremely careful that their samples are representative of the important aspects of the population relevant to the research question. For example, a sample which assessed only children from middle-class homes would not be able to tell us much about the development of the general population which includes children living in poverty and children who are brought up in more affluent areas. In contrast, issues of social class are much less important in the study of questions such as visual development. When a representative sample is obtained, survey methods can provide extremely useful information about important issues in child development. In one large-scale survey conducted in the United States, the National Longitudinal Survey of Youth (NLSY), some 12,000 individuals between the ages of 14 to 24 were interviewed about topics such as school performance and employment. Seven years later, approximately 5,000 of the children of women who participated in the first wave of assessment were interviewed. Data from this study have been used to address very important questions such as the impact of daycare and maternal employment on children's development (Chase-Lansdale, Mott, Brooks-Gunn, & Phillips, 1991). Although useful, survey studies are limited in their ability to provide detailed explanations of how the factors surveyed influence child development. They are best suited to revealing broad patterns among the factors studied in a particular survey.

Observational methods

Jean Piaget (e.g., 1926) was a keen observer of children's behaviour. Much of his work on children's cognitive development was informed by careful observations of his own children. In current research, behavioural observation continues to be a powerful method for assessing theories of child development (e.g., Rubin et al., 1999). Observational research can take place in both *naturalistic settings*, such as a playground, daycare, or classroom, or it can take place in *laboratory settings*, where the experimenter can arrange conditions so as to gain more control over them.

In order to be useful to a researcher, observational data must satisfy certain conditions. One such criterion is that the study should allow for the gathering of an adequate sample of children's behaviour. A study which attempted to make generalizations about how children's social competence impacted on their classroom behaviour on the basis of a ten-minute observation of the child in their classroom would be suspect because the researcher would not obtain an adequate sample of the child's classroom behaviour. Most importantly, the data gathered in an observational study must not be influenced by the presence of the observer or observers. In other words, children and other participants in an observational study should not alter or distort their behaviour because they are being observed, so that what is observed is a **representative sample** of their typical behaviour. A group of observers in a classroom who stare at children and continually make notes may cause the children to alter their behaviour, perhaps acting better than they otherwise might! This is an example of children showing **reactivity** to being observed; high reactivity leads to less valid conclusions. Similarly, in laboratory settings, it is important that the situational demands imposed in the laboratory do not exert influences on the behaviour of the participants. For example, factors such as conspicuously placed video cameras may cause parents to interact differently with their children than they might if they were less conscious of being videotaped. As you might guess, it is difficult to overcome these obstacles in observational research. When you read about developmental studies which employ observational methods, it is important to ask yourself whether or not the experimenters made adequate attempts to control or account for the presence of the observers or the setting.

In observational studies, the researcher must make some important decisions about the way in which the behaviours that are observed will be recorded, a decision that is primarily influenced by the researcher's goals for the study. If the researcher is interested in everything that a child does in a given period of time, they may create a **specimen record**, in which everything that happens in a fixed period of time is recorded (Bakeman & Gottman, 1997). Most researchers will specify the behaviours of interest beforehand, so that the observed behaviours can be coded efficiently and quickly. Specimen records are very useful for studies which examine questions about the range of behaviours that children use in a particular situation. For example, researchers interested in how children modulate their emotions while engaged in a challenging task may choose to examine various behaviours which have been identified as being related to the child's ability to modulate their emotion (Rothbart, Ziaie, & O'Boyle, 1992). When the researcher is more specifically interested in how children react to particular events, a technique called **event sampling** may be employed (Bakeman & Gottman, 1997). In this technique, behaviours are measured whenever a particular event occurs. If you were interested in how maltreated children react to aggressive behaviours, you could use event sampling to make observations of the children's behaviour whenever an aggressive event occurs. **Time sampling** methods are often used when studying groups of subjects (Bakeman & Gottman, 1997). For example, imagine you want to study incidents of aggression in all the interactions between a group of brothers and sisters. Using a time sampling approach, you might divide your 60 minute observation into five-minute chunks or 'windows' and note whether or not particular forms of aggressive behaviour (defined in advance of the study) occur in a given five-minute window. While this approach makes it easier to study behaviour in groups of subjects such as families and play groups, it leads to a loss of information, such as what happened after an incident or how the other siblings responded.

Laboratory observations are often used when the experimenter wants to ensure that a particular behaviour will be observed and that certain conditions are controlled for. For example, imagine that a researcher wants to examine the reactions of toddlers to brief separations from their mother. One way the researcher could design the study would be to observe the mother and toddler in the home environment. However, there are some problems that might be encountered if this research strategy is selected. For example, it would be difficult to ensure that certain conditions could be met, such as ensuring that the mother behaves in a natural fashion. Also, it may be difficult to arrange equal separations across the participants in the study and to create separations where the infant is free of distractions from other children or pets. By utilizing a laboratory observation procedure, the researcher can create separations that are standardized in length and that control for other extraneous variables. The environment can be designed so that the child and mother are relatively unaware that their behaviour is being recorded, for example, through the use of one-way mirrors and hidden microphones. For many of the research questions that researchers would like to ask, the use of laboratory settings is the only way in which meaningful data can be gathered. Also, the use of specialized data collection techniques imposes its own set of requirements on the environment. Techniques that involve recording physiological data, such as the electrical activity of the brain, require an environment free of electrical interference that could alter the data collected, and these may also constrain behaviour in important ways. Other techniques require the child to remain focused on a particular stimulus item but to remain immobile for a long period of time. Clearly, when employing such techniques, the use of a controlled setting, which can only be achieved in the laboratory, is desirable.

Interviewing children

When many of us want to know something about another person, we simply ask them for the information. Not surprisingly, when we want to know something about children, one of the best methods available is simply to ask them questions. Asking another for information about themselves, what is called **self-report**, can take many forms. One common method is the **clinical interview**, where children are asked to describe their thoughts or feelings about some issue. Clinical interviews differ from other interview formats in that they are conducted in a flexible, open-ended fashion that allows the interviewer to gather as much information about a topic as possible and to follow up on any promising trains of thought the child may express. Jean Piaget (1926) used this method to great effect and was extremely adept at getting information about young children's conceptions of the world through the clinical interview method. The clinical interview method is very useful in that it allows the interviewer to gather a very large amount of information about a topic in a relatively short time. It is also useful in that the clinical interview method may allow us to obtain information that closely approximates the way in which children really think.

However, getting information from young children presents some difficult problems to the interviewer. First of all, children's verbal abilities may limit or impede their capacity to understand the interviewer or to express themselves clearly, limiting the usefulness of the information obtained. Second, as Siegal (1991) has argued, because of their difficulties with the social conventions surrounding conversations (see Chapter 7 for a discussion of this issue), young children may fail to understand the interviewer's intention in asking a question and may unwittingly provide unwanted or irrelevant information.

Most importantly, clinical interviews may be *inaccurate*. Children's recollections of an experience may be simply incorrect or distorted, or may be influenced by a tendency to respond in **socially desirable** ways, that is, the participant may say what they think the interviewer wants to hear. This last point is also applicable to **structured interviews** and to questionnaire formats as well.

A structured interview differs from a clinical interview in that each participant is asked the exact same set of questions in the same order. Structured interviews help to avoid the possibility that interviewers may treat individual participants in different ways. They also have the advantage of being more efficient forms of interviews for situations where one's time with a child is short or where the child's attention span and willingness to talk may be limited. Structured interviews can also be adapted to employ multiple choice responses (e.g., *Did you feel good or bad about that?*) or rating scales (e.g., *Is this description really true of you or just sort of true of you?*) to help children respond. Of course, structured interviews sacrifice the depth of information that could potentially be obtained by a good clinical interviewer.

Finally, questionnaires are useful methods for obtaining information from older, literate children. In this format, the participant reads through a list of questions and responds in written form or by answering in a specific fashion dictated by the questionnaire format such as *true/false* or *multiple choice*. Questionnaires are useful in that they can be widely distributed at a relatively low cost; however, the lack of personal contact with participants makes it difficult to ascertain whether the participants respond in a truthful or socially desirable fashion.

Reports on children by others

So far, we have considered some of the issues involved in having children report on their own thoughts or feelings about a topic of interest to the researcher. Another common method used in the study of child development is to obtain reports from *third parties*, such as family members, peers, or teachers. It is very often the case that others who are well acquainted with the child can provide very useful information about them. Reports from third parties also have the potential advantage of providing a perspective on the child when viewed in different environments. For example, teachers spend much time with the child in a unique and significant context for development: the school environment. For this reason, teachers will be able to provide critical information about the child's behaviour in this context. Parents also have the potential to provide the experimenter with information about their children that is unique. An additional advantage in using their reports is that they have also had the opportunity to view the child across many different contexts and at different points in time. Moreover, the parent is in a position to discuss their thoughts and feelings about how their behaviours or parenting practices might impact on the child.

Third party reports suffer from many of the same limitations as children's self-reports. For instance, parents may not be particularly accurate about their own parenting practices with a child, or teachers may exaggerate the negative characteristics of children with whom they do not get along well while exaggerating the positive qualities of children with whom they do have a positive relationship. However, while there are potential problems with third party reports, they do offer the researcher an opportunity to gain valuable information about children. As well, discrepancies between children's self-reports and third party reports may be an important source of information for the researcher.

Psychophysiological methods

An increasingly popular means of gathering data about children is through the use of **psychophysiological methods**. These are diverse sets of research methods which have the common feature of measuring some aspect of the child's physiological functioning in order to examine how these processes contribute to children's behaviour. Psychophysiological methods are also extremely useful in that they can help us to identify feelings in very young children or infants who may not otherwise be able to tell us about their feelings. Researchers who use psychophysiological methods can often make strong inferences about which aspects of our physiology – for example, the brain, central nervous system, or autonomic nervous system – may underlie the development of some observable behaviour.

One potent psychophysiological technique is to record the electrical activity of the brain using an **electroencephalograph** (**EEG**) while a child performs a particular task. An electroencephalograph is a device that amplifies and records electrical activity from the scalp using a number of small electrodes which are temporarily adhered to the scalp. Such methods can provide insight into which parts of the brain underlie performance on some task. In addition, particular aspects of brain activity known as *event-related potentials*, or ERPs (Segalowitz, 1995), can be measured in relation to task performance. For example, Molfese and Molfese (1979) used ERP techniques to show that speech sounds elicit a faster response from the left hemisphere of infants than from the right hemisphere, data which are consistent with the suggestion that the left hemisphere is most responsible for the processing of linguistic stimuli.

Another psychophysiological technique which is proving to be increasingly useful in research on child development is **functional magnetic**

resonance imaging or **fMRI**. fMRI is a noninvasive technique which allows the researcher to detect changes in the blood flow to the brain, using magnetic fields to provide exceptionally clear images of the areas of the brain that are activated during a cognitive task. fMRI techniques have been used to identify the areas of the brain which are activated and presumed to be important to performance on a wide variety of psychological tasks, from memory to computational tasks. In one such study, children were asked to perform tasks that involve reasoning about another's mental states (Baron-Cohen et al., 1994). The data from this study indicated that the frontal areas of the brain are of particular importance to performance on tasks that involve mental state reasoning. Imaging techniques such as fMRI help the researcher to assess which areas of the brain are most likely to underlie cognitive performance, helping us to obtain a better picture of the relationship between brain development and behaviour.

Other psychophysiological techniques have been developed which measure changes in aspects of our physiology. These include measures such as: heart rate variability (often referred to as **vagal tone**; Porges, 1991); changes in the electrical conductance of the skin or **galvanic skin response**; and changes in the baseline level of hormones such as **cortisol** (released into the bloodstream in response to stressful events) in the bloodstream after a stimulus event. In a classic study, Joseph Campos and his colleagues used heart rate information to make inferences about the development of depth perception in young infants (Campos, Langer, & Krowitz, 1970). When an infant notices something of interest, there is a tendency for their heart rate (measured in beats per minute) to slow from its normal resting rate. Campos showed that when 1½-month-old infants were placed on a clear glass covering over a deep trench the infants showed a slowing in their heart rate, indicating they perceived the depth of the trench and found it an interesting experience. Physiological differences have also been linked to important differences in socioemotional development and personality (Kagan, 1998). For example, shy or inhibited children tend to show distinctive patterns of heart rate variability when compared to children who are rated as less inhibited.

While psychophysiological methods provide the researcher with a powerful means of examining development, they also suffer from a number of limitations. First of all, changes in physiological indices such as heart rate can be *difficult to interpret.* The researcher hopes that these indices change in relation to the stimulus they have introduced, but there is always the possibility that other factors such as boredom, anxiety, or even hunger and sleepiness could alter heart rate as well. Thus, the researcher using a psychophysiological method must be careful to ensure that such extraneous factors have been controlled. Second, the use of psychophysiological methods is *inferential.* That is, the researcher is measuring a physiological process (such as brain electrical activity) in relation to some behaviour (for example, making a decision about whether a target stimulus is present in a display or not). On the basis of correlations between the physiological data and the behaviour, the researcher makes inferences about how the physiological indices may underlie the behavioural processes. Of course, there is room for error in this procedure. The researcher who observes a specific pattern of brain activity in response to some stimulus cannot be entirely certain how the information has been processed. However, psychophysiological methods are proving increasingly popular in the study of child development and are helping to provide a better understanding of the relationship between physiology and behaviour. (See Table 3.1 for an overview of measurement techniques.)

Research design

When a researcher decides to tackle a particular research question, an issue with which they must come to grips very early on in the process is how to design a research project that will give them the best chance of properly examining the question. The researcher's goal is to provide a test of the hypothesis which produces valid results. Researchers attempt to design their studies so that they can test their hypotheses while controlling for other variables which may potentially provide **validity threats** to the study (Campbell & Stanley, 1963). Validity threats are factors related to the design of experiments which can cause problems with how the data from a study should be interpreted. A discussion of each of the different types of validity threats associated with scientific studies is beyond the scope of this text (but see Haslam & McGarty, 1998). However, you should think critically about the research you read about, and attempt to evaluate it in terms of whether the findings are valid, that is, free of validity threats.

While no experimental design is perfect and entirely free from validity threats, the goal of scientific research is to minimize threats to the validity of one's study in order to provide as adequate a test of the hypotheses as possible. One way researchers meet this goal is to conduct multiple studies, using a variety of research designs and methodologies to test their hypotheses. Findings that stand up across repeated testing are considered both reliable and valid. Reliable findings are findings which we are confident could be reproduced again, or replicated. Research findings which are reliable and valid are the bedrock of psychological science.

Controlled experiments

Controlled experiments are the most powerful form of research designs in terms of their ability to let us make *causal statements*, that is, statements about

TABLE 3.1 Common measurement techniques

Measurement technique	Strengths	Limitations
Surveys	• Most effective for revealing broad patterns in child development • Researchers are able to provide wide-reaching information about important issues in child development	• Unless the sample is representative of the population, it is difficult to make generalizations about the findings • Limited in their ability to provide detail
Observational methods	• The researcher is able to obtain a sample of natural behaviour • Depending on the goals of the study, researchers can record data in different ways (e.g., event sampling and time sampling) • Laboratory settings can be employed when the researcher needs more control over the environment than can be attained in a naturalistic setting	• Must have an adequate sample of the children's behaviour, which can be time consuming • Data may be subject to the influence of the observer and the instruments of observation (e.g., video cameras) • It is sometimes difficult to ensure that all relevant criteria are met when employing naturalistic settings
Interviews	• Information is obtained first hand from the individual • **Clinical interviews** allow the researcher to gather a large amount of information in a short period of time. Also enables the researcher to be flexible and follow promising leads • **Structured interviews** allow researchers to treat individual children in the same way, and are useful for children with short attention spans • **Questionnaires** are useful for obtaining information from older, literate children	• Young children may not be cognitively or linguistically advanced enough to provide information about themselves • Young children may fail to understand the researcher's intention, and provide unwanted information • Children's memory of certain experiences may be inaccurate or distorted • Children may answer in socially desirable ways, and not according to the actual state of affairs (e.g., tell the researcher what he or she thinks the researcher wants to hear)
Third party reports	• Other people may be able to accurately comment on the child's behaviour • Significant others have the opportunity to view the child at varying stages of development • Reports from different people may provide perspectives on the child in different contexts (e.g., at home and school)	• Parents and teachers may be biased when reporting the child's behaviour (e.g., be negative about a child they consider to misbehave) • Parents and teachers may not remember certain episodes in the child's life • Parents and teachers may also respond in socially desirable ways
Psychophysiological methods	• Help researchers to identify feelings in very young children or infants who may be too young to report themselves • Provide some understanding of the ways that physiology and brain development underlies the development of observable behaviour	• Changes in physiological indices (such as heart rate) may be difficult to interpret • The use of psychophysiological methods is inferential (e.g., based on correlations, the researcher makes presumptions about how the child's physiology underlies behaviour), and such inferences are subject to error

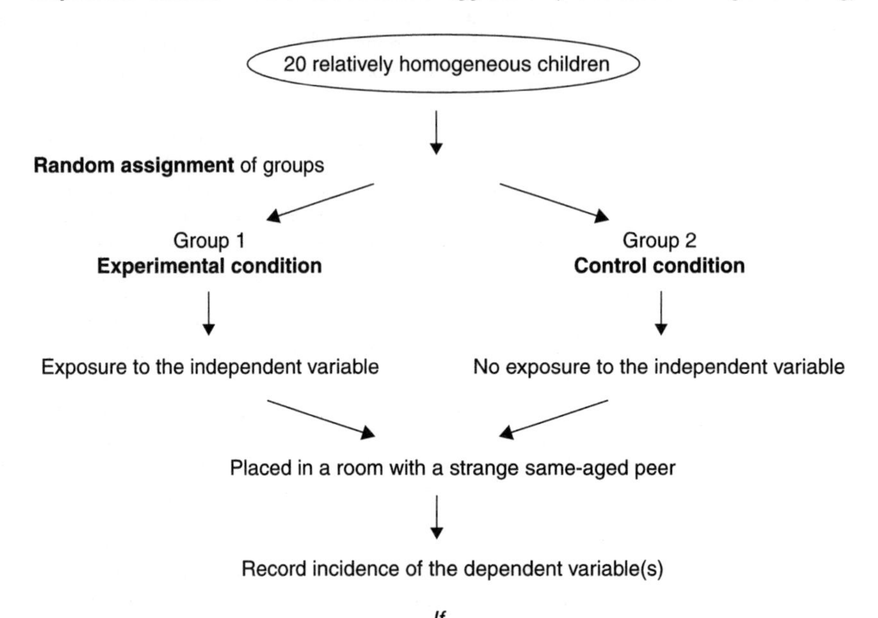

FIGURE 3.1 The controlled experiment

whether one thing causes another (Hartmann & George, 1999) (see Figure 3.1). There are two types of variables in an experimental design: **independent variables** and **dependent variables**. In general, independent variables are variables which are expected or thought to affect other variables (the dependent variables). In controlled experiments, however, independent variables are those variables which are manipulated by the experimenter. For example, imagine a study where two groups of children are observed individually in a play situation with a strange, same-aged peer. The experimenter in this study is interested in whether a child's exposure to aggression will produce aggressive behaviour in the child; thus, the experimenter designs a study in which some children are exposed to an aggressive incident while some children are not. Before the observation period begins, one group of children is exposed to a mock argument between the child's mother and a strange female (an accomplice of the experimenter's). The second group of children simply see the mother and the strange female act normally. Whether or not children are exposed to the mock argument is a variable which is under the experimenter's control and is therefore what we call an independent variable. In addition, the age and sex of the child are independent variables because these two factors are expected to have important effects on the dependent variable (e.g., boys might be expected to show higher levels of physical aggression than girls).

All children are measured on the dependent variable. The dependent variable is the factor that the experimenter expects to be influenced by the independent variable. In our example, the researcher might choose to measure acts of aggression exemplified by hitting and kicking initiated by the target child during the play session. The researcher could generate an 'aggression score' such as the number of aggressive acts demonstrated by each target child in five minutes of play with the strange child. In some studies, multiple dependent variables are assessed. In our example, the researcher could measure both physical aggression and verbal aggression.

Children who are assigned to the condition where they receive exposure to the independent variable are in what is called the **experimental condition**. Children who do not receive exposure to the independent variable are part of the **control condition**. Critical to the design of a controlled experiment is that children in the two groups are assumed to be equal before the study begins. Generally speaking, the best way to achieve this is through the **random assignment** of subjects to the experimental and control conditions. For example, the experimenter might place the names of subjects in a hat and randomly draw ten to participate in the experimental group and ten to participate in the control group. Alternatively, the experimenter may flip a coin or use any other method which guarantees that there is no bias in how subjects are assigned to the experimental and control conditions.

When properly conducted, the controlled experiment allows the researcher to make conclusions about cause and effect. Consider our example: if children in the experimental condition show significantly higher levels of aggression when playing with the peer than children assigned to the control condition, the researcher is able to state conclusively that exposure to an aggressive model causes aggressive behaviour in young children (once again, assuming the experiment is properly controlled and within the limits of the statistical techniques used).

Quasi-experiments

In contrast to controlled experiments, **quasi-experiments** are investigations where the experimenter has instituted appropriate controls over variables which might influence the results, but is unable to randomly assign participants to experimental conditions (Hartmann & George, 1999). Many developmental studies are not truly controlled experiments because it is impossible to completely randomize the assignment of subjects to conditions when certain variables such as age are the variable of interest in the investigation. In other words, when comparing children of different age groups on some variable, the assignment to conditions is obviously dictated by the child's age. This means that the causal inferences which can be made from quasi-experiments are much less clear than in true controlled experiments (Hartmann & George, 1999).

Nonexperimental designs

Nonexperimental designs, often known as **correlational methods**, are research designs in which neither the random assignment of subjects to conditions nor the use of a control group is employed (Hartmann & George, 1999). The goal of nonexperimental designs is to inform the researcher about potential relationships among variables or sets of variables. For example, a researcher might wonder whether a child's intelligence is related to their social skills. To answer this question, a researcher could administer measures of intelligence and social skills to a sample of children and look for a statistical relationship between the measures, known as a **correlation**. Nonexperimental designs are often known as correlational methods because of the frequency with which this statistical technique is employed, but it is important to note that nonexperimental/correlational designs can be carried out without the use of correlations.

A correlation coefficient measures the strength of relationship between two variables. When two variables are perfectly related, such that an increase in variable X is associated with a predictable increase in variable Y, we say that the variables show a perfect **positive correlation**. Perfect positive correlations are expressed by a correlation coefficient of +1.00. In contrast, when an *increase* in variable X is always accompanied by a completely predictable *decrease* in variable Y, we have an instance of perfect **negative correlation** which is expressed by a correlation coefficient of −1.00. When the scores of two variables are completely *unrelated*, there is no correlation, expressed by a correlation coefficient of zero (0.00). Moreover, the strength of a relationship can be assessed by the magnitude of the correlation coefficient: a correlation of 0.70 between two variables indicates a stronger relationship between them than a correlation of 0.20.

Getting back to our example, if we found that children's scores on our measures of IQ and social skills showed a correlation of 0.30, we have evidence that children's intelligence and their social skills are related. There is an important fact to notice here. Note that we do not say 'intelligence *causes* social skills' but only that the two variables are associated in a positive fashion. This is because nonexperimental or correlational research designs do not allow us to say anything about the *causal* relationship between the variables. This fact is often summed up by the catch phrase *correlation does not equal causation*. In our example, we are unable to ascertain whether intelligence causes the development of social skills, whether the reverse is true (that is, social skills may cause intelligence), or whether the two constructs are caused by some other common factor.

This last possibility is known as the **third variable problem**. A correlation between two variables, X and Y, could be caused by the presence of a third variable Z, which is responsible for the relationship between X and Y. For example, reading skill and speed at naming objects might show a positive correlation such that children who are better readers are able to name common objects more quickly than children who are poor readers. However, research has suggested that a third variable, changes in the child's speed of information processing, might underlie the changes in both reading skill and memory span (Kail & Hall, 1994). That is, the faster a child can process information, the faster they can name objects, and the better they are at tests of reading skill. One way in which researchers can deal with the issue of a possible third variable relationship is to control for the variable by including measures of it in the study.

Case studies

In the other approaches to research design that we have examined so far it is common to focus on groups of children rather than on individuals. This fact may lead you to wonder about the usefulness of studying a single individual. Can we learn anything worthwhile from the intensive study of a single child as opposed to looking at average levels of behaviour or knowledge across groups? **Case study methods** allow the researcher to focus on a single child, looking at their development in an in-depth fashion that is not practical with larger groups. Case studies have been used to examine unusual cases such as children with rare diseases or exceptional talents in some area. For example, Camras (1994) has used a case study methodology to look at the development of emotional expressions in her infant daughter. Camras created extensive video records of her daughter which captured emotional expressions produced in a wide variety of situations. Camras' work has proven extremely influential to theorizing on the nature of emotional development and the ties between facial expressions and emotional experience.

Case study methods have also been developed to provide a kind of experimental research design which is particularly useful for studying the effects of interventions on behaviour change. In these **ABAB designs**, the letter A represents a control condition or **baseline phase** of the study where the researcher simply measures the frequency or rate of occurrence of the behaviour they wish to alter. After collecting sufficient baseline information, the second phase of the experiment, the **treatment phase** (represented by the letter B), is begun. During the treatment phase the researcher employs some treatment to each incidence of the target behaviour, often a reward or punishment. The researcher is particularly interested in whether their manipulation has the effect of increasing or decreasing the frequency of the target behaviour in relation to the baseline phase. After some predetermined point in the treatment, the researcher stops implementing the treatment and looks to see whether the behaviour returns to its baseline frequency. Finally, the researcher will then reinstate the treatment, looking to see whether the behaviour increases/decreases in frequency. If the behaviour changes reliably as a function of the treatment, the researcher can be fairly confident that their treatment is effecting change in the target behaviour. Of course, a limitation of the case study method is the inability to generalize to the wider population. Simply because the treatment works with a single child does not mean it will be successful with all children. Another problem is that the target behaviour may not return to baseline levels in the third phase of the study; the behaviour may continue to exist at a different frequency than in the baseline phase, making it difficult to clearly assess whether the treatment was the cause of the behaviour change. (See Table 3.2 for an overview of the strengths and limitations of the various research designs.)

Research designs to study development

Developmental psychologists employ a wide range of research designs to study child development. Given that the goal of developmental studies is most often an examination of change over time in some aspect of behaviour or functioning, research designs which incorporate time as a variable are particularly relevant here. We will examine four such research designs: the cross-sectional study, the longitudinal study, the microgenetic study, and the sequential study. This is only a selection of the full range of research designs used in the study of child development, and you should be aware that there are many research designs available (see Schaie, 1965).

The cross-sectional design

One of the most common methods for studying age-related differences in behaviour is the **cross-sectional method**. In a cross-sectional design, researchers compare groups of children who are of different ages but are studied at the same point in time. For example, we may be interested in the

TABLE 3.2 Research designs: strengths and limitations

Research design	Strengths	Limitations
Experimental designs	• Allows the researcher to make *causal statements* about the relationship between two or more variables	• The findings of carefully controlled laboratory experiments may not generalize to real world settings
Quasi-experimental designs	• Allows the researcher some degree of control • Allows the researcher to take advantage of unique opportunities or natural experiments	• Because assignment to treatment conditions is not random, the ability to make *causal statements* is weakened
Nonexperimental designs	• Allows the researcher to study the relationships among a set of variables • Useful designs for the exploration of new areas and for generating new hypotheses	• These designs do not permit the experimenter to make *causal statements* about the relationships between variables
Case studies	• Allows for an in-depth examination in a way that is not practical with large groups • Can be set up to provide a quasi-experimental design	• Because assignment to treatment conditions is not random, the ability to make *causal statements* is weakened • Unable to generalize to the wider population

way children develop their notions of what a friend is. Thus, using this design, we would compare conceptions of friendship in children of two or more age groups, for example, 5-, 10-, and 15-year-olds. A cross-sectional study such as this one would allow us to compare whether or not children's conceptions of friendship change over time. That is, we might find that older children view intimacy as the most important aspect of friendship while younger children see shared interests as defining their conception of friendship (Rubin & Coplan, 1992).

However, the cross-sectional is only a convenient short-cut to the study of developmental change, and, as you might expect, short-cuts often come with limitations that restrict the conclusions that can be drawn from the findings. For instance, information about how an *individual child* changes is not available from a cross-sectional design. This is because the cross-sectional design only assesses group differences, such as the group of 5-year-olds compared to the group of 10-year-olds or to the group of 15-year-olds. As a consequence, we learn nothing about whether children's early conceptions of friendship influence their later conceptions or how stable conceptions might be over time. Cross-sectional designs are also open to the possibility of **cohort effects**. In our last example, imagine our 5-year-olds were born in 1995, our 10-year-olds were born in 1990, and our 15-year-olds in 1985. Differences between the three age groups might not reflect developmental differences at all; instead, the differences might be due to the historical time period in which these children were born. For example, children growing up in the 1980s may have experienced different social conditions than children growing up in the 1990s, factors which could impact on their conceptions of friendship. While historical effects are not always an issue, they can impact on development and we can't know from cross-sectional studies whether they are an issue in any given study. Interpreting the findings of cross-sectional studies, therefore, requires careful consideration.

Longitudinal designs

In a **longitudinal design**, a sample of children is observed repeatedly at different points throughout their lives. One clear advantage of longitudinal designs is that they allow us to observe individual differences in functioning over time. Because longitudinal designs allow the researcher to follow individuals' (as well as groups') progress, it becomes possible to examine individual patterns of stability and change in the behaviour of individuals. When we have large groups of subjects with clusters of similar variability, we can begin to identify what we call **developmental pathways**. By developmental pathway, we mean a particular pattern of movement through the life course, evidenced by groups of participants who follow a similar course of development.

While the obvious advantages of longitudinal designs are powerful incentives for researchers to find the resources to design and conduct them, they also have a number of disadvantages. First, they can be difficult to conduct and can take a great deal of time to complete. While short-term longitudinal studies get around this latter point, not all questions are amenable to their use, and require a much longer period of study. Second, longitudinal studies are open to the possibility of cohort effects. Third, **practice effects** can be an issue in longitudinal designs. Because the participants in a study may receive the same measures on repeated occasions, they may learn how to respond to the measure, meaning that the measure will not provide an accurate estimate of children's knowledge or abilities. Moreover, practice effects may emerge as children become accustomed to the experimenters; that is, having seen the experimenter on repeated occasions, the child may become more comfortable with them and provide more information than they did initially. Thus, what might seem like developmental change is, in reality, attributable to the child's increasing level of comfort.

Attrition (or mortality) is another problem faced when designing longitudinal studies. Attrition refers to the tendency for subjects to drop out of a study due to illness, a lack of interest, or other factors such as relocation.

Attrition can reduce the power of a study through the reduction in the size of the sample. The effects due to subject attrition can also be more insidious: in many studies, attrition occurs more often among particular groups of subjects than in others. For example, imagine that families who are in a lower socioeconomic group are more likely to drop out of a longitudinal study than are families who are in middle or higher socioeconomic groups. This fact could have a dramatic impact on the results of the study, such as reducing the variability in the original sample. In longitudinal studies, it becomes important to assess whether there are detectable patterns among the subjects who drop out of a study.

Microgenetic designs

The **microgenetic design** is a special form of longitudinal study. Microgenetic studies are designed to allow a very fine-grained analysis of developmental change, particularly for behavioural developments which occur rapidly and over a short period of time (Kuhn, 1995). A common feature of all microgenetic studies is that they involve a high density of observations; that is, the researcher looks repeatedly at an emerging development over a short period, trying to measure change in the smallest possible increments. This allows the researcher to form a more complete picture of the development of a given phenomenon. Microgenetic designs are generally short term, lasting from a few days to a few weeks, but this aspect is determined in large part by the nature of the developments the researcher wishes to study. Of course, like longitudinal studies, microgenetic studies are open to the possibility of practice effects and researchers must be careful to check for these.

The time-lag design

A **time-lag design** attempts to control for time of measurement effects such as historical effects associated with a particular birth cohort. As we have seen, historical factors can have a profound influence on child development. There is an abundance of possible factors which can impact on child development, such as war, disease, economic depressions and booms, the development of technologies such as television or computers, and health-related concerns. In a time-lag study, the researcher is generally more interested in identifying cultural changes that might impact on development rather than in studying the development of individuals. For example, a time-lag study might compare sexual attitudes and behaviours in sample of 18-year-olds born in 1950 (and thus, who were 18 years of age in 1968) to a sample of 18-year-olds born in 1980 (18 years of age in 1998). Such a study would allow the researcher to see how historical factors may have influenced change at the societal level.

A limitation of time-lag designs already noted is their inability to answer questions about the development of individuals. One important use of the time-lag study is as a supplement to longitudinal studies where time of measurement effects or cohort factors may be influencing the outcome. For example, a researcher might want to study the change in the sexual attitudes and behaviours of adolescents as a function of age. However, it would be difficult to be certain that any developments in sexual attitudes and behaviours observed were not simply the result of changes over time in society's values towards sexuality. By conducting a time-lag study along with the longitudinal study, the researcher would be able to say something about the extent to which these attitudes and behaviours have actually changed, and, thus, is in a better position to interpret the findings of the longitudinal study. (See Table 3.3 for an overview of research designs.)

Ethical issues in research on child development

The student undertaking the study of child development needs to be aware of ethical issues of relevance to the study of children. Guidelines or standards for conducting ethical research with children have been produced by a number of organizations such as the Society for Research in Child Development and the American Psychological Association.

The most obvious ethical issue is the need to avoid any harm to children who participate in the study. One of the main concerns of a formal ethical review process will be to evaluate the proposed research for any possible harm to the participants. Harm, whether physical or psychological in form, must be avoided as much as is possible. Some studies will involve procedures that are unpleasant to the child, such as arm restraint procedures which are designed to elicit some negative emotion. Ethics committees must consider whether the costs and benefits of the procedures are justified in relation to the potential of the research to add to our knowledge of child development. If unpleasant procedures are employed, the researcher must endeavour to alleviate any negative effects which the participants may experience as much as is possible on the completion of the study.

An important right of children involved in research projects is their right to provide consent before taking part in the research. This is known as **informed consent**, that is, an agreement by a participant to take part in a research project based on a full understanding of the nature of the project, what it entails, and its purpose. Children themselves need to be briefed on the study and what will happen to them. They also need to be informed, and made to understand that they can withdraw their participation at any time during the experiment; that is, if they become uncomfortable during the experiment, they may refuse to participate further. However, even with the

TABLE 3.3 Research designs to study developmental change

Research design	Strengths	Limitations
Cross-sectional designs	• Most efficient design for study of age-related changes in child development. Can be conducted quickly without a need to wait for individuals to change • Useful for studying *group* differences (as opposed to changes in individuals)	• Unable to address issues about the *individual* child • Only provides a short cut to the study of developmental change • Conclusions tempered by the possibility of *cohort* effects
Longitudinal designs	• Allows the researcher to study individual differences in functioning across time • Useful for identifying *developmental pathways* • Provides information about important developmental issues such as *stability vs. change* and the relationship between early behaviours and later outcomes • Identifying whether dependent variables change as a function of age or birth cohort aids in the search for the *mechanisms* underlying development	• Require a great deal of time and effort (especially large-scale, long-term studies) • Conclusions tempered by the possibility of *cohort* effects • Developmental change may be confused with *practice effects* • The *attrition* of subjects from the sample can make interpreting the results difficult
Microgenetic designs	• Allows the researcher to obtain a fine-grained analysis of developmental change • Useful for developing a more complete picture of developmental change which occurs rapidly	• Developmental change may be confused with *practice effects*
Time-lag designs	• Allows the researcher to control for cohort effects • Useful as a supplement to longitudinal studies where cohort effects are likely to be a factor	• Unable to address issues about the development of the *individual* child • On their own, time-lag designs do not address sources of developmental change other than cohort effects

researcher's best efforts, some children may be too young to fully understand their rights, and more importantly, may be unable to give fully informed consent. Because many children are too young to give fully informed consent, we rely on their parents to provide this consent for them. Thus, it is critical to ensure that the child's parents fully understand the nature of the research if the parents are to act as the child's guardians, safeguarding their interests.

All research projects should undergo a formal ethical review process. This means that the research project must be scrutinized by a board of experts whose goal is to ensure that the proposed research project meets the highest ethical standards. Most universities have an ethics committee that oversees all projects conducted under the auspices of the institution. Many hospitals and psychiatric institutions also have their own ethics committees. Finally, it is often the case that research projects submitted to school boards undergo an ethical review by the board's own committee. The net effect of this scrutiny by a group of people trained to evaluate research projects is to head off any potential ethical problems before the project is conducted. In addition to this, many scientific journals in the field of child development now require a statement from the researcher that the project meets ethical guidelines for research in child development and that no ethical principles were violated in conducting the research.

Confidentiality is also an issue. A researcher must maintain the confidentiality of the information obtained from each of the participants in their study. For example, information that could identify individuals involved in a project must be removed from their records. In addition, researchers must not publish findings in such a way as to identify an individual child. Finally, the findings of a research project need to be made available to the participants. This should take place in a form which they can understand; generally, this will consist of a report specifically designed for parents, which is made available to them after the completion of the project. Researchers also have an obligation to consider the broader ramifications of their findings on social attitudes, public policy and the like. The researcher should give careful consideration to how their findings could be misinterpreted or misused before publication, in order to lessen or avoid the chances of such an event taking place.

SUMMARY

A variety of methodologies (e.g., survey, observational and psychophysiological methods) and research designs (e.g., nonexperimental and quasi experimental designs) are employed within the study of child development. Methodology is a fundamental issue in the study of child development, however, many students are tempted to devote relatively less time to this topic or to skip over it entirely. Sound methods underpin research in this field and without a knowledge of the *hows* and *whys* of these methods, understanding the research which contributes to our knowledge of children is far more difficult.

Glossary

ABAB designs are a kind of experimental research design which is particularly useful for studying the effects of interventions on behaviour change. Baseline measures of a behaviour are obtained, an experimental treatment is introduced and is then withdrawn and reintroduced.

Attrition refers to the tendency of subjects to drop out of a longitudinal study.

Baseline phase is the phase of ABAB research design in which the researcher documents the frequency of occurrence of a particular behaviour.

Case study methods are research designs which focus on a single child, looking at their development in an in-depth fashion that is often not practical with large groups.

Clinical interview is a flexible, open-ended interview format that allows the interviewer to gather as much information about a topic as possible and to follow up on any promising trains of thought.

Cohort effects refer to differences which are due to the historical time period in which a cohort of same-aged children were born.

Confidentiality refers to an obligation on the part of the researcher to maintain the confidentiality of the information obtained from each of the participants in their study.

Control condition refers to the condition in an experiment where participants are not exposed to the independent variable.

Controlled experiments are research designs where the researcher manipulates one or more independent variables and measures their effect on one or a set of dependent measures, while controlling for confounding variables.

Correlation refers to a statistical measure of the association between two variables.

Cross-sectional designs are used when researchers compare groups of children who are of different ages but are studied at the same point in time.

Cortisol is a hormone which is released into the bloodstream in response to stress. It is often used as a psychophysiological index of stress.

Dependent variables are the factor(s) that the experimenter expects to be influenced by the independent variable.

Developmental pathways refer to a particular pattern of movement through the life course, evidenced by groups of participants who evidence similar patterns of development.

Electroencephalograph (EEG) is a device which amplifies and records electrical activity from the scalp using a number of small electrodes.

Event sampling used in observational research, is a technique where a set of predetermined behaviours are recorded whenever a particular event occurs.

Experimental condition refers to the treatment condition in an experiment where participants receive exposure to the independent variable.

Functional magnetic resonance imaging (fMRI) is a noninvasive technique which allows the researcher to detect changes in the blood flow to the brain, using magnetic fields to provide exceptionally clear images of the areas of the brain that are activated during a cognitive task.

Galvanic skin response is changes in the electrical conductance of the skin, a psychophysiological measure.

Independent variables are those variables which are manipulated by the experimenter.

Informed consent is an agreement by a participant to take part in a research project based on a full understanding of the nature of the project.

Longitudinal design is a method where a sample of children is observed repeatedly at different points throughout their lives.

Microgenetic designs are research designs which allow for a very fine-grained analysis of developmental change by using a high density of observations. They are particularly useful for studying behavioural developments which occur rapidly and over a short period of time.

Negative correlation when an increase in one variable is accompanied by a decrease in a second variable, we say the two variables are negatively correlated.

Nonexperimental designs (or **correlational methods**) are research designs in which neither the random assignment of subjects to conditions nor the use of a control group is employed.

Positive correlation when an increase in one variable is accompanied by an increase in a second variable, we say the two variables are positively correlated.

Practice effects can be an issue in longitudinal designs; participants in a study may receive the same measures on repeated occasions, and may learn how to respond to the measure.

Psychophysiological methods are a diverse set of research methods which have the common feature of measuring some aspect of physiological functioning in order to examine how these processes contribute to behaviour.

Quasi-experiments are investigations where the experimenter has instituted appropriate controls over variables which might influence the results, but is unable to randomly assign participants to experimental conditions.

Random assignment is a quality of experiments where participants are placed in the experimental and control conditions via some random method.

Reactivity occurs when subjects are highly conscious of being observed. This can lead to distorted behaviour and less valid conclusions.

Reliable findings are ones which we are confident could be reproduced or replicated.

Replicable refers to the fact that observations need to be able to be duplicated by other researchers.

Representative behaviour in an observational study the researcher should employ methods which do not lead participants to alter or distort their behaviour because they are being observed. We want a sample of behaviour which is representative of the participant's typical behaviour in that situation.

Representative sample is a sample in which the population surveyed resembles the larger population about which data are being gathered.

Self report a method in which the child is asked to report on their own thoughts, feelings or behaviours. A commonly employed method is the clinical interview.

Socially desirable responding occurs when a research participant responds in a way that they think the interviewer would like, that is, telling the interviewer what they want to hear.

Specimen record is a record of everything that happens in a fixed period during an observational study.

Structured interviews are interview formats wherein each participant is asked the exact same set of questions in the same order.

Third variable problem refers to the fact that a correlation between two variables, X and Y, could be caused by the presence of a third variable, Z, which is responsible for the relationship between X and Y.

Time sampling methods are observational techniques where a set of predetermined behaviours are recorded during a particular window of time.

Time-lag designs attempt to control for time of measurement effects such as historical effects associated with a particular birth cohort.

Treatment phase is a phase of an ABAB research design in which the experimenter employs some treatment designed to increase or decrease the frequency of a particular behaviour.

Vagal tone refers to the variability in heart rate, a commonly used psychophysiological technique.

Validity threats are factors related to the design of experiments which can cause problems with the interpretation of data.

The Biological Foundations of Development

4

LEARNING AIMS

At the end of this chapter you should:

- **be able to describe the developmental course of physical growth and articulate the principles which growth follows**
- **be familiar with the factors which can influence physical growth and sexual maturation**
- **be able to describe the course of motor development and recognize the difference between *gross* and *fine motor* development**
- **be able to recognize and label the major parts of the human brain and understand the neuron**
- **be familiar with concepts such as *hemispheric specialization* and *experience-expectant* and *experience-dependent* development**
- **be able to explain the logic of behaviour genetics, twin designs, and associated concepts such as *heritability*, *niche picking*, and *range of reaction***

The course of physical growth

In comparison to other species, the course of physical growth in human beings is a long drawn-out process. Evolutionary theorists have suggested that our lengthy period of physical immaturity provides us with added time to acquire the skills and the knowledge which are required in a complex social world. This suggestion emphasizes the fact that physical growth is not simply a set of maturational processes that operate independently of input from the environment: rather, physical growth occurs within an environmental context. Environments, including factors such as cultural practices, nutrition and opportunities for experience play an important role in physical development.

The patterns of growth

Physical growth does not proceed randomly; instead, it follows orderly patterns known as **cephalocaudal** and **proximodistal** development. The cephalocaudal pattern of development refers to the fact that growth occurs in a head to toe direction. For example, two months after conception, the human infant's head is very large in contrast to its total height and by birth, this ratio is much smaller as the rate of growth in the rest of the body begins to catch-up. Within the head itself the eyes and the brain grow faster than the jaw. These examples illustrate the head to toe direction of physical growth. The proximodistal pattern of development refers to the fact that development occurs outwards from the centre of the body. For example, a baby will acquire control over the muscles of the neck and trunk before it acquires control over the fingers and the toes.

Body size

Changes in body size are the most obvious manifestation of physical growth. During infancy, changes in growth are extremely rapid. An example which readily comes to mind is the dramatic changes in height. By 1 year of age, infants average a growth of approximately 11 inches (approximately 32.5 cm) over their size at birth (Malina, 1975). Similarly impressive gains are noted in weight. At 2 years of age, an infant's weight will have quadrupled since birth. In general, physical developments in height and weight tend to occur very rapidly in infancy, continue at a relatively steady pace throughout childhood, and then slow down towards puberty.

At puberty, there is a marked *growth spurt*, that is, a very rapid increase in size and weight. The pubertal growth spurt varies from person to person in terms of its intensity, its duration, and its age of onset. The pubertal growth spurt tends to last around 4½ years, girls usually showing their pubertal growth spurt around age 11, whereas in boys the same process begins at approximately age 13. According to Tanner (1990), girls finish pubertal growth by about age 16 whereas boys continue to grow until approximately 18 years of age; however, in both sexes growth may still take place after the completion of the pubertal growth spurt.

A number of studies have provided evidence that hereditary factors play a strong role in physical growth. Work by Wilson (1986) examining correlations in a variety of physical indices showed that the correlation in height between identical twins was approximately 0.94 at 4 years of age, and this correlation remained stable after this time. For fraternal twins, the correlation for height was relatively high at birth but became increasingly smaller over time, moving from 0.77 at birth to 0.49 at 9 years of age (at which point it became stable). The large and stable correlations observed in identical twins and the smaller correlations observed for fraternal twins suggests that genetic factors play an important role in determining height. Similar patterns are observed for weight as well as for the timing of growth spurts (Wilson, 1986).

Environmental factors in physical growth: nutrition

Of course, genetic factors are unlikely to tell the entire story of physical growth. Not surprisingly, growth is highly dependent on our nutritional intake, that is, what kinds of food we eat, and how much of them we eat. Height and weight are clearly affected by nutritional intake. Studies during World War II showed that the restrictive diets imposed by wartime conditions in Europe led to a general decline in average height, reversing a trend towards increasing height which had been apparent since the end of World War I (Tanner, 1990). However, more than just our height and weight can be affected by nutritional intake: research has indicated that dietary restrictions during the war also had an effect on puberty. Studies of French women showed that **menarche**, the onset of menstruation, was delayed by up to 3 years (Tanner, 1990).

Cognitive development has also been related to nutrition. For example, *anaemia*, the condition where a person suffers from low levels of iron in the bloodstream, has been associated with a slowing of intellectual development (Pollitt, 1994). A striking example of nutritional effects on cognitive development comes to us from the examination of intestinal worms. Intestinal worms sit in our digestive tract and rob us of valuable nutrients which fuel our growth. Watkins and Pollitt (1997) showed that children who have high levels of intestinal worms show reduced performance on psychometric tests of cognitive ability. In some cases, studies have shown that these effects can be quite severe.

Hormonal influences

In large part, the physical changes observed at puberty are controlled by **hormones**. The hormones are a set of chemical substances manufactured by glands and are received by various cells throughout the body to trigger other chemical changes. The most important of these glands is the **pituitary gland** located near the base of the brain. The pituitary gland triggers changes both directly, via the hormones it secretes into the bloodstream, which act on various tissues to produce growth and indirectly by triggering other glands to release different hormones.

The physical changes associated with puberty, specifically **primary sexual characteristics** (growth involving the reproductive organs: the penis, scrotum and testes in males and the vagina, uterus and ovaries in females) and the **secondary sexual characteristics** (visible changes which are associated with sexual maturation such as the development of breasts in females, facial hair in males and pubic hair for both males and females) are also controlled through the pituitary gland which stimulates the release of the sex hormones. In boys, **testosterone** is released in large quantities, leading to the growth of male sexual characteristics, while in females **oestrogens** are associated with female sexual maturation. Both types of hormones are actually present in both sexes although in quite different amounts.

Sexual maturation

In terms of sexual maturity, the most important changes to result are **menarche** and **spermarche**, that is, the first menstruation in females and the first ejaculation in males. These two milestones are commonly believed to indicate a readiness to reproduce although in actuality, there is often a short period of sterility which can last about one year in both females and males in which menstruation and ejaculations occur but no eggs or sperm are released (Tanner, 1990).

The factors which determine the timing of puberty are multiple and complex, ranging from genetic determination to the nature and quality of family relationships. Genetic factors are certainly involved in determining when the pituitary gland begins releasing the hormonal signals which begin the physical transformations, but interestingly, they are not the sole cause of when pubertal timing occurs for an individual. In young women, physical exercise can delay the onset of the physical changes associated with puberty. For example, Brooks-Gunn (1988b) found that very few ballet dancers actually had their first menstruation at the 'normal' time. Family factors can also play an important role in pubertal timing. Moffitt et al. (1992) found that family conflict and the absence of fathers predicted an earlier onset of menarche. Steinberg (1987) found that an increased psychological distancing between girls and their fathers also predicted an earlier menarche. A more recent study by Ellis et al. (1999) showed that the quality of fathers' investment in their daughters was positively associated with the timing of puberty; when fathers had good quality relationships with their daughters, the onset of pubertal maturation in their daughters came later. Together, these studies highlight the importance of environmental factors in sexual maturation, demonstrating the necessity of examining interactions between genetic and environmental causes in studying development.

Besides examining the questions of when and why adolescents enter puberty earlier or later than their peers, we can ask what effects early or late maturation has on individuals. A classic study by Jones and Bayley (1950; see also Jones, 1965) suggested that early maturation carries distinct advantages for boys but not for females. Jones and Bayley tracked 16 early-maturing and 16 late-maturing boys for a six-year period. Late-maturing boys were characterized as lower in physical attractiveness, masculinity, and were rated as more childish, eager and attention seeking than early-maturing boys. In contrast, early-maturing boys were characterized as independent, self-confident, and as making better leaders and athletes. Jones showed that for women, the reverse effects obtained (Jones & Mussen, 1958): early-maturing girls were more likely to show social difficulties than late-maturing girls. They were also less popular, less self-confident, held fewer leadership positions and were more withdrawn than late-maturing girls. More recent research has confirmed and extended these findings. Early-maturing girls tend to have a poorer body image than normally maturing or late-maturing girls (Brooks-Gunn, 1988a), at least in part because the normal weight gains which accompany pubertal maturation violate the cultural ideal for thinness. This trend is exactly the reverse for males: early-maturing boys tend to have a much more positive body image, in large part because many cultures seem to value traits like height and muscularity.

Behavioural problems have also been associated with early versus late maturation, particularly in girls. The explanations for these problems seem to reduce to two types. Caspi and Moffit (1991) argue for a dispositional account, believing that it is not early maturation *per se* that creates problems for girls, but rather, early maturation on top of a previous history of behaviour problems. Their argument is that when stressful events such as early maturation occur, they may highlight dispositional factors (tendencies to behave in a particular fashion, possibly due to genetic factors or previously acquired habits). It is these dispositions which Caspi and Moffit believe are ultimately responsible for the behaviour problems. In contrast, Graber, Brooks-Gunn and Warren (1995) believe that *psychosocial factors* – factors such as parental warmth, parental approval, and the level of family conflict – play an important role in how girls react to early maturation. Research from Sweden has tended to support the view that psychosocial factors play an important role in the effects of early maturation on girls (Stattin & Magnusson, 1990). These researchers found that early-maturing girls tended to have smaller networks of friends, to associate with older friends who often engaged in deviant behaviours, and were more likely to engage in risky behaviours such as smoking, drinking alcohol, and sexual intercourse. While the findings to date do suggest a risk to early-maturing girls, it is clear that contextual and psychosocial factors play an important role: not all early-maturing girls will experience problems and some early-maturing girls may show very positive developmental outcomes (Brooks-Gunn, 1988a).

TABLE 4.1 Selected milestones in motor development

Age	Milestone
6 weeks	Hold head upright while in a prone position
2 months	Roll from back onto side
3 months	Directed reaching for objects
5 to 7 months	Sit without support
9 to 14 months	Stand without support
8 to 12 months	Walk with support
12 months	Use of pincer grasp when reaching
12 to 14 months	Walk alone

Motor development

Human infants start life with very limited motor skills, yet by about 1 year of age, they are walking independently. In between birth and learning to walk a great many skills are acquired. What does the course of motor development in infancy look like? Nancy Bayley (1969) provides us with a description of the average age at which infants and toddlers acquire many of the most common motor skills. According to Bayley, infants can hold their heads upright by 6 weeks of age; by 2 months they can roll from their sides onto their back; by 3 months of age they can grasp an object; by 7 months infants can sit alone and begin to crawl; by 12 months they walk on their own (see Table 4.1).

Also included in Bayley's work is a description of the age range at which 90 percent of children achieve a particular skill. For example, while the average infant sits upright alone by 7 months of age, 90 percent of infants will acquire this skill somewhere between 5 and 9 months of age. Bayley's data highlight an important fact regarding the variability of motor development: while the sequence of motor development is relatively uniform, progress in the acquisition of motor skills is highly variable. For example, some infants will learn to walk as early as 9 months while others will not take their first steps until 17 months. It is important to remember that individual children will not conform exactly to any description of the average age at which developmental milestones are achieved; some variability is normal and early progress or lack of the same is not a good predictor of the final level of development.

A principle known as **differentiation** comes into play when we try to describe the acquisition of motor skill (Bühler, 1930). Differentiation refers to the fact that, initially, motor skills are rather global reactions to a particular stimulus; only with time and practise do motor behaviours become more precise and adapted to particular ends. Consider the reaction of an infant to having an unwanted blanket placed on top of her. A very young infant might twist and writhe in a random fashion which may or may not achieve the desired effect. Older infants will grasp the blanket and pull it away; they use a more specific, more precise behaviour to accomplish their goals. The principles of cephalocaudal and proximodistal development also apply to the acquisition of motor skills. For example, infants learn to hold their head upright before they learn to sit upright or to pull themselves to a standing position.

Maturation vs. experience

The maturation of the neural and muscular systems determines, to a large extent, when children will acquire a particular skill. Early research on motor skill highlighted a maturationist viewpoint, that is, that development is under the control of inherited programmes that are genetic in origin (Gesell & Thompson, 1929; McGraw, 1935). These researchers were reacting against behaviourists like John B. Watson (see Chapter 2) who believed that motor skills like walking were simply conditioned reflexes. In contrast, maturationists like Gesell and McGraw believed that motor behaviours like walking emerged according to a preprogrammed genetic timetable.

Gesell devised a simple design to demonstrate the effects of maturation. Using identical twins allowed Gesell to control for biological factors since identical twins share 100 percent of their genes. One twin would be given extra practise at a particular motor task while the control twin received no extra training. When tested after a period of training, *both* twins showed significant evidence of acquiring the motor skill, not simply the twin who had been given extra practise as might be predicted (Gesell & Thompson, 1929). Such findings led Gesell to the conclusion that maturation and not experience is the prime factor in determining when children acquire skills.

However, as Thelen (1995) notes, the development of motor skill is not simply the outcome of genetic programming: transactions with the environment must play a crucial role in the timing of motor skill acquisition. Thus, an important aspect of when children acquire a particular motor skill is experience. In contrast to the work of Gesell, opportunities to practise particular motor skills have been shown to promote their earlier appearance (Zelazo, Zelazo, & Kolb, 1972). The acquisition of motor skills also varies across cultures in ways which are not consistent with genetic factors. Some cultures emphasize practices which encourage the earlier or later appearance of a skill. For example, Hopkins and Westra (1988) found that mothers in the West Indies have babies which walk considerably earlier than the average North American infant. West Indian mothers use a particular routine, passed down to them by other members of their culture, which encourages the early development of walking and other motor skills. As this example shows, environments can have important effects on when skills are acquired.

Gross and fine motor development

Bertenthal and Clifton (1998) note that control over one's motor behaviour ranks among the infant's greatest achievements. Psychologists who study the acquisition of motor skills find it useful to distinguish between **gross motor development**, that is, motor skills which help children to get around in their environment such as crawling and walking, and **fine motor development**, which refers to smaller movement sequences like reaching and grasping. The development of motor skill has implications beyond simply learning how to perform new actions: motor skills can have profound effects on development. For example, researchers have shown that infants with locomotor experience were less likely to make errors while searching for hidden objects (Campos & Bertenthal, 1989; Horobin & Acredolo, 1986). The ability to initiate movement about one's environment stimulates the development of spatial encoding abilities, making hidden object tasks easier to solve. Rovee-Collier (1997) has made a similar point in regard to memory development. She argues that the onset of independent locomotion around 9 months of age marks an important transition in memory development. Children who can move about the environment develop an understanding of locations such as 'here' and 'there'. Because infant memory is initially highly dependent on context – that is, the similarity between the situation where information is encoded and where it is recalled – infants who have experience moving about the environment and who learn to spatially encode information become less dependent on context for successful recall. These examples show that motor development has implications beyond the immediately apparent benefits of crawling or walking.

Piaget (1952) argued that the development of reaching and grasping was a key aspect of cognitive development because it forms an important link between biological adaptation and intellectual adaptation. Reaching and grasping are voluntary actions under the infant's control, and as such, they open up exciting new possibilities in the infant's ability to explore their environment. The infant who reaches for and grasps an object so as to explore it pushes his development forwards as he engages in processes such as adapting his grip to the size and shape of the object. Piaget argued that these early processes of assimilation and accommodation to objects drive cognitive development in the sensory motor period.

The development of reaching begins early in life. Newborn infants seated in an upright position will swipe and reach towards an object placed in front of them, a behaviour labelled **prereaching**. These poorly coordinated behaviours start to decline around 2 months of age (Bower, 1982) and are replaced by **directed reaching**, which begins at about 3 months of age (Thelen, Corbetta, Kamm, Spencer, Schneider, & Zernicke, 1993). At this time reaching becomes more coordinated, efficient, and improves in accuracy

(Bushnell, 1985). According to research conducted by Clifton, Rochat, Robin, and Berthier (1994) the infant's reaching does not depend simply on the guidance of the hand and arm by the visual system but is controlled by **proprioception**, the sensation of movement and location based on stimulation arising from bodily sources such as muscle contractions. By about 9 months of age, infants can adjust their reaching to take into account a moving object. However, 9-month-olds are far from expert reachers and a good deal of skill remains to develop.

Once infants begin reaching they also begin to grasp the objects that are the target of their reaches. The **ulnar** grasp is seen when infants first engage in directed reaching. The ulnar grasp is a primitive form of grasping in which the infant's fingers close against their palm. The fingers seem to act as a whole, requiring the use of the palm in order to hold an object. Shortly after this accomplishment, when infants can sit upright on their own, infants acquire the ability to transfer objects from hand to hand. By around the end of the first year, infants have graduated to using the **pincer** grasp (Halverson, 1931) wherein they use their index finger and their thumb in an opposable manner, resulting in a more coordinated and finely tuned grip. This allows for the exploration of very small objects or objects which demand specific actions for their operation, such as the knobs on a stereo system which require turning to the left or right to adjust volume.

The development of motor skill beyond infancy

Beyond infancy, not a great deal is known about the development of motor skill. Gallahue (1989) suggests that, beyond infancy, three fundamental sets of motor skills emerge in the child's repertoire. These are *locomotor movements*, which include walking, running, jumping, hopping, skipping and climbing; *manipulative movements* including throwing, catching and kicking; and *stability movements* (centered around controlling one's body) including bending, stretching, rolling, balancing, and walking on one's hands.

The development of motor skill progresses through three stages (Gallahue, 1989). Consider an example such as learning to swing a tennis racquet. Initially, a child tries to execute the motor skill, however, they fail to follow through with the movement. They also fail to engage in any sort of anticipatory movements which prepare them to execute the action. Young children's stroke often looks more like a swipe, barely resembling the straight-armed, locked-wrist style that mature players use. By the second stage, what we might think of as a transitional stage in the development of the skill, children can execute the individual components of the swing more competently, however, they fail to organize the components into a smoothly sequenced whole. At this stage, children may adopt a straight arm, start with their racquet well behind their body and follow through, but on any given swing they are unlikely to execute all three of these aspects of an accomplished stroke together. Finally, by the third stage all components of the behaviour are integrated into a coordinated whole. Motor skills continue to improve as related developments in the sensory and perceptual skills, as well as the maturation of the nervous system, take place. However, increased practise will speed children's acquisition of a skilled behaviour.

Brain development

Perhaps the most obvious change in the developing brain is its size. At birth, an infant's brain is approximately 400 grams or 25 percent of the weight of an average adult brain, which weighs in at about 1,400 grams (Segalowitz, 1995). By the time the infant is 6 months old the brain weighs about half as much as an adult brain, and by age 2 it is 75 percent of the weight of an adult brain (Restak, 1984). Like many other aspects of development, brain growth is not smooth and continuous, but rather, occurs in spurts (Segalowitz, 1995).

The structure of the brain

The brain is made up of two **hemispheres**, together known as the **cerebrum** (see Figure 4.1). These hemispheres are connected by a set of nerve fibres known as the **corpus callosum**. The left and right hemispheres of the brain are anatomically distinct and control different functions (Segalowitz, 1983b; Springer & Deutsch, 1993). For example, the temporal lobe, an area associated with language, seems to be larger on the left side of the brain than on the right. However, whether these anatomical differences are related to functional differences remains a question which is open for further research.

The cerebrum is covered by a layer known as the **cerebral cortex**. This layer of cells is extremely convoluted giving rise to the distinctive look of brain tissue. The cerebral cortex accounts for approximately 90 percent of the brain's total number of cells. It is also the most advanced part of the brain, supporting complex functions such as language, vision and motor skills. The cerebral cortex is divided into four main areas called **lobes**, and two other areas known as the **association areas**. The four lobes of the brain are known as the **frontal lobe** (which supports planning, organization, and other higher mental functions), the **temporal lobe** (involved in language, hearing, and smell), the **parietal lobe** (involved in the processing of bodily sensations) and the **occipital lobe** (which is involved in visual processing). The **anterior association** area (located at the front of the brain) and **posterior association area** (located near the rear of the brain) are involved in linking up information from various parts of the brain.

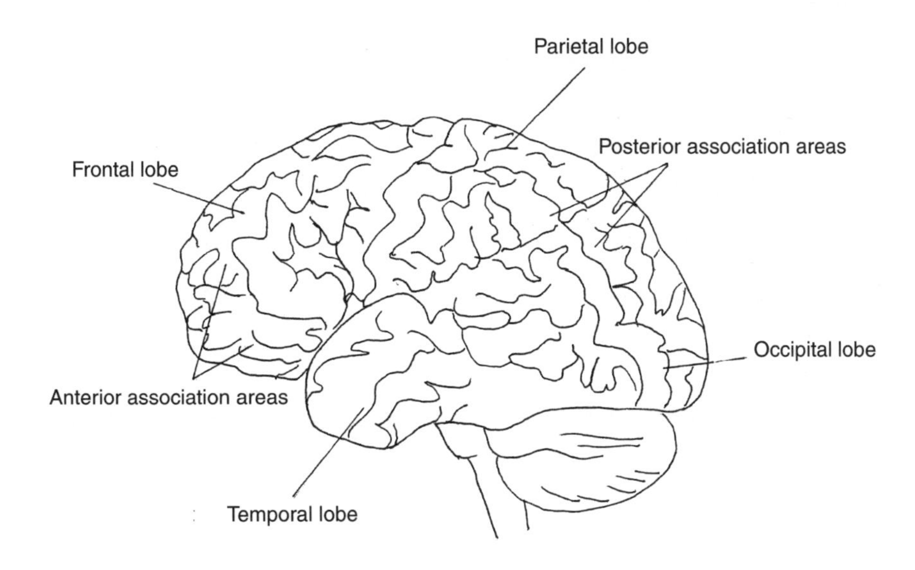

FIGURE 4.1 The human brain

Neuronal development

So far we have described the structure of the brain at a macro level. Let us now consider the micro level structure of the brain. The brain is made up of a number of different types of cells. **Neurons** are the name given to the nerve cells which send and receive neural impulses (electrical signals) throughout the brain and the nervous system. The average human brain is made up of some 100 billion neurons, each with as many as 15,000 connections to other cells. The second type of cell which make up the brain are **glial cells**. These are the cells which provide structural support to the neurons, regulate the nutrient concentrations delivered to neurons, and are important to the task of **myelination**, in which neurons are covered with an insulating layer of *myelin* (a fatty substance) which makes the neuron a more effective transmitter of electrical information (Johnson, 1998).

The neuron itself is made up of **dendrites**, a **cell body**, an **axon**, and **terminal buttons** (see Figure 4.2). The dendrite is the part of the cell which receives signals from other neurons and which transmits this information to the cell body. The information collected is than transmitted along the axon to the terminal buttons which send information across the **synapse** (the gap between the terminal buttons of one neuron and the dendrites of another neuron) to other neurons. This transmission across the synapse is carried out by means of special chemical signals known as **neurotransmitters**.

The development of neurons begins the embryonic period, with most neurons present by the 7th month after conception (Rakic, 1995). Recall that an average human brain is made up of about 100 billion neurons. This

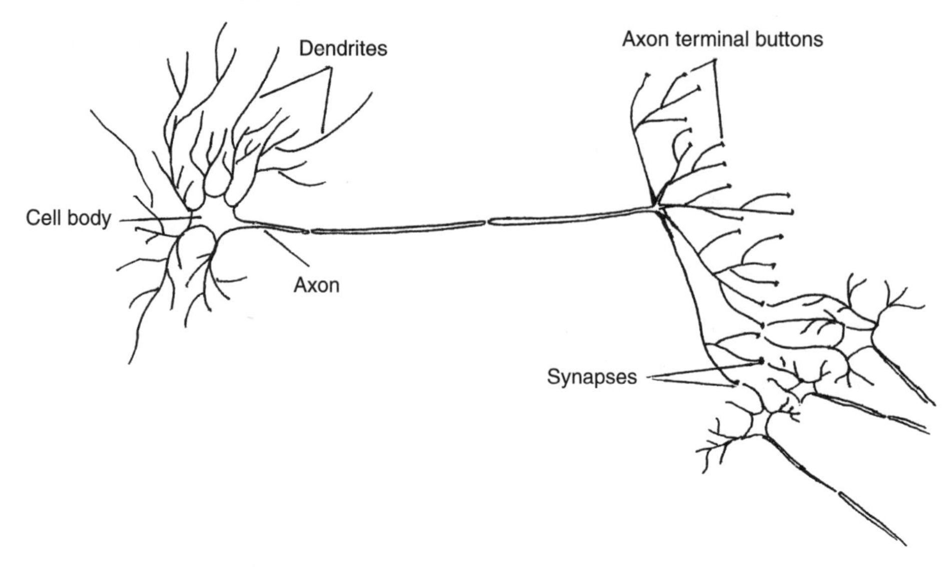

FIGURE 4.2 The neuron

means that neurons are being generated in the brain at the rate of about 250,000 per minute in a process known as *neuron proliferation*. Neurons which are generated often travel to other locations in the brain, guided by a set of complex neurochemical processes.

The brain has a peculiar property of overproducing both neurons and synaptic connections between neurons. Segalowitz (1995) argues that while the purpose of this overproduction is not completely known, two functions are presumed to result from this process. First, it allows experience to dictate which connections between neurons are kept and which connections are lost, thereby ensuring that the child acquires all of the skills and information required to enable development to take place. Second, the overproduction of neurons and synapses ensures *plasticity*. By plasticity, it is meant that the brain can compensate for early damage by either replacing connections which have been lost or transferring functions to other areas of the brain. The available evidence suggests that, if brain injury occurs reasonably early in life, the likelihood of recovering the function is good (Fox, Calkins, & Bell, 1994). However, while the brain is genetically programmed to overproduce synapses and neurons in the early years, this overproduction is soon curtailed. This **thinning** of neurons and synapses (Huttenlocher, 1990; 1994a, b; Segalowitz, 1995) is accomplished through two processes: **neuronal death**, in which some neurons are programmed to die, apparently to provide more space for crucial cell clusters, and **synaptic pruning**, in which the brain disposes of a neuron's connections to other neurons. According to Huttenlocher (1994a, b), the goal of both processes is to increase the efficiency of transmission between neurons.

Hemispheric specialization

One of the most important aspects, and often one of the most misunderstood (Segalowitz, 1983b), is the left–right organization of the brain across its two hemispheres. **Hemispheric specialization** refers to the differential functions carried out by the two cerebral hemispheres. Hemispheric specialization begins at birth and the differences between the two hemispheres remain largely the same into adulthood. This belief, that there is a lack of change in the organization of function across the two hemispheres, has come to be known as the **invariance hypothesis**. However, as Segalowitz (1995) notes, what *will* change is what the child is able to do with the information that is processed by the two halves of the brain. Also of note is the fact that the two hemispheres of the brain mature at different rates, with the evidence suggesting that the right hemisphere of the brain matures earlier than the left (Best, 1988). Interestingly, this earlier maturation of the right hemisphere mirrors the growth of functional differences carried out by the two hemispheres (Segalowitz, 1995).

So, what are these functional differences attributed to the left and the right hemispheres? Movement and sensation are each controlled by a single hemisphere. The left side of the brain controls movement and sensation of the right side of the body while the right side of the brain controls movement and sensation for the left side of the body. The only exception to this pattern is the eyes which send input to both sides of the brain. The left side of the brain is specialized for language processing. In contrast, the right side of the brain is specialized for processing spatial information, music and the perception of faces. The two hemispheres are also believed to be differentially involved in the processing of emotion. According to Davidson (1994b) the left hemisphere of the brain is responsible for the expression of emotions associated with approach to the external environment, emotions such as *interest*, *anger* and *joy*. In contrast, the right side of the brain is responsible for processing emotions associated with withdrawal from the environment such as *fear*, *distress* and *disgust*. While the evidence is clear that some functions are associated with a particular hemisphere, it is important to note that the separation of function across the hemispheres is not absolute. For example, a number of studies conducted with individuals who have right brain damage have demonstrated that these people have difficulty processing nonliteral forms of language such as sarcastic speech (Kaplan, Brownell, Jacobs, & Gardner, 1990), suggesting that the right hemisphere may be associated with particular aspects of language processing such as *pragmatics* (Siegal, Carrington, & Radel, 1996). **Lateralization** is the term used to describe the processes by which the two halves of the brain become specialized to carry out specific functions. Research in developmental neuropsychology suggests that the lateralization of brain function across the left and right hemispheres is a very complex process which is not yet well understood.

Brain maturation and developmental change

As discussed earlier, the brain undergoes several growth spurts over the course of its development. Recordings of brain electrical activity as reflected in the electroencephalogram (EEG) appear to show correlations between growth spurts and major periods of cognitive development (Fischer & Rose, 1994; 1995). Indeed, many developmental psychologists and neuropsychologists have drawn connections between developments within the brain itself (changes due to the growth of synapses, synaptic pruning, the development of the frontal lobes and the myelinization of neurons) and cognitive development (Case, 1992c; Thatcher, 1994). For example, Case (1992c) argued that major stage changes in children's developing cognitive ability mapped onto changes in brain development. While it is tempting to make such leaps, Segalowitz (1995) provides a caution in doing so, arguing that studying global changes in brain structure is less informative than examining how regional developments in the brain develop to support specific functions.

A related point comes from neuropsychological work on the distinction between **experience-expectant** development and **experience-dependent** development made by Greenough, Black and Wallace (1987). These authors have shown how neural circuitry is related to environmental events. Some neural circuits require input from the environment in order to begin growing, a process which Greenough et al. refer to as experience-expectant development. In contrast, other types of neural circuits are strongly influenced by the types of environmental input they receive, what Greenough et al. term experience-dependent development. The development of the brain is critically dependent on environmental experience. Brain structures in and of themselves do not cause development. (Similarly, experience with the environment will not produce developmental changes if the brain structures which underlie those changes have not yet matured.) Thus, a theory of cognitive development which attempts to relate changes in brain structure to other developmental changes must also factor in the role of experience in this association. Given that experience is involved, the correlation between brain maturation and developmental change will never be perfect.

Genes and behaviour

Heredity: the process of genetic transmission

The processes underlying the hereditary transmission of parental characteristics to their offspring are remarkably complex. Consider your own siblings or a friend you know who has brothers or sisters: are you or your friend exactly the same as your or his/her bother or sister? The answer (even if you have an identical twin) is probably 'no'. Siblings share half their genes with each other; that is, half of your genetic material is the same as your brother or sister, but these shared genes are not enough to ensure a high degree of similarity. This is because genes interact with the environment to produce observable characteristics such as eye colour, and height or behaviours such as personality and intelligence. When we speak of an individual's **genotype**, we refer to their genetic makeup, that is, the particular set of genes which they have inherited from their parents. As a result of development, environments act on individuals to produce their **phenotype**, that is, their observable characteristics.

In our discussion of genetics and human development, we will take for granted that by this point in your career you have acquired an understanding of sexual reproduction and instead will focus on the key genetic aspects of the process. At conception, a single **sperm** from males unites with the **ovum** or egg from the female to create a fertilized egg called a **zygote**. Sperm and egg are unique cells in that they are the only cells in the human body to carry 23 chromosomes (all other cells carry 46 chromosomes). These special cells are known as **gametes**. **Chromosomes** are a very special chemical structure made up of a series of proteins known as deoxyribonucleic acid or DNA. They have a thread-like appearance and are found in the nucleus of a cell. Chromosomes come in 23 pairs; half of these come from the mother and half from the father. The chromosomes carry the **genes** which are the units of hereditary transmission. Genes are sequences of proteins, a part of the DNA molecule. They work by triggering the production of proteins when instructed to do so by environmental signals or by other genes.

Remember that chromosomes come in pairs, one from the father and one from the mother. Thus, a gene on one chromosome has a partner or an alternate form on the other chromosome. This alternate form of the gene is called an **allele**. To further complicate matters, the alleles of a gene from both parents can be similar or dissimilar in their genotype. If the alleles are alike, the child is said to be **homozygous** for the trait coded for by the gene; if the genes are dissimilar the child is **heterozygous**. Homozygous children will display the trait which is coded for by the genes whereas the relationships between the two alleles will determine how the trait is expressed for heterozygous children. Consider eye colour as an example. The genes which code for eye colour can have different forms, an allele which specifies blue eyes and an allele which specifies brown eyes. If the child's parents both carry the brown-eyed allele, the child will have brown eyes.

The relationships between alleles are described in terms of **dominant** and **recessive** alleles. In some cases, one allele is more powerful or dominant than another and will always express its effects over those of another allele. This is the case for hair colour. The brown hair allele is dominant over the red hair allele. Thus a child who inherits a red hair allele from one parent and a brown hair allele from the other will always develop brown hair. If we represent a dominant allele by **A** and a recessive allele by **a** than you should recognize that a person could have the following combinations of alleles: **AA**, **Aa**, **aA**, and **aa**. These reduce to three patterns. **AA** is homozygous and represents two dominant genes. **Aa** and **aA** are heterozygous and represent combinations where the dominant gene will be expressed. The combination **aa** is again homozygous and represents a person with two recessive genes. In our example of hair colour, this is the *only* combination of genes which would result in a red-haired child. There is yet another possibility which can occur, called **codominance**. Codominance occurs when heterozygous alleles both express their traits with equal force. For example, the blood types A and B are codominant alleles such that a person who inherits the A allele from one parent and the B allele from the other will have blood type AB.

Many harmful traits coded for by genes are recessive, a fact which has the happy effect of greatly reducing their occurrence in the population. An example of this is the allele for **phenylketonuria** or **PKU**. PKU is a genetic disorder in which the child is unable to metabolize a protein called phenylalanine, a problem which can lead to brain damage and to profound mental retardation. The allele which codes for the normal metabolizing of phenylalanine is dominant while the gene which leads to PKU is recessive. When both parents carry the recessive allele for PKU there is a one in four chance that their offspring will have the disorder (as we described earlier).

Genes and environments

In contemporary developmental psychology, rarely will one find a psychologist taking up a position that emphasizes either genes or environments as the sole cause of behaviour. Instead, modern psychologists recognize that genes and environments *interact* to shape the course of development. Research has shown clearly how genetic factors serve to restrict the range of possible courses that development can take, while at the same time we have gained an ever more sophisticated understanding of how environments exert a tremendous influence on development, both supporting and restricting it.

We also know that genes can shape environments. This may strike you as an odd idea, one which violates your intuitive notions of the direction in which biological effects should go. According to the work of Sandra Scarr (1992, 1996; Scarr & McCartney, 1983), genes can have effects on the environment in at least three ways. First, genes can have what Scarr referred to as **passive** effects. Children's environments are most often dictated by parents. Because parents and children share some of their genes, it is not surprising that parents will create a home environment which is supportive of the child's genotype. Consider musical talent. Musical parents will likely have musical children. As a result of their own predisposition, musical parents will create a musical environment for their children. Thus, the parent's efforts provide an ideal environment for the child's genes which code for musical talent to be expressed. Second, genes may have an **evocative** relationship with the environment. This occurs when some trait in the child causes others to react in a certain way which has the effect of strengthening the trait. For example, temperamentally 'easy' babies who smile and act sociably will elicit positive social reactions from others which reinforces the baby's behaviours and ultimately strengthens their genetic predisposition. Finally, genes can effect the environment in an **active** way. This occurs when children seek out environments which are compatible with their genetic makeup. For example, athletically talented children will eventually move towards participation in school sports while musically talented children will join the band. This process, which Scarr (1996) calls **niche picking**, is an active process based on one's genetic predisposition. As Scarr notes, niche picking increases in importance as people move towards adulthood and begin to take increasing control over their own environments. This process may also play a role in explaining why correlations for traits such as cognitive ability show increasing concordance over time.

As suggested earlier, environments also have profound effects on genetic factors. One way in which this relationship has been conceptualized is through the concept of **range of reaction** (Gottesman, 1963). According to range of reaction concept, genes do not fix behaviour in a rigid fashion but establish a range of possibilities which depend heavily on environmental circumstances. In a sense, you can think of a person's genotype as placing boundaries on their ability which differ depending on environmental circumstances. For example, if a child is born into an impoverished environment, their genotype may place specific limits on how far their cognitive abilities may develop. This child may show very low ability under impoverished environments, and only slightly higher levels of achievement under more enriched environments. In this case, we would say the child has a small range of reaction. In contrast, another child with a different genotype may perform slightly better in impoverished environments but extremely well under an enriched environment. This child would show a much larger range of reaction.

The reaction range concept has been criticized by Gilbert Gottlieb (1991; Gottlieb, Wahlsten & Lickliter, 1998). Gottlieb suggests that genes play a much less deterministic role than is suggested by the range of reaction concept which emphasizes the limit-setting effect of genes. He suggests that genes and environments engage in a process of *coaction* wherein the relationships between genes, environments, and other levels of behaviour such as neural activity all mutually influence one another. The influences between any levels are bidirectional, that is, they go both ways. Thus, genes are simply part of a system which are affected by events at other levels of the system.

Behaviour genetics

So far we have covered cases of genetic transmission that conform to a simple model where a gene is causally related to a particular trait such as eye colour. However, most behaviours that are inherited are multifactorial, that is, they have more than one cause. When some trait is affected by more than one gene, geneticists speak of **polygenetic inheritance**. Given the state of genetic research, it is very difficult at this point in time to specify exactly which genes contribute to some trait, but researchers are beginning to make some progress in this regard. A recent report (Chorney et al., 1998) identified a particular gene which is associated with cognitive ability. However, more often than not, researchers are only able to specify how important genetic factors are relative to environmental factors in the cause of some particular trait, that is, how much of the variance in a given trait is caused by genetic factors and how much is caused by environmental factors. This area of inquiry, examining the relationship between genetic and environmental factors is known as **behaviour genetics**.

We know genetic factors play a critical role in human development. For example, researchers have identified a form of a gene which, if present in an individual, increases the risk of developing Alzheimer's disease by a factor of four over the normal population (Plomin, DeFries, McClearn & Rutter, 1997). Beyond such high profile cases as a genetic cause for Alzheimer's disease, behaviour geneticists have shown that genetics play important roles in the development of psychological traits such cognitive abilities, school achievement, personality, self-esteem, and drug use. In the following section we will examine some of the findings of behaviour genetic research.

Heritability

Behaviour geneticists employ a concept known as **heritability** to measure the effects of genetic factors on a trait. Essentially, heritability is an estimate of the relative influence of genetic versus environmental factors. According to Plomin et al. (1997: 79), heritability can be defined as 'the proportion of phenotypic variance that can be accounted for by genetic differences among individuals'. It is estimated by examining the correlations for some trait among relatives and is generally expressed as an *intraclass correlation*, that is a correlation which can be straightforwardly interpreted as a percentage. In other words, an intraclass correlation of 0.80 between identical twins for IQ would suggest that 80 percent of the variance in IQ scores between the twins was due to genetic factors.

Heritability has been criticized as a concept by many authors. Bronfenbrenner (1972) demonstrated that heritability cannot be straightforwardly interpreted as simply an index of genetic causation. In his analyses, Bronfenbrenner shows how environmental factors have a clear impact on the calculation of heritability. While not at all refuting the importance of genetic factors in development, Bronfenbrenner's argument is that heritability should be interpreted as reflecting the capacity of the environment to invoke and nurture the development of a trait. In his critique of research on racial differences in intelligence, Block (1995) questions the common assumption that heritability is simply an index of genetic causation. Block points out that heritability is calculated as a ratio of *genetically caused* variation to *total variation* in some trait. Again, while not refuting the importance of genetic factors in human development, Block's argument is that a characteristic can be highly heritable even if it is not caused by genetic factors. Take a trait such as long hair. Block would argue that in 1950, long hair was caused genetically. That is, in Western cultures, only women wore long hair and since women are genetically different than men, the cause of wearing long hair could be construed as genetic. The ratio of genetic variation (sex: men or women) to total variation (women: only women wore long hair) was close to one, indicating high heritability. However, now that variability in who wears their hair long (as both men and women commonly do these days) has increased, the heritability of long hair has decreased. However, neither in 1950 nor today is wearing long hair genetically determined in the normal sense. Men did not usually wear long hair in the 1950 due to strong social pressures to conform (i.e., environmental reasons); when the environmental reasons change, so too does the heritability of the trait. While this example may seem frivolous, the point it makes is very important to how we interpret heritability. The student of developmental psychology needs to remember that heritability does not necessarily imply genetic causation.

Research designs in behaviour genetics

Most commonly, heritability is estimated using **twin studies**. In one common twin study design, the correlation on some trait (for example, intelligence) is measured between pairs of **monozygotic twins** and **dizygotic twins**. Monozygotic twins are born of the same fertilized egg, a zygote which has split in half, and thus they share 100 percent of their genes. Dizygotic, or fraternal twins, develop in the womb at the same time but are of two different fertilized eggs, and, as a consequence, they share only 50 percent of their genes. If one makes the assumption that the environments of identical twins are no different than the environments of fraternal twins, then higher correlations for the trait between identical twins is thought to be the result of their genetic similarity. It is important to note that this conclusion is based on an assumption of *equal environments* between identical and fraternal twins. Bronfenbrenner (1972) highlighted the reasons why this assumption is problematic. Think for yourself about this issue. Do you think identical twins might be treated differently from fraternal twins in some way? If you bring to mind issues such as parents dressing twins exactly alike or friends and relatives confusing identical twins then you have identified some of the factors that Bronfenbrenner felt might be problematic for the twin design, and which violate the equal environments assumption. Again, while such problems pose issues for how exactly we interpret the findings of behaviour genetic research, they by no means suggest that genetic factors are unimportant determinants of human development.

A large number of behaviour genetic studies have been conducted to examine the heritability of intelligence. A review of many of these studies by Bouchard and McGue (1981) showed that the average correlation between same sex pairs of monozygotic twins measured for general intelligence was 0.86. A correlation of 0.62 was obtained for fraternal twins. Both of these results indicate a substantial effect for genetic factors (although keep in mind the potential interpretative problems discussed earlier). When Bouchard and McGue examined the findings for twins reared apart, the correlation dropped to 0.72, again, indicating a substantial role for genetic factors. Further work on the importance of genetic factors across the life span has come to the intriguing conclusion that genetic factors become more salient to explaining the correlations between the IQ scores of twins as time goes on. In other words, as age increases so does the correlation for general intelligence between twins (DeFries, Plomin & Fulker, 1994; Plomin, Pedersen, Lichtenstein, & McClearn, 1994; Plomin et al., 1997). As many of these researchers would note, the findings described, while indicating a substantial role for genetic factors in the development of general intelligence, also indicate the importance of environmental factors in determining intelligence.

Finally, we briefly consider genetic effects on personality. Behaviour genetic research in the area of personality has suggested that as much as 50 percent of the personality differences between people are due to genetic factors (Bouchard, 1994). Loehlin (1992) reported evidence of significant genetic effects on two commonly measured aspects of personality: *neuroticism* (emotional instability) and *extraversion* (sociability). Intraclass correlations for identical twins reared together were around 0.50 for both traits, suggesting a strong link between genetics and personality. Another trait known as *sensation seeking*, which is comprised of behaviours such as thrill seeking, searching out novel experiences, and susceptibility to boredom, showed a correlation of 0.54

in a sample of identical twins reared apart. Plomin et al. (1997) suggest that there is also strong evidence that a variety of personality disorders such as schizotypal, obsessive-compulsive, and borderline personality disorder are all at least partially heritable.

SUMMARY

Acquiring an understanding of the maturation of our bodies, our brain and central nervous system, and the importance of genetic factors to our development is the foundation for understanding other key areas of child development such as perception, cognition, and emotion. While the study of our biology is important in its own right, it is also tied to development in these other domains, and it is necessary to examine this at an early point in our study of children.

Glossary

Active effects are genetic effects which occur when children begin to seek out environments compatible with their genetic makeup. For example, athletically gifted children may seek out athletic environments.

Allele refers to the alternate form of a gene.

Association areas refers to two parts of the brain, the **anterior association** area (located at the front of the brain) and **posterior association area** (located near the rear of the brain) that are involved in linking up information from various parts of the brain.

Axon refers to the part of the neuron which ends in the terminal buttons.

Behaviour genetics is the area of inquiry examining the relationship between genetic and environmental factors in development.

Cell body is the body of the neuron which contains the nucleus and other structures.

Cephalocaudal development refers to the idea that physical growth occurs in a head to toe direction.

Cerebral cortex is the outer layer of cells which covers the cerebrum. It is also the most advanced part of the brain, supporting complex functions such as language, vision, and motor skills.

Cerebrum refers to the two interconnected hemispheres, or halves of the brain.

Chromosomes are a very special chemical structure, found in the nucleus of a cell, which is made up of a series of proteins known as deoxyribonucleic acid or DNA.

Codominance occurs when heterozygous alleles both express their traits with equal force.

Corpus callosum is the bundle of fibres which connects the two hemispheres, or halves of the brain.

Dendrites are the part of the neuron which receives signals from other neurons, and which transmits this information to the cell body.

Differentiation refers to the fact that, initially, motor skills are rather global reactions to a particular stimulus, and only become more precise and adapted to particular ends with time.

Directed reaching describes reaching which has become more coordinated, efficient, and has improved in accuracy.

Dizygotic twins are twins which are born at the same time but which develop from separate fertilized ova.

Dominance refers to the fact that one allele for a trait is more powerful or dominant than another and will always express its effects over those of another allele.

Evocative effects occur when children's traits cause others in their environment to behave towards them in a particular way. For example, temperamentally easy babies may elicit higher levels of social interactions from others which strengthens their disposition to engage in and enjoy social interaction.

Experience-dependent development is a process which describes how the growth of some types of neural circuits are strongly influenced by the types of environmental input they receive.

Experience-expectant development is a process which describes how some neural circuits require input from the environment in order to begin growing.

Fine motor development refers to small movement sequences like reaching and grasping.

Gametes are the specialized sex cells from males and females (sperm and ovum) which combine to form a new life. Each gamete contains only 23 chromosomes, half the number of a regular cell.

Genes are the units of hereditary transmission. A gene refers to a portion of DNA located at a particular site on the chromosome.

Genotype is our genetic makeup, that is, the particular set of genes which we have inherited from our parents.

Glial cells are the cells which provide structural support to the neurons.

Gross motor development refers to the various motor skills such as crawling and walking which help children to move around in their environment.

Hemispheric specialization refers to the differential functions carried out by the two cerebral hemispheres. Hemispheric specialization begins at birth and the differences between the two hemispheres remain largely the same into adulthood.

Heritability is an estimated measure of the effects of the relative effect of genetic factors on a trait.

Heterozygous a child is said to be heterozygous for a trait coded for by the gene if both forms of the gene are different.

Homozygous a child is said to be homozygous for a trait coded for by the gene if both forms of the gene are alike.

Hormones are a set of chemical substances manufactured by glands, which, received by specialized receptor cells throughout the body, can trigger other chemical changes.

Invariance hypothesis the hypothesis which proposes that the functions attributed to the two hemispheres of the brain remain constant, or invariant, across the lifespan.

Lateralization is the term used to describe the processes by which the two halves of the brain become specialized to carry out specific functions.

Lobes the cerebral cortex is divided into four main areas called **lobes** and two other areas known as the **association areas**. The four lobes of the brains are called the **frontal lobe**, **temporal lobe**, **parietal lobe**, and the **occipital lobe**.

Menarche refers to the onset of menstruation.

Monozygotic twins are often called 'identical twins'. Refers to twins who are born of the same fertilized egg. This occurs when a zygote splits into two clusters of cells which develop into two genetically identical individuals.

Myelination is a process in which neurons are covered with an insulating layer of *myelin*, a fatty substance which makes the neuron a more effective transmitter of electrical information.

Neuronal death is a process in which some neurons are programmed to die, apparently to provide more space for crucial cell clusters.

Neurons are the name given to the nerve cells which send and receive neural impulses (electrical signals) throughout the brain and the nervous system.

Neurotransmitters are a special class of chemicals which are released across the synapse by the terminal buttons.

Niche picking is an active process whereby one's genetic predisposition leads one to arrange the environment to suit one's dispositions.

Oestrogens are hormones that are associated with female sexual maturation.

Ovum is the female germ cell which unites with a male's sperm at conception.

Passive effects occur when parents structure the child's environment in ways which are consistent with genetic traits shared by parents and child. For example, musical parents may provide a musical environment for their children which may lead to the expression of genes which code for musical talent.

Phenotype refers to the observable characteristics of an organism, created by the interaction of the genotype with the environment.

Phenylketonuria (PKU) is a genetic disorder in which the child is unable to metabolize a protein called phenylalanine which can lead to brain damage and mental retardation.

Pincer grasp refers to a grasp where infants use their index finger and their thumb in an opposable manner, resulting in a more coordinated, and finely tuned grip.

Pituitary gland is a gland located near the base of the brain which (1) triggers physical growth by releasing hormones, and (2) controls other hormone-releasing glands via its chemical secretions.

Polygenetic inheritance is said to occur when some trait is affected by more than one gene.

Prereaching is a behaviour wherein newborn infants seated in an upright position will swipe and reach towards an object placed in front of them.

Primary sexual characteristics refer to the reproductive organs: the penis, scrotum, and testes in males, and the vagina, uterus, and ovaries in females.

Proprioception is the sensation of movement and location based on stimulation arising from bodily sources such as muscle contractions.

Proximodistal development refers to the idea that physical growth occurs outwards from the centre of the body towards the hands and feet.

Range of reaction refers to the fact that genes do not fix behaviour in a rigid fashion, but establish a range of possibilities which depend heavily on the environment.

Recessive refers to the weaker of the two alleles.

Secondary sexual characteristics refer to the visible changes which are associated with sexual maturation such as the development of breasts in females, facial hair in males, and pubic hair for both sexes.

Sperm is the male germ cell which unites with a female's ovum at conception.

Spermarche refers to the first ejaculation in males.

Synapse is the gap between the terminal buttons of one neuron and the dendrites of another neuron.

Synaptic pruning is a process in which the brain disposes of a neuron's connections to other neurons.

Terminal buttons are the ends of a neuron which release neurotransmitters across the synapse to be received by other neurons.

Testosterone is a male hormone which is responsible for the production of sperm and for the development of primary and secondary sexual characteristics.

Thinning is the process by which the brain reduces the number of neurons and synaptic connections between neurons in early development including neuronal death and synaptic pruning.

Twin studies refers to a class of research designs that employ twins as research subjects. These designs are often used to tease apart the genetic and environmental effects on a particular trait.

Ulnar grasp is a primitive form of grasping in which the infant's fingers close against their palm.

Zygote is a fertilized egg, created by the union of a sperm and an ovum. Refers to the first two weeks of life.

5 Perceptual Development

LEARNING AIMS

At the end of this chapter you should:

- **be aware of the distinction between sensation and perception and the reasons why we study perception**
- **be able to describe the different theories of perception and be able to explain concepts such as *affordances* and *invariances***
- **be familiar with developments in each of the five senses**
- **understand and be able to describe the different cues which aid in the development of vision**
- **describe the concept of *intermodal perception***
- **think about the development of perception across the life span**

Introduction

Psychologists studying perceptual development tend to make a distinction between **sensation**, the act of detecting a particular stimulus event via a sensory system and **perception**, the processes by which we make sense of our sensations. William James (1890), often thought of as the father of American psychology, described the infant's perception of the world as a 'blooming, buzzing confusion'. James believed that newborns (or **neonates**) find the world of sensory stimulation chaotic and argued that perceptual development was required in order for the infant's sensations to become organized and meaningful. In contrast to James's view, perceptual psychologists have learned that infants come equipped with sophisticated abilities that allow them to make much more sense of the world than James would have believed possible. Advances in research methods for studying infant development, such as *preferential looking* and *habituation paradigms*, allow us to better understand the sorts of stimuli that infants are attuned to and how their early perceptual abilities develop.

When studying perceptual development, it is important to keep in mind that there is a close relationship between perception and action. Motor activity provides the infant with an important means for learning about the world and stimulates the development of their perceptual capabilities (Bertenthal & Campos, 1987). In turn, as the infant's perceptual skill develops, so too does their motor skill. In short, perceptual activity and motor activity are inextricably linked, each promoting the development of the other (Stein & Meredith, 1993).

Why study perception?

Research on infant perception has largely been concerned with two key questions: what can infants perceive at birth and how do their perceptual abilities change over the first few months of life? There are a variety of reasons why it is important to answer these questions. Whether infants have adult-like perceptual abilities specified in their genetic inheritance and which develop in a normative manner or whether infants slowly acquire these abilities over time relates to the nature versus nurture controversy. Work on perceptual development has shed light on the relationship between nature and nurture in human development. A second reason for interest in perception and perceptual development is that our capacity for visual, auditory, tactile, olfactory, and taste perception enable us to interact with other human beings. Thus, their development not only has important implications for our biological growth, but it also has a profound effect on our social and cognitive development as well.

Until relatively recently, the amount of research on infant's perceptual development was limited. Early researchers made the argument that although it would be interesting to study young children's perceptual abilities, it was simply not possible to do so because of the limitations of human infants. However, there has been a recent flurry of activity on perceptual development in infancy, research which has done a great deal to change our image of an infants' perceptual competencies (e.g., Kellman & Banks, 1998). Infants' perceptual abilities are undoubtedly more impressive than had been previously assumed. John Flavell (1985) suggests three reasons why developmental researchers underestimated the perceptual competencies of infants. First, Flavell argues that there had been an unwarranted generalization from observations of infants' motor abilities to their perceptual abilities. Because on the motor side of their development infants demonstrate incompetence, it seemed natural to assume a similar level of perceptual incompetence. Second, there has been a strong associationist tradition in both philosophy and psychology that assumes that we begin life with very minimal capabilities which are gradually built up through learning. This view of development, prevalent until the early 1960s, contributed to the negative estimation of infants' perceptual skills. Finally, there was a tendency to extrapolate downwards from the findings of poor perceptual skills in years after infancy. The assumption was that, if preschool children showed marked improvement on perceptual abilities, then infants' perceptual capabilities must be very poor indeed. We now know, as a result of a great deal of painstaking research, that infants come equipped with a much higher level of ability than we originally estimated. In what follows, we survey some of these abilities. The rapidity with which infants' perceptual functioning achieves adult levels is very striking in contrast to their development in other domains such as cognition.

Theories of perceptual development

According to Bornstein and Arterberry (1999), theories of perceptual development need to be viewed in the light of more general theories of the nature of perception itself. There are two prominent perspectives on perception, which lead directly to the two theories of perceptual development described in this chapter (see Table 5.1 for a summary). As we will briefly examine each theory, it should become clear as you read through this chapter that the overwhelming evidence is in favour of **nativist** positions on perceptual development. The very rapid way in which perceptual development occurs suggests that it is, to a large extent, a function of our biological endowment. Even so, learning still occurs, and is central to modern theories of perception.

According to the first view, **nativist theory**, meaningful perceptual structures exist in the world (structures which are independent of how we perceive them). In other words, these structures do not need to be created or constructed from the sensations we receive via our senses, rather, these structures and the information they impart exist independently of us. For those who hold to this view, perception is simply a process of detecting or 'picking up' the information available in these structures (Gibson, 1969; Gibson, 1979). In other words, our perceptual systems have evolved to pick up the information available in the environment. This view, elaborated most articulately by James and Eleanor Gibson, is known as the theory of **direct perception**.

In contrast to this view, other arguments have been put forward that suggest that our interpretations of the physical world are not simply constrained by the nature of our perceptual systems. These theorists make the argument that information gained by the organism through transactions with the environment may influence our perception (Bornstein & Arterberry, 1999); that is, our perceptions are often constructions, the result of prior knowledge used to guide our current interactions with the environment in order to interpret immediate experience. Whereas these **constructivist theories** of perception do allow for some innate perceptual abilities, they emphasize that perceptual

TABLE 5.1 Theories of perceptual development

Nativist theory	
Gibson and Gibson	Perception is a process of picking up information available from structures that are independent of how we perceive them, called *direct perception.* This process occurs via the exploitation of *invariances* in stimuli (their unchanging elements), which occurs by interacting with the object through its *affordances* (properties of a stimulus that allow interaction with it). Perceptual development occurs as the individual absorbs more information from any given stimulus and begins to recognize relationships between stimuli, or *compound invariants*
Constructivist theory	
Piaget	The process of perception is supplemented by the process of perceptual activity, the former being innate and the latter the intellect's correction of initial impressions with reference to previous experience
Neisser	The individual's previous experience, or the *schema* the individual applies to a situation, affects perception of affordances. This perception of the environment in turn changes previous knowledge or schemas, which results in further exploration within the environment

development is largely the result of interactions of the person with their environment, which lead to the construction of our understanding of the world. Piaget's view of perception is an example of this position.

Piaget's theory of perceptual development

Piaget's theory of perceptual development is rather different from other theories of perception in the respect that Piaget believed that perception does not develop, but is 'enriched by the emerging structures of intelligence' (Pulaski, 1980: 108). In his view it is our intelligence which demonstrates a continual pattern of development (Piaget, 1969).

Piaget's (1969) theory of perceptual development makes a critical distinction between **perception** and **perceptual activity**. For Piaget, perception is our initial and immediate sensory experience via modalities such as seeing, hearing, and touching, that occurs when we are exposed to a stimulus. Perceptual activity, by way of contrast, is the 'correction' of our initial impressions by the activity of our intellect (Pulaski, 1980); that is to say, perceptual activity refers to the modification of perception by previous experience.

It is fair to say that Piaget's theory is not so much a theory of perception but, rather, a theory of the cognitive processes by which infants and children come to interpret perception (Bremner, 1994). Piaget was clear in his belief that perception is dependent on intelligence. Like many modern perceptual psychologists, Piaget believed that perception provides direct knowledge of the environment, however, he made it clear that this direct, perceptually based knowledge is prone to error (Piaget, 1969). Thus, for Piaget, perception is not the source of our knowledge, rather, knowledge comes from the combined operation of perception and perceptual activity. In other words, knowledge is a product of the whole organism and not simply a product of the sense organs. Given that Piaget's theory of perception is largely a cognitive theory, with a strong focus on the relationship between action or experience and cognitive development, we will consider Piagetian theory further in Chapter 6 on cognitive development, where we take up Piaget's view on the development of knowledge about objects.

Gibson's theory of perceptual development

According to James and Eleanor Gibson, perceptual development is an active cognitive process in which we interact selectively with the array of possibilities afforded to us by the environment (Gibson, 1969; Gibson, 1979). A key concept in the Gibsonian approach to perceptual development is the notion of **affordances**. Affordances are the properties of objects that offer the individual the potential to interact with the object in a variety of ways. We can perceive affordances by exploiting **invariances** in the visual environment, that is, aspects of the environment which do not change. For example, floors afford walking by virtue of their smooth, continuous, and solid qualities whereas the handle on a coffee mug affords the action of grasping by virtue of its shape and solidity.

Ulric Neisser (1976) suggests that which affordances are perceived is a function of our previous experience, that is, the **schema** we bring to bear on a situation when we first perceive it. A schema is a mental representation or knowledge structure which guides our understanding of the environment. Our schema direct how we explore our environment, and, therefore, which affordances we pick up from the environment. The information we obtain from the environment causes changes in our knowledge or schemas which direct further exploration, and so on, in a cyclical fashion. According to Neisser, affordances need not be limited to objects like floors and coffee mugs. People afford possibilities for interaction as well; for example, think of facial expressions: a person's raised eyebrows, wide open eyes, and dropped jaw afford an attribution of a particular mental state, namely surprise.

If, as the Gibsons suggest, perceptual development is merely a process of taking in information that exists in the environment, the question that naturally arises with respect to perceptual development is, simply, 'what develops?' According to Eleanor Gibson (1969), with development, children take more information from a stimulus. With experience, children learn to perceive more information from a set of stimuli, both about individual objects, and about the relationships between objects. Gibson (1979) refers to the perception of relationships among stimuli that specify more complex or higher order affordances as **compound invariants**. In other words, the relationships among objects give more information to the perceiver than simply picking up the objects themselves in isolation. Thus, with development, older children learn to abstract higher order structures of which younger children may remain entirely naïve.

Consider the following example: have you ever watched an infant try to make his way down a small incline, say, a very short staircase? This situation was studied by Karen Adolph and her colleagues (Adolph, Eppler, & Gibson, 1993). They had two groups of infants try to negotiate a series of ramps which varied in slope. Infants were placed on the top of the ramp, and encouraged to descend by their mother who waited at the bottom. Adolph's subjects were a group of 8-month-old infants who were crawling but not walking, and a group of 14-month-old infants who had learned to walk. On the basis of Gibsonian theory, you would expect the older infants to recognize that gentle slopes afford walking whereas steeper slopes require a different strategy. In contrast, 8-month-olds will not have had enough locomotor experience to have encountered many inclines, and, thus, they will not have developed much in the way of a strategies for dealing with them. This is in fact what Adolph and her colleagues found: 14-month-olds walked down gentle slopes but approached the steeper slopes by sitting down and sliding (usually after a good deal of searching for an alternative method). By way of contrast, the 8-month-olds simply approached each ramp the same way, by crawling down head first. On the steep ramps this often led to the infant sliding down in an uncontrolled manner. The results of this study support a Gibsonian account of perceptual development. Older infants, with appropriate experience, could perceive the affordances offered to them by the different ramps, and adjusted their strategy for descending accordingly. Younger infants were unable to perceive the affordances for walking versus sliding and tended to approach each ramp in the same way.

Ways of studying perceptual development in infants

Given that much of the research on perceptual development is conducted with infants in an effort to understand what perceptual abilities they come equipped with and how these change with age, it is important to briefly examine the particular methods which are used to study what infants know and what they can do. Studying infant development is particularly challenging because of the methodological difficulties entailed; that is, you cannot simply ask babies questions about what they see and what they do not (well, you can, but you should not expect particularly good answers). In short, we need to find other methods of testing that will allow us to learn which aspects of the world infants can perceive. (See Table 5.2 for an overview of children's perceptual development.)

TABLE 5.2 Milestones in children's perceptual development

Age	Milestone
1 to 3 months	A clear preference for human *faces* is in evidence by 3 months of age
	Sense of touch operative
	Newborns can distinguish tastes such as *salty* and *sweet*
	Newborns are able to distinguish their own mother on based on her *smell.*
	Newborns react to noxious smells but learning which smells are noxious takes some time
	Newborns' hearing is much less sensitive (by about 17db) than adults. Most sensitive to sounds within the typical range of the human voice
	Visual acuity in newborns is very poor. Improves dramatically over the first year.
	Visual accommodation reaches adult levels by 2 months of age
	Newborns are unable to discriminate objects on the basis of *colour.* Colour vision develops by about 2 to 3 months of age
	Size and *shape constancy* are present at birth but are refined into the early childhood years
	1-month-olds show evidence of *intermodal perception* in that they can match visual and tactile cues
3 to 6 months	Exploration of objects through *touch.* Reaches its zenith by 6 months
	Can distinguish between a range of musical sounds
	Can use sounds to help locate objects in a darkened room
	Infants show a preference for increasingly complex visual patterns
6 to 12 months	Can distinguish objects on the basis of *touch* alone
	Can distinguish between simple melodic patterns
	Ability to use sounds to locate object improves dramatically
	Can recognize human forms from *point light* displays
	Infants can perceive *depth*; show a reluctance to cross the *visual cliff*
12 months and beyond	Ability to discriminate *pitch* develops to adult levels by 2 years of age
	Visual acuity improves. Reaches adult levels by about 5 years of age
	Refinement of perceptual skill as a function of increasing experience in a domain (i.e., development of *expertise*)

One of the most common and simple techniques employed by researchers examining perceptual development is to make use of an infant's perceptual *preferences* (Fantz, 1961). That is, we try to figure out what it is that infants prefer to look at in a display by measuring such behaviours as looking time (how much they look at a particular stimulus in relation to another). Using measures such as looking time may reveal that the infant prefers to look at one stimulus over another, a fact which gives rise to the name of these methods: **preferential looking techniques** (Miller, 1998).

Generally, the strategy researchers using these techniques take is to observe changes in naturally occurring behaviours, such as *gaze* at an object or display. A researcher will introduce some stimulus to the infant and then look for changes in the *rate*, *duration*, or *intensity* of gazing (or some other behaviour). Importantly, these changes can serve as an index of whether or not the baby has perceived the stimulus. Using a preferential looking technique, the researcher can infer that, because the infant prefers to look at one stimulus relevant to another, the infant *perceives a difference* between two sets of stimuli.

In addition, infants' preferences tell us two important things about their perceptual systems. First, they tell us what sorts of stimuli the infant's perceptual system can distinguish or discriminate. That is, an organism could not systematically attend to, or prefer, one thing rather than another unless it could somehow perceptually discriminate one from the other. For example, if an infant prefers to look at a pattern in fine back and white stripes rather than a plain grey pattern (which are equal in total brightness), that preference tells us that the infant has the ability to see the stripes.

Second, the infant's preferences tell us something about the nature of their perceptual systems; that is, we can observe what the infant is more and less inclined to attend to, which, in turn, tells us about the design of the infant's perceptual, attentional, and related psychological systems. For example, infants may prefer to look more at an object when it is in motion than at the same object when it is stationary. This suggests that the infant's perceptual system is constructed to be more attentive to movement than to nonmovement. Preferential looking methods can thus provide the researcher with a powerful method for examining several aspects of perceptual development.

Habituation studies are similar to preferential looking studies, and are used in many studies of infant cognition, perception, and emotion (Miller, 1998). Habituation studies involve the use of two simple concepts: *boredom* and *novelty*. In general, psychological research has shown that humans prefer novelty; that is, we are designed to look at or attend to things that are new. Once some stimulus display becomes familiar (i.e., it loses its novelty), we become bored with it and stop attending to the display. In psychological terms, we say we have *habituated* to the display. Finally, when we see something new or the stimulus display alters in such a way as to become novel, we show a *release from habituation*, that is, we once again attend to the stimulus. In infant research, habituation paradigms provide us with a tool for learning about infant development. They allow us to contrast various sorts of stimulus conditions and see whether the infant detects changes in them, measured by the amount of time they attend to the stimuli.

As good as these methods are for studying infant development, they have some limitations. For example, using preferential looking methods, it is possible that an infant may, in fact, be able to perceptually discriminate between two stimulus but may not show any preference for one stimuli over the other. As a result, their ability to discriminate between the stimuli would go undetected. In other words, preferences imply discrimination, but discrimination does not imply preference. However, whatever limitations might accompany preferential looking and habituation techniques, these methods represent an important advance in the ability to examine perceptual development from the earliest point in the life span.

The development of the senses

Touch

Our sense of touch is an extremely important sense. The sense organ which allows us to discriminate touch, is of course, the skin. The skin is our largest organ, covering our entire body. Nerve endings, located under our skin, mediate our sense of touch, responding to sensations on the skin. These same nerve endings also respond to dimensions such as temperature. Our sense of touch is also mediated by nerve endings in other specialized surfaces such as the lips.

We know that newborn infants are sensitive to touch. The **rooting reflex**, the tendency for infants to search for objects which touch them on the cheek (a reflex which helps them locate their mother's nipple for feeding), is a sign that the infant is sensitive to touch. Similarly, the **Babinski reflex**, a splaying of the toes and foot, is elicited in newborn infants by a light stroking of the bottom of the infant's foot, from heel to toe. This reflex is useful in detecting early damage to the nervous system as it is absent in infants with spinal cord defects. A study by Reisman (1987) showed that 1-day-old infants are also sensitive to temperature. In this study, infants reacted negatively to having a cold glass tube placed on their cheek, turning their heads to avoid it. In contrast, infants turned their head towards a warm glass tube. In general, newborn infants are sensitive to any stimuli that are colder than their body temperature (Humphrey, 1978).

There is widespread agreement that our sense of touch is operative at birth. In fact, according to Field (1990), our sense of touch may be active well before we are born. Infants in the womb are surrounded by fluid and are in contact with the mother's tissues. It would seem likely that these factors stimulate the infant's sense of touch before they are born.

Before the end of their first year, infants can learn to discriminate objects solely on the basis of touch (Streri & Pecheux, 1986). For example, a study by Gibson and Walker (1984) gave 1-month-old infants one of two stimuli to suck on: either a plastic rod, or a soft sponge made into the same shape as the plastic rod. Then infants watched an experimental display where two rods were shown moving around. One rod remained rigid and did not bend as it was moved about whereas the other rod was shown to bend and flex with movement. The experimenters measured infants' looking times at the two stimuli. The findings revealed that infants looked longer at the type of object they had previously sucked on. If the infants had sucked on the sponge rod, they tended to look more at the rod in the display which bent as it moved. These findings strongly suggest that infants discriminated the rods on the basis of their oral contact with them. In other words, they could remember the feel of the rods by having spent time mouthing them.

Infants' use of touch to explore the world of objects increases as soon as they can successfully grasp them. Babies are frequently observed to mouth objects and, as parents well know, one needs to be especially vigilant to make certain that the wrong sorts of objects do not end up in their mouths. The use of mouthing to explore objects reaches its zenith by about 6 months of age, after which it declines steadily in favour of more complex exploration using the new-found ability to reach for and grasp objects so they can be examined in a multitude of ways (Ruff, Saltarelli, Capozzoli, & Dubiner, 1992).

At one time, it was believed that infants do not experience pain, and as a result, many medical procedures were carried out without administering the infant any pain-relieving medications. For example, male infants were routinely circumcised without an anaesthetic to relieve their pain. The findings we have reviewed on the newborn infant's sensitivity to touch have led to new ways of thinking about pain. One source of evidence that suggests infants do, in fact, experience pain during such procedures is the release of the stress hormone cortisol into the bloodstream. Male infants have been found to show significantly higher levels of cortisol in their bloodstream (when compared to a preprocedure cortisol measure) after a circumcision (Gunnar, Malone, Vance, & Fisch, 1985). While concerns about the safety of pain-relieving drugs with infants have typically meant that their use with infants is limited, newer drugs are being developed which may prove safe for infants. In addition, other methods are being developed to help relieve infant discomfort, such as the use of an artificial nipple which delivers a sweet solution to the infant during the procedure. The sweet solution helps induce calm in the infants, and even produces a reduction in their heart rate (Blass & Ciaramitaro, 1994).

Taste

Are infants sensitive to different tastes such as *sweet*, *salty*, and *bitter*? Research with newborn infants suggests that they are indeed sensitive to taste. Blass and Ciaramitaro (1994) have shown that, like adults, newborns prefer sweet tastes. Rosenstein and Oster (1988) performed an experiment wherein newborn infants, only 2 hours old, were given sweet, sour, bitter, and salty substances. The infants produced distinct facial expressions in response to each. Infants tended to purse their lips in response to sour tastes, and produced a reaction of disgust (an arched mouth and narrowed eyes) to the bitter substances. Infants showed a relaxed response to the sweet substance. Other research has shown that when sucking on a nipple which produces a sweet fluid, infants' sucking changes, showing fewer pauses between each suck (Crook & Lipsitt, 1976). Such findings tend to suggest that taste preferences may be innate. However, work by Menella and Beauchamp (1996) has shown that infant taste preferences can be modified by early experience.

Smell

As we noted earlier, the development of the senses is important in that it provides part of the foundation for later social interaction. In particular, our sense of smell plays an important role in helping the infant to distinguish the key people in their world. Smell helps animals to identify their offspring, providing them with more protection against predators. Human mothers can similarly identify their own babies by smell, although our sense is less well developed than that of other species. Are newborns similarly able to identify their own mother through smell? In a classic study, MacFarlane (1975) showed that 6-day-old infants could distinguish their mother from other females on the basis of smell. MacFarlane used the breast pads which absorb leaking breast milk as the source of the mother's smell. She also used pads from other women who were breast feeding. Infants were placed on their backs on a table with a pad from their mother on one side and a pad from a strange female on the other. Infants turned more to the pad from their mother than to the other pad, suggesting that they recognized their mother's scent. Whether infants are breast fed or bottle fed, they still learn to recognize the distinctive scent of their own mother, although this process may take somewhat longer for bottle-fed infants (Cernoch & Porter, 1985; Porter, Makin, Davis, & Christensen, 1992).

Their sense of smell also provides infants with a measure of protection against odours which may emanate from toxic substances. Rieser, Yonas, and Wilkner (1976) found that newborns would quickly turn their head away from a noxious smell like ammonia. Infants' preferences for smells are not unlike those of adults. For example, they prefer smells such as bananas, honey, and chocolate, and reject smells such as rotten eggs (Maurer & Maurer, 1988; Steiner, 1979). Are infants' preferences for certain smells innate? Research has suggested that, while newborns do seem to have an innate preference for certain smells and are quickly able to learn to distinguish particular scents such as that of their mother, some learning about what 'smells good' still occurs. Studies have shown that preschool children do not respond in the same way as adults when exposed to many odours which adults naturally find unpleasant (Crook, 1987). Even into adulthood we may continue to learn to discriminate on the basis of smell, for example, learning to distinguish different varieties of wine.

Hearing

So far, we have seen that infants' sensory abilities are quite well developed at birth. Perhaps not surprisingly then, hearing is no exception to this trend. In a recent review of infants' perceptual abilities, Aslin, Jusczyk, and Pisoni (1998) found that the data on hearing suggest that newborns' hearing is very well developed. However, this does not mean that infants hear as well as adults. One dimension on which infants' hearing does not match that of adults is **auditory sensitivity**. Adults can hear much softer, quieter sounds than can newborn infants. A sound must be approximately 10 to 17 decibels louder for an infant to hear it than for an adult (a *decibel* is the measure of the loudness of a sound) (Hecox, 1975). According to Maurer and Maurer (1988), infants' auditory sensitivity improves steadily through infancy and reaches its height by the time children are ready for school.

The sounds which infants are most sensitive to are those sounds which come within the typical frequency range of a human voice (Aslin et al., 1998). Infants are also less sensitive to low-pitched sounds. This fact may explain why speech directed to young infants is often done in a higher pitch. Research has further shown that infants are much more attentive to speech uttered with a higher pitch (Cooper & Aslin, 1990; Fernald, 1985). While newborns may have difficulty discriminating sounds that are low in pitch, infants quickly reach adult levels of pitch discrimination, usually by two years of age (Aslin et al., 1998).

Is speech the only type of sound to which infants are attuned? Interestingly, infants seem very well attuned to musical sounds. Newborn infants will increase their rate of sucking if they are rewarded with hearing musical sounds instead of noise. By the time they are a few days old, infants can distinguish patterns of tones in a rising or descending order (Bijeljac-Babic, Bertoncini, & Mehler, 1993). By two months, they distinguish a range of musical sounds and by 6 months of age, they can discriminate between simple melodic patterns (Trehub & Trainor, 1993). Such findings have led to the conclusion that like speech, there seems to be a biological preparedness to perceive music (Kagan & Zetner, 1996).

An important aspect of hearing is its role in the infant's exploration of the environment. A variety of research has shown that infants have impressive capabilities locating the source of sounds. Newborn infants will turn their head in the direction of a sound (Muir & Clifton, 1985; Muir & Field, 1979). Clifton and her colleagues (Clifton et al., 1994) have shown that 4-month-old infants placed in a completely dark room can use auditory cues to help them accurately reach to an object which emits a sound. Soon afterwards, they can use auditory cues to help them judge whether the object is too far away to reach or not (Clifton et al., 1991). Over the first half year, infants generally become increasingly adept at using sound to locate objects (Morrongiello, Hewitt, & Gotowiec, 1991).

One might ask why infants' hearing is so remarkably good at birth. Have newborn infants had some experience with hearing before birth? The research findings on this question suggest that this is, in fact, the case. Consider a study by DeCasper and Spence (1986) designed to address this question, in which pregnant mothers were asked to read a particular book,

The Cat in the Hat by Dr. Seuss, twice a day to their infants for the last six weeks of their pregnancy. After birth, a preferential sucking paradigm was used to measure infant preferences; that is, they measured the rates at which infants sucked on an artificial nipple while listening to different stimuli, in this case, stories. The experimenters had the mothers record themselves reading *The Cat in the Hat* and another story. Over several trials, the infants would learn that if they sucked in a particular pattern (e.g., long, slow sucks), they would hear *The Cat in the Hat*, and if they sucked in another pattern, they would hear the other story. The investigators found that infants sucked such that they listened to *The Cat in the Hat* significantly more than to the other story. The findings suggest that the infants discriminated the stories on the basis of familiarity, that is, they preferred the story they had heard previously. While these findings are impressive, and indicate that infants can hear in the womb, it is clear that further work remains to be done in order to examine what aspects of the sounds they hear infants can use and how prenatal auditory experience affects the development of the auditory system.

The development of vision

It is probably true to say that humans are more reliant on their vision than they are on any of their other senses. Ironically, the visual system is the least developed of any of the five senses in infancy. While newborns can perform impressive visual feats such as detecting motion in the visual field and tracking moving objects with their eyes (Kellman & Banks, 1998), the 'hardware' which makes up their visual system is not fully developed at birth. One aspect of the visual system which undergoes further development after birth is the **retina**, the membrane which lines the back of the eyes and which receives light which is then sent as signals from the eye through the optic nerve to the brain. The cells which make up the retina have not fully matured at birth. Moreover, the pathways this information takes to reach the brain, and indeed, the parts of the brain which are responsible for processing this information parts also undergo further maturation, a process which may take several years (Kellman & Banks, 1998). Given that selected aspects of the visual system require further maturation, there may be certain classes of information which are either handled poorly by the infant or not handled at all (see the following discussion on colour vision).

Visual acuity

The term **visual acuity** refers to the quality of a person's vision, measured in terms of the fineness of discriminations which they can make. Good visual acuity allows one to see the fine details of an object or a scene. Psychologists are interested in visual acuity because it helps to shed light on the development of the components of the visual system. Visual acuity is usually measured in terms of distance and size of the object; tests of visual acuity usually involve attempting to discriminate stimulus items such as letters of the alphabet at standardized distances. For example, if you are able to discriminate a letter only at 20 feet while people with perfect vision can read the same letter at 60 feet, you would have 20/60 vision.

Courage and Adams (1990) used this same index with newborn infants. Typically, infants can see an object at 20 feet as well as adults can at 600 feet (ranging from 200 to 800 feet). According to Kellman and Banks (1998), infants at this age would be defined as legally blind on the basis of their visual acuity. Anything that is not held quite close to a baby will not be seen by them. Using tests of visual discrimination involving black stripes on a grey field, Maurer and Maurer (1988) found that infants ability to discriminate the stripes from the background was one-thirtieth that of a normally sighted adult. In other words, infants could not see stripes that were narrower than 0.1 of an inch from one foot away. Fortunately, their visual acuity undergoes rapid changes over the first few months of life. By 8 months of age, infants see about one fourth as well as an adult (i.e., stripes of about 0.01 of an inch wide from one foot away). Visual acuity reaches adult levels by about 5 years of age (Maurer & Maurer, 1988).

Another aspect of the infant's visual system which limits their acuity and impedes their ability to see very close or very distant objects is the relative immaturity of the muscles which guide eye movements. When viewing distant objects, the muscles of the eye actually change the shape of the lens to provide an appropriate focus on the object. This process of changing the shape of the lens is referred to as **visual accommodation** (Bremner, 1994). The eye movements of infants are less accurate than those of adults and can accommodate only minor changes, initially. Newborn infants focus best on those objects placed about ten inches from their face; objects which are much further or much closer will appear blurry to them. Between two to four months of age, infants become much more practised at visual accommodation and begin to achieve adult levels of performance (Bremner, 1994; Maurer & Maurer, 1988).

Colour vision

One of the most active areas of research in infant perception has been the study of colour vision. The most basic question for much of this research has been when can infants distinguish colours on the basis of hue alone? To answer this question, we first need to define **hue**. Hue refers to the wavelength of light, the primary feature which distinguishes one colour from another. The colour we call red has a different wavelength than the colour we call green. We can discriminate hue from **brightness**, the intensity of a colour. This distinction is important because two stimuli with different hues may also differ in terms of their brightness, thus we cannot be certain on which feature infants might distinguish the stimuli. We know from early research on infant perception that newborn infants can distinguish brightness (Maurer & Maurer, 1988) but what about hue? Studies of newborns have generated strong evidence that they do not perceive colours. When brightness is controlled across a pair of stimuli which differ only in terms of hue, infants cannot discriminate between them. The evidence on when exactly infants do perceive colour is mixed. Some researchers have stated that by 2 months of age, infants are able to discriminate colours across the entire spectrum and by 3 months of age infants are also able to group colours into the basic colour categories such as red, green, and blue (Teller, 1997). In other words, by the time they have reached 4 months of age, infants perceive colours in the same way as do adults.

In a review of the literature on visual development, Kellman and Banks (1998) suggest that infants younger than 7 weeks of age probably cannot process colour information. They argue that this limit occurs because of the relatively immature state of the newborn's visual system. The cells which process colour reside in the middle of the eye and are called **cones**. The cones in a newborn infant's eye are not fully developed at birth and it takes some weeks before they begin to function properly (Bremner, 1994; Maurer & Maurer, 1988). It may be that these deficits in colour processing are related to the immature state of the structure of the infant's eye; colour perception only becomes possible when the neural structures in the eye and the visual cortex begin to perform their functions.

Pattern perception

Recall the quote by William James on the nature of infants' sensory experience mentioned at the beginning of this chapter, suggesting that the infant's world is a 'confusion' of perceptions. Psychologists working since James have been interested in examining whether this claim is in fact true. Do infants experience the world as a confusion, or do they experience more meaningful, organized patterns? If they do experience patterns, do they have to learn to construct their sensations into meaningful, organized wholes?

One of the pioneers of research on perceptual development in infancy, Robert Fantz (1961), showed that newborn infants prefer to look at patterned rather than plain stimuli; for example, infants prefer a drawing of a face to a black and white drawing of a circle. As they age, infants seem to prefer increasingly complex visual patterns (Banks & Salapatek, 1983), however, the attempt to figure out why infants prefer certain patterns has proven to be a difficult exercise for perceptual researchers. One of the features which seems to govern infants' preferences is called **contrast sensitivity** (Banks & Ginsburg, 1985). This refers to the characteristic changes in the brightness across the different regions of a visual pattern, for example, the differences in the black and white squares of a checkerboard pattern. Infants prefer patterns with higher contrasts. Of course, the ability to perceive contrasts is related to visual acuity; very young infants, because of their poor acuity, will prefer the contrasts found in large patterns such as in a checkerboard with very large squares. As their visual acuity increases and they become able to resolve finer patterns, infants will shift their preference to more fine-grained patterns with high contrast, such as checkerboards with smaller squares (Maurer & Maurer, 1988).

Another aspect of pattern perception which develops is the way in which infants visually scan patterns. When looking at a visual pattern such as a human face, infants initially focus on the edges and boundaries of the face (Maurer & Salapatek, 1976), but by 2 months of age, they begin to take in features which reside inside the pattern (Dannemiller & Stephens, 1988; Kellman & Banks, 1998). While initially, infants seem to perceive only the isolated aspects of visual patterns, with time and experience, infants begin to combine these elements so they can perceive more complex, meaningful patterns such as the ability to perceive a human figure in motion from a *point light display*. A point light display is a display created by placing dots on a visual image, for example, the joints of a human figure walking. When the image is removed and only the pattern of moving lights remains, you have a point light image. Research by Bertenthal and colleagues has demonstrated that by about 9 months of age, infants show a distinct preference for a pattern of lights representing a person in motion as opposed to a pattern of randomly moving lights (Bertenthal, Profitt, & Kramer, 1987).

Object perception

A further development in the infant's developing perceptual skills is the ability to perceive the world of objects. Unlike pattern perception, the ability to perceive objects requires perception in three dimensions. Given the fact that learning to perceive and interact with objects is critical to the infant's developing cognitive system, we need to examine the developmental course of the abilities which govern object perception.

One important development in object perception is the ability to perceive an object's size as the same no matter what its distance from the observer and independently of the size of its retinal image. This ability is known as **size constancy**. Research has suggested that newborn infants come equipped with this ability (Slater, Mattock, & Brown, 1990). The ability to perceive size constancy, while present at birth, develops further as the infant's binocular vision improves due to changes in muscular coordination (refer to our earlier discussion of visual accommodation). Indeed, refinements in the perception of size constancy continue to take place through to approximately 11 years of age (Kellman & Banks, 1998). Another aspect of object perception is the achievement of **shape constancy**. Shape constancy refers to the perception of an object's shape as being consistent even though movement may change the shape of its image on the retina. A study by Slater and Morrison (1985) shows that this ability is also present at birth. Both of these findings on object perception serve to underscore the point that, in contrast to theories such as Piaget's (1954; 1969), infants come remarkably well equipped with perceptual capacities that allow them to organize and interpret their perceptual experience from birth.

Face perception

As we saw earlier, infants prefer to look at complex patterns such as faces. In fact, a number of studies have revealed that infants do have a bias for human faces over other sorts of visual patterns. Early work in this field by Fantz (1966) demonstrated that infants prefer to look at schematic illustrations of human faces more so than at other patterns. Fantz showed newborn infants a black and white picture of a schematic human face along with a variety of other visual patterns such as a bull's-eye or plain colours. His data indicated that newborn infants looked longer at the face than at any of the other stimuli. Further work by Fantz revealed that this preference was difficult to interpret. When Fantz showed infants both scrambled human faces (drawings where the arrangement of parts such as the ears, nose and eyes were mixed up) and normal faces, infants below 2 months of age showed no clear visual preference (Maurer & Barrera, 1981). These findings tend to suggest that infants younger than 2 months of age do not see faces as structured wholes, but rather as a collection of parts. Research into the features which guide infants to pay attention to faces, whether arranged correctly or scrambled, is ongoing.

However, by about 3 months of age, infants seem to show a clear preference for correctly arranged human faces (Maurer & Maurer, 1988). Work by Dannemiller and Stephens (1988) illustrates this fact rather nicely. Dannemiller and Stephens presented two groups of infants aged 1½ and 3 months two sets of stimuli, computer-generated faces and computer-generated abstract patterns. Two sets of faces were shown to infants: a 'normal' face and an 'odd' face (a negative image of the normal face). Similarly, infants were shown two sets of abstract patterns, a normal image and its reversed image. In addition, both sets of images, faces and shapes were equated for contour density and complexity. Using a preferential looking paradigm, Dannemiller and Stephens found that 1½-month-old infants were no more likely to look at the face stimuli than they were the abstract patterns. In contrast, the 3-month-old infants preferred the schematic faces over the abstract patterns and favoured the 'normal face' over the 'odd face'. Lest you think infants preference for the normal face was simply because they found the nonreversed image more interesting, Dannemiller and Stephens found that, for the abstract stimuli, there was no such preference: infants were equally likely to look at either the normal or reversed abstract patterns, suggesting infants do not simply find the nonreversed images more attractive.

Interestingly, the preference for faces co-occurs with changes in the way infants scan faces. Maurer and Salapatek (1976) showed that at 1 month, infants scan the edges or boundaries of faces but fail to scan the internal features of the face. Consistent with findings described earlier, infants seem to be attracted to the areas of the face which show high contrast, such as the border between the hairline and the forehead. It is not until 2 to 3 months of age that infants begin to scan the interior of the face, focusing on areas like the eyes and mouth (Cohen & Salapatek, 1975). One problem with most of these studies has been that they have employed static pictures of human faces rather than displays which utilized live, animated faces. Caron, Caron, and MacLean (1988) have suggested that in these real life contexts, infants may be able to extract more information from faces than has been shown in laboratory studies.

Depth perception

An important dimension which infants must learn to perceive is depth. After all, the infant lives in a three-dimensional world. When do infants begin to perceive depth? Gibson and Walk (1960) devised a test of depth perception known as the **visual cliff**. The visual cliff is basically two tables with a gap in between them which creates a drop-off or 'cliff'. The tables are covered in a checkerboard pattern which accentuates the drop, making it clear to the infant. However, rather than allow infants to plummet over the edge, Gibson and Walk covered the cliff with a sheet of clear plexiglass which can easily support the infant should they choose to venture out across the surface. The experimental device creates a very convincing illusion of a cliff. Gibson and Walk arranged the experiment so that infants were placed on one side of the cliff and the mother stood on the other side, with the drop-off in between them. The experimenters asked mothers to try and entice their infants to crawl across the cliff. They found that by 6 months of age, infants were extremely reluctant to cross over suggesting that by this age, they perceived the depth and understood its significance to their well being.

Further work using the visual cliff paradigm has added greatly to our understanding of the development of depth perception. In one set of studies, Joseph Campos and his colleagues employed a visual cliff apparatus which had both a 'shallow' side and a 'deep' side. Campos arranged for 1½-month-old infants to be placed directly on the shallow side of the cliff and then on the deep side of the cliff. The infants' heart rates were measured in order to see how they reacted to being placed on the cliff. The results showed that when placed on the shallow side and then on the deep side, infants showed a slowed heart rate, indicating that they were *interested* in the experience (Campos, Langer, & Krowitz, 1970). In contrast, when 7- to 9-month-old infants were placed onto the deep end of the cliff, they showed heart rate acceleration, indicating, once again, that they were afraid, because they perceived the depth and recognized the situation as threatening (Bertenthal & Campos, 1987; Campos, Bertenthal, & Kermonian, 1992).

Research using the visual cliff paradigm has also demonstrated that locomotor experience is very important to the development of depth perception. In one study investigating the effects of locomotor experience, Bertenthal, Campos, and Kermonian (1994) found that when infants who did not yet crawl were given 30 to 40 hours' worth of experience in infant walkers (wheeled devices which allow the infant to move themselves about a room), they showed fear on the visual cliff. Locomotor experience clearly provides the infant with chances to learn about depth perception and the meaning of heights (Bertenthal & Clifton, 1998).

There are a variety of visual cues which give rise to the perception of depth. One set of cues, known as **kinetic depth cues**, come from the motion of objects through our visual field. This movement provides clues as to how close or distant things are from us by the speed with which they pass through our visual field. Nearby objects move past more quickly than more distant objects (Nánez, 1987). Studies suggest that infants are sensitive to kinetic cues by about 3 months of age (Yonas & Owsley, 1987). The fact that we have binocular vision also provides further cues to depth. One such cue which we use to see depth is **retinal disparity**, the fact that each eye receives slightly different images of a given scene. Our brains are sensitive to this disparity between the two retinal images and use this information to create an awareness of depth. By about 3 months of age, infants are able to use retinal disparity to perceive depth (Birch, 1993; Yonas & Owsley, 1987). Finally, infants are also able to take advantage of what are called **pictorial depth cues**. These are the kinds of information that artists use to convey depth and perspective in two-dimensional art forms such as drawing. Think of how you might draw railway tracks leading off into the distance. You would probably make the lines which represent the rails move closer together until they vanish at a horizon. This effect suggests distance to the viewer. Research has suggested that infants gradually learn to use this sort of information to perceive depth. By the time they are about 7 months of age, infants begin to respond to pictorial depth cues (Arterberry, Yonas, & Bensen, 1989). This development, however, is far from complete (Kellman & Banks, 1998). A sensitivity to pictorial depth cues is one of the last aspects of perception to develop.

Intermodal perception

So far, we have examined each of the senses in isolation. However, it is clearly the case that humans can combine information across the different sensory modalities. It should be clear from your own experience that you combine or integrate various forms of sensory information, for example, sight and sound, so that you perceive a coherent whole. This integration of sensory information from more than one modality at a time is called **intermodal perception**. Of what use is intermodal perception? Intermodal perception is critical to our ability to make sense of the world. For example, matching up lip movements and sounds is an example of intermodal perception, and, moreover, one that is critical to our ability to understand speech. You might think that intermodal perception sounds like a complicated process in that there must be some work involved to integrate the senses; however, research on the development of intermodal perception suggests that this impression would be somewhat mistaken.

Meltzoff & Borton (1979) performed a classic study on intermodal perception. They looked at infants' ability to integrate tactile and visual information. In this study, two groups of 1-month-old infants were given either a normal, smooth infant pacifier or a specially designed pacifier which was covered in knobs. After some experience sucking on the pacifiers, they were removed. Infants were then shown a display which contained pictures of two pacifiers, the smooth one and the knobby one. Infants' looking time at the two displays was measured. Findings indicated that infants who had received the smooth pacifier looked more at its corresponding picture; this same finding applied to the group that had received the textured pacifier. The authors suggested that infants are able to grasp the equivalence of the information obtained by touch and by sight, and, that, given the young age of the infants involved in the study, this ability is probably unlearned. This study was replicated by Kaye and Bower (1994) with newborn infants who ranged in age from 13 to 43 hours, a very young sample. Importantly, these infants were all breast fed and had had no previous experience with pacifiers. As in the Meltzoff and Borton study, the infants in Kaye and Bower's study showed a visual preference for the pacifier on which they had been sucking, even though the time they were given with the pacifier (20 seconds) was very limited. These findings provide support for the nativist position: that intermodal perception is an innate, unlearned ability.

However, infants ability to perceive correspondences across sensory modalities does not appear to be as easy across all the combinations of modalities. Spelke (1987) found that not until 4 months of age do infants learn to match sights and sounds, such as the sound of a voice to a display of faces with moving lips. Such findings have suggested there are rules to be learned which guide the integration of information across sensory modalities and that it takes some time to learn these rules. Moreover, infants require experience with the world before they can be expected to learn to match a sound with an object they have never seen before. Thus, what is of interest to developmentalists interested in perception is not so much the issue of *when* an infant learns to perceive a particular sensory combination but *how* they learn to do so. Further research will be required in order to learn more about the processes that underlie intermodal perception (Haith & Benson, 1998).

Perceptual development across the life span

What about perceptual development across the life span? We tend to think of perceptual ability as something that declines with age, for example, the decline in visual acuity throughout adulthood. However, there is an obvious area where we see perceptual development occur at any age: the development of expertise in a given domain. According to some theories, expertise is the development of perceptual skills or the perception of higher order invariances in the environment (Carey, 1996). People can become more expert at forms of perceptual discrimination at any stage of life. Avid birdwatchers become more able to identify species of birds and the differences among them. Art lovers can learn to identify a painter by her brush strokes and to discriminate among schools of artists based on combinations of properties, such as type of brush stroke and use of colour. Tennis players learn to swing or not swing at a given shot based on how their opponent hits the ball, judging rapidly whether or not a shot will be out of bounds. In fact, some psychologists would argue that developing expertise is a process of being increasingly able to specify the invariances or norms that exist across a set of stimuli. For example, people who become judges at dog shows learn to perceive certain relationships among stimuli such as the shininess of the dog's coat, but they also learn to see relations among various properties (e.g., shininess, stature, and obedience), and can learn to perceive the norms in these properties which allow them to make judgements about individuals and to compare or rank individuals. According to Carey (1996), this process is not particularly *developmental* at all, in that it does not derive from general limitations on a person's cognitive abilities but, rather, reflects their *experience* with a class of stimuli. Once again, the question of interest is how experience is utilized.

SUMMARY

As we have seen, perceptual abilities are surprisingly well developed in infancy, although there are many important changes which follow on from these early abilities. An issue which remains unresolved in the field is the extent to which our perceptual abilities are either learned or innate. The study of perceptual development is also worth our attention given the fact that perceptual abilities provide for the ability to interact with the physical and social worlds, and, thus, are very relevant to the study of children's cognitive and social development.

Glossary

Affordances are the properties of objects that offer the individual the potential to interact with it a variety of ways.

Auditory sensitivity refers to the sensitivity of the infant's auditory system. For example, a given sound needs to be louder for an infant to hear it than it does for an adult to hear the same sound.

Babinski reflex is a splaying of the toes and foot elicited in newborn infants by a light stroking of the bottom of the infant's foot, from heel to toe.

Brightness refers to the intensity of a colour.

Compound invariants are a class of environmental invariants where information is obtained not simply from objects themselves, but from the relationships between the objects. The information afforded by the relations between the objects is more that the information given by the objects in isolation.

Cones are the cells which process colour and that reside in the middle of the eye.

Constructivist theory refers to a class of theory that suggests that development is largely the product of interactions between an organism and its environment. Perceptual knowledge is constructed by the individual as a result of these interactions.

Contrast sensitivity refers to the characteristic changes in the brightness across the different regions of a visual pattern.

Direct perception is a theory of perception associated with James and Eleanor Gibson which proposes that our sensory systems simply detect or pick up information which is already available in the structure of the information we receive from the world.

Habituation studies is a research design which exploits the concepts of novelty and boredom to study infant cognition and perception. Infants are exposed to a display until they become habituated (show boredom). The display is then altered in some way. If the infants perceive a difference between the new display and the old, they will show a release from habituation and begin to attend to the display.

Hue refers to the wavelength of light, the primary feature which distinguishes one colour from another.

Intermodal perception refers to the use of sensory information from more than one sensory modality at a time (e.g., sight and sound) which is combined so that we perceive a coherent whole.

Invariances are aspects of the visual environment which do not change.

Kinetic depth cues arise via the motion of objects through our visual field, providing us with clues as to how close or distant objects are from us.

Nativist theory refers to a class of theories which posit that our biological endowment includes some innate knowledge and abilities which play a role in early learning.

Neonate refers to a newborn baby.

Perception is the processes by which we make sense of our sensations.

Pictorial depth cues are the kinds of information that convey depth and perspective in two-dimensional art forms such as drawing.

Preferential looking techniques a class of research methods for studying infants in which their natural preferences are exploited in order to learn about the sorts of information they can perceive.

Retina is the membrane which lines the back of the eyes and which receives light which is then sent as signals from the eye through the optic nerve to the brain.

Retinal disparity refers to the fact that each eye receives slightly different images of a given scene. These cues help us to perceive depth.

Rooting reflex is the tendency for infants to search for objects which touch them on the cheek (a reflex which helps them locate their mother's nipple for feeding).

Schema is the term used to describe a knowledge structure which guides our understanding and exploration of the environment.

Sensation refers to the act of detecting a stimulus event via a sensory system.

Shape constancy refers to the perception of an object's shape as being consistent even though movement may change the shape of its image on the retina.

Size constancy is the ability to perceive an object's size as the same no matter what its distance from the observer.

Visual accommodation refers to the change in the shape of the lens to provide an appropriate focus on a viewed object.

Visual acuity refers to the quality of a person's vision, measured in terms of the fineness of discriminations which they can make.

Visual cliff is an apparatus designed to test infants' depth perception. It uses patterned materials to highlight a deep 'cliff' over which the infant can crawl. The cliff is actually covered in clear plexiglass to prevent the infant from falling.

6 Cognitive Development

LEARNING AIMS

At the end of this chapter you should:

- **be able to describe the three theories of cognitive development covered**
- **understand and be able to define the key concepts of Piagetian theory, including *adaptation*, *organization*, *equilibration*, *assimilation*, and *accommodation***
- **be familiar with the four stages of development described by Piaget**
- **be aware of evidence both for and against Piaget's theory**
- **understand and be able to define the key concepts of Vygotskian theory, including *elementary* and *higher mental functions*, *internalization*, *zone of proximal development* and *scaffolding***
- **be aware of evidence both for and against Vygotsky's theory**
- **describe the model of the human information processing system covered**
- **understand and be able to define the key concepts of the information processing approach including, *long-term* and *working memory*, *encoding*, *automatization*, and *m-space***
- **be able to articulate some of the similarities and differences between the three theories**

Introduction

Cognition is the study of the thought processes or mental activity by which we acquire and deal with knowledge. The study of human cognition is a vast field, encompassing an extremely wide variety of topics. Examine any cognition textbook and you will find chapters on memory, attention, language, social cognition, reasoning, problem solving, and more. While, ideally, we would review each of these topics, it is simply impossible to do so in one chapter (especially in a book not devoted entirely to cognitive development). Therefore, in this chapter, we will cover three of the most influential theories of cognitive development – the work of Jean Piaget, Lev Vygotsky, and information processing views on cognitive development. Within the discussion of each of theory we consider some of the key aspects of cognitive development across childhood.

Piaget's theory of cognitive development

Piaget's theory of cognitive development is considered the most important to emerge from the study of human development (Siegler, 1998). It is perhaps the most controversial theory as well (Beilin, 1992), since Piaget's theory and ideas are still at the centre of debate in developmental psychology. Ultimately, whether you agree or disagree with his position, the student of human development needs to understand Piagetian theory in order to understand the field of cognitive development. Thus, we start this chapter with a survey of Piaget's theory of cognitive development.

According to Siegler (1998), there are a number of reasons for the longevity of Piaget's theory. First, Piaget's observations of children provide a remarkable 'feel' for what cognitive development looks like. Second, Piaget's theory addresses fundamental questions that are of interest to philosophers and lay people alike. Piaget's theory attempts to provide answers to questions such as 'what is intelligence?' and 'how do we develop knowledge?' Finally, Piaget's theory was notable for its breadth, drawing together seemingly unrelated aspects of development under a coherent theory.

However, the fact that Piaget's theory has been influential in the study of cognitive development does not mean it has been accepted uncritically. A number of serious problems with Piagetian theory have been identified. We will review some of these at the end of this section, but where the research bears on a specific stage of development, we will review evidence that runs counter to Piagetian theory.

An overview of Piagetian theory: key concepts

In contrast to the assumptions of behaviourist theories, that children developed in reaction to their environment and the rewards and punishments it provided, Piaget argued that children actively explore their world, and their thoughts are ultimately derived from the child's actions on the world. Piaget believed that children *construct* their reality as they manipulate and explore their world; what children actually construct are cognitive structures which Piaget termed **schemes**. A scheme is an interrelated set of actions, memories, thoughts or strategies which are employed to predict and understand the environment. Gardner (1973) elaborates this concept, arguing that a scheme is the aspect of an action or a mental operation which can be repeated with or generalized to a similar action or operation. Schemes form the basis for organizing one's reactions to the environment. As children grow, they develop and refine their schemes.

Piaget's early training was in the field of biology. Central to his theory are two biological concepts, **adaptation** and **organization** (Ginsburg & Opper, 1988). Organization refers to the individual's tendency to organize their cognitive structures or schemes into efficient systems (Lutz & Sternberg, 1999). Organization can take place independently of interaction with the environment. Children naturally begin to link together schemes, creating a more organized and interrelated cognitive system. For example, infants eventually begin to link together schemes developed for reaching, grasping, and sucking objects, combining these into more complex structures that can be generalized to other situations, and, thus, further their ability to negotiate the environment. Initially, they cannot combine these actions but through the process of organization, they are able to do so. This brings us to the concept of adaptation.

Adaptation involves the creation of cognitive structures or schemes through our interactions with the environment, allowing us to adjust to the demands posed by the environment. Adaptation takes place through two complementary processes called **assimilation** and **accommodation** (Piaget, 1952). Assimilation refers to the process of integrating the environment into one's current psychological structures (Lutz & Sternberg, 1999). That is, assimilation uses current schemes to interpret new knowledge. When we assimilate something, we mould it to fit in with our existing structures. Accommodation is the opposite process; it occurs when old schemes are adjusted to better fit with the demands of the environment. Assimilation and accommodation often operate simultaneously (Ginsburg & Opper, 1988). Consider the following illustration of how this process works: the infant sees a circular ring; the infant can assimilate this new object into their experience, applying their grasping scheme. Now the infant encounters a much smaller object such as a plastic token. The child cannot grasp it using their standard grip. They are forced to accommodate to the object, altering their grip so as to be able to pick up the token and continue their exploration.

Piaget believed that development occurred as a result of our predispositions to organize and adapt to new experiences. However, there are times when our cognitive structures tend to remain in one state more than another. At some points in time, we will be able to assimilate most new experiences, whereas at others, we will be forced to accommodate and adapt our structures to the environment. Piaget argued that when we can assimilate changes in the environment we are in a state of cognitive *equilibrium*, a 'steady state' which our system aims for. However, when we are forced to accommodate we enter into a state of cognitive *disequilibrium*. States of disequilibrium force us to modify our cognitive structures so that we can assimilate changes and regain equilibrium. Piaget referred to this continual balance between achieving states of equilibrium and disequilibrium as **equilibration** (Piaget, 1952). The process of equilibration leads to the development of more efficient cognitive structures (Lutz & Sternberg, 1999).

Piaget noted that the organization of cognitive structures occurs in **stages**. For Piaget, a stage of development is a period in which the child's cognitive structures are *qualitatively* similar. Piaget also maintained that stages had two important characteristics. First, they occur in an *invariant* order in development; that is, stages are not missed, and children move through them in a fixed order. Second, stages are *universal*, in that they are applicable to all children and are not affected by cultural or social norms. While children may progress through the stages at different speeds as a function of inherited traits or particular environmental influences (Piaget, 1926), the nature of the stages through which they progress does not change. Piaget postulated four stages of development. We will consider each of these stages in turn.

The sensorimotor stage The **sensorimotor stage** encompasses the first two years of an infant's life. During the sensorimotor stage of infancy, children move from responding to the environment in a simplistic, reflexive manner, to being able to think about the environment using symbols. According to Piaget (1954), the major achievement of the sensorimotor stage is the development of **object permanence**. This is the idea that objects continue to exist independently of our ability to perceive them or to act on them. Object permanence is important, as it signals the beginnings of the ability to think using representations rather than through actions. In what follows, we consider each of the six substages (see Table 6.1).

Piaget (1952) argued that the sensorimotor stage of development is comprised of six substages. The first substage, *reflexive schemes*, runs from birth to 1 month of age. For Piaget, newborn behaviour consisted of little more than reflex behaviours. Development during this stage consists of the infant gaining control over these reflex behaviours and practising them. The second substage, *primary circular reactions*, runs from about 1 to 4 months of age. During this stage, infants begin repeating chance behaviours that lead to satisfying results, developing simple motor habits such as sucking their thumbs and opening and closing their hands. Piaget termed these behaviours **primary circular reactions**. Additionally, infants start to vary their newly acquired behaviours in response to environmental demands, as, for example, when they open their mouths differently to a nipple than to a spoon. In other words, they show a limited ability to anticipate events.

TABLE 6.1 Piaget's stages of sensorimotor development

Substage	Age	Significant accomplishments and limitations
Sensorimotor stage	0–2 years	*Infants initially understand the world via action but gradually develop the ability to use symbolic representations*
• Reflexive schemes	0–1 months	Infants gain control over and practise reflex behaviours
• Primary circular reactions	1–4 months	Infants repeat chance behaviours that lead to satisfying results (e.g., thumb sucking), and show a limited ability to anticipate events
• Secondary circular reactions	4–8 months	Infants can combine single schemes into larger structures (e.g., repeatedly grasping and shaking a rattle). This behaviour is not goal directed, however
• Coordination of secondary circular reactions	8–12 months	Secondary circular reactions are combined into new actions, and become intentional. For example, infants can coordinate a means and a goal
• Tertiary circular reactions	12–18 months	Infants begin to repeat actions and vary them in a deliberately exploratory manner. Can solve the **A-not-B** task and develop **object permanence**
• Invention of new means through mental combinations	18–24 months	Onset of the child's ability to think symbolically and mentally represent reality. Also heralds the beginning of **pretend play**

Substage 3, *secondary circular reactions*, runs from 4 to 8 months of age. Now infants perform actions that are more definitely oriented towards objects and events outside their own bodies, what Piaget termed **secondary circular reactions**. Using the secondary circular reaction, they try to maintain, through repetition, interesting effects produced by their own actions, such as creating a sound with a rattle. During this stage, infants move beyond employing one scheme at a time, and begin to combine schemes into larger structures, for example, grasping and shaking. Although they are a great cognitive advance over the previous stage, secondary circular reactions are limited in that they involve undifferentiated connections between actions and objects. Piaget did not view the infant's behaviour as goal directed or *intentional*; infants simply repeat newly acquired actions with respect to that object.

In substage 4, *coordination of secondary circular reactions* (which runs from 8 to 12 months of age), previously acquired secondary circular reactions are combined into new action sequences that are intentional and goal directed. A clear example is provided by Piaget's object hiding tasks, in which he showed the infant an attractive object which was then hidden under a cloth cover or beneath a cup. By substage 4, infants could set aside the obstacle and retrieve the object, coordinating two schemes: a *means* (pushing aside the cup) and a *goal* (grasping the object). Piaget regarded this means–end behaviour as the first truly intelligent behaviour and the foundation of all later problem solving. Also, the fact that substage 4 infants can retrieve a hidden object indicates that they have achieved some appreciation of object permanence. However, Piaget believed that infants' understanding of object permanence is limited at this stage. He claimed that, if an object is moved to a new location, infants of this level of ability will still search for the object in the place in which it was first concealed, revealing that they do not view the object as existing independently of their actions on it. Finally, at this stage infants begin to show a tendency to engage in the *imitation* of behaviour.

From 12 to 18 months of age, infants progress through substage 5, *tertiary circular reactions*, in which they begin to repeat actions and to vary them in a deliberately exploratory manner. In doing so, infants try to provoke new results, as they quickly habituate to results that they are familiar with and are no longer satisfied with them. At this stage, infants can solve the **A-not-B task**. In this task, infants search for hidden objects, but after a set number of trials where they search for an object at one location (the A trials), the object is hidden in a second location (the B trial). Substage 4 infants will continue to search at A on the B trial, whereas substage 5 infants correctly search for the object at the new location. Another aspect of this stage is that infants can imitate more complex and unfamiliar behaviours. Infants also exercise their schemes in play when, for example, they bang blocks together in different ways or drop toys (or food) from their high chair on purpose. Finally, infants begin to distinguish themselves and their own actions from the world around them, showing the first signs of a developing sense of *self* (demonstrated through performance on the *rouge test* – see Chapter 9).

Infants typically reach substage 6, the *invention of new means through mental combinations*, at 18 months (lasting through to 2 years of age). Substage 6 marks the onset of the child's ability to think symbolically, that is to use mental representations of reality. Thus, at substage 6, the infant can think 'in their heads' before they act. In other words, they are able to combine symbols or representations in their heads rather than being tied to acting them out in sensorimotor behaviour, as in the previous stages. At substage 6, infants engage in *deferred imitation*, copying the *past* behaviour of models. As well, infants can pass *invisible displacement tasks*, a more advanced version of the A-not-B task. Finally, at substage 6, infants engage for the first time in **pretend play**, where they act out imaginary activities, and use real objects to stand for imagined objects.

EARLY UNDERSTANDING OF OBJECT PERMANENCE Renee Baillargeon and her colleagues (Baillargeon, DeVos, & Graber, 1989) have found results which stand in sharp contrast to Piaget's findings. Using a violation-of-expectation paradigm, Baillargeon examined infant's understanding of object permanence in 5½-month-old infants. Her study involved two phases: in the first phase, infants watched as two cardboard rabbits moved from a position on one side of screen, and travelled behind the screen (out of the infant's sight), to appear on the opposite side of the screen. Infants watched two types of events in this phase, one involving a short rabbit and a second with a tall rabbit. After infants were habituated to these two displays, they entered into the second phase of the experiment. In this phase, the short and tall rabbits moved behind a screen which had a 'window' cut out in the middle. The window was designed to be high enough so that the tall rabbit would be seen when passing behind the screen while the short rabbit would not appear in the window, remaining invisible while behind the screen. Infants watched two further events in the second phase, a *possible event* and an *impossible event*. In the possible event, a short rabbit moved behind the screen in the same fashion as before, not appearing in the window. In the impossible event, the tall rabbit moved behind the screen and appeared on the other side in the usual fashion, but also did not appear in the window. Baillargeon et al. measured infants' looking times to these two events. Infants did not look any longer at the possible event than they did at the short rabbit in the first phase of the experiment, indicating they remained habituated to the possible event. However, infants dishabituated to the impossible event, looking at this event much longer than they did in the first phase of the study. This finding indicates that the infants recognized that the tall rabbit should have appeared in the window while behind the screen, suggesting that these very young infants have an understanding of object permanence. That is, they understood the tall rabbit continued to exist when occluded by the screen and therefore should have remained in view when passing the window.

The findings of this study and many others (Baillargeon, 1987; 1991; Baillargeon & Graber, 1988; Spelke, Breinlinger, Macomber, & Jacobson, 1992) have shown that infants have a great deal of knowledge about objects and their properties. Moreover, this research has shown that infants seem to come equipped with a rich understanding of the physical world. According to Piaget, this is knowledge infants should not possess until they are much older and able to engage in means–end reasoning. How can we reconcile these results? Ahmed and Ruffman (1998) have suggested that the knowledge tapped by object permanence tasks which employ looking as the measure of understanding may reveal a different type of knowledge than tasks like Piaget's A-not-B task which require the infant to manually search for the hidden object. They distinguish between **implicit knowledge** and **explicit knowledge**. Roughly speaking, explicit knowledge is knowledge which is accessible to consciousness (that is, you can reflect on it) whereas implicit knowledge is knowledge which is not accessible to consciousness but which still plays a role in guiding behaviour. The impossible event paradigms of

Baillargeon et al. may reveal implicit knowledge. In contrast, Piaget's A-not-B task focused on the development of explicit knowledge.

The preoperational stage The preoperational stage of development characterizes children's thinking between 2 to 7 years of age. The major change observed in children's thinking during this period of development is in the growth of representational abilities. Children make great strides in their use of language, number, pictorial representation, spatial representations, and pretend play. Rather than cover development within each of these areas, we focus instead on some key characteristics of children's thinking during the preoperational stage of development.

While children do make much progress in their ability to use representational thought, Piaget focused more on the *limitations* of the preoperational child's thought than on what they accomplish during this stage of development (Beilin, 1992). One of these limitations upon which Piaget focused is what he referred to as **egocentrism**. Egocentrism refers to the child's tendency to think only from their own perspective; egocentric thinking fails to consider other viewpoints. According to Piaget, the preoperational child's thought is egocentric in nature. To demonstrate this quality of preoperational children's thinking, Piaget employed a task called the 'three mountains task' (Piaget & Inhelder, 1956). In this task, the child sits on one side of a table upon which is a three-dimensional model of a number of mountains and some distinctive landmarks such as a cross and a house. Importantly, some landmarks can only be seen from certain perspectives and children were allowed to experience this for themselves by walking around the entire table. The child was then seated on one side of the table and a doll was placed on the opposite side. The child's task was to choose from a set of photographs which best described what the doll could see. Before the age of 6 or 7, children have great difficulties with this task and often respond by picking the photograph which is consistent with their own point of view.

According to Piaget (1926), another aspect of preoperational children's thinking is that it is **animistic**. Animistic thinking refers to the tendency to attribute life-like qualities to inanimate objects such as plants, rocks, or the moon. For example, young children may believe that the moon follows them while driving, or that picking a flower might hurt it. In Piaget's view, animistic thinking was a consequence of the child's tendency to think egocentrically. Animistic thinking declines during the preoperational stage as children acquire a better understanding of the world.

Another important limitation in preoperational children's thinking is the inability to employ mental **operations**. An operation is a procedure that can be carried out on some mental content. For example, preoperational children fail to understand a simple operation like **reversibility**, the idea that a transformation can be reversed by carrying out a second transformation which negates the first. For example, if you have no apples and are given two apples, you can reverse the transformation by subtracting two apples to get back to the original state.

Piaget tested children's ability to employ operations using the **conservation task**. The conservation task tests children's understanding that the physical characteristics of an object or substance or quantity remain the same even though their physical appearance may change. A classic demonstration of the conservation task uses three glasses. Children are presented with two identical glasses, tall and thin in shape, each of which contains an identical amount of water. The experimenter takes one of these glasses and empties it into a third glass which is short and wide. The child is then asked which glass has more water, less water, or the same amount of water as the water remaining in the original tall, thin glass. In this example, the preoperational child will usually answer that the tall, thin glass has more water. They recognize that no water was taken away from or added by the experimenter, yet they insist that the amount of water has changed. Children's failure on this task illustrates a number of the characteristics of preoperational thought. First, the preoperational child's thinking is bound by the perceptual characteristics of the task; that is to say, they focus on appearances rather than on the nature of what occurs. A related characteristic is what Piaget called **centration**. Centration in the preoperational child's thinking leads them to focus on only one characteristic of the task. In our example, the child centres on the *height* of the water in the glass, a perceptual characteristic. Most importantly, children's failure on the task illustrates their inability to reverse the transformation which created the situation; the failure to understand the reversibility of the transformation leads them to mistakenly infer the quantity of water in the glass has changed. Only with the ability to carry out mental operations such as reversibility do children pass the conservation task.

Much like his work on sensorimotor development, Piaget's thoughts on the preoperational stage have also been criticized. For example, using a simplified version of the three mountains task, Borke (1975) showed that Piaget exaggerated children's difficulty with the task, suggesting that they are less egocentric than he may have thought. Research on children's developing social cognition – that is, their *theory of mind* (see Chapter 9) – supports this view, showing that by the preschool years, children are quite adept at perspective taking, recognizing for example, that people can hold different beliefs about a situation or that a person's belief might differ from reality (Wimmer & Perner, 1983).

Similarly, Piaget may have overestimated how much animistic thinking children engage in. By kindergarten, few children attribute the characteristics of living things to inanimate objects (Carey, 1985). Children's incorrect responses tend to result from their lack of knowledge about living things and suggests that they have a theory of what 'alive' means that is different in some respects from the adult norm. Finally, research has suggested that preoperational children can be trained to understand concepts such as conservation (Beilin, 1978), suggesting that Piaget's belief that the development of operational thought is absent in one stage and present at another is incorrect. In summary, research on preoperational thinking has suggested that children's thought is far more complex than Piaget believed.

The concrete operational stage The hallmark of children's entry into the concrete operational stage is the ability to think using mental operations. Operations are mental representations of both the static and the dynamic aspects of the environment (Siegler, 1998). At this stage, the child can now represent transformations carried out mentally. For example, in the conservation problem, children acquire the ability to mentally represent the transformation that helps them to realize that the quantity of water in the glasses was not changed, only its appearance was altered. An interesting aspect of children's development of the concept of conservation is that, once learned, it is not necessarily applied to all types of conservation problems. The liquid conservation problem we looked at in our example is not the only type of conservation problem. Children must also learn to conserve number, for example, recognizing that rearranging a fixed number of jelly beans does not alter how many jelly beans one has. Similarly, if you take a ball of bread dough and roll it into another shape, the amount of dough does not change. Children presented with different types of conservation problems, number, length, mass, liquid, and area, usually pass the tasks in this order (Brainerd, 1978). You may recognize that this fact does not fit well with Piaget's theory. Remember that Piaget argued that each stage is a qualitatively new level of understanding. The logical competencies which underlie a stage should apply to all tasks that are structurally similar, however, the fact that conservation tasks are acquired in a particular order contradicts this assertion. Evidence has accumulated that children at a given stage do not always show only stage-appropriate levels of performance (Case, 1992b; Lutz & Sternberg, 1999); occasionally, children's familiarity or lack of familiarity with the task materials may lead them to show performance above or below what should be expected of them. Piaget recognized this fact and coined the term **horizontal décalage** to describe this unevenness in the mastery of a concept. The existence of horizontal décalage has been pointed to as a failing of Piaget's theory and evidence that cognitive development may not be as stage-like as Piaget suggested.

Conservation is one of the most important achievements of the concrete operational stage, however, it is not the only accomplishment. During this stage, children develop the mental skills which allow them to understand classification hierarchies. For example, the child who collects sports cards can now sort them by team, by the players' positions, or in a multitude of other ways. This understanding of classification hierarchies allows children to solve the **class inclusion problem**. In this problem, children are presented with a picture of a bunch of flowers consisting of some white roses, and a larger number of red tulips. Children asked the question 'are there more tulips or more flowers?' correctly answer that there are, indeed, more flowers; that is, they recognize the tulips are a class by themselves as well as members of the larger class of flowers, and therefore, that there must be more flowers. In contrast, preoperational children will routinely fail this question. Concrete operational children also pass **transitive inference** problems. For example, given the information that *John is bigger than Bob, and Bob is bigger than Allan*, they can correctly infer that John is bigger than Allan.

More recent research on these tasks has questioned Piaget's findings. Class inclusion problems have been criticized for the wording of the test question. Donaldson (1978) simplified the question and found that much younger children were able to pass the task. Similarly, Bryant and Trabasso (1971) argued that preoperational children could pass transitive inference tasks when the memory requirements of the task were reduced. These and other findings suggest that, once again, Piaget's estimates of when children can pass these tasks are incorrect. They also call into question his assumptions regarding the discontinuity of cognitive development, suggesting that development may in fact, be more continuous than Piaget believed.

The formal operational stage Whereas the concrete operational child can solve a variety of logical problems such as conservation tasks, transitive inference problems, and class inclusion problems, they still fail to understand logical problems when they are required to go beyond the concrete and to consider the abstract or the hypothetical. Around 11 years of age, children reach the **formal operational stage** which, in Piaget's view, was the endpoint of cognitive development. By the formal operational stage, children become capable of reasoning in propositional, abstract, and hypothetical ways (Inhelder & Piaget, 1958). Formal operational children reason in a specific way, using what has been called **hypothetico-deductive reasoning**. When trying to solve a difficult problem, adolescents start with a general theory of all of the factors which might impact on the outcome of the problem and then try to deduce specific hypotheses in light of these factors. Next, they test their hypotheses and if necessary, revise their theory. This type of reasoning represents the hypothetical and abstract nature of the adolescent's thinking. According to Keating (1990), these characteristics of adolescent thinking, namely hypothesis testing and hypothetical thinking, are what truly distinguish formal operational thought from the previous stage.

Adolescents also think in a propositional manner; that is, they can reason based on the logical properties of a set of statements rather than requiring concrete examples. Osherson and Markman (1975) did a study in which they gave adolescents and younger, concrete-operational children two types of problems. The participants were shown a pile of poker chips of different colours, and were told that they were going to hear statements about the chips and that they should try and state whether these were true or false. In one condition, the experimenter concealed a chip in their hand and said *Either the chip in my hand is green or it is not green* or *The chip in my hand is green and it is not green.* In this case, only adolescents were able to state that the first statement was true and the second false. In another condition, the experimenter made the same type of statements about a different chip but held the chip in plain view. In this case, both groups were able to correctly state whether the statements were true or false. The concrete operational children were able to pass the task when they could match the statement to a concrete property of the chips; when they unable to do this, they failed the tasks. In contrast, adolescents used the logic of the statements themselves; 'and' statements were always incorrect since a chip could not be one colour and another at the same time and 'either–or' statements were always true.

Criticisms focusing on the idea of a formal operational stage concentrate on two main issues: first, whether all individuals reach the formal operational stage and second, whether children might develop the ability to test hypotheses and think abstractly earlier than Piaget suggested. In regard to the first issue, research has shown that, contrary to Piaget's belief that formal operations are universally attained by all normally developing adolescents, a significant number of individuals fail to attain formal operational reasoning. In one study, Keating (1979) showed that between 40 to 60 percent of college students failed Piagetian formal operations tasks. Research has also shown that in many cases, adults do not reason at the level of formal operations (Neimark, 1975). In addition, cross cultural evidence suggests that in many cases, formal operational reasoning is not naturally achieved in other cultures. While the literature on adolescent reasoning clearly supports a distinction in the nature of reasoning exhibited by adolescents and younger children (Keating, 1990; Moshman, 1998), it seems there is considerable variation in the attainment of formal operations, possibly as an effect of schooling practices in literate societies which emphasize logical thinking and problem solving.

To address the question of whether children might show abstract thinking and reasoning abilities earlier than Piaget suggested, we can turn to a study by Ruffman, Perner, Olson, and Doherty (1993). Ruffman et al. showed that 6-year-olds were able to understand the relationship between hypotheses and evidence, recognizing that one needs appropriate evidence to confirm or

TABLE 6.2 Piaget's stages: the preoperational, concrete operational, and formal operational stages

Stage	Age	Description
Preoperational stage	2–7 years	*The growth of representational abilities* • **Egocentrism**: the child at this stage has a tendency to think only from his/her own perspective • **Animistic** thinking: the child attributes lifelike qualities to inanimate objects • Inability to employ mental operations, such as reversibility and conservation tasks • **Centration**: child only focuses on one aspect of a problem
Concrete operations	7–11 years	*The ability to think using mental operations* • **Conversation**: understanding that the physical characteristics of an object or substance or quantity remain the same even their physical appearance may change • **Classification hierarchies**: flexible grouping of objects into classes and subclasses; allows children to solve class inclusion problems • **Transitive inference**: given two statements, such as John is bigger than Bob, and Bob is bigger than Allan, can infer that John is bigger than Allan
Formal operations	11+ years	*Endpoint of cognitive development. Reasoning in propositional, abstract, and hypothetical ways* • **Hypothetico-deductive reasoning**: the ability to start with a general theory of all the factors involved in a problem, the deduction of specific hypotheses considering these factors, and a testing and possible revision of the hypothesis • **Propositional thinking**: Reasoning based on the logical properties of a set of statements rather than requiring concrete examples

reject a hypothesis. They also recognized that hypotheses would constrain a person's predictions about future events. However, children were only able to come to this recognition for very simple sets of variables and relationships. The results from the study by Ruffman et al. (see also Sodian, Zaitchik, & Carey, 1991) suggest that under the appropriate conditions, even quite young children can show some ability to think in an abstract, hypothesis-driven fashion.

Finally, some theorists have advocated the addition of a fifth stage of cognitive development to Piaget's model, a stage which people begin to recognize that thinking occurs in a continuous and increasingly complex manner (Riegel, 1973). Whether cognitive development continues beyond adolescence, however, is still an open question (Moshman, 1998). (See Table 6.2 for an overview of Piaget's stages.)

Criticisms of Piagetian theory

A good theory should be able to integrate a wide array of information and stimulate new research; Piaget's theory does well on both counts. Piaget integrated a great number of diverse facts about children's cognitive development under a coherent theory. Moreover, his theory incorporated development in domains as diverse as *time*, *space*, *number*, and *physics*, showing how development in each of these areas is related to the child's acquisition of an increasingly powerful mental logic. Piagetian theory has also stimulated a great deal of new research, evident in the vast number of studies influenced by his work since the 1960s when his work first became widely known in North America. Importantly, although the bulk of this research has suggested that Piaget's ideas about cognitive development were incorrect on a variety of points, the inspiration for much of this research was his theory. Even though he may have underestimated children's knowledge in many domains, Piaget was responsible for pushing the field of cognitive development forward.

While Piaget's theory has important strengths, it also has been heavily criticized, as shown earlier in this chapter. Piaget's erroneous conclusions regarding children's cognitive ability stem partly from his reliance on verbal interview methods. New developments in methodology have allowed for a better understanding of emerging abilities. Piagetian theory has also been criticized for its adherence to a conception of development as occurring in stages. Development is not necessarily stage-like (Brainerd, 1978). As Siegler (1998) has argued, whether development appears stage-like or more continuous depends in large part on the level of analysis one chooses. If you assess children's competence every few months, then sudden changes in their level of reasoning will appear abrupt and stage-like. If you assess development on a smaller time scale, development may look more continuous.

Piaget's stage theory has also been criticized for its proposed universality. As we have seen, the sequence of stages might not proceed in as orderly a fashion as Piaget suggested. Some stages may not occur across cultures and their development may be heavily dependent on cultural and social factors (Rogoff, 1998). Children's development within stages can also be altered by experience or training.

Other criticisms leveled at Piaget include the complaint that concepts such as *assimilation* and *accommodation* are too vague to be of any use (Brainerd, 1978). Finally, it is possible that development may not occur in an across-the-board or *domain-general* fashion as Piaget suggested. Recent research in cognitive development has increasingly focused on *domain-specific* developments, that is, development within specific domains of knowledge such as biology and physics (Gopnik & Wellman, 1994). The focus of much of this research has been on how the acquisition of knowledge leads to development within a given domain.

Vygotsky's sociocultural theory of cognitive development

In their review of the wide variety of theoretical positions which guide the study of human development, Dixon and Lerner (1999) identified the work of Lev Vygotsky and his emphasis on the cultural contexts in which human development occurs as one of the main forces behind the spread of the family of theories which they label as *contextualist* theories. Like Piaget, Vygotsky was strongly committed to the idea that children were active explorers of their world who test their ideas against reality, seeking to expand their knowledge.

However, unlike Piaget, who viewed children essentially as solitary figures involved in the construction of knowledge, Vygotsky believed that the child's social environment is an active force in their development, working to mould children's growing knowledge in ways that are adaptive to the wider culture in which they grow up. Vygotsky's perspective on development is often referred to as a **sociocultural** view because of his emphasis on the child's culture and the social environment as forces which shape development.

According to Wertsch (1991), there are three main themes which encapsulate Vygotsky's view of cognitive development. First, Vygotsky maintained that the study of development must rely on 'genetic analyses'. This sounds misleading, as like Piaget, Vygotsky used the term *genetic* to refer to the idea of development, *not* to our biological endowment. His idea is that understanding a mental process is only possible through an examination of the origins and the transformations the process undergoes from its immature to its mature form. In other words, the study of development is, in a very real sense, a historical process. Thus, Vygotsky was a strong advocate of the developmental method, focusing on the origins of mental processes and the transformations which they undergo.

Second, as already mentioned, Vygotsky was adamant in his belief that an individual's cognitive development is largely a social process, not an individualistic construction, as Piaget believed. For Vygotsky, cognitive development occurs as a function of the child's interactions with partners who are more highly skilled than the child. These others interact with the child, and through the instruction and assistance they provide to the child, promote cognitive development (Vygotsky, 1935/1978). Vygotsky did believe that the child was equipped with a set of innate abilities but he maintained that these developed only to a limited extent without the intervention of other members of the child's community. Vygotsky referred to the abilities with which the child is naturally endowed, specifically attention, memory, and perception, as the **elementary mental functions**. He contrasted these with the same functions once they are transformed by social interactions with other, more experienced members of the culture. These **higher mental functions** are the socially transformed products of the child's initial endowment. An important aspect of the higher mental functions is that they are **mediated** processes; they rely on 'mediators' or psychological tools such as language or the number system.

The third major aspect of Vygotsky's theory centres on this notion of mediation. Vygotsky argued that all human cognitive activity, both social and individual, is mediated by the use of symbolic 'tools' such as language, art, numbers, and other culturally derived products. Vygotsky believed that our natural development and our cultural development followed separate lines (Wertsch, 1991); that is to say, the abilities with which we come innately endowed develop to a point without the need for social intervention, following a maturationally based timetable, but then plateau. This halt in the natural line of development comes about because of the child's acquisition of mediators like language. Once children have developed the symbolic capabilities which allow them to interact with other members of their culture, they enter into a dialogue which transforms their innate abilities into the uniquely human, higher mental functions (Vygotsky, 1981).

It is important to note the patterning of development according to Vygotsky's view. Vygotsky stated that: 'Any function in the child's cultural development appears twice, or on two planes. First, it appears on the social plane, and then on the psychological plane' (Vygotsky, 1981: 163). In this statement, Vygotsky argued that development results from processes which occur first *between* people and then occur *within* the individual. Vygotsky referred to this process of functions moving from the interpersonal to the intrapersonal as **internalization**. The development of all higher mental functions occurs in large part, as the result of the internalization. This does not mean that cognitive development is a simple process of copying social processes (Wertsch, 1991). Internalization does involve transformations of social processes by the individual; however, Vygotsky did advocate that our cognition is strongly grounded in social processes.

The zone of proximal development

Vygotsky (1978) believed that the interactions between parents and children which led to intellectual development took place in a specific way. He proposed the concept of the **zone of proximal development** (**ZPD**) as a way of illustrating how social interactions between experienced members of the culture and less experienced children led to development. He defined the zone of proximal development as the difference between the child's 'actual developmental level as determined by independent problem solving' and their 'potential development as determined through problem solving under adult guidance or in collaboration with more capable peers' (Vygotsky, 1978: 86).

There are two aspects of the concept which are important to note (Cole, 1985). First, the zone of proximal development represents a specific way in which more capable members of the culture assist the child's development. This is achieved by working with the child at a level slightly beyond the child's own capabilities. We will examine this aspect further later. Second, the zone of proximal development highlights Vygotsky's concern with how intellectual functioning is measured. Vygotsky felt it was critical to measure the child's *potential* for learning under adult guidance; such a measure of intelligence has a greater utility according to Vygotsky than a simple assessment of what the child is capable of doing alone. Given his belief in the study of developmental processes rather than endpoints, Vygotsky's emphasis on the child's potential as the state we should be concerned with in assessment is extremely appealing.

The zone of proximal development has had a great influence on the study of cognitive development. One way in which it has had an influence is on how developmentalists think about the quality of instruction children receive from others. Vygotsky did not specify how adults and children worked within the zone of proximal development, but later researchers, looking more carefully at the processes involved came up with the term **scaffolding** (Bruner, 1983; Wood, Bruner, & Ross, 1976) to describe the processes involved. Scaffolding is an interactive process in which adults adjust both the amount and the type of support they offer to the child, leading to the eventual mastery of the skill being taught. When adults provide effective scaffolding for a child, they initially try to encourage the child to operate at the limit of their ability. If the child does not respond, the adult will use more specific behaviours to direct the child and, in addition, they may vary the type of instruction offered. As the child begins to experience success, the adult intervenes in more indirect ways, reducing their level of instruction and encouraging the child to move forward. The key to effective scaffolding is a sensitivity to the child's level of development (Rogoff, 1998; Wood & Middleton, 1975). Research has shown that when mothers are more effective at scaffolding their children's behaviours in the context of a problem solving task, the child is more likely to act successfully on their own in a similar task (Berk & Spuhl, 1995).

Language and play

A key question we need to ask is whether or not there is any evidence for Vygotsky's idea that development proceeds from the social plane to the individual? One phenomenon which Vygotsky cited as evidence for this progression was children's speech to themselves. You may have noticed that preschool children often talk to themselves while performing problem solving tasks or while carrying out everyday activities. For example, while playing with toy blocks young children can often be heard uttering things such as '*Now I need a blue one*' or '*That doesn't go here*'. Jean Piaget noticed this tendency as well. He referred to this as **egocentric speech**, believing that because of the preschool child's inability to think from another's perspective, their communications were often profoundly egocentric, that is, not adapted to another's viewpoint. Vygotsky took exception to Piaget's classification of children's speech as egocentric. In contrast to Piaget, Vygotsky (1934/1986) believed children's speech to themselves is a powerful means of regulating their own behaviour. Language gives children the means to reflect on their own behaviour, to organize behaviour, and to control their behaviour. Children's speech to themselves reflects the fact that their thought is organized in the form of dialogues with others and because thought is dialogic, the language which supports it gets expressed. As children become more competent with cognitive tasks, these dialogues become internalized and their speech to themselves declines in frequency. A good deal of research has shown that Vygotsky's view of children's speech to themselves is a better description of children's behaviour than is Piaget's, and have adopted the term **private speech** (in contrast to Piaget's term egocentric speech) to describe this behaviour (e.g., Berk, 1992). Furthermore, in accord with Vygotsky's view, children who use private speech show greater improvement on problem solving tasks than their peers who do not use (or use less) private speech.

Like Piaget, Vygotsky (1978) also took notice of young children's tendency to engage in pretend play, and he pointed to an interesting fact about it. Vygotsky noted that children's pretend play tends to occur at a level beyond their stage in life; that is, in their pretense, children take on roles such as *parent* or *doctor* rather than roles that are appropriate to children. Through pretend play, children place themselves in a zone of proximal development, where they play at a level which is in advance of their real capabilities. Pretend play has the ability to stimulate development in a variety of ways. One way has to do with the child's use of their imaginations. In pretend play, children learn that the objects they use can be separated from their normal referents, and that they can stand for other things. Thus, the child can play with the banana as if it were a telephone. In addition, pretend play tends to be based on rules. The child who pretends to be a baby has to follow the rules and go to sleep when their pretend mummy tells them to, and the child who pretends to be a daddy may have to pretend to cut the lawn. In other words, children's play is constrained by the rules which guide behaviour in these roles, and, because of this, they learn about the social norms that are expected of people. Vygotsky believed that pretend play was an important context in which children learned about the social world.

The implications of Vygotsky's theory for education

Vygotsky's theory has had a major impact on education in recent years, largely because of his stress on the importance of social interactions with more experienced others as a force which drives learning. Vygotsky's belief was not simply that education was a process of refining cognitive structures which the child has already acquired; instead, he maintained that education was a fundamental aspect of human development. Social interactions with more experienced others are essential to our education.

Vygotsky's theory has much to say about how education might best take place. Peer collaboration is a key concept in the Vygotskian approach to education. One educational device that has been developed on the basis of Vygotsky's theory is called **reciprocal teaching**. Reciprocal teaching is a method of using peers to foster dialogues about a subject matter such that they provide a level which is beyond the individual child's capability but within their zone of proximal development (Brown & Palinscar, 1982; Palinscar & Brown, 1984). The method was designed to improve the reading ability of children who were designated as having academic difficulties but it has been extended into other subject areas, such as science. The reciprocal teaching method involves the student in a group with several other students and a teacher. The aim of the group is to engage in collaborative learning, that is, to make certain that the entire group works through and learns a topic. Within the group, students take turns at leading discussions on a particular text. The leader of the group discussion is responsible for ensuring that all the students take part in all phases of the discussion. There are four activities that are required of students within the group: questioning, summarizing, clarifying, and predicting. In a reciprocal teaching group, the leader of a discussion begins the learning process by asking questions about the content of the text. In this phase, group members answer questions, elaborate on others' statements, try to resolve disagreements (by rereading if necessary) and raise questions of their own. This is followed up by the leader's summary of the text and a period of clarification where group members who have trouble grasping certain ideas try to work through these with the group. Finally, the group is asked to use their understanding to predict future content of the text. The idea of reciprocal teaching is to make the processes which a skilled reader engages in automatically more *explicit* so that group members who have problems with these skills can internalize them. As you can see, the practices engaged in by students in reciprocal teaching are very consistent with Vygotsky's theory.

Another way in which Vygotsky's theory is employed in the classroom is through **cooperative learning**. This is a technique in which the child's learning environment is structured into small groups of peers who work together toward a common learning goal. Unlike reciprocal teaching, a teacher is not used to guide each group. Instead, groups are formed from combinations of more and less knowledgeable peers. Cooperative learning environments work best when children truly adopt and share common goals (Forman & McPhail, 1993) and when the group consists of children who are truly accomplished at the particular task and who can provide expert instruction to others who are less skilled (Azmitia, 1988; Rogoff, 1998).

Criticisms of Vygotsky's theory

Vygotsky's theory has proven very influential in recent years and has inspired a great deal of research and speculation regarding the role of culture and social interaction in human development (Rogoff, 1998). However, the relatively recent entry of Vygotsky's theory into the study of human development means that the theory has not yet received the same level of critical analysis that more established theories such as Piaget's have received (Miller, 1993).

One aspect of Vygotsky's work which has been heavily criticised is his almost exclusive focus on the cultural aspects of development. Recall that Vygotsky distinguished between the *natural* line of development and the *cultural* line, however, his theory tells us almost nothing about the natural line of development. Consequently, it is not possible to understand within the confines of Vygotskian theory how exactly the elementary processes such as attention and memory contribute to the development of symbolically mediated forms of cognition (Wertsch & Tulviste, 1992). Importantly, children's cognitive abilities are used as indicators of the kinds of social experiences which will be made available to them. Vygotsky's theory has little to say about how children's developmental level serves to constrain or enhance their opportunities for participation in various contexts. Other issues which are raised as challenges for Vygotskian and other contextualist theories include: the examination of how people determine the goals of their collaborative efforts and the means by which these are carried out; how children and adults collaborate outside the context of experimental settings; the dynamics of groups larger than two persons; and the nature of interactions in cultures other than middle-class, North American, and European groups (Rogoff, 1998). Rogoff has pointed out that, given the typical emphasis in developmental research on the *individual* as the unit of study, it is not surprising that we have little information on some of these questions. The current interest in Vygotskian and other sociocultural theories suggests it is only a matter of time before these and other critical issues begin to be addressed.

Information processing theories

The **information processing approach** to cognitive development is based on an analogy between the digital computer and the human mind. Most information processing theorists share the view that the mind is a system which manipulates symbols according to a set of rules. Like computers, our minds encode information received from the environment, cast it into a symbolic form which the mind can process, and through a variety of operations, processes this information to produce useful output such as the solution to a problem. There are other parallels between human cognition and computers that have been explored by information processing theorists. Like computers, we also have finite resources such as memory which place limits on our cognitive performance. As well, just as computers 'develop' in terms of the sophistication of their hardware, so does the human brain develop, leading to the growth of more powerful thought processes. However, as Klahr and MacWhinney (1998) caution, information processing theorists do not literally believe that the mind is a computer. Rather, they see the computer as a tool for testing models of cognitive development. In essence, the goal is to test whether a theory of intelligent behaviour can be accounted for by a computational system, whether the computations are run in a brain or on a computer.

While there are a large number of information processing theories, all approaches share three basic assumptions (Siegler, 1998). The first belief is that *thinking is information processing*; that is, any thought process such as remembering or perceiving involves the processing of information. Second, information processing theories emphasize the need to study the *change mechanisms* that move development from one state to the next. Third, development within information processing systems is driven by *self-modification*; that is, earlier knowledge and strategies can modify thinking and thus, lead to higher levels of development.

The information processing system

According to Siegler (1998), information processing theories focus on the organization of the information processing system, or what he calls the *structural characteristics*, and the *processes* that provide the means for cognition to adapt to the changing demands of the environment. We examine these two aspects of the information processing system in turn.

The structural characteristics of the information processing system are believed to be universal in that all children share the same basic organization of cognitive structures. Springing from the work of cognitive psychologists (e.g., Atkinson & Shiffrin, 1968; 1971), most theories of information processing are based on a three-part model (known as the **store model**) which consists of a **sensory register**, **working memory**, and **long-term memory**. In this store model, information is believed to flow into the cognitive system through the sensory register. The sensory register is a memory store which allows us to briefly store large amounts of sensory information (e.g., visual images and sounds) for a very short duration, somewhere around one second (Sperling, 1960). If you look closely at something, close your eyes, and monitor your experience you will notice that a visual image of the scene will last for a brief time. From the sensory register, information flows into working memory (also referred to as short-term memory).

Working memory is the area of the system where thinking occurs. That is, working memory allows us a space from which to operate on incoming information, combining it with long-term memory, or transforming it in various ways. A critical point regarding working memory is that it is a limited resource. First, working memory is of limited *capacity*; that is, we can only store so much information in working memory at one time. Estimates of working memory capacity suggest that it can hold approximately 7 units of information (Miller, 1956). Second, information can only be held in working memory for a brief period, somewhere in the order of 15 to 30 seconds (Siegler, 1998). Thus, working memory provides a bottleneck in the system because of this limited capacity. Incoming information pushes information out of working memory such that it is either forgotten or it is moved into long-term memory. An important aspect of working memory is that its capacity can be increased through the application of strategies such as **chunking**, where information held in working memory is organized into more meaningful units. For example, instead of treating the first three digits of a phone number as three separate units of information, you can chunk them into a single unit, remembering '388' instead of '3', '8', and '8'. Chunking allows us to increase our working memory capacity, and, thus, to form more complex mental representations.

Information from working memory can move into long-term memory. Long-term memory is the part of the cognitive system that contains our permanent knowledge base. It is a storehouse of information which seems to have no limit, in terms of either its capacity or in how long information can reside here. Many theorists believe that long-term memory is organized as an *associative network*, in that to retrieve information we need to have cues that allow us to find the stored information (Atkinson & Shiffrin, 1968; Broadbent, 1984). The more associations we form between an item and cues which help us retrieve it, the more likely it is we will remember the item, that is, bring it from long-term to working memory.

As noted earlier, there are a number of processes which may operate on information held in the three memory stores. Unlike the architecture of the information processing system, these processes show considerable development over time; that is, children gain greater expertise with these strategies leading to the more efficient handling of information within the cognitive system. One important process is **encoding**. Given the finite capacity of our sensory register and working memory, we are limited in the amount of information that we can manage to transform into mental representations. Encoding is the process by which we pick out the important features of an object or event so that we can form a representation. Efficient encoding processes allow us to quickly pick out the relevant features that are important to our thinking. In contrast, inefficient encoding processes can lead to the loss of information, producing limitations in the usefulness of the representations children form. Another critical process is **automatization**. Cognitive psychologists (Shiffrin & Schneider, 1977) distinguish between *controlled* processes, that is, processes which require conscious attention, and *automatic processes*, processes which require little or no conscious attention.

The more controlled a process is, the more working memory capacity it requires. Thus, the processes that lead to the automatization of some task are generally beneficial in that they free up mental resources that can be allocated in other ways. Consider a child learning to solve simple arithmetic problems such as 'What is 5 + 3?' At first the child may count off five fingers and then count off a further three fingers, and then count up the total number of fingers which are raised (Siegler, 1998). However, with practise, children begin to memorize the solutions to these simple problems. That is, they have automatized the answer and can simply recall the product of the addition without counting it out. The automatization of a skill leads to increases in the speed of the child's ability to execute it as well as leaving more free working memory capacity so that the child can monitor their cognitive performance and, perhaps, learn to further improve their abilities through the application of strategies.

A neo-Piagetian theory of cognitive development

One of the many information processing theories of cognitive development is that of Robbie Case (1985; 1992b). Case's theory of cognitive development is similar to Piaget's in that it postulated broad, qualitative changes in cognitive development; Case, however, differs from Piaget in that he believes that shifts in cognitive development result from increases in the child's information processing capacity (i.e., working memory). In his theory, Case refers to the growth of information processing capacity as **m-space** and argues that these increases in capacity represent the child's ability to use their limited capacity more efficiently. Case attributes the growth of information processing capacity as stemming from three processes. First, the maturation of the brain leads to increases in information processing capacity through increases in the speed with which mental operations can be carried out. A neural process called myelinization speeds up the transmission of electrical impulses through the brain and thus, increases speed. In turn, speed increases capacity by utilizing working memory more efficiently. Second, the development of cognitive strategies also frees up capacity, speeding up the process of automatization. Finally, automatization of knowledge and schemes leads to the development of *central conceptual structures*. These are networks of concepts and relations between concepts which allow the child to think about some situations in more advanced ways. Case and Griffin (1990) argued that because central conceptual structures lead to the development of more efficient means of thinking about situations, they too free up information processing capacity.

One of the great strengths of Case's theory is its ability to account for the transition from one stage of thought to another. Case argues that the increases in m-space lead to the child moving from one stage to the next; that is, when the child acquires enough m-space to represent a situation in a more complex way, they have progressed to a new level of thinking. In support of this idea, Case has conducted a great deal of research which shows strong correlations between measures of m-space and cognitive performance; the greater one's m-space, the higher is the level of cognitive development. Case's theory represents an important step beyond Piaget, combining concepts from information processing theory with Piaget's ideas, providing us with a more comprehensive and testable account of cognitive development.

SUMMARY

Our survey of the theories of Piaget, Vygotsky and the information processing tradition captures some of the differences in opinion which exist about how to tackle the study of children's cognitive development. Each theory emphasizes different factors as being important to an understanding of cognition. The Piagetian tradition focuses on the nature of children's interactions with their physical environment, whereas Vygotskian theory stresses that social interactions between children and more skilled members of their culture are critical to cognitive development. In contrast to both of these positions, the information processing theorists emphasize the importance of studying the mechanisms which lead to developmental change. As was noted at the outset, covering the whole field of cognition is beyond the scope of this book, but armed with a knowledge of these theories, you should be in a position to understand much of the research in this field.

Glossary

Accommodation is the process of adjusting old schemes to better fit with the demands of the environment (the complement of assimilation).

Adaptation involves the creation of cognitive structures or schemes through our interactions with the environment, allowing us to adjust to the demands posed by the environment. An important aspect of the higher mental functions is that they are **mediated** processes, relying on systems such as language or the numerical system.

Animistic thinking refers to thc tendency to attribute life-like qualities to inanimate objects such as plants or rocks.

A-not-B task in which infants search for hidden objects, first at one location (the A trials) and then later, at a second location (the B trials). Used by Piaget to test for object permanence.

Assimilation refers to the process of integrating the environment into one's current psychological structures, using current schemes to interpret new knowledge (the complement of accommodation).

Automatization is the processes by which behaviours that require conscious, controlled attention are transformed so that they require little or no conscious attention.

Centration refers to the quality of a child's thinking which leads them to focus on only one characteristic or dimension of a task or problem.

Chunking is a process whereby the information held in working memory is organized into a smaller number of more meaningful units.

Class inclusion problem is a problem designed by Piaget to test children's understanding of classification hierarchies.

Conservation task Piaget's task which tests children's understanding that the physical characteristics of an object, substance, or quantity remain the same even though their physical appearance may change.

Cooperative learning is a technique in which the child's learning environment is structured into small groups of peers who work together toward a common learning goal.

Egocentric speech is communication that is not adapted to another's viewpoint.

Egocentrism refers to the child's tendency to think only from their own perspective, failing to consider other possible viewpoints.

Elementary mental functions in Vygotsky's view, the abilities with which the child is naturally endowed, such as attention, memory, and perception.

Encoding is the process by which we pick out the important features of an object or event so that we can form a mental representation.

Equilibration is Piaget's term for the striving of the cognitive system to maintain a state of equilibrium.

Explicit knowledge is knowledge which is accessible to consciousness.

Formal operational stage the stage of cognitive development where adolescents become capable of reasoning in propositional, abstract, and hypothetical ways. In Piaget's view, the endpoint of cognitive development.

Higher mental functions in Vygotsky's view, cognitive functions that have been transformed by social interactions with other, more experienced members of the culture.

Horizontal décalage is used to describe the unevenness in children's mastery of the different forms of a concept such as conservation.

Hypothetico-deductive reasoning is a form of reasoning where a child starts with a general theory of all of the factors which might impact on the outcome of a problem and then tries to deduce specific hypotheses in light of these factors. Next, they test their hypotheses and if necessary, revise their theory.

Implicit knowledge is knowledge which is not accessible to consciousness but which still plays a role in guiding behaviour.

Information processing approach is an approach to the study of cognitive development which focuses on how information is encoded from the environment, cast into a symbolic form which the mind can process, and processed through a variety of mental operations to create useful output, such as the solution to a problem.

Internalization refers to Vygotsky's belief that processes initially carried out at the social level can be internalized by the child and carried out within the individual. For example, dialogues carried out between a parent and child become internalized and can be used by the child to guide their own thoughts and actions.

Long-term memory is the part of the cognitive system that contains our permanent knowledge base. It is a storehouse of information which seems to have no limit, in terms of either its capacity or in how long information can reside here.

m-space refers to the child's capacity to hold information actively in mind. m-space is believed to increase with development through to adolescence.

Object permanence refers to the concept that objects continue to exist independently of our ability to perceive or to act on them.

Operations refer to procedures that can be carried out on some mental content.

Organization refers to the individual's tendency to organize their cognitive structures or schemes into efficient systems.

Pretend play is play where children act out imaginary activities and use real objects to stand for imagined objects.

Primary circular reactions Piaget's term for simple motor habits seen in infants such as thumb sucking that can be repeated and which are pleasurable.

Private speech refers to speech used to guide the child's behaviour. Private speech is more likely to occur when children are faced with a difficult task and becomes less frequent as children get older.

Reciprocal teaching is a method of using small groups of peers to create dialogues about a subject matter, providing a level of instruction which is beyond the individual child's capability but within their zone of proximal development. It emphasizes four cognitive processes: predicting, questioning, summarizing, and clarifying.

Reversibility is the idea that a mental operation can be reversed by carrying out a second operation which is the inverse of the first. For example, the addition of two numbers can be reversed by subtracting an amout equal to that added to the initial quantity.

Scaffolding is an interactive process in which adults adjust both the amount and the type of support they offer to the child, leading to the eventual mastery of the skill being taught.

Schemes is the term used by Piaget to refer to an interrelated set of actions, memories, thoughts, or strategies which are employed to predict and understand the environment.

Secondary circular reactions are behaviours focused on the environment which produce interesting reactions which the infant attempts to maintain through repetition.

Sensorimotor stage refers to the first two years of an infant's life during which the infant moves from responding to the environment in a simplistic, reflexive manner, to being able to think in symbolic forms, and in a goal-directed manner.

Sensory register is a memory store which allows us to briefly store large amounts of sensory information for a very short duration.

Sociocultural theory refers to Vygotsky's perspective on development which places a strong emphasis on the child's culture and the social environment as forces which shape development.

Stage a stage of development is a period in which the child's cognitive structures are qualitatively similar.

Store model a model of the flow of information through the cognitive system which posits a variety of information stores including the sensory register, short-term memory, and long-term memory.

Transitive inference problems are a class of problems where the child must make an inference based on premise information contained in the problem and the concept of transitivity.

Working memory is a mental space from which we operate on incoming information, combining it with long-term memory or transforming it in various ways.

Zone of proximal development is the difference between the child's independently determined developmental level and their potential level of development determined when problem solving under adult guidance, or in collaboration with more capable peers.

7 The Development of Language and Communication

LEARNING AIMS

At the end of this chapter you should:

- **understand the different facets involved in the study of human language**
- **be able to articulate the essential points of learning, nativist, and interactionist accounts of language**
- **be aware of evidence for and against each of the three theoretical accounts**
- **be able to describe the key concepts involved in phonological development**
- **be able to describe the course of semantic development including concepts such as *fast mapping* and the constraints which support the development of children's word learning**
- **be able to describe the course of grammatical development including concepts such as *syntactic bootstrapping***
- **be able to describe the developmental course of pragmatic knowledge and key concepts such as *speech registers*, *conversational implicature*, and the *cooperative principle***

Introduction

When we communicate successfully, we do so because we are able to do at least four different things. First, we need to be able to produce the sounds that make up a language and convey meanings to other people. Second, we need to know what the words of a language mean. Third, we need to know how to put these words together in grammatically appropriate ways such that others will understand us. Finally, we also need to know how to effectively *use* our language to communicate with others. Psychologists who study language refer to these four processes by separate names. How we produce meaningful sounds is the study of **phonology**. The study of **semantics** refers to the developing knowledge of word meanings and how we acquire a vocabulary. The study of **syntax** refers to how we learn the grammar of our language, that is, the rules for combining words into meaningful sentences. Finally, **pragmatics** is the study of how we use our language to achieve our communicative goals. If you want to be *polite*, make a *promise*, or speak in a *sarcastic* way, you need to know more than simply how to string words together.

Note that in what follows, we focus on the development of spoken language. While there are other topics which could be considered, such as the development of written language or nonverbal communication, these will not be addressed in a systematic way in this chapter.

Theories of language development

Two approaches have dominated the study of language. The first of these theories of language were accounts based on the behaviourist approach to psychology, so influential in the 1940s and 1950s. These behaviourist inspired theories of language fell out of favour after a devastating review of learning theory accounts of language published by Noam Chomsky (1959). With Chomsky's review, a new theory of language based on nativist ideas emerged. Simply put, Chomsky and his followers believed that we do not learn a language; indeed, Chomsky has argued that it makes little sense to use the word 'learn' in connection with how we acquire a language. Instead, Chomsky claimed that language quite naturally developed as we matured. Until recently, Chomskian accounts have dominated work on language development, however, a variety of learning accounts have been put forward which stress the importance of environmental influences on language learning. In what follows, we will review each of these positions. (See Table 7.1 for an overview of the theories.)

Learning theory

Learning theory accounts of language development are distinguished from more contemporary theories of language by their adherence to the traditional principles of learning theory, that is, reinforcement and punishment. Learning theory views of language range from the radical behaviourism of B.F. Skinner (1957) to the social learning theory of Albert Bandura (1989) with its emphasis on cognitive processes. Skinner's theory of language was put forth in his 1957 book *Verbal Behaviour*. Skinner argued that language is like any other form of behaviour in that it is acquired through operant conditioning. That is, parents selectively reinforce the child's linguistic behaviours, rewarding only those behaviours which they recognize as words or as appropriate,

TABLE 7.1 Theories of language development

Learning theory	
Skinner	Focus on operant conditioning, with the development of language occurring through parental selective reinforcement of 'appropriate' linguistic behaviours
Bandura	Focus on observational learning, with imitation of others resulting in learning of complex and length utterances. The reinforcement of such imitation and its generalization allows application of newly learnt language to new situations, and feedback helps children understand the appropriateness of such
Criticisms of the theory	Given the rapid nature of language learning and the long period of time over which principles of operant conditioning and observational learning influence behaviours, it appears unlikely that the latter can be applied to the former Positive parental feedback is not limited to the grammar of children's language, but rather to its truth The language children are exposed to rarely includes instances of complex structures, and this *stimulus poverty* means that it would be difficult if not impossible for children to adequately learn how to accurately apply such complex structures in their own language
Nativist theory	
Shared assumptions	Certain grammatical concepts are common to all languages and are thus innate; children have a biological predisposition to language learning; children's innate hypotheses regarding language allow extraction of principles which govern language
Chomsky	The innate mental structure responsible for language is the language acquisition device (LAD). It contains the common grammatical concepts, or universal grammar, which allows its operation with reference to any language. Once the principles of the specific relevant language are extracted by the LAD, these principles are built into the LAD in order to allow interpretation of further speech
Criticisms of the theory	What kind of universal grammar is common to all languages? The lengthy time period over which understanding of grammatical rules emerges suggests that if knowledge is innate, it must be more limited than that proposed by most nativist theorists There is little neurological evidence for a biological predisposition to language learning, such as the LAD
Interactionist theory	
Bruner	The social support and social context of instruction in language acquisition is as important as biological factors. Scaffolding, motherese, and expansion and recast all facilitate the effective operation of the strong biological predisposition towards language acquisition. This collection of strategies has been termed the language acquisition support system (LASS)
Criticisms of the theory	Direct feedback on the appropriateness of language is rare and cannot be regarded as an essential element of any LASS Language acquisition appears to occur at the same rate across cultures, even though not all cultures utilize the techniques that are elements of the LASS

grammatically correct utterances. In Skinner's view, children gradually begin to use only those words or utterances for which they have been reinforced. Through the use of reinforcement, parents gradually shape their children's linguistic behaviour, until over time it begins to sound like adult speech. Essentially then, Skinner's theory was a way to describe how children chain together words to produce grammatically correct speech. These days, Skinner's theory of verbal behaviour has very few adherents, although some psychologists continue to work within this framework (Moerk, 1992).

More commonly observed in the research on language is the influence of Bandura's social learning theory. Bandura (1989) argued that children's learning takes place primarily through observational learning or *imitation*; that is, the child picks up words by overhearing other people and imitating their behaviour. Imitation is an especially important process for describing how a child might learn more complex phrases and longer utterances. According to this view, through processes such as reinforcement and generalization children apply what they have learned to new situations and through feedback about the appropriateness of their speech they learn to use language in an increasingly mature fashion.

Learning theory accounts of language have been criticized on a number of counts (see Pinker, 1994), however, here we consider only three major arguments. First, critics have pointed out that it is simply not possible for parents to reinforce all of the possible utterances a child will use. The amount of time required would amount to a lifetime, yet children come to master most aspects of their language by the end of the preschool years. Second, studies of parent–child interactions (Brown & Hanlon, 1970) have shown that parents do not reward only grammatically correct speech. They are just as likely to reward utterances which are grammatically incorrect but which are truthful. Parents simply do not provide the kind of corrective feedback which learning theory suggests is the main mechanism behind language learning. Third, Chomsky (1957) directed our attention to the nature of the language that children actually hear, highlighting what he called the **poverty of the stimulus**. Analyses of the linguistic data that children actually receive show that they contain too few examples of the complex structures they eventually acquire to suppose that learning accounts could provide a correct model for children's language learning. Only by positing an innate set of specifications can you explain how children actually learn language so quickly.

In the view of many theorists then, learning a language cannot take place *exclusively* through processes such as reinforcement and imitation. It is clear that imitation and reinforcement are important processes in language acquisition (and are perhaps, more important to particular processes such as word learning), however, on their own, they are unable to explain complex developments such as the acquisition of grammar (Chomsky, 1959; Pinker,

1994). Does learning theory have any useful contribution to make to the study of human language then? The answer to this question is 'yes'; a variety of programmes designed to help language-delayed children catch-up to their peers have successfully incorporated learning principles (Ratner, 1993; Zelazo, Kearsley, & Ungerer, 1984).

Nativist theory

The nativist view of language development is traced back to the work of Noam Chomsky (1957; 1968). In contrast to the perspective offered by learning theory, Chomsky argued that language is the product of an unlearned, biologically based, internal mental structure. Chomsky reasoned that the rules which govern the proper use of a language were too complex to be acquired by children in the few short years it takes them to learn a language. Therefore, some aspects of language must be innately specified, meaning that these aspects of our language are not learned but are, in fact, a part of our biological heritage.

All nativist theories of language development share certain elements. First, they assume that certain grammatical concepts are common to all languages and are therefore innate. For example, the fact that all human languages contain concepts such as *subject* (what the sentence is about), *verb* (what the subject does), and *object* (the object of the subject's actions) is consistent with this view. Second, nativist views propose that children are biologically predisposed to learn language. Finally, all children come to the task of acquiring a language with a set of innate *hypotheses* which guide their attempts to abstract the principles which govern their language. These hypotheses constrain the hypotheses children will form about the rules which underlie the language they hear, helping to reduce the complexity of learning a language.

Chomsky (1968) proposed that children come equipped with an innate mental structure which makes the task of learning language feasible. He called this structure the **language acquisition device** (**LAD**). According to Chomsky, the LAD contains a set of features common to all languages, which he termed a **universal grammar**. Universal grammar refers to the entire set of rules or linguistic parameters which specify all possible human languages. The learning of grammar occurs when the LAD operates on speech to abstract out the linguistic parameters which underlie the particular language used in the child's environment. Chomsky termed this process of determining the parameters or rules of one's native language **parameter setting**. Parameter setting is akin to flipping a switch; once the LAD abstracts out a rule or parameter, the parameter is fixed, and the newly learned rule is now used to interpret further speech. For example, one parameter that needs to be set is the word order of the language. In the English language, the basic order of words is Subject – Verb – Object, whereas in Japanese, the word order is Subject – Object – Verb. In this view, learning grammar is much like the game of 20 questions, where children are given data and gradually refine their guesses until they have determined the answer, except that children are acquiring something much more complex: the set of rules which comprise their language.

In support of nativist accounts of language development, nativists would point to the ease and rapidity with which children acquire some very complex sets of rules (Maratsos, 1998; Pinker, 1994). Given the *poverty of the stimulus* argument described by Chomsky, it is certainly an impressive accomplishment that we acquire so complex a system of rules by the early preschool years. The rapidity with which we acquire language despite poor examples from which to learn provides support for the theory that much of what we learn is innately specified. In addition, nativists also have also argued that there is a **critical period** for language learning (Hoff-Ginsburg, 1997), that is, a period during which children are particularly sensitive to language but after which it is difficult or perhaps impossible to acquire language normally. For example, case studies have revealed that people who have suffered extreme neglect by being locked away from social contact during their childhood have great difficulty learning language beyond puberty. Similarly, brain damage to areas responsible for language production and comprehension can be recovered from if the damage occurs before puberty; after this time, however, recovery is incomplete and usually quite poor (Lennenberg, 1967).

Nativist views have also been criticized on a number of counts. One problem with Chomsky's theory in particular is that linguists have failed to specify the universal grammar or set of parameters that could specify all possible human languages. Some critics of Chomsky have doubted whether a universal grammar can ever be specified (Maratsos, 1998). Another criticism of the nativist position is that grammar is not acquired as rapidly as might be expected if a great deal of innate knowledge is specified. Such criticisms suggest that more general learning mechanisms might be required to learn language than are typically specified in nativist theories. Finally, although Chomsky proposes the existence of a biologically based LAD, there is little neurological evidence to support the existence of such a device (Bates & MacWhinney, 1989). Whereas some parts of the brain have been clearly identified as supporting linguistic functions (see Chapter 4), no complete picture of how these and other parts of the brain which are involved in processing language has emerged.

Interactionist views

A variety of theories have arisen in recent years which attempt to reconcile the roles of biology and environment in children's language learning. These

interactionist theories are concerned with the interplay between environmental and biological factors in the process of acquiring language. Interactionists tend to view children as having a strong biological predisposition to acquire a language; however, in contrast to nativists, interactionists stress the importance of both the social support that parents provide the young language learner, as well as the social contexts in which the language-learning child is instructed (Bloom, 1998; Bohannon, 1993; Bruner, 1983). According to Bruner (1983), one advocate of an interactionist position, parents provide their children not with an LAD but with a **language acquisition support system** or **LASS** (notice the parody of Chomsky's view here).

According to Bruner, the LASS is simply a collection of strategies that parents employ to facilitate their children's acquisition of language. One of these strategies involves scaffolding, the deliberate use of language pitched at a level that is slightly beyond what children can comprehend at a given point in time. With support from the parent, scaffolding leads the child to acquire complex language more quickly then they might on their own. Bruner also pointed out that parents provide support for their child's learning by introducing names for things in the context of play, by carefully monitoring their children's understanding, and by finding new ways to convey rules when children fail to grasp a particular instance. Another method which parents use to teach support language is **infant-directed speech**, or what has often been referred to as **motherese**. When using infant-directed speech, parents speak in a higher pitch, stress important words, and talk more slowly to their infants (Fernald & Kuhl, 1987). Research has shown that very young infants show a clear preference for infant-directed speech whether it is employed by women or men (Pegg, Werker, & McLeod, 1992). Such techniques both gain an infant's attention and increase the chances of their understanding the message. Finally, we consider a pair of techniques that adults employ known as **expansion** and **recast** (Bohannon & Stanowicz, 1988). Expansion occurs when an adult takes a child's utterance and expands on the complexity of it. For example, when a child might utter something like '*Felix eated*', the parent might expand on the complexity, adding '*Yes, that's right, Felix ate his dinner*'. Notice here that the parent, while increasing the complexity of the utterance, has also corrected the child's grammar, changing *eated* to its appropriate past tense form, *ate*. When parents expand, as in this example, they often *recast* the child's utterance as well, correcting the grammatical form of the utterance. Through such methods, adults offer subtle, indirect feedback about the child's language. Children often imitate the expansions and recasts of their parents, and, while doing so, gain valuable experience with more complex forms of speech.

A variety of criticisms of interactionist theories have been made. For example, deVilliers and deVilliers (1992) argued that parents rarely offer their children *direct* feedback on the appropriateness of their grammar. Other critics have pointed out that practices regarding linguistic and social interactions between parents and children vary widely across cultures, and some cultures do not use any of the practices described above, yet their children still learn language at similar rates to children in cultures that do employ these practices (Hoff-Ginsburg, 1997). At the same time, it is clear that social interaction has an important influence on language development; German children learn to speak German and Italian children learn to speak Italian not because of any biological differences but because of social interactions between parents, children, and other members of the culture. It seems clear that further study of the effects of social interaction on language development are required before any firm conclusions about how specific types of interaction affect the growth of linguistic skill can be drawn.

Preverbal communication

While the development of language is an extremely impressive achievement, there are a number of nonverbal precursors to language development which are important phases in children's acquisition of a language (Adamson, 1995). For example, Fogel (1993) has illustrated the ways in which infants' first communicative exchanges take place with their parents. Parents and infants often engage in a kind of dialogue which includes sounds, movement, touch, and a variety of facial expressions. Schaffer (1996) has argued that while these exchanges may appear to take the form of 'conversations', they are really under the control of the parent who maintains the interaction, serving as a lesson in communication and conversation for the infant. By about 12 months of age, infants have become much more active participants in this process, taking over a greater share of the responsibility for maintaining the interaction (Schaffer, 1979). These early interactions help the child develop the skills required to become a good communicative partner later in life.

One of the most important of these early nonverbal behaviours is the child's ability to use gestures as a method of communication. By the end of their first year, infants begin to communicate by pointing at objects (Adamson, 1995). These gestures are communicative in that they are used to influence the behaviour of the person the infant is gesturing to. Infants' pointing tends to take two forms (Bates, 1976). **Protodeclarative pointing** occurs when the infant uses pointing gestures to bring an object to another's attention. The infant may point to an object or hold it up to someone, while at the same time, monitoring the other's attention to make sure they have seen the object. Infants seem to use protodeclarative pointing to make statements about things that interest them and to share these things with other people. However, sometimes infants use pointing to get another to do something for them, such as pointing to the cookie jar or to an object that has been placed out of their reach. This form of pointing has been called **protoimperative pointing**. Further developments in gestural communication occur when children begin to use gestures to represent or stand for things they want to communicate (Acredolo & Goodwyn, 1990). For example, a child may use flapping gestures to mimic a bird or may stretch their arms above their head to convey the notion of height. By using gesture in this way, children learn that meanings can be symbolized and shared with others, an insight that they will apply to their use of spoken language.

Phonological development

Most of us are familiar with the ways in which infants pronounce (or often *mis*pronounce) their first words. A classic example of children's early mispronunciation for *banana* is *nana*. Another comes from my own niece who called me *unk*, meaning *uncle*. Phonological development, the process of learning to hear and make the sounds of one's language, is a complex and challenging process for young children. Every language has its own set of speech sounds, some of which are unique, and some of which are shared with other languages. The sounds which make up a specific language are called **phonemes**. Phonological development requires the child to attend to and separate out the sounds they hear in the speech around them, learn to create these sounds for themselves, and to string these sounds together in meaningful units. Not surprisingly, this process takes some time. Between the end of the first year and the beginning of their fourth year, children make considerable strides in this.

Categorical speech perception

As early as 1 month of age, infants can distinguish a variety of speech sounds. Infants are first able to distinguish consonants such as *d* and *n*. Slightly later, at about 2 months of age, they begin to distinguish vowel sounds such as *a* and *i* from one another. An interesting aspect of infants' speech perception abilities is that infants perceive the sound of some consonants in a categorical way, that is, as one sound or another. They do not hear shades of sound that lie in between. This phenomenon has been referred to as **categorical speech perception** (Hoff-Ginsburg, 1997). Findings such as this tend to suggest that infants may be born with an innate mechanism for perceiving the sounds of their language, that is, they do not have to learn these discriminations. However, further research has shown that infants may naturally search for categories for all sounds, and not just for speech (Aslin, 1987). Moreover, some authors have suggested that the ability to perceive sounds in a categorical way is simply a product of our aural system, a property which language may have evolved to exploit (Hoff-Ginsburg, 1997).

While very young infants can distinguish between sets of phonemes when presented in isolation, it takes a greater amount of time for them to pick these sounds out of naturally occurring speech, and for them to recognize more *meaningful* units of speech, that is, *words*. Segmenting the words of a speaker's utterance is critical in learning to comprehend language. Research suggests that figuring out the boundaries between the words in a sample of fluent speech requires considerable experience with language. deVilliers and deVilliers (1979) argued that the evidence on phonological perception suggested that it is not until about 24 months of age that children are able to readily accomplish this task. However, a more recent examination of the literature on phonological perception suggests that by the start of their first year, infants are able to segment naturally occurring speech such that they can begin to pick out individual words. To do this, infants use cues such as the rhythmic properties of speech (Jusczyk et al., 1993), pauses, pitch, and the stresses of particular syllables. Each of these cues helps them to pick out the boundaries between words in fluent speech.

Of course, more than just the ability to perceive and comprehend speech occurs during the first year (Ingram, 1986). From birth, infants are creating their own sounds. Crying is the first of these sounds to be employed. Infants' cries signal their distress but soon come to be modulated to serve a communicative function. By about one month of age, infants begin *cooing*, which involves the production of vowel sounds such as *oo*. By six months of age, infants begin the process of **babbling**. Babbling occurs when infants begin to string consonants and vowels together. A third development in the early production of speech occurs when infants begin to engage in **patterned speech**. Around the end of their first year, infants begin to string the phonemes of their language together in combinations which at first hearing may sound like meaningful words but on closer inspection, turn out to be simple strings of sounds with no meaning. Across cultures, these three stages of phonological development tend to occur in the same sequence, suggesting that these changes may be a function of the maturation of the motor cortex (the part of the brain that controls the production of speech) and the vocal tract.

Finally, children begin to utter their first words. Children's first words are usually of the form *consonant–vowel* (Ingram, 1986). Examples include *mama*, *dada*, and *bye-bye*. Interestingly, the words for *mama* and *dada* in most languages are sounds which the young language learner can readily pronounce. In fact, the first words children learn in so many languages seem to have the developing child's phonological limitations in mind. Parents also seem to recognize their children's phonological limitations and choose simplified versions of words (e.g., *tum-tum* for *tummy*) to communicate with their children.

Phonological development does not end with the child's use of their first words. Another aspect of phonological development which extends into the school years is what has been termed **phonological awareness**. This is the ability to be aware of and analyze speech sounds. One method of measuring phonological awareness is by asking children questions such as name a word that rhymes with *blame*, the word that would remain if you took the last sound off the word *gump*, or what the first sound is in the word *phonology*. Greater phonological awareness is associated with better spelling and with reading ability and training in phonological awareness has been shown to improve reading ability in children labelled as poor readers (Wimmer, Landerl, & Schneider, 1994). (See Table 7.2 for an overview of children's language development.)

Semantic development

For most adults, learning the meaning of a new word is a simple process; we may easily look the word up in a dictionary, and commit its meaning to memory. However, we take for granted the host of other developments that have made this achievement possible: for example, a rich network of other concepts, the ability to read, and so on. For young children, the process would seem to be far less simple. Children often hear a word spoken at the same time as a variety of other events occur. Sometimes they hear words spoken about things that are not present in their immediate environment or about past events. Even in seemingly straightforward cases, closer inspection reveals hidden complexity. Consider the parent who points in the direction of the family dog and says '*What's that? That's a dog*'. How does the child know which aspect of the situation the word 'dog' refers to? Does *dog* specify the fact that the object is four-legged, that it is furry, or that it is an animal? The philosopher Quine (1960) called this problem the *gavagai* problem, and illustrated just how difficult it is for philosophers, let alone children to solve. Even with these and other difficulties, children do learn words, beginning slowly, and doing so in an increasingly rapid fashion throughout childhood.

First words

Children's first words are generally believed to occur sometime between 10 to 13 months of age. It is often very difficult to pick up on children's very first words and to distinguish these from their everyday babbling. Across cultures, the first words that children learn are remarkably similar; their first words refer to important people in their lives and to familiar objects and actions (Nelson, 1973). In addition, some of an infant's new words such as '*all gone*' or

TABLE 7.2 Milestones in children's language development

Age	Milestone
Birth	Infants show a preference for human voices *Cries* initially used to signal distress but are quickly modulated to serve communicative functions
1 to 6 months	Infants begin to distinguish *consonant* sounds. Slightly later they learn to distinguish *vowel* sounds Infants begin *cooing* which quickly turns into *babbling* Infants respond to *motherese* (child-directed speech)
6 to 12 months	Emergence of *patterned speech* in babbling. Babbling begins to resemble speech Infants show an increasing preference for their speech in their native language Infants become increasingly adept at speech perception
12 to 18 months	Emergence of first words. These usually take a *consonant–vowel* form (e.g., *mama, dada*) *Gesturing* is used to refer to objects or the child's desires. Often combined with first words First use of one-word sentences
18 to 24 months	The *naming explosion* begins. Children learn new words at a very rapid rate First appearance of two-word sentences, often referred to as *telegraphic speech* Show the correct use of word order but often drop important grammatical function words
24 to 36 months	Two-year-olds use *fast mapping* to learn new words. Errors in word learning include *overextension* and *underextension* Beginning of the *grammar explosion.* First use of three-word sentences and increasing facility with *grammatical morphemes* Show evidence of *pragmatic knowledge* in early conversational skills
36 to 48 months	Construction of more complex linguistic constructions such as combined sentences, embedding of clauses, and complex question forms Use of appropriate *speech registers* Increasing understanding of pragmatics. Sensitivity to *conversational maxims*
Beyond 5 years	By adolescence, children's vocabulary reaches about 30,000 words Use of more complex grammatical constructions such as *passives.* More sophisticated understanding of *pronoun reference* Increasing sensitivity to verbal *ambiguity*, the *say-mean distinction* and development of *metalinguistic* knowledge Comprehension for nonliteral forms of speech such as *sarcasm* and *metaphor*

'*uh oh*' are linked to cognitive achievements such as the understanding of object permanence (Gopnik & Meltzoff, 1987).

Reznick and Goldfield (1992) argue that in the period from 12 to 18 months of age, infants are learning approximately three new words per month. However, by about 18 months of age, children are acquiring words much more quickly. This growth spurt in word learning has been called the **naming explosion** (Fenson et al., 1994). Research suggests that, by this age, children have a vocabulary of approximately 22 words and they begin to add from 10 to 20 words per week to their vocabularies (Reznick & Goldfield, 1992). By the time children reach six years of age, they have a vocabulary of approximately 10,000 words (Anglin, 1993), suggesting that children acquire approximately five new words each day.

When considering semantic development, it is important to distinguish between two kinds of comprehension that children can show. Research has shown that children's *comprehension*, the words for which they understand the meaning, develops ahead of their *productive vocabulary*, the words which they actually use in their speech. In early word learning, there is a 5-month gap between the time when they comprehend 50 words (at about 13 months of age) and the time when they can produce 50 words (Menyuk, Liebergott, & Schultz, 1995). Producing a word is clearly the more difficult task and depends on the state of children's phonological development. Comprehending a word depends more on recognition memory (Kuczaj, 1986).

Theories of semantic development

One question raised by the naming explosion is *how* children can begin to learn new words so quickly? For example, 2-year-olds can learn a new word after only a single, brief exposure to it, a process which Carey (1978) referred to as **fast mapping**. What sorts of information might children use in order to infer the meaning of a new word? That is, how do children solve the *gavagai* problem?

Research on children's word learning (Markman, 1989; 1992) has suggested that children never consider the full range of hypotheses about what a given word could mean; instead, they narrow the range of possible meanings for a word based on built-in *constraints*. In Markman's view, these constraints are innate processes that force the child to consider only certain relevant cues when trying to map a new word onto an object. By narrowing the range of possible hypotheses for a word's meaning, the constraints make the *gavagai* problem a solvable one. Markman proposed three constraints on word meaning: the **whole-object constraint**, the **taxonomic constraint**, and the **mutual-exclusivity constraint**. These are best described by illustrating how they work.

When children see an adult point at an object and name it, they almost never assume the word refers to some part of the object; instead, they assume the person is naming the *whole* object, thus the name *whole-object constraint* (Markman, 1989). The whole-object constraint describes a bias in which children focus on object properties such as boundaries and shape, leading them to consider that names often refer to whole objects. Similarly, the *taxonomic constraint* narrows children's guesses about word meaning by helping them to figure out the level of generality for which an object name is intended

(Markman, 1989). In other words, the taxonomic constraint points children to the fact that a new word refers to a known *class* of things: *dog* refers to all members of the class of dogs and not to this particular dog. Finally, consider the case where a child encounters two objects, one for which they already know a word, and is told to 'Show me the *bik*' (a nonsense word which avoids the problem of different vocabulary levels across children in the study). In this case, children generally assume that the novel word applies to the object for which they do not already know a name (Markman, 1989). In other words, the fact that an object already has a name means that it is less likely that the new word will apply to it – in other words, names for things are *mutually exclusive*.

Notice that Markman's constraints are geared toward understanding how children learn *nouns*; they have little to say about how children learn verbs. Gleitman and her coworkers (1990; Landau & Gleitman, 1985) have addressed this problem. Gleitman proposed a theory of how children learn verbs, called **syntactic bootstrapping**. According to Gleitman, children also gain information about the referent of a word from syntactic information, that is, from how the word is used in a sentence. For example, some verbs only require two noun phrases to complete a sentence, whereas other verbs may require three noun phrases. Consider the verb *to see*. Seeing requires only a subject (the observer) and an object (the thing observed). In contrast, the verb *give* requires a subject, an object, and a receiver. Such syntactic clues can help the child who hears a verb occur in context figure out to what action it refers to. Syntactic information is yet another very useful constraint on the induction of a word's meaning (deVilliers & deVilliers, 1992).

Critics of Markman's nativist position such as Nelson (1988), have suggested that Markman is incorrect in assuming such built-in constraints. Nelson argues that much could be learned by attending instead, to the social and communicative contexts in which children learn words. The use of the word constraint suggests that these principles operate in an 'all or none' fashion, yet the data on word learning show that this is not the case (deVilliers & deVilliers, 1992). Moreover, research has found that parents influence their children's vocabulary growth, which is at odds with a nativist position (Huttenlocher, Haight, Bryk, Seltzer, & Lyons, 1991). A compromise position acknowledges that these constraints are important, but only work within the context of the social and communicative experiences provided by parents and others who interact with the child (Hoff-Ginsburg, 1997).

Errors in early semantic development

Even with the constraints on word learning and the social support provided by parents, children's first attempts to learn words are not always successful;

children do, in fact, make a number of errors. Here we will consider two of the most common errors that children make. Of particular interest is what these errors tell us about the processes behind children's word learning.

Two of the most characteristic errors in semantic development are **overextension** and **underextension**. Underextensions, where children use a particular word in a highly restricted way, occur much less frequently than errors which take the form of overextensions. In underextension, a child might use the word *doggie* to refer only to his dog and not to other dogs that he encounters (Bloom, 1998). In contrast, overextension occurs when a child uses a single word to label a variety of different objects. Overextentions occur almost exclusively in the production of speech; they rarely occur in children's comprehension (Naigles & Gelman, 1995). A classic example of an overextension is the use of the word *doggie* to cover everything from dogs to cows. Overextension is a particularly common error; about one third of children's words become overextended at some point. Overextensions are often based on perceptual similarity: the child may extend the use of the word *doggie* to animals with four legs and a tail, or *ball* to anything which is round, such as a clock or the moon. As children's vocabularies and conceptual categories develop, overextensions become increasingly rare (deVilliers & deVilliers, 1992). The presence of both of these errors suggest that children's word learning is an active process in which children attempt to learn words based on their hypotheses about the relations between objects and their labels.

Semantic development beyond the preschool years

Semantic development does indeed occur beyond the preschool years, although children's accomplishments are generally less salient to parents. Children typically add about 20,000 words to their vocabulary during their school years, and by adolescence, know some 30,000 words. Moreover, older children can acquire words simply by reading the definition of a word in a dictionary; they no longer directly experience the referent of a particular word. During the school years, children also begin to acquire an appreciation of the ambiguity of word meaning, recognizing that one word can mean different things. For example, the word *bank* can refer to either a river bank or to a financial institution. This burgeoning recognition of ambiguity allows children to appreciate humor based on it. Thus, in the school years children begin to enjoy riddles, puns, and jokes (McGhee, 1979). Try presenting a joke such as '*What has four wheels and flies?*' (Answer, a *garbage truck*) to a preschool child and to a school-aged child. Most younger children will fail to appreciate the humor, whereas the older children usually find the joke funny. To grasp this joke, the child needs to recognize that the word *flies* has two meanings: *to fly* and *an insect that likes garbage.*

Finally, school-aged children begin to appreciate nonliteral speech such as *metaphor* (Winner, 1988). Metaphor requires comprehension of the fact that one thing can be described as another. For example, Shakespeare's metaphor, *Juliet is the sun* compares Juliet to the sun, using one concept to help clarify another. Understanding metaphor requires both an understanding that a speaker can say one thing to mean another (Olson, 1988) and an appropriately developed knowledge base (Winner, 1988). Throughout childhood, the understanding of metaphor develops as children gain both a broader knowledge base and the ability to gauge the communicative intentions of a speaker.

The development of syntax/grammar

A number of issues are apparent within the study of the child's acquisition of grammar. According to deVilliers and deVilliers (1992), some of these issues are: to what extent is children's grammar a function of development in other cognitive abilities? Does experience with language play a role in the development of grammar? Are there biases or constraints which play a role in the ability to learn a grammar? As we shall see, research has not yet offered a definitive answer to any of these questions.

First sentences

Around 18 months to 27 months of age, children typically begin to utter their first combinations of words (deVilliers & deVilliers, 1992). These first sentences often use correct word order but they tend to omit many of the important grammatical function words. Thus, their speech appears sparse, as if they are trying to conserve words, leading to the dubbing of such speech as **telegraphic speech** (Reich, 1986). Examples of such speech include *Daddy read*, *Give juice*, and *More shoe*. Features of telegraphic speech are that it omits the marking of tense (e.g., past tense or future tense), infrequently excludes articles (e.g., *a* or *the*) and does not employ a special syntax to mark *questions*. However, at this stage children do not omit all function words. In particular, they are likely to include pronouns such as *me* and *you* and possessive adjectives such as *mine* and *yours*, demonstrative pronouns such as *this* and *that*, and verb particles such as *put down* or *take off* (Reich, 1986). Despite its limitations, telegraphic speech allows children to communicate a great deal to others because of our ability to infer the child's communicative intent, that is, the meaning they are trying to get across to the listener. In other words, adults 'read into' the utterances of young children and base their responses on what the child intended to say (deVilliers & deVilliers, 1992).

Between 27 to 36 months of age, there is a very rapid development of grammar appearing in children's speech, leading some to refer to this period as the 'grammar explosion', which makes reference to the similar period in children's semantic development (deVilliers & deVilliers, 1992). At this time, three-word sentences make their first appearance, with the extra content being comprised of grammatical terms. Children begin to use *modal verbs* such as *I will do it* or *Daddy can read*; they learn to use negations, such as *I won't do it*; and they begin to apply *tense markings* to words, for example, *Mummy liked my picture* or *I went to the game.* Research by Roger Brown (1973) suggests that children learn to add **grammatical morphemes** – the small changes to a word which change the meaning of the sentence – to their utterances, and that they do so in a very particular order. Brown suggested that this ordering comes about because of two factors which have to do with the complexity of the grammatical morphemes and how much change is required; for example, some changes only require the child to make a small change to a word, such as adding *ing* to a verb to indicate the present tense (as in *He is dancing*). Other grammatical morphemes require more complex changes, such as making the subject and the object of a sentence agree (as in *I am dancing* versus *He is dancing*). Brown's findings on grammatical development have been confirmed by other investigators (Maratsos, 1998).

At around 30 to 48 months of age, children begin building more complex linguistic constructions, combining sentences, embedding clauses within other clauses, and producing complex questions. In each of these attempts, children are sometimes successful and sometimes not. In part, this is because they encounter words which prove to be exceptions to the rules they have learned and which they need to take into account. Another reason is that they encounter words which have special properties, for example, the verb *to promise* (deVilliers & deVilliers, 1992, p.380). In the sentence, *John promised Mary to mow the lawn*, unless Mary is a slave who can be lent out, John is the person who will mow the lawn. That is, the subject makes the promise and must carry out the action promised. Similarly, the verb *to promise* requires that the subject actually be able to carry out the action promised; promising that the weather will be perfect tomorrow is an incorrect usage of the verb because one cannot control the weather and thus ensure the conditions of the promise are fulfilled. Astington (1988) showed that learning the specialized conditions of promising takes children some years to master; in fact, they usually do not grasp these until 9 years of age.

Other grammatical achievements that extend well into the school years include understanding *passive* constructions and coping with **pronoun reference**. Most often we use linguistic constructions such as *The boy kicked the ball* to express ourselves. However, we could also legitimately say *The ball was kicked by the boy*, using a construction which linguists call the passive voice. In the passive voice, a speaker changes the subject–verb–object structure of the language, reversing the position of the object and the subject. According to Horgan (1978), passive sentences are rarely uttered by children until after age 6 and, even then, are used in a restricted way. The development of the passive structure (deVilliers & deVilliers, 1992) involves the gradual application of this form to a wider variety of subject matter and an increasing use of the full passive form (seen in the earlier example).

Pronoun reference involves understanding the rules which govern to whom or to what a pronoun refers. Consider an example from Smyth (1995) which illustrates how difficult this can be: in the sentence *Batman told Superman that he liked Wonderwoman*, the pronoun *he* refers to Batman, however, in the sentence *Batman told Superman that Wonderwoman liked him*, the pronoun *him* refers to Superman. Confused? Perhaps, not surprisingly, it takes young children some time to learn these rules. This developing ability to understand the complexity of pronoun reference is partly a function of development in perspective-taking skill (Smyth, 1995).

In summary then, grammatical development in the school years is linked to the child's developing knowledge base, experience with the language, and to new cognitive achievements. While the most fundamental grammatical forms are in place by approximately 5 years of age, specific aspects of grammatical development continue into the school years (Maratsos, 1998).

The development of pragmatics

As we noted at the outset of this chapter, language is a social behaviour: it is one of the things that we *do* to communicate with other people. To be effective communicators, children have to learn more than the phonology, semantics, and grammar of their language; they must also learn how language is used within their culture. Among other things, they need to know how to engage in conversations with other people, how to select the right language for a situation, and how to interpret a speaker who is deliberately not telling the truth. This knowledge about the social conventions of language use which lead to effective communication is called **pragmatics** (O'Neill, 1996). When we examine the development of pragmatic knowledge, we shift the focus from the study of meaning and syntax, to the study of how language is used to communicate with others.

Becoming an effective communicator

One of the earliest skills that children must acquire in order to communicate effectively is the ability to maintain a conversation with another person. There are a number of components to conversational skill which we will examine in turn. Two requirements for effective conversation are the abilities to engage a listener's attention and to respond appropriately to the feedback provided by a listener. A study by Wellman and Lempers (1977) showed that by 2 years of age, children clearly demonstrated these skills. For example, if they received no response from a listener, 2-year-olds would repeat the message. If the listener showed signs that they did not comprehend, such as a puzzled facial expression, children made further attempts to communicate. Based on their findings, Wellman and Lempers suggested that 2-year-olds are quite effective at the rudiments of conversation. By the time they reach preschool, children are able to take turns in conversations, make eye contact, and respond appropriately to their conversational partner's remarks (Garvey, 1974). Children also adjust their speech depending on their conversational partner; such as when speaking to a younger child, children adjust their speech, exaggerating and simplifying it, so as to engage and hold their attention and ensure comprehension (Dunn, 1988; Shatz & Gelman, 1973).

Preschool-aged children are not consummate communicators; while they are able to maintain a conversation, conversational skills do continue to develop. For example, preschoolers are better at communicating in one-to-one situations than they are at communicating with a group. Ervin-Tripp (1979) showed that preschoolers are more likely to interrupt others and to be interrupted when speaking in the context of a group than when speaking to one other person. The ability to converse with groups continues to develop through to adolescence and perhaps beyond. Another aspect of language use which progresses throughout childhood is children's ability to use **speech registers**. Speech registers are the adaptations that occur when we adjust the level of our speech to our audience. For example, a child might talk to her teacher in a certain tone of voice and choose a particular style of language. In contrast, when speaking to friends, these aspects of language use will change. When speaking to a younger child, the school-aged child will provide more redundant information in their communication, attempting to ensure that their message is comprehensible (Sonnenschein, 1988).

Clearly, children do attempt to take their listener into account in their speech, but how good are they at doing so? According to Reich (1986), many of the problems young children have in communicating information to another have to do with children's relative inexperience and skill. In his view, this ability develops slowly and continuously throughout childhood. One of the means used to measure the growth of this skill is the **referential communication task**. In a referential communication task, children are given a set of stimuli, for example a series of complex geometric shapes, printed on blocks. They are told that their partner, seated opposite them but separated by a screen, has an identical set of shapes presented in a scrambled order. Their job is to describe the shapes to the listener so that the listener can arrange their blocks in the same order. According to Glucksberg, Krauss, and Weissberg (1966), when preschoolers were presented with pictures of animals they could perform this task easily. However, when the stimuli were random geometric shapes, their performance was dismal; the preschool children failed to provide the listener with enough information in order to be able to accurately pick out the block to which they were referring; in fact, many of their utterances were ambiguous, failing to distinguish one block from another. Older children are better able to provide the listener with some unambiguous clues as to the block they intend for the listener to pick. In further research using the referential communication task, Glucksberg and Krauss (1967) showed that it is not until they reach early adolescence that ability on the task reaches an adult level.

Another aspect of pragmatic understanding which develops during the school years is the ability to distinguish between what a speakers *says* and what the speaker really *means*, termed the **say–mean distinction** (Olson, 1994; Torrance & Olson, 1987). Everyday speech is often marked by a discrepancy between what people say and what they mean; for example, a sarcastic speaker usually says one thing but means the opposite. In order to communicate effectively, children must learn to recognize that their own or another person's intentions may not always be clearly articulated. Adults are relatively good at recognizing that a message may not convey the intended meaning. In contrast, young children's understanding of the very possibility of a distinction between what was said (what is called the *literal meaning* of the message) and what was meant (the *intended meaning*, i.e., what the speaker tried to convey) remains somewhat tenuous (Beal & Flavell, 1984; Bonitatibus, 1988; Robinson, Goelman, & Olson, 1983).

Consider the following study by Robinson et al. (1983), who presented a child speaker and a listener with identical arrays of pictures of differently coloured flowers. The speaker picked the red flower from his array and then requested the listener to select a matching flower, but instead of providing a complete unambiguous description such as the 'red flower', the speaker's utterance was ambiguous, telling the listener to pick the 'flower'. When they were asked what the speaker had told the listener to choose, 5- to 7-year-old children tended to accept as correct a phrase which described the speaker's intended meaning (e.g., 'red flower') rather than what had actually been said. Robinson et al. argued that children equated the literal meaning of the message (what was said) with the intended meaning (what was meant). Further research by Bonitatibus (1988) has since replicated these findings. The ability to distinguish between the literal meaning of a sentence and the speaker's intended meaning is an important development which is strongly tied to the child's developing theory of mind (Olson, 1994; see Chapter 9 for a description of *theory of mind*).

In summary, we find that while children's pragmatic ability is sufficient to allow some advanced communication from an early age, there are skills which require further development, a process which lasts until late childhood or early adolescence. Some of these achievements are tied to other cognitive developments, such as in the say–mean distinction, while other areas only require further experience and opportunity for children to refine their skills.

Speech act theory

One of the many ways of understanding pragmatics that has come to guide research within pragmatics is **speech act theory** (Austin, 1962; Searle, 1969). Speech act theory holds that language is a form of *action*. Speech act theorists recognize the essentially social and cooperative nature of communication and stress the importance of considering the intentions and beliefs of speakers and listeners. Austin (1962) proposed that the act of saying something, which he called the **locutionary act**, can be subdivided into two further components: the way in which an utterance is expressed or the **illocutionary force** of an utterance, and the effect an utterance has on its audience, or the **perlocutionary effect**.

Austin's analysis of speech acts focuses on the types of speech acts that we can perform and the effects these acts are intended to cause. Examples of speech acts are *promises*, *assertions*, *denials*, and *warnings*. Each act has a distinct tone or force and is used in different ways. Moreover, as we saw earlier in the chapter in our discussion of the verb to *promise* (Astington, 1988), children gradually acquire this knowledge throughout the school years.

You will notice that speech act theory focuses on the uses or *functions* of language (Halliday, 1975). Proponents of speech act theory argue that we cannot understand language development without understanding the various functions of language. While not all researchers agree on how to best classify the functions of children's communications (O'Neill, 1996) they do agree on the fact that people perform a variety of different functions with language. For example, recall the earlier discussion of protodeclarative and protoimperative pointing: even prelinguistic children use gestures for a variety of functions. By distinguishing the illocutionary and perlocutionary aspects of language, Austin provides us with a useful framework for understanding the development of effective communication.

Conversational implicature

One of the fundamentals of the study of pragmatics is the recognition that the comprehension and usage of language is strongly influenced by the contexts in which language occurs, contexts which may have little or nothing to do

TABLE 7.3 The conversational maxims

Conversational maxim	Description
Quantity	Make your contribution as informative (but not more informative) as is required for the current purpose of the exchange
Quality	Try to make your contribution one that is true; do not say that which you believe to be false or for which you have no evidence
Relation	Make your contribution relevant to the current exchange
Manner	Try to avoid obscurity and ambiguity in your language

with the actual wording of a sentence (O'Neill, 1996). This recognition was exploited by the philosopher of language, H.P. Grice (1975), who formulated a theory about how people use such contextual information to make inferences about what a speaker really means. Grice called this **conversational implicature**. Conversational implicature works by exploiting a principle which guides communicative exchanges, the idea that in conversation, we typically cooperate with our conversational partners. Grice (1975) referred to this as the **cooperative principle**. The cooperative principle states that participants in a communicative exchange are expected to make contributions to a conversation as required, keeping in mind the mutually accepted purpose or direction of the exchange. The cooperative principle is represented by four further *maxims* which Grice termed the maxims of *quantity*, *quality*, *relation*, and *manner*. These maxims are outlined in Table 7.3.

You will probably notice at this point that there are many occasions on which you have violated these maxims; occasionally, you may have done so deliberately. It was Grice's belief that when a speaker deliberately violates one or more of the maxims, they invite the listener to make inferences about *why* they may have done so, that is, to generate a conversational implicature. The generation of conversational implicature allows the listener to go beyond the semantic content of the words in the message and to infer what the speaker really meant.

Consider the following example of conversational implicature in action. Your flatmate comes in from a date. Being friendly, you inquire '*How was your date?*' Your flatmate responds, '*He had nice shoes*'. How should you take this response? If you take her at face value, you might wonder whether she misunderstood you, or whether she recently became delirious. However, if you assume the remark was made deliberately, then a variety of possibilities present themselves. Notice that your flatmate has flouted the maxim of *relation*, in that she seemingly made a response which is not relevant to the current exchange. Assuming that she intended you to recognize this violation as intentional, her response might communicate '*I had a bad time with him*' or '*It was a rotten night*'. Your flatmate's response can be taken as sarcastic in that she expresses a critical attitude towards the situation but does so in a nonliteral way. Now imagine you are a young child. How would you expect a child to take such an utterance? Would they view it as sarcastic? A good start would be to examine whether or not young children are sensitive to the conversational maxims which Grice (1975) identifies as crucial to the process of communication. Conti and Camras (1984) have produced data to suggest that children as young as 6 years of age have some understanding of when Gricean conversational maxims are violated. More recently, Perner and Leekam (1986) have shown that children as young as 3 years of age have the ability to adjust the content of their responses in accordance with the maxim of quantity. Also, as noted earlier, by 2 to 3 years of age children are relatively adept at minding the maxim of relation, keeping their contributions to a conversation in line with the agreed-upon topic (Wellman & Lempers, 1977). In short, these results suggest that by the time they reach preschool, young children seem to adhere to the cooperative principle and its attendant maxims. Given that even young children are relatively adept at recognizing violations of Grice's conversational maxims, can they go onto infer a speaker's meaning? In what follows, we briefly consider some of the work on children's comprehension of nonliteral language.

Nonliteral language

Consider this curious fact: in a great deal of our everyday speech, we fail to say exactly what we mean, for example, we often use *indirect speech.* If we want someone to close a window, we might simply ask '*Is the window open?*' in the hope that the listener might close it. In this example, rather than ask directly, the speaker is indirect, and asks the listener to infer what it is they mean or want. Another form of nonliteral language is *idiomatic speech.* In the case where a friend has made public some secret, we might ask '*Why did you spill the beans?*' As we noted earlier, we also have *sarcasm,* where the speaker says one thing to mean the opposite. Each of these is a common form of **nonliteral language**, language where the speaker does not say what they mean. Let's consider the case of sarcasm as an example of some of the issues involved in the development of nonliteral language.

The comprehension of sarcasm requires the child to appreciate that speakers can say one thing but intend to be taken in a different way: as meaning the opposite of what they say. What kinds of processes are required for a listener to grasp sarcasm? First, children must detect the **incongruity** of the utterance, that is, the inconsistency between what the speaker says and what the speaker means. In other words, children need to make the say–mean distinction (described earlier). Second, the listener must infer the speaker's **communicative intent**, that is, how did the speaker want to be understood? Children's goal here is to ascertain whether the speaker's purpose was to be sarcastic or to be taken in some other way. Notice that the two steps are successive: if children fail to note the incongruity of an utterance, they are unlikely to see a need for inferring the speaker's communicative intent. In other words, inferences about the speaker's meaning are made only when this discrepancy is perceived by the listener.

Ackerman (1981) found that, by around age 6, children have some ability to recognize both sarcastic utterances and lies as deliberately false. In spite of this achievement, it is not until age 12 that children were able to correctly infer the sarcastic speaker's communicative intention. Using a simplified procedure that relied less on children's productive language skills, Winner and Leekam (1991) showed that by age 6, children could recognize that a sarcastic speaker wanted to be understood as meaning the opposite of what they said. Demorest, Silberstein, Gardner and Winner (1983) studied sarcasm comprehension in children aged 6 to 11. They found that children made two types of comprehension errors: they made literal interpretations of the statement, indicating a failure to recognize the incongruity of the remark, or they correctly perceived the incongruity of the sarcastic remark but failed to identify the speaker's communicative purpose. Only the oldest children were very adept at correctly stating the speaker's communicative intention. Finally, Keenan and Quigley (1999) have shown that children make great strides in their ability to comprehend simple instances of sarcasm around 8 to 10 years of age. They demonstrated that features of the utterance such as an exaggerated mocking or nasal intonation can help the child to recognize when someone is being sarcastic. Older children, however, are much less reliant on such features and were able to use more subtle linguistic cues to detect the speaker's true meaning. In sum, these findings suggest that the comprehension of sarcasm can take some time to fully develop, but by the time they reach adolescence, most people are very adept at sarcasm.

SUMMARY

The growth of language skills is one of the most noticeable aspects of children's development. Within a very short period of time, we move from babbling infants to competent native speakers. Researchers investigating the development of language are striving to understand how exactly these changes come about: as the result of general-purpose learning mechanisms, a specific language faculty, or some combination of social influences and biological predispositions. The evidence for each of these positions is by no means complete, and psychologists continue to examine children's language learning.

Glossary

Babbling occurs when infants begin to string consonants and vowels together.

Categorical speech perception refers to the tendency of infants to perceive the sound of some consonants in a categorical way, that is, as one sound or another.

Communicative intent refers to the speaker's intention in communicating something to another; for example, how the speaker wants to be understood by the listener.

Conversational implicature refers to Grice's notions regarding how people use context to understand a speaker's meaning.

Cooperative principle is a principle which Grice believed to underlie conversations. It states that participants in a communicative exchange are expected to make contributions to a conversation that are in keeping with the accepted purpose or direction of the exchange.

Critical period a window in time during which an organism needs environmental input in order for development to proceed. Without input during this period, learning may become difficult or impossible. On some accounts, there may be a critical period for language during childhood.

Expansion is a technique in which adults take a child's utterance and expand it, usually increasing the complexity of the original statement.

Fast mapping refers to children's ability to learn a new word after only a single, brief exposure to it.

Grammatical morphemes are the smallest changes to a word which can change the meaning of a sentence.

Illocutionary force refers to the way in which an utterance is said.

Infant-directed speech (or **motherese**) is a simplified style of speech in which parents speak to the infant using a higher pitch, repetition, stressing important words, and talking more slowly to their infants.

Interactionist theories of language development focus on the interplay between biological and environmental factors. These accounts tend to argue that while children have a strong predisposition to learn language, social interactions with others are of critical importance.

Language acquisition device (**LAD**) Chomsky proposed that children come equipped with an innate mental structure which makes the task of learning language feasible.

Language Acquisition Support System (**LASS**) is a collection of strategies (e.g. scaffolding) that parents employ in order to facilitate their children's language learning.

Locutionary act is the act of saying something.

Mutual exclusivity is a word-learning constraint in which children generally assume that a novel word applies to the object for which they do not already know a name.

Naming explosion is the spurt in vocabulary growth occurring around 18 months of age.

Nonliteral language refers to forms of language where the speaker does not say what they mean, such as sarcasm, metaphor, idiomatic speech, and indirect speech.

Overextension refers to instances where children use a single word to label a variety of different objects.

Parameter setting refers to the process of determining the parameters or rules of one's native language.

Patterned speech refers to pseudospeech wherein infants begin to string the phonemes of their language together in combinations that initially sound like meaningful words.

Perlocutionary effect refers to the effect an utterance has on its audience.

Phonemes are the set of speech sounds which make up the phonetic system of a language; the smallest units of speech which can affect meaning.

Phonological awareness is the ability to be aware of and analyze speech sounds.

Phonology refers to the system of sounds that make up a language.

Poverty of the stimulus is the argument made by Noam Chomsky that the language which children actually hear contains too few examples of the syntactic structures which they eventually acquire. This argument was used by Chomsky to counter claims that language is acquired by learning.

Pragmatics refers to the study of the rules which govern how we use our language in particular social contexts and to achieve particular communicative goals.

Pronoun reference involves understanding the rules which govern to whom or to what a pronoun refers.

Protodeclarative pointing is when the infant uses pointing gestures to bring an object to another's attention.

Protoimperative pointing is pointing that an infant engages in to get another to do something for them.

Recast is a technique wherein adults restate the child's utterance while correcting its grammatical form.

Referential communication task is a language task in which a speaker is required to give instructions to a listener in order to help the listener order a set of objects in a particular way. The task requires the speaker to take the listener's perspective into account and to avoid ambiguous instructions.

Say–mean distinction refers to the ability to distinguish what a speaker says from what they actually mean.

Semantics refers to the study of word meanings and how they are acquired.

Speech act theory holds that language is a form of action and that a consideration of the intentions and beliefs of speakers and listeners is critical to understanding communication.

Speech registers are the adaptations that occur when we adjust the level of our speech to our audience.

Syntactic bootstrapping is a theory of how children learn the meaning of verbs. According to Gleitman, children gain information about the referent of a verb from how the word is used in a sentence.

Syntax refers to the study of the rules for combining words into meaningful phrases and sentences (also known as **grammar**).

Taxonomic constraint is a word-learning constraint that points children to the fact that a new word refers to a known class of things and not only to a particular instance.

Telegraphic speech children's first sentences often omit all but the most essential words required to convey their meaning, leading to speech which appears sparse, as if they are trying to conserve words.

Underextensions refer to instances where children use a particular word in a highly restricted way.

Universal grammar refers to the entire set of rules or linguistic parameters which specify all possible human languages

Whole-object constraint is a word-learning constraint in which children focus on object properties such as boundaries and shape, leading them to consider that names often refer to whole objects.

Emotional Development

8

LEARNING AIMS

At the end of this chapter you should:

- **be able to describe the developmental course of emotion expression, emotion understanding, and emotion regulation**
- **be able to explain key concepts such as *social referencing*, *basic emotions*, and *emotional display rules***
- **be able to describe the important aspects of attachment theory, know the four phases of attachment, and be able to describe the differences between securely and insecurely attached children**
- **understand and be able to define the concept of temperament and key concepts such as *goodness of fit***
- **be able to comment on evidence for and against the stability of temperament**

Introduction

Emotions are one of the most salient aspects of our experiences and it is not surprising that the study of emotion has captured the attention of developmental researchers of nearly all theoretical persuasions. Emotions play an extremely important role in our behaviour, a role of which psychologists have only recently become aware. The study of emotion has recently been undergoing a series of dramatic changes (Saarni, Mumme, & Campos, 1998). While there are a variety of theoretical perspectives that guide the study of emotion, the most important theory to emerge is the **functionalist** approach. Functionalist theories stress that emotions are adaptive processes which organize functioning in a variety of domains of human development including the social, cognitive, and perceptual (Barrett & Campos, 1987; Campos, Barrett, Lamb, Goldsmith & Stenberg, 1983). While emotions may interfere with or undermine an individual's functioning, emotion can also guide and motivate adaptive processes (Thompson, 1991). In most current work on emotional development, emotion is viewed as a regulator of both social and cognitive behaviour.

Taking a functionalist approach in their review of the study of emotional development, Saarni et al. (1998: 238) defined emotion as: 'the person's readiness to establish, maintain, or change the relation between the person and the environment on matters of significance to that person'. The authors note that this definition may strike the reader as odd because of its lack of emphasis on what are seen as the traditional components of emotion such as internal states, feelings, and facial expressions. Instead of focusing on these aspects of emotion, functionalist theories emphasize the relevance of emotions to a person's goals, the close ties between emotion and actions, and the consequences of emotional states. In the following review of emotional development, functionalist views on emotion dominate much of the research.

The development of emotional expressions

Early emotions

A number of researchers have argued through the years that infants are born with a set of readily observable and discrete emotions. The belief that infants enter into the world with the ability to experience and communicate a set of emotions within the first few weeks of life is a belief in the presence of a set of **basic emotions**. The basic emotions which most psychologists seem to agree on are *disgust, happiness, fear, anger, sadness, interest,* and *surprise* (Campos et al., 1983). The evidence for basic emotions is the presence of facial expressions corresponding to the hypothesized emotional states, and, somewhat later, the correspondence between facial expressions, gaze, tone of voice, and the relation between emotions and situations. The argument for the presence of basic emotions is controversial, but most psychologists would agree that by 6 months of age, most of these emotions have made their appearance (e.g., Izard, 1994; Sroufe, 1996). According to Izard (1994; Izard & Malatesta, 1987), the first emotional expressions to appear in the infant's repertoire are *startled, disgust,* and *distress.* Around the third month, infants begin to display facial expressions of *anger, interest, surprise,* and *sadness. Fear* develops at around 7 months of age (Camras, Malatesta, & Izard, 1991). Sroufe (1996) has described a developmental progression of emotional expression which is very similar to that proposed by Izard and his colleagues. Let us briefly consider the development of some emotions appearing early in infancy.

Expressions of happiness are often observed when infants master a new problem or develop a new skill. They also have the positive effect of creating stronger ties between the infant and other people. *Smiles* and *laughter* generate similar responses in the caregiver, creating feelings of warmth and increasing the strength of the bond between parent and infant. Initially, an infant's smiles do not occur in reaction to external stimulation. In fact, very young infants will often smile mysteriously in their sleep. However, by 6 to 10 weeks of age, infants smile in response to social exchanges, such as smiling human faces, and to interesting events that capture their attention. By 3 months of age, an infant's smiles are elicited most often by a responsive person who interacts contingently with the infant (Ellsworth, Muir & Hains, 1993). In the first 6 months of infancy, repeated exposure to a stimulus may be required to generate a smile or other positive response, but after 6 months, emotional reactions are more immediate (Camras, Oster, Campos, Miyake, & Bradshaw, 1992; Sroufe, 1996). Laughter appears first around 3 to 4 months of age and reflects the infant's increased cognitive ability to perceive discrepancies, such as changes from their normal experience, for example, daddy talking in a funny voice or making a face (Sroufe & Wunsch, 1972). By the beginning of their first year and throughout their second year, infants laugh increasingly in response to their own activities and actions; by the preschool years, laughter becomes more and more of a social event, occurring in the presence of others.

Of course, the infant's emotional expressions are not all positive. In the first 6 months expressions of *anger* and *fear* are evident in the infant's emotional repertoire. Perhaps the most salient of these expressions (much to the chagrin of many parents) is the fear aroused in an infant by strangers. Through their interactions with the world, infants naturally start to differentiate the familiar from the unfamiliar and as a result, infants' reactions to unfamiliar people change over time. Whereas a 3-month-old will smile indiscriminately at strangers and parents alike, by 4 months of age infants begin to smile preferentially at caregivers and show some *wariness* to unfamiliar people (Sroufe, 1996). However, somewhere in between the age of 7 to 9 months, infants begin to show a genuine fear of strangers, what has been termed **stranger distress** (Sroufe, 1996). Typically, stranger distress lasts for 2 to 3 months and may continue into their second year (Emde, Gaensbauer, & Harmon, 1976; Waters, Matas, & Sroufe, 1975). Stranger distress has all the aspects of a true fear reaction including crying and whimpering, avoidance reactions such as pulling away from the stranger, and a general wariness of the stranger. As Sroufe et al. (1974) point out, it is not simply *novelty* which engenders stranger distress from an infant, as mothers can perform novel actions (such as approaching the infant while wearing a mask) which do not upset them. Contextual factors such as whether the infant meets the stranger in their own home or in unfamiliar surroundings make an important difference to whether or not distress is elicited (Sroufe et al., 1974). The characteristics of the stranger also play an important role in eliciting distress: infants are less afraid of young children than they are of adults (Lewis & Brooks, 1974) and infants react poorly to strangers who are sober and quiet as opposed to strangers who smile, gesture, and interact in an active, friendly manner. Importantly, each of these points shows that infants react not simply to the occurrence of an event but, rather, on the basis of its meaning; that is, they evaluate situations and appraise the threats they pose.

Emotional development beyond infancy

The development of emotional expression clearly extends beyond infancy and in fact, continues well into adolescence. Emotions such as shame, guilt, pride, and envy are first seen in toddlers (Campos et al., 1983). These developments seem to go hand in hand with developments in their cognitive abilities. Of course, many changes in emotional expression have little to do with cognitive changes but instead, reflect the **socialization** attempts of people in the child's life such as parents, siblings, peers, and others. Work on mother–infant interactions has shown that mothers selectively reinforce their infant's emotional expressions, rewarding expressions of positive affect and not responding to negative expressions (Malatesta & Haviland, 1982). They also shape emotional expressions differently for boys and girls. Mothers tend to reinforce a wider range of emotional expression in female infants than they do in male infants (Malatesta & Haviland, 1985). Socialization is also carried out by the wider culture in which the child is raised. Different cultures have varying standards for the appropriate expression of emotion and thus, we find large differences in emotion socialization across cultures (Gordon, 1989). Emotion socialization is a powerful means of shaping the growing child's emotional expressions and adults use a wide variety of means to accomplish this.

As we will discuss later in this chapter, one of the child's major challenges with respect to emotional development is the process of learning how to control their emotional expression and experience (Saarni, 1990). Much of the early development in the control of emotion is due to adults' attempts at emotion socialization in children. During the preschool years, children begin to learn to control their emotional expressions, adopting these to fit with what is expected of them. In essence, children learn a series of 'rules' about emotional expression, what we call **emotional display rules**. Simply put, these are rules which dictate which emotions are appropriate to express in a given circumstance (Saarni et al., 1998). For example, toddlers learn to substitute one emotional expression (e.g., pouting) for another more appropriate expression (e.g., crying). Later on, children gain a deeper understanding of display rules as they come to learn the social norms of their culture. They come to understand situations where it is inappropriate to laugh or to cry. Moreover, they learn to feign a variety of emotional expressions to accomplish certain ends, such as deceiving a sibling. In summary, learning to follow display rules is an important accomplishment for the developing child.

As we have seen, early on children put display rules into use but they have little understanding of the gap between what they feel and what they actually express (Harris, 1989). Somewhat later, children learn to separate their true feelings from the emotions they express. In one study, Gross and Harris (1988) showed that 6-year-olds were able to distinguish between how a story character would look and how that same character would really feel. In contrast, 4-year-olds were unable to make this distinction, conflating how the character would really feel with how they looked. In other words, the children failed to distinguish between real and apparent emotions. These data support Harris's conclusion that preschool children can employ display rules but have little understanding of them.

The development of emotional understanding

Using emotional information: social referencing

It is not only the range of emotional expressions that infants are capable of expressing which develops throughout infancy and early childhood, but also their *understanding* of emotion. One of the first examples of a developing understanding of emotion is a phenomenon which has been labelled **social referencing** (see Table 8.1). Social referencing, simply put, is the use of another's emotional expressions as a source of information, allowing a person to interpret events or situations that are either ambiguous or too difficult to grasp (Sorce, Emde, Campos, & Klinnert, 1985). Before we explore this phenomenon in infants and young children, think about your own experience with respect to social referencing. Many people have found themselves in a situation where, for example, someone makes what appears to be a joke, and you are not sure whether laughter is appropriate. What do you do? One common strategy is to look to other people's behaviour. Are they laughing or smiling? Other people's emotional expressions can provide us with a valuable source of information for making sense of such situations, and deciding on the appropriate course of behaviour. Recall our discussion of functionalism for a moment; one of the important functions of emotion is their ability to serve as a signalling system about our own and other peoples' internal states. Social referencing exploits this fact about emotion.

Social referencing is first observed at about 12 months of age. One tool used to study how infants employ social referencing is the experimental paradigm known as the visual cliff (see Chapter 5). In this work by Sorce et al. (1985), 12-month-old infants were placed at the top of the visual cliff, on the shallow side of the apparatus. Infants' mothers stood on the opposite side of the cliff and were asked to pose either *happy* or *frightened* emotional expressions at the time when their infants approached the edge of the cliff (remember, the

TABLE 8.1 Milestones in the development of emotional expression and understanding

Age	Emotional expressions	Emotional understanding
0 to 3 months	Startle, disgust, distress, the social smile	
3 to 6 months	Laughter, anger, interest, surprise, sadness	
7 months	Fear	
7 to 9 months	Stranger distress	
12 months		Social referencing
18 to 24 months	Shame, pride	
2 to 3 years	Envy, guilt, embarrassment	
3 to 5 years		Emotional display rules
6 to 8 years		Awareness that two emotions can occur in sequence
9 years and beyond		Awareness that emotions of the same valence can occur simultaneously
11 years		Awareness that one event can elicit a range of feelings

cliff is covered by plexiglass so infants are in no actual danger). The results of the study showed an effect of the emotional expression: when mothers posed happy expressions, most of the infants crossed the cliff. In contrast, when mothers posed frightened expressions, most infants refused to cross. Other studies have shown that mothers' facial expressions can affect how their infants react to new toys or to new people (Klinnert, Emde, Butterfield, & Campos, 1986). Recent research by Ruffman (2000) has demonstrated that young children continue to use emotional information in their understanding of social situations.

The development of complex emotions

Of course, emotions continue to develop after infancy. Another development in the nature of the emotions that we experience is the appearance of what are sometimes called the **self-conscious** emotions (Barrett, 1997; Campos et al., 1983; Lewis, Sullivan, Stanger, & Weiss, 1989). This term is used to describe emotions such as *guilt*, *shame*, *envy*, *embarrassment*, and *pride*, emotions which typically emerge in the second half of the second year. What makes these emotions different from others such as anger or happiness is that they emerge out of the child's developing sense of self-awareness, that is, their sense of having a unique self which is different from the world around them. Moreover, they require the child to consider multiple factors which may influence a given situation, for example, integrating or differentiating more than one perspective. This can be made clear by considering a specific example of a self-conscious emotion – embarrassment. Think of what goes on when you are embarrassed: typically you feel embarrassed when you have done something which you think others may judge to be silly, wrong, or at a level which does not suit you. You evaluate your behaviour against a social standard or a perceived point of view and find your behaviour wanting in some way. Other self-conscious emotions such as envy occur when the child evaluates themselves against particular others. Pride occurs when children feel good about their accomplishments, comparing their performance to specific others or to perceived standards. The developing understanding of emotions such as pride also goes hand in hand with cognitive development in other areas. Children's conceptions of pride, for example, are closely tied to their ability to evaluate the difficulty of an activity. By 3 years of age, children know that they are more likely to feel pride if they solve a difficult task as opposed to an easy task (Lewis, Alessandri & Sullivan, 1992).

Understanding multiple emotions

Throughout childhood and into early adolescence, children gradually become aware that people can experience multiple emotions at the same time (Harter & Buddin, 1987; Wintre & Vallance, 1994). Whereas toddlers and young children clearly *experience* conflicting emotions or blends of emotions, the ability to *understand* these multiple emotions in one's self and others lags well behind. According to Harter and Buddin (1987), there are five stages in the development of multiple emotions. Between 4 to 6 years of age, children can conceive of a person holding only one emotion at a time. They can imagine situations that will arouse one emotion but see it as impossible to provoke two simultaneous emotions. From about 6 to 8 years of age, children begin to grasp that people can hold two emotions, but see these as occurring in sequence rather than simultaneously. Around 8 to 9 years of age, children can describe another as holding two different emotions simultaneously as long as they are of the same valence (e.g., 'If she hit me I'd be *angry* and *upset*') or if they arise in response to two different situations (e.g., 'I would be happy if I did well but proud if I won'). At age 10, children start describing opposing feelings in response to different aspects of a single situation and finally, by age 11, children are able to understand that a single event can cause very different sets of feelings. Harter and Buddin's work shows a clear developmental progression in the complexity of children's emotional understanding, the development of which is not complete until early adolescence.

Emotion scripts

As we have seen, children's understanding of emotional experience undergoes significant developments between infancy and adolescence. Similar developments are observed in the meaning of emotion-specific words and the typical situations that evoke these emotions. This development can be viewed as the child's acquisition of emotion-specific knowledge which takes the form of **scripts** (Lewis, 1989), that is, knowledge of what kinds of emotions a particular event or situation might arouse. Research by Borke (1971) showed that even 3- to 4-year-old children were able to match possible emotional reactions (using depictions of facial expressions printed on cards) to particular stories about events such as a birthday party or an argument. Children can also work backwards, specifying the types of situations that might arouse particular emotions such as *happiness*, *surprise*, or *anger* (Trabasso, Stein & Johnson, 1981). Of course, as they mature, children's emotional scripts increase in complexity (Harris, 1989) to the point where eventually adolescents are able to attribute emotions to others even when there are no obvious behavioural manifestations such as facial expressions.

Children also learn that emotions are intimately tied to a person's *desires*, *intentions*, and *beliefs* (Harris, 1989). For example, in a study by Harris and his colleagues (Harris, Johnson, Hutton, Andrews & Cook, 1989) 4- and 6-year-old children watched as the investigator acted out a story with two puppets. For example, in one story, they are shown a puppet called Ellie the Elephant with a carton of milk and are told that Ellie only likes to drink milk. While Ellie is temporarily absent, another puppet, Mickey the Monkey comes along and pours Ellie's milk out and fills the carton with a orange juice. Children at both ages were accurate at predicting how Ellie would feel when she took a drink and found juice. However, when children were asked to state how Ellie would feel *before* she took a drink, 4-year-olds failed to take Ellie's mistaken belief into account and predicted she would be sad on being presented with the deceptive milk carton. Only by age 6 were children able to take Ellie's mistaken belief into account, recognizing that she would feel happy on seeing the milk carton because she was unaware of the true contents. Harris (1989) argues that understanding and predicting another's emotions requires the child to do more than simply acquire script-like knowledge; they must also view emotions as psychological states which depend on a consideration of their desires and beliefs. More recent work by Ruffman and Keenan (1996) has examined children's understanding of *surprise* and has confirmed that the ability to predict and understand the conditions under which another will be surprised follows a similar developmental course to that described by Harris.

Emotion regulation

Recall that, in functionalist accounts of emotional development, emotions have the potential to organize or to disrupt functioning. The extent to which emotions can organize or interfere with functioning on a given task is, to a large extent, governed by the individual's capacity to *regulate* their emotions. The disruptive effects of a negative affect such as *anxiety* on cognitive performance has been well documented. You can probably recall a time when anxiety has interfered with your ability to think clearly about a problem, for example, during an exam. However, positive emotions can have similar effects. Try and recall a time when excitement has led to someone you know behaving in unacceptable ways, for example, the child who gets too excited on Christmas morning and cannot sleep. Clearly, emotions, both positive and negative, need to be maintained within certain limits. **Emotion regulation**, the processes by which an individual's emotional arousal is maintained within their capacity to cope is defined by Thompson (1991: 271) as 'the extrinsic and intrinsic processes responsible for monitoring, evaluating, and modifying emotional reactions, especially their intensive and temporal features'. Thompson argues that the study of emotion regulation is critical to an understanding of emotional development in that it provides a window into the growth of personality and social functioning. Let's examine Thompson's definition of emotion regulation as well as its development throughout childhood.

One key aspect of this definition is the inclusion of a role for both **extrinsic** and **intrinsic** processes of emotion regulation. By intrinsic processes, Thompson refers to the developments within the individual which allow for the regulation of emotion. Developments in the nervous system and brain, changes in cognitive abilities, and the growth of linguistic skill are all examples of intrinsic processes which promote emotion regulation. In contrast, extrinsic processes refer to those processes which stem from outside the individual and which serve the goal of regulating emotion. The soothing and comforting provided to an infant in distress by its parents, the chance to talk about one's feelings to a close friend, or the cultural prescriptions for how one should feel in a given situation are examples of extrinsic processes by which emotion is regulated. As Thompson (1991) notes, the extrinsic regulation of emotion continues throughout the life span, but is most prevalent during infancy. Infants are initially highly dependent on their caregivers to regulate their emotions but become increasingly able to take over the regulation of their affect.

At birth, the nervous system is far from mature. Therefore, the ability to exert control over the emotional processes is still immature. Two processes are particularly important in developing emotional control. The ability to regulate emotion via the parasympathetic nervous system (Porges, 1991) is one such process. These changes, which occur primarily in the first year of life, allow the infant to gain some control over its feelings, responding in degrees rather than in an 'all or none' fashion (Thompson, 1991). The second change occurs in inhibitory controls over emotional responding. Inhibitory development allows for the suppression or modulation of an emotional response. These developments rely on maturational changes in the cortex and the frontal lobes of the brain. Both developments allow for the infant to tolerate a greater degree of stimulation and to regulate their degree of responding to a particular event or interaction, for example, suppressing a desire to cry or changing the tone of a cry to attract the caregiver's attention.

Changes in the child's cognitive functioning also lead to new developments in the ability to modulate emotional processes. The development of the child's representational abilities, occurring during the preschool years, allows them to evoke memories in order to alter emotional responses. For example, the child experiencing separation anxiety when briefly removed from their caregiver can think about the caregiver in order to soothe themselves and reduce their anxiety (Miller & Green, 1985; Thompson, 1990). Older children can use their cognitive processes in even more sophisticated ways. Whereas preschool children understand that their emotions can be altered by simply avoiding thinking about something, by redirecting their thought processes, or by refocusing their attention, older children understand that a situation or event which makes them feel a particular way can be reframed and thought about in an entirely different way (Band & Weisz, 1988). Thus, older children learn that they can choose to reinterpret a situation as a method to alter their feelings.

Changes in language ability also play an important role in emotion regulation. Language allows us to conceptualize and convey our emotional experiences to others. As a consequence of this, we can encourage extrinsic forms of regulation by discussing our feelings with others. Verbal interactions around emotion can effect changes in emotion regulation in several ways (Thompson, 1991). First, parents can direct their children's regulatory processes through commands (e.g., 'don't get so excited', or 'please stop crying'). Second, parent–child talk about emotion can also suggest to the child new ways of thinking about their feelings allowing them to better manage them. Finally, parents can suggest emotion regulation strategies directly to the child, such as getting them to think about a comfortable image, to rethink their goals, or to engage in some sort of self-soothing behaviour.

By adolescence, the developments in self-understanding which have occurred lay the groundwork for the development of what Thompson (1991) referred to as a **theory of personal emotion**. A theory of personal emotion is essentially a coherent network of beliefs about one's own emotional processes. For example, an adolescent may recognize that they naturally shy away from social interaction and realize that in order to be accepted by their peers, they need to find ways in which to overcome this tendency, such as expressing more positive affect to others, and making a conscious effort to smile and make eye contact. In middle childhood, children begin to appreciate the fact that their emotional experiences may differ from those of others, they start to acquire general knowledge about their own emotional processes, such as the particular idiosyncrasies that may characterize their own emotional experiences. In addition, as they grow children acquire more refined knowledge about coping strategies, and, more specifically, which coping strategies work best for them depending on the situation. However, it is during adolescence that the theory of personal emotion acquires its coherence. As adolescents develop a progressively more complex network of self-referential beliefs, their theory of personal emotion is incorporated into their conception of themselves.

The development of attachment

Bowlby's theory of attachment

Like the young of many species, human infants are relatively helpless at birth, and for the first few months thereafter. We are born with very limited sensory abilities, little in the way of physical motor skills, and few cognitive abilities. This fact means that human infants are vulnerable at birth, and for sometime thereafter. While it is unlikely that in these modern times an infant is likely to be carried off by a predator, our situation was not always so secure. During one point in our evolutionary history, conditions were such that this threat was a very real one. Thus, it is not surprising that we have developed behaviours which help us to adapt to such conditions.

The study of bonding between parents and infants owes much to the pioneering work of John Bowlby (1958, 1960). Bowlby formulated a theory of the relationship between the caregiver and the infant – what he called an **attachment relationship** – drawing largely from work in psychoanalytic theory, ethological theory, and work in cognitive and developmental psychology (Ainsworth et al., 1978). Attachment theory focuses on both the processes which lead to the bonding of parents and children, and the impact of this relationship on psychological development. Furthermore, attachment theory focuses our attention on the development of affectional ties between the caregiver and infant, and on the behaviours and cognitive structures by which these ties are maintained over time.

In contrast to Sigmund Freud who believed that an infant's affectional tie to his caregiver was developed on the basis of being fed by the caregiver, Bowlby believed that selection pressures acting over the course of human evolution led to infants having an innate set of behaviours which caused them to seek an appropriate level of *proximity* to the caregiver. Proximity refers to the physical distance between the infant and the caregiver. By staying close to a caregiver who can protect them against dangers such as predators, an infant has a better chance of survival. Thus, these behaviours are passed on from generation to generation. Human infants also come equipped with a communicative system of cries and facial expressions which allows them to signal for the caregiver to increase their proximity. In other words, we can initiate proximity through means such as crying or smiling. Bowlby argued that both affectional ties and the behaviours that promote proximity to one's caregiver have an evolutionary basis (Campos et al., 1983) in that they are unlearned and instinctive, that is, part of our biological heritage.

Of course, the effectiveness of the infant's communicative signals depends on the ability of the adult to receive and interpret them, thus, human adults must also have a complementary system by which to interpret these signals (e.g., Frodi & Lamb, 1978). Attachment is a two-way process, a relationship between two people; it is *not* simply a set of learned behaviours emitted by infants or adults (Ainsworth et al., 1978; Sroufe, 1996). The effectiveness of the infant's signals depends on the ability to the caregiver to understand and react appropriately to them. In an important way, attachment theory extends the study of emotional development into the social realm, breaking down traditional barriers that focus solely on the individual as opposed to the individual as situated in relationships with other people.

Bowlby's attachment theory was also influenced by work in control systems theory (Ainsworth et al., 1978). According to control systems theory, behaviours which serve a common function are grouped together with the purpose of achieving a particular goal. The behaviours are activated to achieve the goal of the system; if the goal changes, the behaviours are altered to achieve the new goal. Consider the example of an infant that is placed in an unfamiliar room. Given the unfamiliar surroundings, the initial goal of the control system will be to maintain proximity to the caregiver. After some time, as the infant begins to feel comfortable, the goal of the system is altered and the need to maintain proximity is relaxed, freeing the infant to move about and explore. This move away from the mother may be interrupted by the entrance of a stranger. If the infant interprets the stranger as threatening, the need for proximity will be reasserted and the infant will seek out the caregiver. If the infant feels secure with the stranger, exploration will continue and no increase in proximity will be called for.

Another major contributor to attachment theory, Mary Ainsworth (1973), noted that infants use adults both as a **safe haven** and as a **secure base**; that is, infants organize their attachment behaviours so that they use the adult as a refuge and source of comfort when they are distressed but also as a safe vantage point from which to explore their environment. One of Ainsworth's major contributions to attachment theory was the study of how infants' secure base behaviour can be used to inform us about the quality of an infant's attachment relationship with its caregiver, a topic explored in the next section.

Much of the research in attachment focuses on the attachment between mothers and infants. However, Bowlby recognized that infants form attachments to other people as well. Infants form attachment relationships with fathers, grandparents, siblings, and peers, among others (Lamb, 1981; Lewis, 1987; Schaffer, 1996). These attachments differ in important ways across individuals, yet at the same time, Bowlby argued that the nature of the infant's attachment to its primary caregiver has a profound effect on its other relationships. Bowlby claimed that this influence is exerted by the development of what has been called an **internal working model** (Bowlby, 1973). An internal working model is a mental representation or 'mental model' of the infant's experiences with their primary attachment figure. Internal working models are relatively stable over time, however, Bowlby chose the term *working model* to highlight that they are updated on the basis of experience. Importantly, internal working models serve to combine cognitive representations of the infant's relationship with their caregiver with an affective component, that is, how the infant *feels* about the attachment relationship. Bowlby believed that the child's attachment relationship with their primary caregiver influenced all of the child's subsequent relationships. A child who is not securely attached to their primary caregiver is more likely to have difficulty in forming and maintaining other relationships.

The development of the attachment relationship

Attachment relationships do not occur suddenly but, instead, emerge gradually throughout the first 2 years of life. There are four phases in the development of attachment (Ainsworth et al., 1978; Schaffer, 1996). Initially, infants show little preference for particular others; their social behaviours are indiscriminately directed towards others. This phase, called *preattachment*, encompasses the first two months of the life span. In the second phase, *attachment-in-the-making*, which runs from 2 to 7 months of age, infants begin to discriminate familiar from unfamiliar people and show a distinct preference for the attachment figure. At about 7 months of age, the third phase, *clear-cut attachment*, begins. At this time, infants develop marked attachments to particular people with whom they have regular contact, such as their mother and father, grandparents, and daycare workers. Infants actively seek out these people and often protest or are upset when they leave. The final phase of attachment, which begins at 2 years of age, is called a *goal-corrected partnership*. In this phase, the child begins to take into account the feelings and plans of the attachment figure when planning their own actions. The responsibility for the attachment relationship begins to shift from the mother to the child as the child develops the ability to communicate their thoughts and feelings through language. The child has truly become a partner in maintaining the relationship between themselves and their caregiver. At this final phase, the attachment relationship between caregiver and child has reached a new level of sophistication (Ainsworth et al., 1978).

Quality of attachment and the strange situation

Ideally, the attachment relationship serves as a source of affection and nurturance. The attachment relationship allows the infant to feel confident and secure while exploring and learning about the world. Ainsworth was among the first to highlight the importance of parenting in fostering the development of a secure attachment in children (Ainsworth, Bell and Stayton, 1974). The caregivers of securely attached infants usually show a high degree of **sensitivity**. That is, these parents are generally responsive to their infant's needs and engage in consistent patterns of behaviour (Cassidy & Berlin, 1994). Their caregiving allows the infant to play a role in these daily interactions. Ainsworth et al. (1978) argued that when mothers are *insensitive* to their infant's needs, either by being overly *intrusive* or by *neglecting* them, the infant can develop an **insecure attachment**. Insecure attachments are attachment relationships that fail to provide the infant with a sense of confidence and security. Interestingly, the suggestion has been made that the various forms of insecure attachment may actually be *adaptive* solutions for these infants, in that they allow the infant to make sense of a difficult relationship (e.g., Cassidy, 1994; Main & Solomon, 1990). For example, an avoidant attachment relationship helps to minimize the importance of the caregiver for the infant and allows the infant to avoid the negative affect associated with being rejected or neglected by their caregiver.

The quality of an infant's attachment to its caregiver can be measured using a testing paradigm known as the **strange situation** (Ainsworth et al., 1978; Waters, Vaughn, Posada, & Kondo-Ikemura, 1995). Briefly, in the strange situation, the infant is separated from its mother, exposed to a stranger, and then reunited with the mother. The use of the strange situation allows the experimenter to examine differences in attachment behaviour which differ as a function of the infant's quality of attachment to the caregiver. Using a classification system designed by Ainsworth and her colleagues (Ainsworth et al., 1978), infants' attachment relationships with the caregiver can be described as falling into one of three categories. Most commonly observed in a sample of normal children is a **secure attachment**. Securely attached infants are only minimally disturbed by separations from the caregiver, continue to explore the environment while the caregiver is present, and show positive affect on the caregiver's return after separation. In contrast, infants classified as showing an **insecure-avoidant** attachment tended to show little distress on separation from the caregiver. However, they are clearly upset by her departure as a study by Spangler and Grossman (1993), which measured the infant's heart rate, revealed. In addition, when the caregiver returns, insecure-avoidant infants typically pay no attention to her and actively *avoid* contact with her. A third type of insecure attachment is the **insecure-resistant** type (this type is sometimes labelled **insecure ambivalent**). These infants are most often extremely distressed by separation from the caregiver, showing high levels of crying and upset. However, when the caregiver returns insecure-resistant children show a pattern of alternately seeking contact with her and then resisting contact or pushing away from the caregiver. Ainsworth's research with the strange situation showed that for American samples, some 60 to 65 percent of infants were classified as secure, 20 percent as insecure avoidant, and some 10 to 15 percent as insecure resistant. Work by Main and Solomon (1990) revealed a fourth type of insecure attachment which they called **insecure-disorganized**. Insecure-disorganized infants display extremely peculiar behaviours in the strange situation: they often engage in repetitive movements such as rocking, show a tendency to freeze (i.e., remain extremely immobile) in the middle of a movement, and in general, seem confused or disoriented during the reunion with the mother. Sadly, researchers have found that insecure-disorganized attachments often co-occur with child mistreatment (Carlson et al., 1989; Lyons-Ruth et al., 1990) and maternal depression (Field, 1990). In the study by Carlson et al., 82 percent of a sample of mistreated infants developed insecure-disorganized attachments whereas only 19 percent of children who were not mistreated showed this pattern. Unfortunately for these infants, insecure-disorganized attachment has been associated with negative developmental outcomes (Main & Solomon, 1990).

The stability of attachment

An aspect of attachment theory suggested by Bowlby, and confirmed by many researchers, is the assertion that the quality of attachment relationships is stable over time. Waters (1978) studied the stability of attachment classifications in children from 12 to 18 months of age. He found a near-perfect consistency in the classifications across this time span. Similarly, Main and Cassidy (1988) studied a sample of infants who were seen in the strange situation at 12 months of age and were then observed again at 6 years of age. At 6 years the children were given a measure of attachment security used with older children. Main and Cassidy found a high level of consistency for attachment classifications from infancy to 6 years. These and other findings suggest that attachment is highly stable across time (Sroufe, 1979; Vaughn et al., 1979).

These early studies have been criticized on a number of grounds, one of these being that early research on the stability of attachment tended to use largely middle-class samples in the hopes of reducing factors such as stressful life events which might impact on the consistency of attachment classifications. What happens when researchers take into account the effects of stressful life events such as changes in employment (e.g., becoming unemployed or being forced into a lower paying job) or changes in marital status (e.g., divorce or separation)? When such factors are examined, the results provide less evidence for stability in attachment classifications over time. Studies have found that stressful life events as reported by parents were associated with changes in attachment classifications in their children (Thompson et al., 1982; Vaughn et al., 1979). Interestingly, changes in attachment classifications were bidirectional, that is, they could move from secure to insecure or vice versa. Thus, improvements in family life can lead to the development of secure attachments. More recently, Thompson (1998) and Sroufe (1996) have suggested that attachment relationships continue to develop over time and that changes in the stability of a child's attachment relationship is a function of their environment. Stable environments will tend to lead to stable attachment relationships.

The consequences of attachment relationships

Many attachment theorists including Bowlby argued that the quality of an infant's attachment to their caregiver has important consequences for development. One such theory is that the quality of the attachment relationship will act as an organizer for further development (Erikson, 1963). That is, attachment security is associated with different developmental pathways: securely attached children will tend to follow certain pathways through life whereas insecurely attached infants will follow different paths. According to Sroufe (1979), secure attachments are the foundation of healthy psychological development. Infants who form secure attachments should develop into competent, healthy children who are able to form satisfying relationships with others, whereas infants with insecure attachments will have a basic distrust of themselves and their social world, feelings of anxiety and guilt, and difficulties in forming relationships (Bowlby, 1969). A fundamental prediction of attachment theory is that our early social experience has a profound effect on later development in the social, emotional and cognitive domains.

One of the first studies to demonstrate the effects of secure attachments on later outcomes was carried out by Matas, Arend, and Sroufe (1978). In this study, a sample of toddlers were seen at 18 months of age and their attachment quality to their mother was assessed. These same children were then observed at 24 months of age and were asked to engage in a series of problem-solving tasks and a play task. In general, securely attached children were less negative, cried and whined less often, and showed less aggression during the tasks than did insecurely attached children. Securely attached children were more enthusiastic on the problem solving tasks, were frustrated less easily, and were more persistent in trying to find a solution than insecurely attached infants. Securely attached infants also tended to engage in more symbolic play than did insecurely attached children. Finally, securely attached children were more compliant: when their mother made suggestions for solving the tasks, securely attached children were more likely to make use of these suggestions than were insecure children.

Further research showed that these same benefits associated with a secure attachment relationship held into the preschool years, with preschool teachers rating securely attached children as less aggressive toward their peers, less dependent on help from the teacher, and more competent than insecurely attached children (Lafreniere & Sroufe, 1985; Waters, Wippman, & Sroufe, 1979). Recent work by Elizabeth Meins (Meins, Russell, Fernyhough & Clark-Carter, 1998) showed that securely attached children did better on theory of mind tasks at age 4; these children were more likely to pass the false belief task (see Chapter 9) than insecurely attached children. Finally, Lyons-Ruth et al. (1997) found that infants who were judged to be securely attached at 18 months of age were highly likely to be functioning well in interpersonal contexts at school when measured at age 7. In contrast, children assessed as showing disorganized attachments at 18 months were likely to develop *externalizing behaviours* such as hostility towards their peers, and acting up in class. Children whose attachment relationships were classified as avoidant were likely to show *internalizing behaviours* at age 7, such as depression, anxiety and self-criticism. (Internalizing and externalizing behaviours are discussed in greater detail in Chapter 10.) In general, the research by Matas and her colleagues, as well as a host of studies by other researchers, has demonstrated several important benefits to emotional, cognitive, and social development following the formation of a secure attachment relationship.

Temperament

Defining temperament

Early studies of children (e.g., Gesell, 1928) noted that there were striking individual differences between children in terms of their 'core of personality' (Shirley, 1933). Importantly, these researchers recognized that these differences in infants' traits were not fixed and often showed considerable change over time, yet they seemed to be constant enough in most cases that one could plausibly argue that these traits were constitutionally based, that is, rooted in the child's biological makeup. Another aspect of this early research was the examination of how these differences across children led to a variety of possible developmental outcomes. For example, Gesell described how particular traits such as sociability might predispose one towards generally positive outcomes later in life. Much of this early work on what we now call **temperament** has been confirmed by current research. These early observations of individual differences in infants and children highlight three issues central to the study of temperament today: temperamental traits are inherent, constitutionally based characteristics that make up the core of personality; although stability is a feature of many temperamental traits, it is widely recognized that stability greatly depends on the social context in which the child grows; temperament is related to a variety of possible long-term outcomes such as the quality of relationships with peers, psychological adjustment, and psychopathology.

So what is temperament? Temperament involves the study of individual differences in the basic psychological processes that constitute 'the affective, activational, and attentional core of personality and its development' (Rothbart & Bates, 1998: 108). Temperament is strongly tied to emotion, hence its inclusion in this chapter. For example, Allport (1937: 54) described temperament as the characteristics of an individual's emotional nature, such as his susceptibility to emotional stimulation, the nature of his typical emotional responses, and the quality of his prevailing mood. Most recently, temperament has been defined as 'constitutionally based individual differences in emotional, motor, and attentional reactivity and self-regulation' (Rothbart & Bates, 1998: 109). Note that the most recent definition of temperament stresses the inclusion of *attention* and *self-regulation* as critical to the construct of temperament, since these two characteristics of an individual's behaviour have strong implications for one's emotional life. Self-regulatory processes are those processes such as attention which serve to modulate reactivity to a stimulus. For example, when distressed by a particular thought, you can consciously distract yourself by thinking about other more pleasant thoughts. As research has shown, differences in self-regulatory behaviour seem to have a constitutional basis and show a degree of stability which has led many researchers to view them as fundamental aspects of temperament.

Temperament is considered central to an individual's emerging personality and indeed, there is a great deal of overlap between the characteristics identified as being related to temperament and those related to personality. However, it is important to note that temperament and personality are not identical. Although researchers have identified links between early temperament and later personality (e.g., Caspi & Silva, 1995), much work remains to establish exactly how these are linked (Rothbart & Bates, 1998).

Most, if not all, theories of temperament argue that the individual differences which are central to the study of temperament are genetically or biologically rooted (see Chapter 5 for further discussion on the genetic and

TABLE 8.2 Temperamental dimensions and types

Dimension	Description
Activity level	The frequency and tempo of an infant's motor activity
Rhythmicity	The extent to which activities (like sleeping) are regular
Approach/withdrawal	How the infants reacts to novel situations
Adaptability	How easily a response is modified to fit a new situation
Intensity	How energetic the infant's usual reactions are
Threshold	How intense stimulation needs to be before the infant reacts
Mood	The general quality of the infant's mood (e.g., friendly and cheerful vs. unfriendly behaviour)
Distractibility	How easily the infant's activities can be interrupted
Attention span/persistence	How long the infant remains engaged in an activity
Typology	
Easy	Cheerful, rhythmic, and adaptable
Difficult	Low on rhythmicity, easily upset by novelty, cries often
Slow to warm	Adjusts slowly to new experiences, negative mood, and inactive

biological basis of behaviour), attested to by the focus on 'constitutionally based' in our two definitions (Kagan, 1998). Of course, genetic and biological predispositions are strongly influenced by maturation and experience (Bates, 1989; Goldsmith et al., 1987). Thus, all temperamental effects on behaviour represent a combination of biological and environmental effects and are best characterized as *interactions* of the two factors. It is important to keep this fact in mind as we discuss research on temperament and its role in emotional and social development.

Initial work on temperament in infancy by Thomas and Chess (1977) identified nine dimensions of temperament. These are: *activity level* (the frequency and tempo of an infant's motor activity); *rhythmicity* (the extent to which activities such as sleeping and eating are regular or predictable); *approach/withdrawal* (how the infant reacts to new situations); *adaptability* (how easily a response is modified to fit a new situation); *intensity* (how energetic the infant's typical reactions are); *threshold* (how strong a response needs to be before the infant reacts); *mood* (the general quality of the infant's mood); *distractibility* (ease with which the infant's activities can be interrupted); *attention span/persistence* (the extent to which an infant remains engaged in activity) (see Table 8.2). Recent research has gone beyond these descriptive categories of behaviour to focus on additional qualities such as the ability to regulate one's own behaviour (Rothbart, 1989) and makes finer subdivisions between the variability within the broad dimensions identified by Thomas and Chess (1977) and other researchers (Rothbart & Bates, 1988).

Based on their analysis of these dimensions, Thomas and Chess (1986) proposed a typology of temperament that has gained wide acceptance, perhaps largely due to its intuitive appeal. Under their scheme, infants can be classified as **easy**, **difficult**, or **slow-to-warm**. *Easy* infants are sociable, happy, rhythmic, and adaptable. In contrast, *difficult* infants are easily upset by novelty, tend to fuss and cry often, and are low on rhythmicity, having difficulty sleeping and eating regularly. *Slow-to-warm* infants fall in between easy and difficult. These infants tend to initially respond to novel experiences poorly but over time or repeated contact show a pattern of gradually warming to and accepting the experience. Thomas and Chess found that easy children constituted approximately 40 percent of their sample while difficult and slow-to-warm infants made up 10 and 50 percent of the remainder.

The measurement of temperament

A wide variety of methods have been developed to measure temperament. These include: caregiver reports for infants and young children; teacher reports for the preschool and school-aged child; self-reports for older children and adolescents; naturalistic or observational assessments; and laboratory procedures. Not surprisingly, each methodology has its own benefits and its own limitations. For example, parent reports of temperament provide a unique insight from the people who spend the most time with the child, yet they are also open to bias as the parents' report is a function of their own characteristics. Laboratory assessments get around this issue of bias by subjecting children to standard procedures, however, they suffer from particular limitations such as carryover effects from repeated testing, and the constraints placed on the type of responses children can give. Accordingly in their review of research on temperament, Rothbart and Bates (1998) suggest that all measures of temperament require further refinements.

The continuity of temperament

Research evaluating the continuity of temperament over time has produced mixed assessments. While most early research in the field emphasized the stability of temperament across assessments (e.g., Buss & Plomin 1975), more recent work has suggested that temperament develops throughout childhood and is thus modified over time (Goldsmith, 1996). The course of this development reveals that initial individual differences in motor activity and emotionality are modified as developing self-regulatory systems 'come online' (Rothbart & Bates, 1998). The stability of temperamental classifications also varies depending on the temperamental dimension being measured, and the time periods across which it is measured. For example, research with a sample of New Zealand children (Caspi & Silva, 1995) reported that 3-year-olds rated as shy and subdued tended to describe themselves at age 18 (using a personality inventory) as shy or reserved. In contrast, work on the temperamental dimension of *distress proneness* showed little stability for distress measured over the first 3 months of life (Worobey & Lewis, 1989). Rothbart (1986) showed that positive and negative affects measured at 3 months of age were not correlated with the same measures at 9 months of age. However, distress measured later in infancy tended to show stability well into the school years, at 6 to 7 years of age (Rothbart, Derryberry, & Hershey, 1995). In a sample of 5- and 6-year-old Australian children (Pedlow, Sanson, Prior, & Oberklaid, 1993), those who were difficult to soothe showed the same characteristics later in childhood. Clearly, research on this question has produced mixed results.

The attempt to show stability in temperament is hampered in at least two ways. First, measures of temperament appropriate for one age group (e.g., infants) are not necessarily appropriate for another (e.g., school-aged children). For example, infants show their distress by crying while school-aged children are much more likely to demonstrate distress in a wide variety of ways. This means the temperament researcher needs to develop different measures for different age groups. Using different measures for different age groups means there is a possibility that somewhat different things are being measured and thus, it remains uncertain how much change is a function of development and how much is associated with measurement error. Second, a variety of developmental phenomena may interfere with attempts to show stability. For example, during the period between 1 and 3 months of age, infants find it extremely difficult to disengage their attention from a location and, as a consequence, tend to show a high degree of irritability. Measures of temperamental dimensions (such as *mood*) given during this time when infants are naturally irritable may not present an accurate picture of their core temperament, but rather, reflect a perfectly natural state in the infant's development (Johnson, Posner, & Rothbart, 1991). For these and other reasons, further research remains to be done on the question of whether temperament remains stable over time.

Genetic influences on temperament

As we have seen, most theories of temperament assume a biological basis. What evidence is there that this is indeed the case? Behaviour genetic research (see Chapter 4 for a discussion of behaviour genetics) has established reasonable evidence that many aspects of our temperament have a genetic basis. For example, Plomin (1987) has shown that in the first year, monozygotic (i.e., identical) twins show significantly greater similarity in their activity levels, their sociability, and their proneness to fear than do dizygotic (i.e., fraternal) twins. Monozygotic twins also show higher correlations for traits such as shyness, behavioural inhibition, and irritability (Emde et al., 1992; Goldsmith & Gottesman, 1981; Plomin, 1987). Studies in which children are adopted out to foster families show that by 2 years of age, there are significant correlations between adopted children and their biological mothers. In short, a wide variety of evidence points to a genetic basis to many temperamental traits.

However, it is not simply the case that a child's temperament is fixed and unchangeable. Behaviour genetic studies strongly suggest a biological basis to temperament, but these studies should not be taken as suggesting temperament is fully determined by our genetic inheritance. In fact, behaviour genetic research suggests that there are important environmental effects on temperament. Rothbart and Bates (1998) summarize a variety of studies that highlight aspects of temperament which show that a child's environment plays an important role in determining the nature of her temperament. As they suggest, the time is past when we can think of temperament as genetically determined. Instead, we need to recognize that both biological and environmental processes contribute to shaping behaviour.

Goodness of fit

An important aspect of theories of temperament is the idea that temperament is rooted in our biology. As we have discussed in this chapter, behaviour genetic research suggests that temperament is not fixed but, rather, is modified by experience. Therefore, it is not the case that a difficult infant will necessarily remain a difficult infant, although temperament is often stable and resistant to change. A difficult temperament can be modified over time with the provision of appropriate caregiving. Thomas and Chess (1986) introduced the concept **goodness of fit** to the study of temperament in order to explain how temperament can change. By goodness of fit, Thomas and Chess referred to the fit between a child's temperament and their parents' expectations and behaviours towards the child. For example, parents who had strong expectations for a quiet, sociable, and happy child may have difficulty adapting to their difficult infant. They may lack the resources (e.g., coping skills, social support) to deal with a difficult infant and may behave towards the infant in ways that do little to promote change in the infant's behaviours. As a consequence, their behaviours may reinforce the undesirable aspects of that infant's temperament. In contrast, the same infant, when born into a family where the parents are able to respond calmly, positively, and warmly to their child's temperamental traits have a much greater chance of altering the infant's behaviour. As Thomas and Chess point out, with patience and caring, parents help the child to make the most out of their traits.

To date, research on the goodness of fit hypothesis has been mixed. The idea itself seems intuitively appealing and provides a useful explanatory tool for developmentalists interested in temperament and behaviour but researchers have found it a difficult hypothesis to confirm (e.g., Crockenberg, 1986). Further work remains to be done in this area.

Temperament and adjustment

As we noted earlier, since the earliest research on temperament, psychologists have attempted to examine exactly how early temperament leads to later behavioural outcomes. That is, are the observed individual differences in adjustment among children predictable as a function of their temperamental classification? Studies of the developmental outcomes associated with temperamental classifications vary in their assessments of whether there are demonstrable relationships between early measures of temperament and later measures of children's level of adjustment. For example, in work based on the Dunedin Longitudinal Study in New Zealand, Caspi and Silva (1995) showed that children who were rated as inhibited at 3 years of age were more likely to score low on *aggression* and low on *social potency* (a measure of how effective one is in social situations) at 18 years of age. In a study of temperament and social behaviour in 6- and 7-year-olds, Rothbart, Ahadi, & Hershey (1994) found that negative affectivity measured using parent reports was associated with particular social traits such as aggressiveness. They also found that a small subsample of the children in this study who had been through a laboratory assessment of temperament as infants showed a similar pattern: infant measures of negative affectivity were associated with higher levels of aggressiveness and help seeking at 6 to 7 years of age. Eisenberg at al. (1996) showed that school children identified by teachers' reports as showing low self-regulation were more likely to show behaviour problems such as acting out in class. In regard to the relationship between temperament and positive behaviours, Kochanska (1995) provided evidence that temperament was also related to children's moral development. In summary, there is some evidence that specific temperamental dimensions are related to internalizing behaviours (e.g., shyness, depression and anxiety) and externalizing behaviours (acting up, aggressiveness) in childhood as well as to some positive behaviours (Rothbart & Bates, 1998).

SUMMARY

It should be clear to you that the study of emotional development takes in a wide variety of topics, from the study of changes in emotional expressions and understanding to how we learn to control our emotions. Also current in the study of emotional development are the topics of attachment and temperament, constructs which emphasize the importance of our emotional nature to growth in other areas. You should recognize that the study of emotional development is intimately tied to developments in cognition and social understanding. In many ways, these overlaps between areas such as cognition and emotion are among the most interesting areas of study in child development.

Glossary

Attachment relationship is the emotional bond which is formed between an infant and a caregiver.

Basic emotions refers to the set of emotions which most psychologists would agree are innate and develop within the first few weeks of life. This list normally includes disgust, happiness, fear, anger, sadness, interest and surprise.

Difficult according to Thomas and Chess, a temperamental style where infants are easily upset, react poorly to novelty and are not rhythmic. Difficult babies can be challenging children to parent. Difficult infants can become easy infants given an environment which allows them to express themselves and is supportive of their behaviours.

Easy according to Thomas and Chess, a temperamental style where infants are sociable, happy, rhythmic and adaptable. Easy babies are so-called because they tend to be easy children to parent.

Emotion regulation refers to the processes by which an individual's emotional arousal is maintained within their capacity to cope.

Emotional display rules are the rules which dictate which emotions are appropriate to express in a given circumstance.

Extrinsic regulation processes are ways of regulating emotion that depend on factors outside of or external to the individual, such as soothing and comforting interventions given by a caregiver.

Functionalist theory of emotion functionalist theories stress that emotions are adaptive processes which organize functioning in a variety of domains of human development.

Goodness of fit refers to the fit between a child's temperament and their parents' expectations and behaviours towards the child.

Insecure attachments are attachment relationships which fail to provide the infant with a sense of confidence and security and comprise three subtypes: infants who show an **insecure-avoidant** attachment typically avoid contact with the mother during reunion; infants who show an **insecure-resistant** attachment show a pattern of alternately seeking and resisting contact with the caregiver; infants who show an **insecure-disorganized** attachment seem confused or disoriented during the reunion with the mother.

Internal working model is a mental representation of the infant's relationship with their primary caregiver.

Intrinsic regulation processes are ways of regulating emotions that depend on processes internal to the individual. Developments in language abilities, the brain and cognitive abilities are all examples of intrinsic processes.

Scripts are a form of mental representation which includes a knowledge of what kinds of behaviours and emotions are appropriate to a particular event or situation.

Secure attachment securely attached infants show only minimal disruption during separations from the caregiver and positive affect on reunion with the caregiver.

Secure base/Safe haven refers to the function of the caregiver as a refuge and source of comfort from which to explore their environment.

Self-conscious emotion is the term given to emotions such as guilt, shame, envy, embarrassment, and pride.

Sensitivity refers to the parental behaviour that is consistent and responsive to the infant's needs.

Social referencing is the use of another's emotional expressions as a source of information, allowing the child to interpret the meaning of events and situations.

Socialization refers to the processes by which parents, siblings, peers, and others work to shape children's behaviour.

Strange situation is a situation for testing attachment wherein the infant is separated from the caregiver, its mother, exposed to a stranger, and then reunited with the mother in order to assess the quality of the attachment relationship.

Stranger distress is a fear of strangers shown by infants that first emerges around 7 to 9 months of age.

Temperament refers to constitutionally based, individual differences in emotional, motor, and attentional reactivity and self-regulation.

Theory of personal emotion is a coherent network of beliefs about one's own emotional processes.

9 Social Development

LEARNING AIMS

At the end of this chapter you should:

- **understand the role of play in social development, the functions associated with play, and the different types of play**
- **be able to describe the developmental course of peer interaction and define key concepts such as *dominance hierarchies*, *cliques* and *crowds***
- **understand the importance of peer acceptance for social development, the consequences of low peer status, and be able to describe the various categories of peer acceptance based on *sociometric techniques***
- **be familiar with the processes of friendship formation and the development of conceptions of friendship across childhood**
- **be able to define *theory of mind* and describe the course of theory-of-mind development**
- **be able to describe the development of a sense of self and explain the importance of the *rouge test***
- **be able to explain Selman's model of the development of perspective taking**

Introduction

The study of social development has a rich history within developmental psychology. Developmental research in the 1920s and 1930s focused heavily on children's groups as important agents of socialization, and researchers developed a number of new and influential methodologies by which to study children's social development. This early work focused largely on individual differences in sociability, assertiveness, aggression, leadership, group dynamics, peer acceptance and the correlates of individual differences in social skills (Rubin & Coplan, 1992). The focus on children was put aside briefly during World War II but was more permanently ousted during the cognitive revolution and the discovery of Piaget in the United States. Piagetian theory characterized young children as *egocentric* and thus, as incapable of understanding others until middle childhood, a characterization which effectively put a halt to most of the research in social development. However, a growing recognition of the key role of social development to children's cognitive achievements has forced a reconsideration of the importance of studying children's social development. For example, research has shown that one of the best predictors of academic failure is rejection by the peer group. In addition to the relationship between social and cognitive development, there is a growing list of the important functions which friendship and peer relations serve in children's development. In the following chapter we will examine these and other issues.

Theories of social development

A number of theories have been used to understand the typical course of social development and, more specifically, the importance of friendships in social development. Piaget (1932) argued that children's relationships with adults were qualitatively different from their relationships with other children. Piaget believed that children's relations with adults were structured along what we could call a **vertical dimension**. That is, relations with adults are asymmetrical and fall along a vertical dimension of power assertion and dominance, with children falling below adults. In contrast, children's relationships with other children are somewhat more balanced and egalitarian and, thus, are structured on a more **horizontal** plane. Piaget believed it was on this plane where children's relationships are more or less equal that they could explore conflicting ideas, perspectives, and learn to generate compromises. Piaget's ideas have influenced many researchers interested in social development (Rubin & Coplan, 1992).

Another early theorist who influenced many current researchers was Harry Stack Sullivan (1953). Sullivan emphasized the role of friendships in children's development and the special functions which friendship served for the child. In Sullivan's view, children are initially insensitive to peers but eventually move towards entering into complex, reciprocal relationships with peers. Children's early relationships help to shape their personality and the later relationships they will go on to form in adolescence and adulthood, according to Sullivan.

Social learning theorists have also been concerned with peer relations, arguing that children learn about their social world and how to behave within it through their interactions with peers (Bandura & Walters, 1963). This learning can take place either *directly*, through children teaching one another concepts and behaviours, or it can take place *indirectly*, through the child's observation of their peers' behaviours. From a social learning perspective, children are viewed as agents of behavioural control who positively reinforce and punish those behaviours which they regard as appropriate or inappropriate. Social learning theories have been very influential in the study of peer relationships and children's social behaviours (Hartup, 1983).

Ethological theories have also proven important to current research within the domain of social development. Ethological theories are concerned with the biological and evolutionary bases of behaviour. An important aspect of ethological theory for the study of social development is the methodologies developed by ethologists for the observation of animal behaviour. The methods employed by ethologists such as naturalistic observation are important elements in the study of social development. Ethological theorists argue that all behaviours are 'limited by the biological constraints related to their adaptive evolutionary function' (Rubin et al., 1998, p.632). According to Tinbergen (1951) when the ethologist observes a particular behaviour of interest she must ask: (1) Why did the individual demonstrate the behaviour at that particular point in time? (2) How did the individual produce the behaviour? (3) What is the function or survival value of the behaviour? Asking such questions focuses the developmentalist on how we learn a behaviour, the developmental course of the behaviour, what biological constraints guide the emergence of the behaviour, and the behaviour's adaptive significance.

Types of play and their functions

On the basis of an observational study of preschool children during their play periods, Parten (1932) observed six different types of play that preschoolers engaged in (see Table 9.1). She also measured the frequency of each type of play and how the frequency of play changed as a function of age. Parten argued that different types of play she observed involved differing levels of complexity. In the following, we begin with the most complex form of play and work our way downwards.

Cooperative play was the most complex form of play Parten observed. Cooperative play includes behaviours like playing formal games, social pretend play where children take on pretend roles, and constructive play, where children build things together such as models out of Lego blocks. Parten found the cooperative play was rare before the age of 3 years. **Associative play** occurs when children talk to one another and share the same materials in their play but do not take on different roles within the same imaginary context or work towards completing a joint project. Associative play was found to be the most common form of play among 4-year-old children. **Parallel play** occurs when children play *beside* other children

TABLE 9.1 Types of play

Play type	Description
Cooperative play	Cooperative play includes behaviours like playing formal games, social pretend play (where children take on pretend roles), and constructive play (where children build things together such as block models). Cooperative play is rare before the age of 3 years
Associative play	Associative play occurs when children talk to one another and share the same materials in their play but do not take on different roles within the same imaginary context or work towards completing a joint project
Parallel play	Parallel play occurs when children play *beside* other children rather than *with* other children. They use the same toys and materials but do not interact with each other
Onlooker	Onlooker behaviour occurs when a child watches other children play but does not join in
Unoccupied play	Unoccupied play occurs when the child does not play with anything but simply watches other interactions, events, and objects that are of interest
Solitary play	Solitary play is when children play by themselves in a way which is noticeably different from those around them

rather than *with* other children, using the same toys and materials but not interacting. Parallel play was the most common form of play observed among 2-year-olds and was almost as common among 4-year-olds as associative play (Parten, 1932). Parten also defined three categories which are non-social and reflect an absence of play. **Onlooker** behaviour occurs when the child is watching other children play but is not joining in. **Unoccupied play** occurs when the child does not play with anything but simply watches whatever interests them. **Solitary play** is when children play by themselves in a way different from those around them. Subsequent research has provided additional evidence for the validity of Parten's categories although researchers typically draw quite different conclusions from those of Parten (Hartup, 1983; Rubin, Fein & Vandenburg, 1983). Whereas Parten's focus on play was on the level of children's *social interactions*, modern researchers have also examined the *cognitive* complexity of children's play (Piaget, 1962). While Parten's categories do not capture all of the variations in children's play, her data are important in demonstrating significant changes in the nature of peer interactions through the preschool years.

A wide variety of functions have been attributed to play (e.g., Saracho & Spodek, 1998). Classical theories of play saw it as a means of *exercising skills* that will be required later in life. In essence, play is an instinctive way of acquiring and rehearsing future skills. Many aspects of children's play such as the rough and tumble play of middle childhood resemble the play of our primate ancestors which suggests that children practise skills which are adaptive for survival (Biben & Suomi, 1993). Other theories of play focus

TABLE 9.2 Milestones in children's social development

Age	Milestone
Birth to 6 months	By 6 months of age, infants are aware of and take an interest in other infants Increase in rates of vocalization and smiling around peers
6 to 12 months	Infants show a clear interest in their peers Displays emotional expressions to peers and responds to peers in a contingent fashion
12 to 24 months	Mainly engages in *parallel play* Social interactions increase in length and complexity and involve the use of language Development of *self-understanding* around 18 months as evidenced by success on the *rouge test* Understanding of the rules of social exchange First evidence of *prosocial behaviours* such as *empathy* Child operates according to a *desire* psychology
3 years	Begins to engage in *cooperative* play Child operates according to a *belief–desire psychology* *Dominance hierarchies* observed in children's peer groups
4 years	Most commonly observed in *associative play* Has acquired a *representational theory of mind* indicated by performance on the *false belief task* *Conflict* is observed in children's relationships
6 years	Sharp increase in time spent with peers. Peer groups increase in size. Peer interactions take place in a wider range of settings and are less under the control of adults The goal of friendships is typically defined by *shared interests* and the maintenance of coordinated and successful play Child can understand *second-order mental states*
7 to 9 years	The goal of friendships is gaining *peer acceptance*
Early adolescence	Friendships are centered on *intimacy* and *self-disclosure* Peer groups become organized around *cliques* and *crowds* First appearance of *adolescent egocentrism*
Late adolescence	Friends are increasingly seen as a source of emotional and social support *Adolescent egocentrism* declines

instead on the *content* of play. Piagetian theorists believe that the social interactions which occur within the context of play are essential for driving cognitive development. Vygotskian theorists suggested that play builds mental structures through the child's use of tools acquired from the culture around them such as language and number. For example, the child playing at being a shopkeeper utilizes several concepts such as buying and selling and the role of money in commercial transactions. Play also allows children to explore their social world by adopting various roles and interaction patterns, thereby promoting social development (see Table 9.2). In some theories, play promotes the development of social competence (Haight & Miller, 1993).

The developmental course of peer interaction

Infancy (birth to 1 year)

Early researchers who examined social interaction in infancy regarded infants as having some significant 'social shortcomings' (Rubin, Bukowski & Parker, 1998: 633). Early researchers (Bühler, 1935) held that until about 6 months of age, an infant was unaware of the presence of another infant. While it is clear that infants do have some significant social limitations, however, it is also true that careful and detailed observation of infants reveals that they do show an interest in social exchanges with other infants. At 2 months of age, infants will gaze at one another (Rubin et al., 1998). At 6 months of age infants are aware of and take interest in other infants (Rubin & Coplan, 1992) indicated by the increased rates of smiling, vocalizations and gaze in the presence of other infants. By their ninth month, infants show a clear interest in peers, challenging the widespread belief that infants are not social. By the end of their first year, infants have consolidated several important behaviours: they intentionally display smiles, frowns and other gestures to their interaction partners, they attend carefully to their play partner's behaviours, and they respond in a contingent fashion to their interaction partner's behaviours. Of course, infants' interactions are very rudimentary and are limited by their *cognitive*, *motoric*, and *linguistic* capabilities.

Early childhood (2 to 5 years)

By the second year of life, new forms of social interactions are made possible by the infant's increased locomotor and physical abilities as well as by the toddler's developing cognitive and language skills. Using words to communicate with an interaction partner opens up a whole new dimension for interacting. Social interactions become more complex, more reciprocal, and the interactive sequences are sustained over significantly longer periods of time than in infancy (Ross & Conant, 1992).

Rubin and Coplan (1992) note that many researchers believe that there also seems to be an elementary understanding of the rules of social exchange demonstrated during the second year, mainly in the form of games toddlers play. Toddlers show an understanding of turn-taking and tend to coordinate their play with a partner. They imitate behaviours displayed by others and recognize when others are imitating their behaviours (Eckerman, 1993). The emergence of pretend play in individual children is seen in the second year but by their third year, young children are much more likely to share in pretend play. Moreover, during the third year, the first signs of prosocial behaviour such as sharing and helping emerge (Radke-Yarrow, Zahn-Waxler, & Chapman, 1983). Children share symbolic meanings with each other and assign imaginary roles in their pretend play (e.g., Astington & Jenkins, 1995;

Howes, 1987). These developments reflect the preschooler's evolving ability to take another's perspective, reflecting what is termed their **theory of mind** (Astington, 1994; Wellman, 1990). In early childhood the emergence of *conflict* is noted (Rubin et al., 1998). Interestingly, sociable toddlers are the most likely children to enter into conflicts. Finally, toddlers develop *relationships*, that is, reciprocal relations with another child over a succession of encounters (essentially, a shared history of interactions) which involve both positive and negative exchanges. In the early years, children's relationships do not equal true friendships, although by the end of the early childhood period, children do go on to form true friendships.

Also of interest to social development is the emergence of social **dominance hierarchies** during the preschool years (Rubin & Coplan, 1992). Dominance hierarchies are rankings of individuals in terms of their dominance (i.e., their *toughness* and *assertiveness*) within the group. Research examining dominance hierarchies in preschoolers has consistently revealed that more dominant children are the winners of conflicts and less dominant children tend to lose conflicts (e.g., Strayer & Strayer, 1976). However, the preschool child is not aware of these dominance relations, often nominating themselves as the most dominant individual.

In summary, by the end of the early childhood period, children have learned skills that comprise the ability to coordinate their play with another, to imitate and recognize that they are being imitated, and turn-taking. However, it is also important to note that in the early childhood years, children's opportunities for social participation are largely controlled by their parents. Their parents determine who they will see, when they will see them, what kinds of friends they will have, and so on. In addition, various aspects of the child's social ecology also control the formation of peer relationships; for example, the nature of the child's community (e.g., rural versus urban, violent versus safe), religious participation, and ethnic background can have a marked effect on the kinds of opportunities for social participation that children are exposed to.

Middle to late childhood (6 to 12 years)

According to their review of the social development literature, Rubin et al. (1998) suggest that a simple indication of the changing nature of children's social interactions can be found in examining *who* is involved in children's interactions. The developmental trend is towards increasing contact with peers as children age. For 2-year-olds, approximately 10 percent of their time spent in social interactions is spent with peers whereas in middle childhood this figure rises dramatically to around 30 percent. In addition, the preference for interacting with peers rises sharply (Ellis, Rogoff & Cromer, 1981). Children's peer groups become larger and more diverse as children are brought into contact with new groups of peers. In addition, children's groups become less supervised. Much of this change is a function of the onset of formal schooling and of the other group activities (e.g., sports, band, cultural activities) which children enter into. Thus, the settings for children's social interactions change from the home and preschool settings to reflect a wider variety of locations and institutions. Verbal aggression becomes more prominent in middle and late childhood, replacing earlier forms of physical aggression, and play tends to take the form of games with rules. Social dominance hierarchies also tend to become more stable in middle childhood (Strayer & Strayer, 1976) and most children are able to agree on which children in a group are dominant.

Adolescence (12 to 18 years)

Peer relationships in adolescence continue the trend towards increased time spent with peers. As the adolescent's relationships with family are restructured, peer relationships multiply and become more intense as new demands and social expectations are made apparent to the adolescent by the peer group. While the overall number of friends decreases in adolescence, peer relationships often surpass parents as the adolescent's primary sources of social support (Adler & Furman, 1988). Friendships take on new significance in adolescence and are centred on *intimacy* and *self-disclosure* (Buhrmester, 1996; Parker & Gottman, 1989). In addition, sexuality adds a new dimension to the adolescent's social life as dating begins and new possibilities for intimacy develop.

Adolescent social life is organized around two primary social structures, the **clique** and the **crowd** (Dunphy, 1963). Cliques are close-knit groups of friends ranging in size from three to nine, who are held together by mutual acceptance and common interests. Cliques generally contain same-sex members, although initially same-sex cliques may build strong ties to opposite-sex cliques, affording new types of social activity (Dunphy, 1963). Eventually, toward the end of adolescence, these cliques dissolve into smaller, more tightly knit groups when members 'pair off' in dating relationships. Clique membership comprises an important part of adolescents' psychological well being. Dunphy formulated his ideas regarding crowds and cliques based on observations of adolescent cliques conducted in Sydney, Australia. To date, these observations have not been replicated in other cultures and in other contexts (e.g., rural settings as opposed to urban settings) and thus may not provide an entirely accurate or generalizable picture of adolescent social life.

Another important social structure for the adolescent is crowds. Crowds are groups of adolescents who organize on the basis of reputation, are comprised of similarly stereotyped individuals, and who are defined on the basis of the attitudes held by the members (Rubin et al., 1999). Examples of the sorts of groups pointed to as crowds by adolescents include *punks*, *brains* and *druggies*. Crowds are less cohesive than cliques but have the function of bringing together a more extended set of adolescents. Initially, adolescents describe the members of crowds in terms of their behaviours but through adolescence there is a shift to describing crowds in terms of the dispositions and the values of their members. These changes in the perception of crowds seem to reflect the importance of crowds in adolescents' social lives. Crowds have the function of exposing the adolescent to a wider range of activities such as parties and other social functions and serve to introduce members of same-sex cliques into an environment where they meet members of opposite-sex cliques (Dunphy, 1963).

Determinants of peer acceptance

Children's social skills are important determinants of their acceptance by their peers. Children's judgements of their peers, however, are not simply made on the basis of social skills and other personal characteristics but on the basis of less rational qualities over which children themselves have very little control. One such surface characteristic on which children base their impressions of others is *names*. Names are an important factor in children's judgements about each other. Children with unfamiliar names are likely to be poorly regarded by their peers (Rubin et al., 1999). Of course, the familiarity of names varies from culture to culture and across time, so it is difficult to give examples of names that are universally unfamiliar to children. Yet it is the case that unfamiliar names will often generate an adverse response from children, especially if there are other factors that set the child apart from his or her peers.

Another factor on which children base their judgements of the acceptability of peers is *physical attractiveness* or beauty. Beauty may only be skin deep, however, for children who are judged to be physically attractive, the benefits of their beauty are many. Both children and adults are likely to attribute more desirable characteristics to attractive people than to unattractive people (Langlois, 1985). Children who are viewed as less physically attractive are judged to be aggressive, antisocial, and mean while children viewed as physically attractive are seen as independent, pleasant, honest, fearless, and friendly. Physical attractiveness seems to be more important to a girl's popularity than it is to boys' popularity (Vaughn & Langlois, 1983). Langlois and Downs (1979) examined the social behaviour of 3-year-old and 5-year-old children judged to be attractive and unattractive. Whereas there were no differences in the social behaviour of the 3-year-olds, unattractive 5-year-olds were more likely to aggress against other children. The authors interpreted the results to suggest that the age trend in the data, that is, the difference between the 3-year-olds and the 5-year-olds, reveals the existence of a self-fulfilling prophecy at work. The 5-year-olds' aggressive behaviour may be a result of peers' and adults' negative perceptions of them; their bad behaviour is caused, in part, by the characteristics which are attributed to them and the expectations that others hold for them.

Two other factors are important determinants of peer acceptance, *sex* and *age*. Children generally prefer to play with peers who are the same sex as they are. This is especially evident after the age of 7 years. Before this time, children will play with both boys and girls although they tend to prefer playing with same-sex partners. However, the tendency to choose same-sex partners increases throughout the school years (Maccoby, 1990). Maccoby and Jacklin (1987) suggest that one reason for the preference for same-sex play has to do with personality differences between boys and girls. Boys tend to be more aggressive, having higher activity levels and engaging in more rough and tumble play (Humphreys & Smith, 1987). With the onset of adolescence, more cross-sex mixing occurs. Age may also be an important factor in who children choose to play with, although across cultures there are wide differences in this trend. The majority of children in Western cultures spend most of their time playing with children who are the same age as they are (Ellis et al., 1981) while in many other cultures, older children will play with children much younger than they are. You may have noticed that there is a commonality to many of these factors, namely, *similarity*. On the whole, we tend to accept and like people who are similar to us. Berndt (1988) argues that similarity of another person to themselves is the key factor behind many of children's judgements.

Peer status

Adults, such as coaches or teachers, who are familiar with a group of children, generally have good insights into issues such as which children are well liked by their peers or which children are popular. It may surprise you to learn that even very young children have a good understanding of which children in a group are popular and which children are unpopular. Researchers interested in social development have been able to exploit this knowledge using **sociometric techniques**. Sociometric techniques involve asking children to nominate a specific number of their peers who fit some criterion. For example, *name three classmates who you really like*. The number of times that children are nominated by other classmates can give the researcher a picture of the relative status of an individual within the group. Sociometric nominations have a number of strengths. First, peers are likely to have information about other children that adults are simply unable to access. Second, peers tend to have a broader range of experiences with other children in a group. Third, peer nominations and ratings represent a group perspective which is not reliant on the ratings of a single source, such as a teacher.

The use of sociometric nominations allows the researcher to classify children into one of a number of sociometric categories. One such system described by Rubin and Coplan (1992) and which is popular among researchers uses five categories. **Popular** children are children who are rated highly on a dimension of *most liked* and rated low on a dimension of *least liked.* Popular children are good at *initiating* new relationships and at *maintaining* the relationships which they have built. They tend to be viewed as socially competent. In general, their status within the groups is clear cut. **Controversial** children are those individuals who are rated high on *most liked* and high on *least liked*; simply put, controversial children are both liked and disliked. **Neglected** children are children who score low on *liked most* and low on *liked least.* Neglected children are friendless children but importantly, are not usually actively disliked. **Average** children fit somewhere in the middle, receiving some positive and some negative evaluations; they are not as popular as popular children and not as disliked as neglected children. **Rejected** children score low on *liked most* and high on *liked least* and tend to cluster into two subcategories (French, 1988, 1990). *Aggressive rejected* children have high levels of behaviour problems, poor self-control and show high levels of aggression. *Nonaggressive rejected* children are rejected by their peers for different reasons than aggressive rejected children, in large part, because they are socially unskilled, withdrawn, and socially anxious. Extremely anxious withdrawn children are noted by their peers as socially deviant and are rejected on these grounds. Rejected children report feeling more lonely and more isolated than their popular peers (Asher, Parkhurst, Hymel, & Williams, 1990).

A number of researchers have shown that the categorizations *popular* and *rejected* are extremely stable over time. Popular and rejected children tend to remain popular or rejected children (Coie & Dodge, 1983). When changes do occur they tend to be to closely related categories: popular children may become average children but only rarely do they become rejected (Rubin & Coplan, 1992).

Consequences of low peer status

What are the consequences of being unpopular or disliked by one's peers? Many of the consequences that researchers have focused on are developmental outcomes related to academic matters such as academic difficulties, truancy, and dropout (Rubin & Coplan, 1992). This connection is not particularly surprising. Clearly, school is less pleasant when a child has serious troubles with their peers, perhaps even becoming the target of their hostility. Outcomes such as truancy may seem adaptive when faced with such difficulties. In one study by Wentzel and Asher (1995), children rated as *rejected* by their peers were shown to be perceived by teachers and peers as weak students. *Rejected aggressive* children (relative to *average* children and *rejected withdrawn* children) showed low interest in school and were viewed by their teachers as noncompliant, troublesome, and disruptive. Parker and Asher (1987) reported that children who were unaccepted by their peers were significantly more likely than their accepted peers to drop out of school. Finally, Kupersmidt and Coie (1990) reported that children identified as *rejected* were twice as likely as the rest of the sample to engage in delinquent acts in adolescence.

Unpopular children also tend to feel social dissatisfaction and loneliness as a consequence of their lack of peer acceptance. Rejected children are especially likely to feel lonely, with nonaggressive rejected children feeling the loneliest of all (Parkhurst & Asher, 1992). In a study of the consequences of peer rejection in Australian schoolchildren, Renshaw and Brown (1993) followed groups of third and sixth grade children for 1 year. They found that children who moved towards being less accepted by their peers were more likely to have lost friends and to report that that they were poor at developing friendships. In general, nonaggressive rejected children feel more poorly about their own social competence and their difficulties with social skills and peer relationships (Rubin, 1985).

Some recent evidence suggests that for children identified as rejected by their peers, even one quality friendship can act as a buffer against the negative effects of their social status (Parker & Asher, 1993). This finding suggests that **friendship quality** is an important variable to consider when measuring children's social networks. Interestingly, other research has suggested a somewhat more counterintuitive finding regarding the value of friendships for rejected children. Studies by Hoza, Molina, Bukowski and Sippola (1995) and Kupersmidt, Burchinal, and Patterson (1995) showed that the presence of a best friend increased the severity of negative outcomes for children identified as *rejected aggressive*. One explanation for these findings is that the friendship networks of rejected aggressive children are likely to comprise other aggressive children as suggested by Patterson, DeBaryshe, and Ramsey (1989) in their model of the developmental progression of antisocial behaviour. The involvement in a deviant peer group comprised of other children with behaviour problems reinforces and supports the rejected aggressive child's inappropriate behaviours.

Friendship

Friendship formation

Friendship can be defined as a relationship between two (more or less) equals which involves *commitment* to one another and *reciprocity* (Hartup, 1989;

Shantz, 1983). *Liking* is an important part of friendships but it is not a sufficient condition for the development of friendship (Shantz, 1983). The seemingly simple question, '*How do children become friends?*' has proven to be a difficult problem for psychologists interested in the development of peer relations and social processes to untangle. However, many inroads have been made into the processes involved in the development of friendships.

John Gottman (1983) set out to examine this question in a series of studies. In the first of these studies, Gottman tape recorded the conversations of children aged 3 to 9 who played either with a stranger or with their best friend. One of the central findings of this study was the identification of a set of social processes which were related to friendship formation and which distinguished between the play patterns of children with their best friends or with the strangers. The processes identified were: connectedness in communication (i.e., making communicative exchanges clear and relevant to the topic at hand); exchanging information; establishing common ground (e.g., exploring similarities and differences and working jointly); successfully resolving conflicts; showing positive reciprocity (e.g., responding to another's behaviours and comments in a positive manner); self-disclosure (e.g., sharing information about one's own feelings). Best friends were more likely than strangers to score highly on these six dimensions. Moreover, in a second study, Gottman showed that when children were introduced to a same-aged stranger for a series of play sessions, those children who got along well were more likely to score highly on these six dimensions than children who did not get on well.

Parker and Gottman (1989; Gottman & Mettetal, 1986) argued that the focus of friendships changes with age. In early childhood, around 3 to 7 years of age, the goal of peer interaction is to achieve successful, coordinated play. The social processes employed to achieve this goal are those centred around play. Around 8 to 12 years of age, the goal of children's friendships changes with the gaining of acceptance from one's peers taking precedence. At this stage, children are concerned with figuring out which behaviours will lead to acceptance by their peer group and which behaviours lead to rejection. Finally, around adolescence (13 years of age onwards), the goal of friendships changes to developing a better understanding of the self, with a corresponding increase in a focus on self-disclosure.

Conceptions of friendship

These changes in the focus of friendships correspond closely with children's developing conceptions of friendships, that is, what characterizes a friendship. Damon (1977) interviewed children about their knowledge of friendship and found evidence for three levels of friendship. At level 1 (ages 5 to 7 years), friends are seen in a momentary or transient way and are defined by how the child interacts with them. Friends are *playmates*, people who *share* toys and other things, and who are *fun*. At level 2 (8 to 10 years), children's conceptions of friends are focused on issues surrounding *trust* in one another, and on the *dispositions* or *traits* which one likes about another person. At level 3 (age 11 and beyond) conceptions of friendships are centred around *intimacy*, revealed in the disclosure and the sharing of thoughts, feelings and attitudes, and the development of *mutual understanding* (Youniss, 1980). A number of other 'stage theories' of friendship show similar developmental patterns in children's conceptions of friendship (Selman, 1981; Youniss & Volpe, 1978), however, Berndt (1981) maintains that children's conceptions of friendship do *not* develop in a stage-like manner. Rather, their conceptions represent an accumulation of dimensions such as commonalities in favoured modes of play and an increasing interest in intimacy and self-disclosure. Further research on these issues is required in order to sort out exactly how such development in children's conceptions of friendship takes place (Rubin & Coplan, 1992).

The maintenance of friendships

Children's early friendships are often fragile bonds which can be quickly formed, and just as easily terminated. As children grow older, their friendships become more stable and enduring as the characteristics on which the friendships are based evolve. In a study of fourth- and eighth-grade children (approximately 9 and 13 year of age, respectively) in the United States, Berndt, Hawkins and Hoyle (1986) found that over two thirds of children who reported that they were close friends at the beginning of the school year were still close friends at the end of the year. The friendships which endured the year were characterized by the children as involving frequent interaction and a high degree of mutual liking. Unstable friendships were characterized by a lack of intimacy. Children's friendships do not differ from their lesser relationships or acquaintanceships in terms of conflict experienced with the relationship but friends are more likely to be concerned with resolving conflict than are acquaintances (Newcomb & Bagwell, 1995).

The functions of friendship

Friendships play a number of important functions in children's development. According to Sullivan (1953), friendships in childhood serve to: offer consensual validation of one's feelings and interests; bolster the child's feelings of self-worth and importance; provide affection; provide opportunities for intimacy and disclosure; promote the growth of interpersonal sensitivity; offer prototypes for later relationships. According to Rubin and Coplan (1992), a number of other functions for friendship have been suggested, from providing companionship and offering a context for transmitting social norms, to promoting a sense of loyalty and alliance. Friendships also offer a 'secure base' (Ainsworth et al., 1978) outside of the family. As Parker And Gottman (1989) suggest, friendships are at the heart of the development of social and emotional competence.

Social cognitive development

Piaget's focus was on cognitive development and, as a result, he had little to say about the child's developing social awareness. However, Piaget's theory was the inspiration for a great deal of research which attempted to examine whether the changes in children's cognitive development identified by him could explain the development of children's social understanding and behaviour, particularly, their understanding of themselves and others (Damon & Hart, 1992). This focus on children's social cognition has become a major area of research, with many facets (Flavell & Miller, 1998). Here we examine research in two of these areas: the child's developing 'theory of mind' and the development of a sense of self and other.

The child's 'theory of mind'

Consider the following scenario adapted from Simon Baron-Cohen (1995): John walks into the kitchen, looks around, and then leaves. How do we explain John's behaviour? According to Baron-Cohen, we effortlessly generate explanations for John's behaviour based on his **mental states**, that is, internal states such as *beliefs*, *desires*, *intentions* and *emotions* which exist in the mind. For example, we might say that *John came to the kitchen because he* WANTED something, but he FORGOT what it was so he left. Alternatively, we might argue *John was* LOOKING for something but could not find it. Both explanations seem natural and plausible. However, consider an explanation such as *John walks into the kitchen everyday, looks around, and then leaves*. Such explanations sound odd and do not seem to really explain the facts. As Baron-Cohen argues, it is hard for us to make sense of behaviour in any other way than via the attribution of mental states to others. We engage in such processes automatically and often unconsciously and they form an important piece of the puzzle in our understanding of the social world.

The attribution of mental states to others is a kind of common-sense psychology that we all employ. Developmental psychologists interested in this area have used the term **theory of mind** to describe the attribution of mental states to explain behaviour in both ourselves and other people (Astington, Harris & Olson, 1988; Perner, 1991; Wellman, 1990). This ability to infer the existence of mental states and to use them as explanatory devices for human behaviour is an important step in the child's developing understanding of the social world. Holding a theory of mind allows us to easily understand our own and other's actions and to predict and control their behaviour by manipulating their mental states. Thus, the child who has acquired a theory of mind is in a good position to *deceive* someone by making them think something that is false or to *empathize* with someone in order to comfort them. Holding a theory of mind is a crucial step in the child's participation in the social world. As you will recall, we briefly discussed the development of a theory of mind in Chapter 6. In this chapter we will examine how a theory of mind is related to children's **social cognitive development**, that is, their thinking about social interactions.

Why call it a 'theory of mind'?

Before we go on, let us consider an important question we have not yet addressed. Why do researchers call the child's developing knowledge of mental states a 'theory' of mind? There are at least three reasons for doing so. First, like in all scientific theories, the concepts that make up the child's theory of mind – beliefs, desires, intentions and emotions – are defined in relation to one another. Thus, *beliefs* are mental states which can be true or false, while desires are states which are either satisfied or not. Second, like any scientific theory, the child's theory of mind applies to a particular domain – the domain of mental states, a domain which is quite different from, say, the world of objects which the infant is so concerned with. Third, like scientific theories, the child's theory of mind is used to predict and control phenomena in the world, in this case, people's behaviour.

According to Gopnik (Gopnik, 1996; Gopnik & Meltzoff, 1996), one of the pioneers of theory of mind research, children act like young scientists, *forming* theories about people's behaviour, actively *evaluating* the evidence for their theory, and *revising* or *discarding* their theory when they encounter evidence that the theory cannot adequately explain. Gopnik and many others (e.g., Carey, 1985; Wellman, 1990) believe that the child's development of ever more complex theories is explained by the same basic processes of theory change which characterize how scientists work, in other words, by the construction and revision of theories. Of course, children's theories are different in that they are not explicitly held as scientific theories are. However, the comparison of children and scientists has led to some important findings regarding children's developing understanding of the mind.

Desires and beliefs

Around age 2, children begin to talk about their mental states. Bartsch and Wellman (1995) analyzed a database of linguistic transcripts providing daily samples of preschool children's talk. Bartsch and Wellman found that around age 2, children's everyday speech is littered with examples of mental state talk, in particular, talk about their *desires* and their *intentions*. Young children are notoriously good at making clear what it is they want. According to Wellman (1990), the child's first theory of mind can be called a **desire theory** because 2-year-old children understand that people have internal states which correspond to desires, and, furthermore, they understand that people's actions and emotional reactions can be predicted on the basis of these states. Knowing that someone wants an apple, it is easy to predict that they are likely to go to the kitchen and get an apple as opposed to going to the playground. The 2-year-old recognizes that people act to satisfy their desires. Wellman suggests that while the 2-year-old's understanding of desire is still not exactly the same as an adult's conception, it is very similar and allows the child to make many of the same predictions as an adult.

By age 3, children have elaborated their basic theory to include an understanding of *beliefs*. Wellman calls this theory a **belief–desire psychology** since it incorporates both concepts. The child who is equipped with a belief–desire psychology can make much more complex predictions about behaviour; they explain behaviour using the concepts of belief and desire Wellman (1990). In other words, children show an ability to relate a person's actions to his beliefs and desires. Bartsch and Wellman (1989) performed a series of experiments that showed 3-year-old children readily engage in this sort of reasoning, sharing at least the rudiments of an adult theory of mind. Moreover, with a belief–desire psychology, the 3-year-old child can understand that two people could have the same desire, but might act in different ways, in accordance with their beliefs. This sort of phenomenon would be extremely difficult for a child equipped only with a simple desire psychology to accommodate. Thus, by age 3 the child reasons about their own and other's behaviour in a way very similar to adults. There is, however, one crucial difference between 3-year-olds and adults, a fact about mental representations which 3-year-olds have not yet grasped: the notion that one's beliefs are not always true of the world, that is, that beliefs can be *false*.

Understanding misrepresentation: the case of false beliefs

Around age 4, children begin to conceive of the fact that beliefs can be false, that a person's mental states can *misrepresent* a situation. As children get older, they begin to appreciate that people's beliefs depend on their perceptions and are not direct copies of the environment (Carpendale & Chandler, 1996; Keenan, Ruffman & Olson, 1994). In other words, we act on the basis of our representations of reality and not on the basis of reality itself. The 4-year-old has developed a much more sophisticated theory of mind, a theory which includes the idea that our beliefs, desires, and intentions are mental representations, and that these representations can differ in their relation to reality. Furthermore, 4-year-olds begin to understand that people act on the basis of their beliefs and *not* simply on the basis of reality. Many psychologists refer to this level of understanding as a **representational theory of mind** (Perner, 1991; Wellman, 1990).

How do developmentalists test whether or not a child holds a representational theory of mind? Wimmer and Perner (1983) devised a task known as the **false belief task** which has become the litmus test for demonstrating that children understand that people act on the basis of their representations of the world. In the false belief task, a child watches as one of two puppets places an object like a piece of candy in a distinct location, say a red box. This puppet then leaves the scene. In the next part of the story, a second puppet takes the object from the red box and places it in a second location, a green box. Finally, the first puppet returns and the child subject is asked, 'Where will puppet look for her candy?' or 'Where will she think her candy is?' Wimmer and Perner (1983) found that most 3-year-olds failed the false belief task, incorrectly claiming that the puppet would look where the chocolate really is. These children erred on the task because their theory predicts that people's beliefs tend to directly reflect reality, so the person acting in accord with their beliefs will search for the object where it is really located. By way of contrast, most 4-year-olds correctly understood that the puppet would look for her candy in the location where she originally put it. These older children understand that the puppet would hold a false belief, and moreover, would act on the basis of this false belief and not based on the actual situation.

Early social experience and the development of theory of mind

There are a number of factors in children's early social interactions that help them take steps towards the acquisition of a theory of mind. One line of research has examined the role of family structures in children's acquisition of a theory of mind. Perner and his colleagues (Perner, Ruffman, & Leekam, 1994) showed that the age at which children passed the false belief task was positively correlated with the number of siblings which the child had. Three-year-old children with older siblings were as likely to pass a false belief task as 4-year-old children with no siblings. On the account of Perner et al., having an older sibling seems to be worth about a year's experience. Presumably, children in larger families receive more 'exposure' to theory of mind through the kinds of talk and social interchanges which take place in sibling interactions. Adults also provide opportunities for children to acquire a theory of mind too, thus only children are not entirely disadvantaged (Lewis, Freeman, Kyriakidou, Maridaki-Kassotaki, & Berridge, 1996).

Recent work by Meins, Fernyhough, Russell, and Clark-Carter (1998) has examined how parents may play a role in the child's acquisition of a theory of mind. Meins et al. found that children who passed the false belief task at an early age tended to have parents who were what she called *mind-minded*, that is, who often spoke to children of mental states or used mental state terms in their speech to children. Ruffman, Perner and Parkin (1999) showed a similar finding. In their study, mothers of 2-year-olds were asked to imagine what they would say to their child after some transgression, such as hitting another child. Mothers wrote their responses and these were coded for whether they showed evidence of mental state talk. Ruffman et al. found that children whose mothers used mental state terms in their responses, for example, saying things like, '*Imagine how that child feels? Would you like to be hit?*', were more likely to pass the false belief task at age 3 than children whose mothers talked to their child in other ways such as '*You shouldn't do that*' or '*Was that a nice thing to do?*' In another study conducted by Dunn, Brown, Slomkowski, Tesla, & Youngblade (1991), family discourse about feelings measured when they were 43 months of age predicted children's later performance on both false belief and affective perspective-taking tasks (measured 7 months later). The authors of this study argue that talk about the social world mediates children's social cognitive development. Clearly, parents' socialization efforts with their children can have a profound effect on the nature of their children's development; in this case, when their children acquire an understanding of a fundamental aspect of the social world.

Theory of mind and later social development

A final question which we will consider in relation to the child's developing understanding of the mind is how it relates to other developmental achievements. While there is relatively little evidence on the impact of acquiring a theory of mind on children's social development, Keenan and Harvey (1998) have suggested that the child's theory of mind acts as a **developmental organizer** for subsequent social development. That is, aspects of theory-of-mind development such as whether children acquire the concepts relatively early or relatively late can play a role in shaping later development. In other words, when children develop a theory of mind might affect aspects of later social development such as children's ability to form friendships, thus, theory of mind organizes the nature and course of later development. What evidence is there that the acquisition of a theory of mind really does lead to a reorganization of how children understand the social world?

Recent work by Watson and her colleagues has addressed this question. Watson et al. (1999) showed that 3- to 5-year-old children's performance on a false belief task was positively correlated with their peer social skills as assessed by the child's teacher. This relationship held even when the researchers controlled for the effects of individual differences in language development across children. In a second study, Capage and Watson (in press) showed that performance on a false belief task was negatively correlated with children's level of aggression and positively correlated with social competence. Thus, the results of both studies show a significant relation between the development of a theory of mind and social behaviour. However, given the correlational nature of the studies, it is impossible to do more than speculate on whether an understanding of false belief causes changes in social behaviour or vice versa. Further longitudinal work on this issue is required.

Perner (1988: 271) argued that 'the social significance of human interactions depends on the mental states of the interacting parties, particularly their higher-order mental states'. By 'higher order mental states', Perner refers to what psychologists call **second-order mental states**. Second-order states are simply embedded mental state expressions such as *Jill wants Jack to believe that there is someone behind him*. You can see from this example that Jill has a *desire* to create a particular *belief* in Jack. The acquisition of an understanding of second-order mental states lags behind the understanding of false belief as children do not typically understand second-order mental states until about age 6.

An understanding of second-order mental states is particularly important in understanding nonliteral language (speech where someone doesn't say what they mean). For example, when a story character (Jill) tells another character (Jack) a lie such as *I had a really nice day*, the child who watches the interaction needs to recognize that Jill wants Jack to believe what she says (that she had a nice day). This is because Jill wants to influence Jack's beliefs, that is, to create in him the false belief that Jill had a nice day. When the child acquires this level of understanding, they are in a position to understand quite complex social interactions (Harris, 1989). Imagine for example that Jill had a car accident, lost her wallet, and missed an important appointment. Jack asks how Jill's day was and she replies, *I had a really nice day*. The child who understands second-order mental states is in a position to recognize that Jill's utterance was meant *sarcastically*. Jill does not want Jack to think she had a good day but instead wants the opposite – for him to recognize she had a horrible day. Notice that in both cases the speaker makes the same remark but can mean quite different things by it depending on how they intend the listener to understand them. The child observer of such interactions needs to appreciate second-order mental states in order to differentiate between speech acts such as *lies* and *sarcasm* (Keenan & Quigley, 1999; Perner, 1988). The complex quality of linguistic interactions is but one of many possible examples of where a child's theory of mind plays an important role in their developing social understanding.

LaLonde and Chandler (1995, p.182) have argued that once children acquire an understanding of the mind and its role in behaviour, children may begin to frame their social judgements. Children may put their newly acquired understanding to use in tasks such as choosing friends, manipulating other people, making interpersonal comparisons. Lalonde and Chandler argue that what is required to evaluate this claim is longitudinal research which tracks the consequences of acquiring a representational theory of mind. It is a certainty that future work on theory of mind and social development will undertake this challenge.

The development of self and the differentiation of self from others

At some point in our development, we begin to differentiate ourselves from others. In the view of many, a notion of *self* cannot develop without a notion of *other* (Damon & Hart, 1992). At the same time, the concepts of *self* and *other* are distinct and independent categories which serve distinct functions. In other words, our understanding of self is different from our understanding of others. Developing a sense of self is a central process in the development of social cognition (Harter, 1998). How then, does the development of a sense of self take place, and what is its developmental course?

The differentiation of self from other begins in infancy. This is illustrated in a clever study by Murray and Trevarthen (1985). These researchers devised a procedure using a closed circuit television where 2- to 4-month-old infants could interact with their mothers via the television (infants saw the mother on a screen at the same time as mothers, in another room, saw the infants on their screen). For a few minutes, interactions went on normally and the infants reacted with pleasure and with interest to their mothers. However, after a few minutes, Murray and Trevarthen interrupted the live interaction and instead played a videotape to the infants of the mother during her first minute of interaction. Infants became quite distressed by this. According to the authors of the study, this was because of the lack of *contingency* in the interaction between infant and mother; the mother's actions were no longer tied to their infant's and were thus, unsynchronized. According to Damon and Hart (1992), these findings show that even very young infants are both aware of their own actions and sensitive to the presence of others.

Using a test of self-awareness, researchers have been able to show that a true sense of self develops sometime between 18 to 24 months of age

(Amsterdam, 1972; Lewis & Brooks-Gunn, 1979). This is done using the **rouge test**. In the rouge test, an experimenter carefully marks an infant's face with rouge (or in variants of the task, places a bright yellow sticker in the child's hair) in such a way that the child does not feel this act occur. Then the infant is seated in front of a mirror and their behaviours are recorded. If the infant moves to explore or try and remove the spot, they are credited with having a sense of self because the infant who removes the mark recognizes that their face looks different now than it has in the past. In a study by Amsterdam (1972), it was found that infants younger than 20 months of age rarely moved to remove the spot. Note the parallel between the development of self and when children acquire a concept of object permanence; developing a concept of object permanence may be a prerequisite for the development of a sense of self.

Throughout the rest of childhood, there are changes in the development of the sense of self and the sense of other. Preschool-aged children describe themselves largely in terms of physical attributes or preferences, for example, *I am 5-years-old; I am tall; I like to play with my dog.* As they move past early childhood, their self-descriptions become more complex, involving more descriptions of psychological characteristics (e.g., *I am an outgoing person*; *Sometimes I feel shy*) and values (e.g., *I am an honest person*) and the first use of trait labels such as *smart*, *lazy*, and *mean* (Harter, 1998; Livesly & Bromley, 1973). Children at this stage of their development are creating a description of their personality, trying to integrate their various characteristics into a meaningful whole, that is, a theory of their own personality (Damon & Hart, 1992). By adolescence, the growth of cognitive abilities which allow the adolescent to think abstractly, supports them in their attempts to forge a more coherent view of the self which integrates their various characteristics (Harter, 1998). Adolescents develop an explicit theory of the self which aids them in the task of better understanding themselves and their own thoughts, feelings, and behaviours.

Understanding others' perspectives

An important aspect of learning to interact with others is the ability to take another person's perspective, what has often been referred to in the literature as **role taking**. Role taking is the ability to reason from another person's perspective, or in other words, to refrain from thinking egocentrically. The theory of mind literature attests to the fact that children become less egocentric in their thinking about other people by the preschool years and it also provides important information about the understanding of representation which makes this feat possible. However, theory of mind has relatively little to say about the development of social cognition beyond the preschool years. As we have seen already, in middle childhood, the use of psychological statements about the self increases dramatically; this also applies to the way children think about others (Livesly & Bromley, 1973). Selman (1980) has proposed a five-stage model of the development of role taking ability. In this model, Selman describes how children learn to differentiate between their own and other peoples' perspectives. At stage 0, the child does not distinguish between their own and another's perspective, that is, they reason egocentrically. At stage 1, the child can recognize that they and another may have different perspectives, but they have difficulty describing what the other's perspective might be like. At stage 2, children can see themselves from another's perspective and they know that others are similarly capable. By stage 3, the child recognizes how a third person might view both their own and another's perspectives on a situation. Finally, at stage 4, children understand that a network of perspectives exists that binds individuals into a social system. Selman's research has shown that there is a steady progression in role taking ability through to adolescence. Other research has shown that the development of role taking ability is associated with other sorts of social behaviours such as children's tendency to engage in altruistic or unselfish acts (Eisenberg & Fabes, 1998).

Finally we consider an aspect of adolescent social cognition, a kind of side-effect of their developing ability to think abstractly. Elkind (1967) described an aspect of adolescent cognition that was termed **adolescent egocentrism**. Adolescent egocentrism is the emerging recognition that one may be the focus of another's attention. Adolescents tend to overgeneralize this new understanding, leading to a high degree of self-consciousness because of the mistaken belief that that their behaviours are constantly the focus of others' thoughts. The available evidence suggests that egocentrism decreases as adolescence progresses (Elkind & Bowen, 1979) and beliefs about others' perspectives of one become more realistic. This development is important, because an excessive preoccupation with the self may interfere with the necessary attention to others' perspectives that underlies social competence.

SUMMARY

The study of social development is one of the busiest areas of research in child development at present, particularly because the task of understanding how children get on in a highly social environment is so important to their overall well being. Social development is strongly tied to changes in cognitive development, although the issue of cause and effect (i.e., do changes in cognition underlie social developments or vice versa?) is still unresolved. The development of friendships and peer relationships are examples of topics which are relevant to other areas of study, such as developmental psychopathology and emotional development, where researchers are often interested in trying to better understand the processes by which people negotiate a very complex social environment.

Glossary

Adolescent egocentrism is the recognition that one may be the focus of another's attention which leads to a high degree of self-consciousness.

Associative play according to Parten, occurs when children share toys and materials within a play context but their play is not directed towards a common or joint goal.

Average children are liked by some of their peers, but are not as well liked as popular children. Average children are also disliked by few of their peers.

Belief–desire psychology refers to Wellman's term for the child's theory of mind at age 3. Children understand that people act to satisfy their desires in light of their beliefs, however, they do not yet understand that beliefs can be false.

Cliques are close-knit groups of friends, ranging in size from three to nine members, who are held together by mutual acceptance and common interests.

Controversial children are both well liked by some of their peers and least liked by others.

Cooperative play as defined by Parten is a form of play in which children share a common goal within the context of the play. Games with rules and pretend play, and joint play to construct a block model are examples of cooperative play.

Crowds are groups of adolescents who organize on the basis of reputation and defined on the basis of the attitudes held by their members.

Desire theory refers to Wellman's description of the 2-year-old child's theory of mind. Two-year-olds understand that people have internal states which correspond to desires and furthermore, they understand that people's actions and emotional reactions can be predicted on the basis of these states.

Developmental organizer refers to the notion that some developmental changes have a significant impact on subsequent changes and functioning in that they organize later development.

Dominance hierarchies are orderings of individuals within a group with respect to their dominance or status within the group. Dominance hierarchies tend to become more stable across middle childhood and adolescence.

False belief task which has become the litmus test for demonstrating that children understand that people act on the basis of their representations of the world. In the false belief task, a child watches as one of two puppets places an object like a piece of candy in a distinct location, say a red box. This puppet then leaves the scene. In the next part of the story, a second puppet takes the object from the red box and places it in a second location, a green box. Finally, the first puppet returns and the child subject is asked, 'Where will puppet look for her candy?' or 'Where will she think her candy is?'

Friendship quality a measure of the nature and quality of children's friendship that goes beyond simply measuring how many friendships children have.

Horizontal dimension refers to children's relationships with other children because of their balanced and egalitarian nature.

Mental states are the states of mind that we infer in others as a function of our theory of mind. Mental states that are important to social behaviour include beliefs, intentions, desires and emotions.

Neglected children are not liked or disliked by many children in their peer group. These children have few friends but are not actively disliked by many.

Onlooker behaviour refers to a situation in which a child watches other children play but does not join in with them.

Parallel play according to Parten, is seen when children play in proximity to other children but do not play with other children. They may use similar toys or materials but their play does not involve social interaction.

Popular children are liked by many others within their peer group and disliked by few.

Rejected children are disliked by many in their peer group and are liked by few.

Representational theory of mind refers to a theory of mind which includes an understanding of the mind as a representational medium. When children recognize the possibility of false beliefs, they are said to hold a representational theory of mind.

Role taking is the ability to reason from another person's perspective, or in other words, to refrain from thinking egocentrically.

Rouge test is an experimental task used to test for self-recognition. The infant is surreptitiously marked with a sticker, seated in front of a mirror, and their behaviours are recorded. If the infant explores or tries to remove the sticker, they are credited with having a sense of self.

Second-order mental states are simply embedded mental state expressions such as *Jill wants Jack to believe that there is someone behind him.*

Social cognitive development is the domain of development which includes children's developing ability to think about themselves, other people and their social relationships.

Sociometric techniques are procedures for measuring children's status within their peer group. Sociometric techniques involve asking children to nominate a specific number of their peers who fit some criterion such as friends.

Solitary play according to Parten, occurs when children play by themselves in a way that is different from those children around them. They do not interact with other children.

Theory of mind refers to the child's developing knowledge of the mind and its role in behaviour. A theory of mind is an organized set of concepts, namely, mental states, which are used to predict and explain other people's behaviour.

Unoccupied play according to Parten, occurs when a child does not play with any toys but simply watches things of interest.

Vertical dimension refers to children's relationships with adults because of their asymmetrical nature.

10 Developmental Psychopathology

LEARNING AIMS

At the end of this chapter you should:

- **be able to describe the *developmental psychopathology* approach to the study of psychopathology**
- **be familiar with the issues surrounding the measurement of psychopathology in childhood and some of the instruments used by psychologists**
- **be able to describe some of the central forms of psychopathology encountered in children, including *depression*, *anxiety disorders*, *attention deficit/hyperactivity disorder*, *conduct disorder*, and *autism***
- **be able to explain the concepts of *risk*, *resilience*, and *protective mechanisms***
- **be familiar with the issues involved in the prevention and treatment of childhood psychopathology**

Introduction

One conceptualization of psychopathology is that it is the study of normal development gone askew (Wenar & Kerig, 2000). Based on this conceptualization of psychopathology, an area of study known as **developmental psychopathology** has arisen to capture the important relationship between the study of psychopathology and normal development. The study of developmental psychopathology can be thought of as a marriage between developmental psychology and the study of childhood disorders. Psychologists who adopt the developmental psychopathology framework stress that it is important to look at a range of functioning to fully understand developmental psychopathology, including the 'ontogenetic, biochemical, genetic, biological, physiological, cognitive, social-cognitive, representational, socioemotional, environmental, and societal influences on behaviour' (Cicchetti, 1993: 473).

Importantly, psychologists adopting a developmental psychopathology approach to the question of mental disorders generally assume a continuum of behaviour, with normal behaviour at one end of the scale and abnormal behaviour at the other end. Under this model, developmental principles are important to both normal and psychopathological behaviour, as the same life-course principles apply along the continuum. Take the development of attachment, as discussed in Chapter 8: becoming securely attached to a primary caregiver in infancy provides a base for the child's future well being and healthy exploration of the world. However, becoming overly attached may lead to high separation anxiety and a difficulty with new endeavours such as school and forming friendships with peers. This kind of reservation would have serious consequences for the child's successful social development. Thus, the same mechanism that leads to healthy development is also involved in adverse functioning, at the other end of the spectrum. It has therefore been argued that an understanding of normal development is important for the development of knowledge about psychopathology, and likewise, that understanding psychopathology leads to further knowledge about normal functioning (Cicchetti, 1990). Cicchetti (1993) has further pointed out that to understand normal development is to be as interested in the children who are at risk of developing a disorder and do not, as those who do actually develop a disorder. Therefore we will look at the issues of risk and resilience later in the chapter.

Rutter and Garmezy (1983) have suggested that the discipline of developmental psychopathology is based on a number of tenets arising from a dual consideration of child development issues and the study of child psychiatric disorders. First, the child's developmental level, or age, is of central importance to understanding the onset, significance, and course of psychopathology. The age at which a behaviour becomes manifest is perhaps the primary question; to illustrate, *enuresis* (bed-wetting) takes on very different meanings depending on whether the individual is 2, 10, or 20 years of age when it starts. A related point is that susceptibility to stress or risk of psychopathology is linked to the child's age, such that individuals are more vulnerable at different times in their lives. The second major tenet is that the development of a disorder, such as depression, is often based on experiences at an earlier point in development, which calls for a life-span approach. Third, developmental psychopathologists are interested in individual differences, examining the many different paths that may lead to the development of psychopathology in general, as well as to specific disorders. There are many different ways that children come to manifest disturbed behaviour, a concept known as **equifinality** (Cicchetti & Rogers, 1996). A related idea is **multifinality**, which means that a particular risk factor (risk factors are discussed later in this chapter) can have a number of different developmental outcomes depending on the characteristics of the individual, previous experiences, and the environment. The fourth tenet is concerned with the continuity and discontinuity of bchaviour. For example, the presence of a problem in childhood is often associated with a continued vulnerability in adulthood, but this is not always the case. Thus, a significant issue in the study of developmental psychopathology is discovering which factors promote or prevent a childhood disorder from continuing or reoccurring.

The measurement of psychopathology

The primary issue in the diagnosis of psychopathology is the achievement of an effective and accurate working definition. In the introduction we saw that normal and psychopathological behaviour can be conceptualized as based along a continuum. However, it is questionable under this model where normality ends and psychopathology begins. Indeed, there is no one definition of psychopathology that has been readily accepted by all, as would be clear from the different approaches taken in the various models already reviewed. Therefore, a number of classification systems of childhood psychopathology have been developed, each focusing on slightly different criteria according to how psychopathology is conceptualized, and whether developmental considerations are addressed. Two of the more well-known diagnostic systems, the Diagnostic and Statistical Manual of Mental Disorders (DSM) and the Child Behaviour Checklist (CBCL), will be reviewed here.

Before tackling the issue of how exactly psychopathology is defined, it is important to note that the classification of disorders is not straightforward, and it is often unclear to which specific diagnostic category a child belongs to. **Comorbidity**, that is, the presence of two or more disorders at once, is quite high in children, meaning that multiple diagnoses are often required. Thus, it is not uncommon for a child to suffer from depression as well as anxiety (Nilzon & Palmerus, 1997), although different classification systems deal with this issue in different ways.

The most common and widely used form of diagnosing psychopathology is the **Diagnostic and Statistical Manual of Mental Disorders (DSM-IV)**, which is now in its fourth edition (American Psychiatric Association, 1994). The proper use of the DSM-IV is dependent on a clinician's skills in determining whether a client's symptoms match those listed in order to diagnose a particular disorder or syndrome. The DSM-IV is not concerned with classifying people, but focuses instead on their behaviour. Thus, you will not see reference to a 'juvenile delinquent' but rather, to a 'child with conduct disorder'. This focus on behaviour helps to remove the negative stigma of certain terms, such as 'alcoholic' and 'delinquent', which are sometimes used to label people in a derogatory and uninformed way. The DSM-IV is an attempt to provide an objective diagnostic tool to be used by all kinds of clinicians, whether they are psychiatrists or psychologists, and it is therefore guided by empirical work and not grounded in any one model or theory.

A number of aspects of people's functioning are targeted in the DSM-IV, through a multiaxial classification system. Axis I is concerned with the *classification of specific disorders*, such as depression, which is the most well known role of the DSM-IV. Axis II deals with the *personality disorders* and *mental retardation*, as these have a pervasive, often lifetime impact on the individual's behaviour. In Axis III, the clinician notes any *medical conditions* that could potentially have an effect on the person's functioning, such as a physical injury. The individual's *psychosocial and environmental problems*, such as insufficient social support, are the focus of Axis IV. Axis V is finally concerned with a *global assessment of functioning*, which is a score based on the clinician's judgement of an overall level of functioning, ranging from 1 (the lowest) to 100 (the highest).

To get an idea of how the DSM-IV works, it may be useful to use an example of how it sets out a particular disorder under Axis 1. For a sleep-walking disorder, the diagnostic criteria include: (A) repeated episodes of rising from bed during sleep and walking about (B) while sleepwalking, the person has a blank, staring face, is relatively unresponsive to others, and can be awakened only with great difficulty (C) on awakening, the person has amnesia (D) within several minutes of awakening, there is no mental impairment of mental activity (E) the sleepwalking causes clinically significant distress or impairment in social, occupational, or other important areas of functioning (American Psychiatric Association, 1994).

There has, however, been some question as to whether the DSM-IV deals with developmental issues. There is no provision for changes in the behaviour underlying a disorder which may occur as a function of age. Research has shown that as children develop, their symptoms of a disorder tend to change as well. For example, younger children with attention deficit hyperactivity disorder (which we will look at in the next section) show more hyperactivity or physical disturbance, whereas older children are more inattentive (Hart et al., 1995). Despite the many strengths of the DSM-IV, it seems that this diagnostic system does not adequately classify children's and adolescents' changing behaviour. It is thus worth making note of other diagnostic approaches, and in particular, the **Child Behaviour Checklist (CBCL)**.

Whereas the DSM-IV uses categories to classify behaviour, that is, an individual either has a disorder or not, the CBCL is dimensional in nature and thus provides information about the extent to which an individual shows disturbance. This approach fits more neatly with the definition of psycho-pathology outlined in the introduction, where deviation was viewed as continuous from normality. The CBCL, as devised by Thomas Achenbach, is comprised of 118 items which create a profile of eight *narrow-band* and two *wide-band* factors. The narrow-band factors include withdrawal, physical (or *somatic*) complaints, anxiety/depression, social problems, thought problems, attention problems, delinquent behaviour, and aggressive behaviour. The more general wide-band factors, which encompass a number of the narrow-band factors, are the **internalizing** and **externalizing** scales. These two terms have actually been adopted in a general way in developmental psychopathology. Internalizing disorders refer to an inward suffering or distress and include disorders such as anxiety and depression. Externalizing disorders are a more outward and 'acting-out' form of distress and include aggression and delinquent behaviour. It is possible, and actually common, for children to behave in a way that would be considered along both internalizing and externalizing dimensions. A child may, for example, be sulky and aggressive at the same time.

Norms that differ by age and gender are available for the CBCL, so that comparisons can be made with an individual's scores. Based on this comparison, a clinician can determine how close to normality the individual's behaviour is and thereby classify the extent of their psychopathology. Three different forms of the CBCL, namely, the self report, parent report, and teacher report forms, are available for the clinician to gather information about the child's behaviour. There are often important differences between these sources of information, although it seems that parents and teachers provide more reliable reports of the child's externalizing behaviour, while the child her or himself is able to provide a more accurate comment on their internalizing behaviour (Cantwell, 1996).

A significant problem with the CBCL is that it does not include some of the major childhood disorders, such as autism, certain learning disabilities, and eating disorders (Wenar & Kerig, 2000), all of which are covered in the DSM-IV. The CBCL is concerned with degrees of normality, and it is arguable that certain disorders, such as autism, are either clearly present or absent. Such disorders are thus best dealt with by the DSM-IV, which is able to provide information about the severity of a disorder, but assumes that the disorder is distinct from nonpathological behaviour. Both the DSM-IV, Axis 1, and the CBCL will be used to examine some of the major developmental disorders in the next section, so that disorders which are clearly a continuum of normal behaviour will be represented as well as those which are not. Please bear in mind that we only look at five disorders here, simply to provide you with a sense of the kinds of disorders that can affect children; there are many more important and significant forms of psychopathology that are not covered here. (See Table 10.1 for an overview of these five disorders.)

TABLE 10.1 The development of some significant childhood disorders

Disorder	Common features	Gender differences	Outcomes in adulthood
Depression	Sadness, fatigue, self-pity, recurrent thoughts of death, decrease in interest and pleasure, and a loss of appetite	Childhood: equal rates Puberty: more females affected	Depression is a fairly stable disorder (although the *form* of depression may change with age)
Anxiety	Intense fear of a situation (social phobia) or thing (specific phobia) which is maladaptive, persistent and beyond the individual's voluntary control	Depends on the anxiety disorder, e.g., for obsessive-compulsive disorder, boys > girls, but for panic disorder, girls > boys	Anxiety in childhood often predisposes the individual to either anxiety in adulthood, or other forms of psychopathology
Attention deficit/ hyperactivity disorder	Inattention and or hyperactivity and impulsivity that is frequent and severe. Impairment is often seen in social, academic or occupational functioning	More males than females are affected (ratios have been estimated from 3:1 to 5:1)	The disorder persists into adulthood for many children. Later antisocial problems and drug abuse may also be associated
Conduct disorder	A pattern of antisocial behaviour which is persistent and repetitive, e.g., aggression to people and animals, destruction of property, deceitfulness and theft, and a serious violation of rules	More males than females are affected by conduct disorder (approximately 4:1)	Childhood onset CD is often associated with problems, such as antisocial personality disorder, criminal behaviour, and drug and alcohol abuse later in life
Autism	A disturbance in social interactions, a host of unusual behaviours and problems with communication, e.g., the child may not engage in eye-to-eye gaze, be mute, and engage in repetitive behaviours. The disorder has a very early onset (infancy)	More males than females are affected by the disorder (approximately 4:1). Females with autism are more likely to display mental retardation	The disorder is most often life long, and over half of children affected continue to be completely dependent on caregivers in adulthood

The development of some significant childhood disorders

Depression

The criteria in the DSM-IV for depressive disorders are the same, or very similar, for children and adults. There are, however, some important differences in the way that children of varying ages manifest these disorders, and a developmental approach is therefore of great benefit to studying depression in children.

Feeling depressed is fairly common. Most people feel 'down in the dumps' every now and then. However, in order to actually be diagnosed with a *depressive disorder*, or what is otherwise known as **clinical depression**, the normal depressive symptoms that many of us experience on occasion, such as sadness, fatigue, and self-pity, have to be marked and quite severe. As with most disorders, the hallmark of clinical depression is an impairment of day-to-day functioning and/or the presence of significant distress. Thus, an individual suffering from depression may have these symptoms, as well as recurrent thoughts of death, an obvious decrease in interest and pleasure, and a loss of appetite, all at the same time. Depression exists in varying levels of severity and this description is based on the criteria for *major depression*, which is a debilitating form of depression marked by a single or multiple episodes. Another type of depression is **dysthymia**, which is characterized in children by a chronically depressed mood, or irritability, for at least one year.

Although it has been noted that the symptoms of depression in childhood are very similar to those seen in adulthood (Cicchetti & Toth, 1998), there are nevertheless some important developmental differences. For example, in infancy and toddlerhood, depression may be distinguished by a loss of developmentally appropriate behaviour such as toilet training and intellectual functioning. During the preschool years, equivalent symptoms include a sad appearance, a return to earlier stages of development, such as intense separation anxiety and sleep problems. The school-aged child is better able to vocalize their distress, and therefore their depression is more in line with adult symptoms. Eating and sleep disturbances are often present, as are self-criticism and a loss of motivation.

There are also important gender differences in the development of depression. In childhood, the rate that depression affects boys and girls is fairly equal. However, once puberty strikes, females increasingly experience more severe and frequent episodes of depression than males, and this is a pattern that persists into adulthood. Reasons for this gender difference include a general tendency for girls to internalize their stress, and for boys to externalize it, and increased negative life events for females, such as sexual abuse, as well as more intense family and peer control and expectancies than boys are subject to (Nolen-Hoeksema, 1994).

Depression ratings taken during the early school years have been found to predict the presence of depressive disorders up to six years later for both males and females (Achenbach, Howell, McConaughy & Stanger, 1995). It has further been reported that depressed children who no longer show signs of that particular type of depression in adolescence and adulthood, very often develop another form of depression (Harrington, Rutter, & Fombonne, 1996).

There are many theories of what causes depression, known as the **etiology** of depression. An interesting approach that integrates many of these ideas is the attachment perspective, which suggests that insecure attachment leads to depression in infants, children and adolescents (Cicchetti & Toth, 1998). Insecure attachment causes the individual to feel unworthy and that others are unloving. These feelings, in turn, make the individual vulnerable to the cognitive (thoughts about worthlessness and hopelessness), emotional (fear of disapproval and being abandoned), and biological (heritability) processes that are often associated with depression.

Anxiety

A disorder that often accompanies depression in both childhood and adulthood is **anxiety**. There are a number of different types of anxiety disorders listed in the DSM-IV, such as *specific phobias* (as in a fear of heights, for example), *separation anxiety disorder*, *obsessive-compulsive disorder*, *social phobia*, and *panic disorder*. All of these disorders have a number of things in common, like the presence of intense fear, which is maladaptive, persistent, and beyond the individual's voluntary control. Like some of the depressive symptoms, being fearful is a fairly common feeling that happens to most of us from time to time. However, where fear becomes an actual anxiety disorder, the individual's normal and adaptive functioning is severely impaired. So, for example, many of us may fear social appraisal to the point that a sinking stomach and beating heart are associated with giving a class presentation, but when this fear becomes so intense that a person is unable to go to school, or even leave the house, we are likely to classify it as an anxiety disorder. Using the continuum model for psychopathology outlined at the beginning of the chapter, anxiety disorders are situated at the extreme end of the fear spectrum.

Although the developmental course of each of the anxiety disorders differs, it is generally the case that anxiety increases with age. For example, Vasey and colleagues (Vasey, Crnic, & Carter, 1994) examined anxiety in children aged between 5 and 12 years of age. The presence of worrisome thoughts was more prevalent in children aged 8 and older. In particular, the 11- to

12-year-olds displayed significantly more evidence of anxiety than the younger children did.

Some children with anxiety disorders outgrow them, but in many circumstances early susceptibility to anxiety problems means continued problems in later life. In a study of the course and outcome of children diagnosed with an anxiety disorder, many of the children no longer had the disorder after a four-year follow up, however, 30 percent of these children developed another psychiatric disorder, in many cases another type of anxiety disorder (Last, Perrin, Hersen, & Kazdin, 1997). There are a number of reasons why a child might initially develop and continue to display anxiety, including internal factors, such as a genetic predisposition, as well as external factors, like a stressful environment or overprotective parents. As will be revealed in the following section on risk and resilience, however, the factors which guide the development and outcome of a disorder are very rarely straightforward.

Attention deficit/hyperactivity disorder

In contrast to the internalizing disorders of depression and anxiety, **attention deficit/hyperactivity disorder (ADHD)** and conduct disorder (to be discussed in the next section) are externalizing forms of maladjustment. The core features of ADHD can be inferred from its name. The disorder involves the ongoing presence of *inattention* and/or *hyperactivity–impulsivity* that is both more frequent and more severe than can be accounted for by developmentally appropriate behaviour. To constitute a diagnosis of ADHD: some symptoms must have been evident before the age of 7 years; impairment must cross contexts so that, for example, behaviour at school and at home is affected; and there must be sufficient evidence of significant impairment in social, academic or occupational functioning (American Psychiatric Association, 1994).

As is the case with many disorders, a relatively common range of behaviours must clearly cross the boundary from normal to psychopathological, in order to reach a diagnosis of ADHD. Thus, an inability to sit still for long periods of time is common, and indeed, expected during the preschool years (and has been known to follow many of us into adulthood), but children with ADHD often cannot engage for any length of time in even fun activities.

There are currently three different types of ADHD, which perhaps reflects past difficulties in reaching a single accurate definition of the disorder. The first form of ADHD is one based on inattention; the second on hyperactivity–impulsivity; and the third involves a combination of the first two. The *inattention* type of ADHD reflects the behaviour of children who have great difficulty keeping their attention on tasks, compared to age-appropriate levels of concentration. Thus, such children may be described as easily distracted, not seeming to listen, as daydreamers, and as continuously losing things. Children characterized by *hyperactivity* appear to have boundless levels of energy and are constantly on the move. These children very often fidget or squirm when seated, run and climb at any opportunity, and talk excessively. Children with impulsivity can't seem to hold themselves back, and frequently blurt out answers, can't wait their turn and interrupt other people's conversations or games. It is once again important to note that these behaviours may be common at earlier times in development, but children with ADHD clearly do not display developmentally appropriate levels of attention and/or action–impulse control.

The prevalence of ADHD is thought to be somewhere in the range of 3–5 percent of the general population of children (Wenar & Kerig, 2000). Estimates vary for gender differences in ADHD with some suggestion that the ratio of boys to girls with ADHD is about 3:1 although a recent study (Gomez, Harvey, Quick, Scharer, & Harris, 1999) employing children from an Australian primary school, revealed the male to female gender difference to be slightly higher at a ratio of 5:1.

ADHD can be quite difficult to detect during the toddler and preschool years, as short attention spans and a tendency to get into everything are characteristic of young children. However, the severity, frequency and chronicity of the child's behaviour are important identifiers of ADHD at this age (Campbell, 1990). The disorder is easier to detect in middle childhood, as standards for self-control and concentration abilities are more perceptible and firmly set. The continuation of ADHD into adolescence and adulthood is not uncommon. It is estimated that between 30 and 50 percent of children with ADHD continue to have the disorder as adults (Jackson & Farrugia, 1997).

Children with ADHD do not appear to develop any significant cognitive deficits later in life, but they do tend to end up, on average, with two years less schooling and a lower occupational ranking than average (Mannuzza, Klein, Bessler, & Malloy, 1993). It is perhaps surprising that many children with ADHD grow up to function in such a relatively successful way, when considering the time and important issues that their inattention and/or hyperactivity may have caused them to miss at school. There is some evidence that children with the hyperactive-inattentive type of ADHD fare the worst. These children are at least 7 times more likely than others to have antisocial problems in adulthood or a drug abuse problem (Manuzza et al., 1993). This may stem, at least in part, from a comorbid antisocial problem in childhood. It has been noted that criminality in adulthood is related to childhood ADHD *and* conduct disorder, but not to ADHD alone (Lie, 1993). Therefore, our discussion now turns to the range of problems that are associated with conduct disorder.

Conduct disorder

Conduct disorder is defined in the DSM-IV as, 'a repetitive and persistent pattern of behaviour in which the basic rights of others or major age-appropriate societal norms or rules are violated' (American Psychiatric Association, 1994). Antisocial behaviour thus defined refers to the extreme end of relatively standard childhood behaviour like stealing, lying, and fighting. The activities of children with conduct disorder (CD) therefore constitute a serious and severe deviation that affects many aspects of the individual's life. Estimates for the prevalence of CD in the community range between 2–6 percent, and the disorder affects boys almost four times more often than it affects girls (Kazdin, 1997). There have been a number of reasons proposed for this gender discrepancy, such as differences in predispositions to acting aggressively, and parent–child socialization that encourages boys to be active and girls passive, boys to freely express their anger, and girls to feel empathy and guilt (Zahn-Waxler, Cole, & Barrett, 1991).

There are a number of main criteria that the DSM-IV lists to guide the clinician's diagnosis of conduct disorder. Included is: *aggression to people and animals*, such as bullying; the *use of a weapon to cause harm* to others or forcing another into sexual activity; *destruction of property*, like fire-setting; *deceitfulness or theft*; and a *serious violation of rules*, such as staying out late at night, running away from home, or playing truant. Antisocial activity obviously varies in degrees of severity as we can see with the merging of 'normal' and 'naughty' behaviour in most children. Likewise, there are various levels of conduct disorder that the clinician can identify, ranging from mild, through to moderate and severe. Conduct disorder can also be defined in terms of childhood onset (before 10 years of age) and adolescent onset (absence of CD before 10 years of age). This is an important distinction in terms of the outcomes for children with conduct disorder.

Childhood-onset CD seems to constitute a more serious and pervasive form of the disorder, as these children are more likely than the adolescent-onset youths to persist in aggressive and criminal behaviour and continue their dysfunction into adulthood. In fact, in order to meet a diagnosis of antisocial personality disorder (an adult disorder that constitutes an axis 2 diagnosis and is characterized by unlawful, aggressive, deceitful and generally severe antisocial behaviour), conduct disorder must have been present in youth. Longitudinal studies have shown that conduct disorder in childhood predicts similar levels of deviance up to 30 years later (Farrington, 1991).

Not all children with CD continue their antisocial behaviour into adolescence and adulthood. In a classic study, Robbins (1978) found that less than 50 percent of children displaying conduct disorder carried on with their antisocial behaviour into adulthood. However, while some children may escape a protracted course of conduct disorder, they are still at risk of developing a range of other disorders later in life. Kazdin (1997) has identified a range of difficulties that individuals with a history of CD are prone to, including: *psychiatric problems* such as anxiety and alcohol abuse; *criminal behaviour*; *occupational problems*, as in difficulty getting and keeping jobs; *marital problems*, characterized by high divorce rates; and *physical illness*, such as a higher mortality rate, and hospitalization for physical problems. An important development issue in identifying whether CD and related problems continue over an individual's life is the transmission of conduct disorder from one generation to the next. Some evidence suggests that a child is more likely to engage in antisocial behaviour if his or her grandparents evinced antisocial behaviour (Glueck & Glueck, 1968).

Autism

Autism is a fairly rare disorder that has a genetic basis (Bailey, Phillips, & Rutter, 1996) and affects between 0.1 and 0.3 percent of the population (Wing, 1993). The hallmarks of the disorder are a disturbance in *social interactions*, *problems with communication*, a host of *unusual behaviours*, and *very early onset* (Klin & Volkmar, 1997). As an example of each of these characteristics, children with autism often do not engage in eye-to-eye gaze and simply look through people when being spoken to, they may be *mute*, engage in repetitive behaviours such as rocking over and over again or display an inflexible adherence to rituals, and develop the beginnings of this behaviour in infancy or toddlerhood.

Autistic children seem to have problems with the fundamental developmental issues such as emotional, social and cognitive maturity, which allow us to successfully interact in this world of others. In severe cases of autism, it is almost as though the child cannot conceptualize of those around them as people who are capable of thoughts and feelings. Indeed, there is now fairly concrete evidence to suggest that autistic children have a deficient or non-existent theory of mind that cannot be explained by a more general cognitive impairment (Frith & Happé, 1999). As you may recall from Chapter 9, theory of mind refers to the ability to take another's perspective, and to understand mental states, such as beliefs, desires, intentions, and emotions. Thus, children with autism seem to be incapable of understanding what others think and feel, a process which nonimpaired children develop naturally in the early preschool years.

Indeed, the DSM-IV diagnostic criteria for autism refer to *qualitative* differences in social interaction and communication; that is, the deviant behaviour that characterizes autism is generally not found in either nonimpaired children or children with other developmental disorders. Thus, certain behaviours that characterized autism, such as a complete lack of interest in human emotions or faccs, are not present in other babies and children, and therefore do not have a corresponding counterpart in nonimpaired development. There are also *quantitative* differences in the social behaviour of children with autism, which is more congruent with the definition of psychopathology as a continuum of normal behaviour. Thus, some children may have odd habits or a preference for routine, but these behaviours are marked and severe in autism. An associated feature of autism that can be seen to vary in quantitative terms is self-injurious behaviour. Children with autism often inflict injury on themselves, such as head banging, and hitting or biting themselves. Not only are these sorts of behaviours present in children with other forms of disturbance, but anyone who has witnessed a toddler's temper tantrum can verify the occasional occurrence of self-injurious behaviour in nonimpaired children.

The long-term effects of autism are profound, with 60 percent of children diagnosed with autism continuing to be completely dependent in adulthood. Only 5 to 15 percent of children grow up to have well-adjusted social and work lives (Lotter, 1978). The outcome is especially poor if a child with autism has failed to develop communicative speech by 5 years of age, and if their IQ is below 60. The autistic adults who do manage to cope relatively well generally do so by rigidly keeping to the rules they have learnt for acceptable behaviour. They rarely engage in spontaneous activity, or have insight into their own or others' thoughts and behaviour. Therefore, people with autism are generally incapable of experiencing empathy, and show little interest in sexuality (Paul, 1987).

Risk and resilience

Why do some children emerge from a highly stressful and harmful situation psychologically intact, while others are subject to significantly less adversity and cope much less effectively? These are the kind of questions that work into **risk** and **resilience** address. Some have identified these two concepts as flip sides of the same coin (Rutter, 1987), as research on resilience is usually concerned with the first scenario whereas research on risk looks at the second. These notions are important complements of each other, and each will therefore be examined in turn.

Risk

Risk or **vulnerability** factors are fairly enduring characteristics of an individual's external and internal worlds that are likely to lead to maladaptive and negative functioning. Put simply, a risk factor is any factor that increases the chance of an individual developing a psychopathological condition.

External factors include the family, social dynamics, and more generally, the environment of the individual. Internal factors relate to influences such as genetics, biology, and temperament.

Rutter and others (1979; 1985; Rutter & Quinton, 1987) have identified six significant risk factors that are commonly involved in the development of psychopathology; these are primarily chronic family problems, and are thus factors extrinsic to the individual. Note that this list is by no means exhaustive, and is simply meant to provide examples of the types of risk which may lead to psychopathology. The factors include: severe marital discord, maternal psychiatric illness; low socioeconomic status; overcrowding or large family size; parental criminality; and the placement of a child out of the family home. Such distal risk factors are important so far as they directly influence proximal factors that lead to problems more directly. To illustrate, severe marital discord may not in itself cause problem behaviour in a child, rather, it is likely that the ineffective parenting, resulting from the discord, poses a risk for the development of problem behaviour (Dubow, Roecker, & D'Imperio, 1997).

Another example of this distinction between distal and proximal risk is the mechanism that leads from a maternal psychiatric illness, such as depression, to problems in the child. Goodman and Gotlib (1999) have recently proposed that maternal depression does not in itself comprise a risk factor. Depression leads to risk mechanisms, such as the heritability of depression, exposure to the mother's negative behaviour and emotions, and exposure to a stressful environment. Any one of these mechanisms could in itself, or in combination, lead to depression and other psychopathological disorders in children.

It seems that the sheer number of risk factors that apply to an individual's life is a more significant determinant of future pathology than specific combinations of risk factors (Garmezy & Masten, 1994). For example, Williams et al. (1990) found that when children experienced fewer than two risk factors from a list similar to that just given, only 7 percent showed problem behaviour. Where children were subject to at least eight such risk factors, that figure rose to 40 percent. It has similarly been found that the likelihood of an ADHD diagnosis rose as a direct function of the number of family problem risk factors the child was subjected to (Biederman et al., 1995).

Intrinsic risk factors are equally likely to impact on the child's level of adaptive functioning. This is especially clear in a study of the effects of children's temperament and behaviour (Tschann et al., 1996). Children with difficult temperaments who lived in families characterized by adversity exhibited more internalizing and externalizing disorders than children who lived in families with a similar level of conflict, but who had easy temperaments.

The child's age or developmental level, and thus their intellectual and social-cognitive skills, are core developmental considerations in the assessment of risk. It has, for example, been proposed that older children generally cope with a first case of depression in their parents more effectively than younger children. This is likely to be due to older children's matured behavioural systems (Goodman & Gotlib, 1999) and their increased level of competency to effectively cope with the stress (Sroufe & Rutter, 1984). Contrariwise, it has been suggested that the very increase in complexity of thought and affect that is achieved in later childhood may cause an increased level of distress for the child, and therefore be associated with higher levels of psychopathology (Cicchetti & Toth, 1998).

It is also significant that children do not live in a one-way environment, and their behaviour may itself be a risk factor. Gerald Patterson (1996) has made the following notable observation: antisocial children are generally coercive and not very effective in dealing with others. This is, at least in part, a result of poor parental discipline and management of behaviour, however, the children's coercive style and poor social skills feed back into the risk process as provocation for negative parental behaviour, which in turn, intensifies the child's existing antisocial behaviour. Patterson's observation makes it clear that models of risk should consider how the complete dynamics of the environment and the individual interact to produce an effect. It is also evident from Patterson's work that we should be careful when making inferences about the causes and effects of behaviour; the determination of cause and effect in the development of psychopathology (or developmental psychology more generally) is a complex task.

Resilience

The term **resilience** basically refers to an individual's ability to rise above an adverse or stressful situation to function both competently and successfully (Rutter, 1990). A number of **protective factors** have been identified as contributing to the development of resilience in children. These have been grouped into three broad sets of factors by Garmezy (1985): *personality features* such as easy temperament and self-esteem, *family unity* and minimal family conflict, and lastly, the *presence of support networks*, such as the emotional availability of peers and elders in the community. However, the presence of such factors is not adequate to explain why certain children display resilience. Protective factors may not act in the same ways for all children, and they may be differentially significant at each stage of development. For example, the early primary years are considered to be a developmentally sensitive time (Meyer, 1957), when resilient children emerge from the stress of the new environment of school relatively intact. Rutter (1990) has therefore proposed that we look at **protective mechanisms**, which go beyond a simple list of factors to help us to understand how a child may become resilient. The first mechanism he has identified is *reduction of risk impact*, which applies to children who are buffered from a risky situation. For example, having a caring and trusted older sibling may lessen the negative impact of an emotionally unavailable and distanced parent. The second mechanism is *reduction of negative chain reactions*, and basically refers to ways in which a vicious cycle can be cut short. For example, a common ring of adversity involves poverty, living in an underprivileged area, the presence of deviant peers, and crime. However, identification with a positive peer group can prevent the link to crime. The third mechanism is the *fostering of self-esteem*, which helps children to feel like they can deal with their problems, and have the confidence to see that parts of their lives might not be okay, but they still are. The fourth and final mechanism is the *emergence of opportunities*. There are turning points in everyone's lives when it is important to take advantage of the opportunities at hand, such as the option to stay at school and receive a higher education, as opposed to dropping out and leaving oneself with fewer alternatives.

Another consideration identified by Rutter (1987) is the differential interaction of various risk and protective factors. For example, it has been found that shyness in boys is related to poor social interactions, and may thus be classed as a possible risk factor for problem behaviour. However, the same characteristic in girls is related to positive interactions with others, and consequently is more of a protective factor (Stevenson-Hinde & Hinde, 1986). Therefore, the ways in which children may be protected from, and at risk of, psychopathology are complex, and dependent on a number of interacting processes that do not necessarily have the same effect in isolation from each other.

Resilience is not an all-or-nothing concept covering every aspect of functioning; children may be protected from certain problems in one context, but not another. For example, children may function poorly at school, but nevertheless be successful in other situations, such as their interactions with peers (Cicchetti & Toth, 1998). This highlights the need in resilience research to make distinctions between functioning in a number of areas, such as behaviour at home, school, and peer relationships. A related point is that resilience is not a static concept. Just because an individual is resilient at one stage of their lives, does not mean they always will be. If the person's situations alters, so too does their protection from adversity (Rutter, 1987).

It has been documented that children who function well in the face of stressors often internalize their stress, in the form of depression and anxiety (Luthar, 1991). It thus appears that even resilient children do not completely escape the negative effects of their adversity, although they are able to inhibit outward expressions of disturbance. Ongoing support for resilient children is often required, and not limited to individuals who clearly display psychopathological tendencies. Indeed, it is possible that the *continued* availability of help for resilient children is a factor in whether they continue to display resiliency in later life. Such a life-span consideration is the kind of tangible benefit that a developmental perspective brings to the study of psychopathology.

In fact, it is largely due to the adoption of a developmental perspective on psychopathology that there is a growing increase in resilience research (Cicchetti & Toth, 1998). Knowledge about both normal and so-called abnormal development is enhanced by understanding how a child may be able to successfully adapt in an otherwise negative environment and allows for the application of 'resilience-promoting' factors to children's lives, helping to promote healthy developmental outcomes. In short, the study of resilient children is very important to *prevention* and *treatment* of psychopathology. By understanding what has prevented certain children from developing psychopathology in the past, it is possible to develop early intervention efforts to halt psychopathology in the future. Resilience factors may also be applied to the treatment of existing psychopathology, although the prognosis or outcome of such retrospective interventions is less certain.

Prevention and treatment

Prevention and treatment efforts differ according to the theoretical viewpoint that the clinician or therapist adheres to. For example, psychodynamic psychotherapists use techniques such as **play therapy** with children. Play therapy describes the process by which the therapist observes and interacts with the child in the context of play, interpreting fantasies and behaviour as an indication of stresses or problems the child may be experiencing. In contrast, the therapist guided by behaviourist-oriented beliefs uses techniques guided by the general principles of behaviour change, such as instructing parents to consistently reward desired behaviours by their child in order to shape the child's behaviour, getting them to display these behaviours more often. Finally, cognitive therapists look to internal or mental processes, rather than overt behaviour, as the focus of their interventions. Thus, the primary goal of cognitive therapy is to change the way that the child thinks about things. As a consequence, behavioural changes are predicted to follow.

Previously each of the techniques covered by the various models of psychopathology were argued by their respective proponents to be the best form of treatment. However, in recent years there has been a recognition of the strengths and weaknesses of each approach, and there has consequently been a more unified and sophisticated attempt to understand which kinds of therapy are most effective with whom and under what circumstances. Thus, many present day therapists use a combination of techniques borrowed from a number of theoretical positions to most effectively help a client. There is, however, an important distinction between interventions that are provided to treat already present psychopathology, as opposed to the *prevention* of psychopathology appearing in the first place.

Treatment obviously differs according to the disorder or problem that is the focus of intervention. For example, when treating depression, a combination of antidepressant drugs, correcting the child's negative thinking, and an increase in the chances of the child receiving positive reinforcement (such as praise from the parents) may all be employed (Mufson & Moreau, 1997). In contrast, when helping children with conduct disorder, a predominantly behavioural family intervention, where parents are trained in such areas as child management, problem solving, and family communication, may prove to be effective (Dadds, 1997).

It is important for the clinician to keep in mind the child's developmental level when considering treatment options. For example, it has been found that cognitive-behaviour therapy is more effective for 11–13 year old children, who are presumably more adept at thinking abstractly, than for younger children. It has been argued that younger children, in the preoperational and concrete operations stages of cognitive development, do not have the same level of cognitive sophistication which is needed to think about the premises of cognitive-behavioural therapy (Durlak, Fuhrman, & Lampman, 1991). Thus, simpler methods of treatment are needed for younger children. Regardless of the form of treatment, however, it has been found that the outcome for children who receive help is better than for control groups, or children with equivalent difficulties who do not receive treatment (Shapiro & Shapiro, 1982).

There are a number of general problems that may arise in the treatment of children under stress. Initial access to help may be a difficulty, as children don't usually present themselves for treatment, and rely on their parents or teachers to seek help, which does not always happen as quickly as it should. Family breakdowns may also make it difficult for the child to receive help, as the child's problem may fade into the background when the parents or caregivers are facing personal hardships of their own. Once treatment has actually been sought, there are a whole host of reasons why help is discontinued, and dropout from treatment is actually quite high. For example, dropout rates for children being treated with CD have been reported to be as high as 50 percent (Kazdin, 1990). Reasons for treatment termination include low expectations of treatment, limited skills of the therapist, personal factors like low family and peer support, and environmental factors, such as poverty and unavailability of nearby clinics or centres for treatment (Prinz & Miller, 1991).

Regardless of the type of intervention techniques used, there are a number of developmental considerations that may be useful to guide therapy and prevention efforts with children (Wenar & Kerig, 2000). First, an understanding of normal development is important for an accurate distinction between normal and pathological behaviour. Second, treatment and prevention programmes should be tailored to the child's cognitive, emotional, and social level of development, as we have already seen in the preceding chapters that the differences between a preschool- and school-aged child can be profound. Thus, a therapy which is effective at one age may not be quite so useful with children of an earlier or older age group. For example, limits on children's language abilities may restrict the usefulness of some types of therapy. Third, knowledge about the various developmental challenges a child of any given age may face can put their behaviour into context and make it more understandable. For example, seeing the conflict between a desire to be autonomous, and the constraints presented by their parents and their physical immaturity, can shed light on the cause and seriousness of a 2-year-old's temper tantrums. An understanding of key points in development can provide a guide to the best time for intervention. Thus, an adolescent just starting high school who is very much aware of the tasks of 'fitting in' and making friends in a new environment, may be vulnerable to the demands of an antisocial peer group and therefore a candidate for preventative interventions.

SUMMARY

As we have seen, the developmental psychopathology approach has made a number of important contributions to the study of abnormal development. Two key aspects of this approach are the emphasis on the study of normal development in relation to the treatment of psychopathology, and the conceptualization of development as taking place on a continuum from normal to abnormal. From our brief survey of this area, it is evident that the study of psychopathology in childhood poses some particularly difficult issues for the clinical psychologist.

Glossary

Anxiety refers to disorders which have an intense, maladaptive, and persistent fear that is beyond the individual's voluntary control.

Attention deficit/hyperactivity disorder (ADHD) involves the ongoing presence of inattention and/or hyperactivity–impulsivity that is both more frequent and more severe than is appropriate for the child's developmental level.

Autism is a rare disorder with a genetic basis which causes a disturbance in social interactions, problems with communication, repetitive or stereotyped behaviours, and has an early onset.

Child Behaviour Checklist (**CBCL**) is a parent-report measure of psychopathology for children and adolescents.

Clinical depression refers to an impairment of day-to-day functioning and/or the presence of significant distress, resulting in depressed mood, an obvious decrease in interest and pleasure, and a loss of appetite, all at the same time.

Comorbidity refers to the presence of two or more disorders at one time.

Developmental psychopathology is a discipline which takes a developmental approach to the study of psychopathology, focusing on the course, change and continuity in maladaptive behaviours.

Diagnostic and Statistical Manual of Mental Disorders (**DSM-IV**) is the most common and widely used method of diagnosing psychopathology.

Dysthmia is a chronic state of depression, characterized by a depressed mood and irritability, that lasts for at least one year.

Equifinality refers to the notion that there are many developmental pathways that can lead to the same outcome.

Etiology refers to the origins or cause of a disorder.

Externalizing disorders are a more outward or 'acting-out' form of distress and include aggression and delinquent behaviour.

Internalizing disorders refer to an inward suffering or distress and include disorders such as anxiety and depression.

Multifinality refers to the notion that a single developmental pathway can lead to multiple outcomes.

Play therapy describes a set of processes by which a therapist observes and interacts with the child in the context of play, using the child's expression of fantasies and behaviours as an indication of the stresses or problems the child may be experiencing.

Protective factors are factors or mechanisms that are identified as contributing to the development of resiliency in children.

Resilience refers to an individual's ability to rise above an adverse or stressful situation, maintaining competent and successful levels of functioning.

Risk or vulnerability factors are enduring characteristics of an individual's disposition or environment that are likely to lead to maladaptive and negative functioning; a risk factor is any factor that increases the chance of an individual developing a psychopathological condition.

Afterword

Having finished this text, you may find yourself reviewing the large amount of material you have covered and realizing that you have more questions about research in child development for which there are seemingly no answers provided. While this may disturb you, it is considered by many scholars a good thing to come away from a book or an article with more questions than when you started. Although I have tried to provide a review of some of the key areas in the study of child development, the field is far too vast to cover in more than a limited fashion in a book of this size. All that can be hoped is that you now have acquired a broad-based knowledge of the field which helps you to undertake more study in this area and to gain some further insights into both the questions you may have had when you originally undertook to read this book, and the more recent questions which may have developed as a function of entering into the study of child development.

It is also important to recognize that this book presents a somewhat static picture of a field that continues to follow its own developmental progression. Recently, the field of developmental psychology has seen the rise of a theoretical framework known as *developmental science* (Cairns, Elder, & Costello, 1996). Developmental science incorporates many of the insights generated by research into development and organizes them into an overarching framework which helps scientists to understand and find new ways to approach the complexity which is inherent in studying human development. Adherents of the developmental science framework advocate a strong emphasis on creating a deeper understanding of the processes and mechanisms which underlie the transition from infancy to adulthood. They also argue that an individual develops in a 'dynamic, continuous and reciprocal process of interaction with his or her environment' (Magnusson & Cairns, 1996: 13). The developmental science perspective is a life-span one – the study of development is not limited to infancy or childhood – and thus, follows the principles outlined by Baltes (1987). Within the developmental science framework there is also a recognition of the multidisciplinary nature of human development; that is, the study of human development goes beyond the confines of developmental psychology and branches into areas such as neurobiology, comparative psychology, sociology, and evolutionary biology (Magnusson & Cairns, 1996). The name *developmental science* follows directly on from this recognition of the multidisciplinary approach that must be taken if the complex questions that arise in the course of studying human development are to be answered and suggests that the study of development is itself, a new field of scientific inquiry which crosses traditional boundaries. The approach has already proven to be an extremely useful way of approaching research on human development.

The developmental science perspective is only the beginning of the evolution of research and theory in child development. It is highly likely that the field will undergo further transformations as developments in theoretical perspectives, new empirical findings, and methodological advances accumulate and reshape the field. Of course, to keep up with the transformations which are likely to occur, it is important that the beginning student has a strong foundation on which to construct an understanding of these new developments.

One of the many aims of this book is to help the student of child development identify and grasp the key issues and theoretical perspectives which represent how we understand child development. In Chapter 1, you were introduced to the field of life-span development, and exposed to the principles which underlie the thinking of developmental psychologists. After finishing this book, you should be able to point to many instances of the life-span approach in action across the diverse content areas represented in this text. For example, you should recognize that the study of childhood psychopathology embraces Baltes' (1987) principle that development is *multi-directional*; that is, there is more than one route that may lead to the development of an illness such as depression or an anxiety disorder. To take a rather different example, after finishing Chapter 4 on the biological foundations of development, you should recall that the development of the human brain is very *plastic*; that is, its organization can change in response to changed conditions. One final example: Baltes stresses the importance of *contexts* for human development. Having read this book, you should be able to point to a number of instances of the importance of context in children's development. For example, consider the research on the scaffolding of children's learning by adults discussed in Chapter 6, the role of friendships in children's social development discussed in Chapter 9, or the effects of environmental influences on the development of cognitive abilities discussed in Chapter 4. In short, you should now be able to articulate the principles of a life-span developmental approach and to provide examples of these from the various domains of development covered in this text.

Another aspect of Chapter 1 which 'sets the stage' for your reading of the remaining chapters of this text is the discussion of the central themes which have guided research and theorizing within the study of child development. As you will recall, these issues included: the question of whether development is best characterized as being *continuous* or *discontinuous*; the issue of whether development typically shows *stability* or *change* over time; the question of whether *early experiences* play a critical role in development; and finally, the debate over whether a particular aspect of development is best characterized as the result of *nature* or *nurture*.

By now these issues should be familiar to you. A key aspect of your learning about child development is to be able to both articulate these positions clearly and to highlight the importance of each. Moreover, you should also be able to say something about the current status of each issue within child development research. For example, in Chapter 1, we noted that it is rare for current researchers in child development to take an extreme position on either side; instead, virtually all developmentalists view the effects of nature and nurture on children's development as interacting and inseparable. Finally, in regard to these issues, you should be able to cite examples of each issue from the different developmental domains covered in Chapters 4–10.

Another important aspect of your own progress as someone studying child development is to be able to articulate the various theoretical positions which researchers have put forward over the years. You should know the functions of a theory; that is, why we have theories and how they work. Now, take a minute to recall the various theories of child development which you have read about in this text. Some of the major theories were described in Chapter 2. An important aim for your learning is to be able to describe the essence of each of the major theoretical positions on child development. For example, you should recognize that Bandura's *social learning theory* is a variant of the learning theories advocated by B.F. Skinner and J.B. Watson but emphasizes the importance of *modelling* and *imitation* as mechanisms for how children acquire new knowledge and skills. Others, such as the *developmental psychopathology* approach to the study of psychopathology (covered in Chapter 10) or *attachment theory* (covered in Chapter 8) were discussed with respect to a specific content area, such as the study of psychopathology or parent–child relationships. Finally, with specific regard to cognitive development, you should be able to articulate the key aspects of the cognitive developmental theories of Jean Piaget and Lev Vygotsky, and the more modern *information processing* theories, as well as comparing and contrasting each of these. Another goal of your learning should be to see if you can identify the theoretical position of any research which you might encounter in the media. If you can ascertain the theory which underlies a given piece of research reported on television or in the newspaper, it is likely that you have a good grasp of the theories described in this text.

I have one further suggestion for you which is sure to enhance your appreciation of the study of child development. Go out and watch some children for yourself. Try to find some time to sit in a park and watch a group of children at play, or look for an opportunity to observe a mother and infant as they interact, perhaps in a shopping mall or a cafe.

First of all, watching children will remind you of what we are interested in attempting to explain. Second, engaging in some careful observation will remind you why the study of children's development is so rewarding. Finally, you will have a chance to put to use some of what you have learned in an immediate and satisfying way. Hopefully, you will begin to see children in a way that you might not have previously. As I noted at the outset of this book, the study of child development is both extremely challenging and very enjoyable. After some intensive study, it is a good idea to remind yourself of this.

References

Achenbach, T., Howell, C.T., McConaughy, S.A., & Stanger, C. (1995). Six-year predictors of problems in a national sample of children and youths: I. Cross-informant syndromes. *Journal of the American Academy of Child and Adolescent Psychiatry*, *34*, 336–47.

Ackerman, B.P. (1981). Young children's understanding of a speaker's intentional use of a false utterance. *Developmental Psychology*, *17*, 472–80.

Acredolo, L.P., & Goodwyn, S.W. (1990). Sign language in babies: The significance of symbolic gesturing for understanding language development. In R. Vasta (ed.), *Annals of child development* (Vol. 7, pp. 1–42). Greenwich, CT: JAI Press.

Adamson, L.B. (1995). *Communication development during infancy*. Madison, WI: Brown & Benchmark.

Adler, T., & Furman, W. (1988). A model for children's relationships and relationship dysfunctions. In S.W. Duck (ed.), *Handbook of personal relationships: Theory, research and interventions* (pp. 211–28). London: Wiley.

Adolph, K.E., Eppler, M.A., & Gibson, E.J. (1993). Crawling versus walking infants' perception of affordances for locomotion over sloping surfaces. Special Section: Developmental biodynamics: Brain, body, behaviour connections. *Child Development*, *64*, 1158–74.

Ahmed, A., & Ruffman, T. (1998). Why do infants make A not B errors in a search task, yet show memory for the location of hidden objects in a nonsearch task? *Developmental Psychology*, *34*, 441–53.

Ainsworth, M.D. (1973). The development of infant–mother attachment. In B. Caldwell, & H. Ricciuti (eds.), *Review of child development research* (Vol. 3). Chicago: University of Chicago Press.

Ainsworth, M.D., Bell, S.M., & Stayton, D.J. (1974). Infant–mother attachment and social development: 'Socialization' as a product of reciprocal responsiveness to signals. In M.P.M. Richards (ed.), *The integration of a child into a social world* (pp. 91–135). Cambridge: Cambridge University Press.

Ainsworth, M.D., Blehar, M., Waters, E., & Wall, S. (1978). *Patterns of attachment*. Hillsdale, NJ: Erlbaum.

Allport, G.W. (1937). *Personality: A psychosocial interpretation*. New York: Holt.

American Psychiatric Association. (1994). *Diagnostic and statistical manual of mental disorders* (4th edn). Washington, DC: APA.

Amsterdam, B. (1972). Mirror self-image reactions before age two. *Developmental Psychology*, *5*, 297–305.

Anglin, J.M. (1993). Vocabulary development: A morphological analysis. *Monographs of the Society for Research in Child Development*, *58* (10, Serial No. 238).

Arterberry, M.E., Yonas, A., & Bensen, A.S. (1989). Self-produced locomotion and the development of responsiveness to linear perspective and texture gradients. *Developmental Psychology*, *25*, 976–82.

Asher, S.R., Parkhurst, J.T., Hymel, S., & Williams, G.A. (1990). Peer rejection and

loneliness in childhood. In S.R. Asher & J.D. Coie (eds.), *Peer rejection in childhood* (pp. 253–73). New York: Cambridge University Press.
Aslin, R.N. (1987). Visual and auditory development in infancy. In J.D. Osofsky (ed.), *Handbook of infant development* (2nd edn, pp. 5–97). New York: Wiley.
Aslin, R.N., Jusczyk, P.W., & Pisoni, D.B. (1998). Speech and auditory processing during infancy: Constraints on and precursors to language. In W. Damon (Gen. ed.), D. Kuhn, & R. Siegler (Vol. eds.), *Handbook of child psychology: Vol. 2. Cognition, perception and language* (pp. 147–98). New York: Wiley.
Astington, J.W. (1988). Children's understanding of the speech act of promising. *Journal of Child Language, 15*, 157–73.
Astington, J.W. (1994). *The child's discovery of the mind.* London: Fontana.
Astington, J.W., & Jenkins, J. (1995). Theory of mind development and social understanding. *Cognition & Emotion, 9*, 151–66.
Astington, J.W., Harris, P.L., & Olson, D.R. (1988). *Developing theories of mind.* New York: Cambridge University Press.
Atkinson, R.C., & Shiffrin, R.M. (1968). Human memory: A proposed system and its control processes. In K.W. Spence, & J.T. Spence (eds.), *Advances in the psychology of learning and motivation* (Vol. 2, pp. 90–195). New York: Academic Press.
Atkinson, R.C., & Shiffrin, R.M. (1971). The control of short-term memory. *Scientific American, 225*, 82–90.
Austin, J.L. (1962). *How to do things with words.* Oxford: Oxford University Press.
Azmitia, M. (1988). Peer interaction and problem solving: When are two heads better than one? *Child Development, 59*, 87–96.
Bailey, A., Phillips, W., & Rutter, M. (1996). Autism: Towards an integration of clinical, genetic, neuropsychological, and neurobiological perspectives. *Journal of Child Psychology and Psychiatry and Allied Disciplines, 37*, 89–126.
Baillargeon, R. (1987). Object permanence in 3½- and 4½-month-old infants. *Developmental Psychology, 23*, 655–64.
Baillargeon, R. (1991). Reasoning about the height and location of a hidden object in 4.5- and 6.5-month-old infants. *Cognition, 38*, 13–42.
Baillargeon, R., & Graber, M. (1988). Evidence of location memory in 8-month-old infants in a nonsearch AB task. *Developmental Psychology, 24*, 502–11.
Baillargeon, R., DeVos, J., & Graber, M. (1989). Location memory in 8-month-old infants in a non-search AB task: Further evidence. *Cognitive Development, 4*, 345–67.
Bakeman, R., & Gottman, J.M. (1997). *Observing interaction: An introduction to sequential analysis* (2nd edn). New York: Cambridge University Press.
Baltes, P.B. (1987). Theoretical propositions of life span developmental psychology: On the dynamics between growth and decline. *Developmental Psychology, 23*, 611–26.
Baltes, P.B., Reese, H.W., & Lipsitt, L.P. (1980). Life-span developmental psychology. *Annual Review of Psychology, 31*, 65–110.
Band, E.B., & Weisz, J.R. (1988). How to feel better when it feels bad: Children's perspectives on coping with everyday stress. *Developmental Psychology, 24*, 247–53.
Bandura, A. (1977). *Social learning theory.* Englewood Cliffs, NJ: Prentice-Hall.
Bandura, A. (1989). Social cognitive theory. In R. Vasta (ed.), *Annals of child development: Six theories of child development* (Vol. 6, pp. 1–60). Greenwich, CT: JAI Press.
Bandura, A. (1992). Perceived self-efficacy in cognitive development and functioning. *Educational Psychologist, 28*, 117–48.

Bandura, A., & Walters, R.H. (1963). *Social learning and personality development.* New York: Holt, Rinehart & Winston.

Banks, M.S., & Ginsburg, A.P. (1985). Early visual preferences: A review and new theoretical treatment. In H.W. Reese (ed.), *Advances in child development and behaviour* (Vol. 19, pp. 207–46). New York: Academic Press.

Banks, M.S., & Salapatek, P. (1983). Infant visual perception. In M.M. Haith, & J.J. Campos (eds.), *Handbook of child psychology: Vol. 2. Infancy and developmental psychobiology* (pp. 435–571). New York: Wiley.

Barkow, J.H., Cosmides, L., & Tooby, J. (1992). *The adapted mind: Evolutionary psychology and the generation of culture.* Oxford: Oxford University Press.

Baron-Cohen, S. (1995) *Mindblindness: An essay on autism and theory of mind.* Cambridge, MA: MIT Press.

Baron-Cohen, S., Ring, H., Moriarty, J., Schmitz, B., Costa, D., & Ell, P. (1994). The brain basis of theory of mind: the role of the orbito-frontal region. *British Journal of Psychiatry, 165*, 640–49.

Barrett, K.C. (1997). The self and relationship development. In S. Duck (ed.), *Handbook of personal relationships.* New York: Wiley.

Barrett, K.C., & Campos, J.J. (1987). Perspectives on emotional development II: A functionalist approach to emotions. In J.D. Osofsky (ed.), *Handbook of infant development* (2nd ed., pp. 83–108). New York: Routledge.

Bartsch, K., & Wellman, H. (1989). Young children's attribution of action to beliefs and desires. *Child Development, 60*, 946–64.

Bartsch, K., & Wellman, H. (1995). *Children talk about the mind.* New York: Oxford University Press.

Bates, E. (1976). *Language and context: The acquisition of pragmatics.* New York: Academic Press.

Bates, E., & MacWhinney, B. (1989). Functionalism and the competition model. In B. MacWhinney & E. Bates (eds.), *The cross-linguistic study of sentence processing.* New York: Cambridge University Press.

Bates, J.E. (1989). Applications of temperament concepts. In G.A. Kohnstamm, J.E. Bates, & M.K. Rothbart (eds.), *Temperament in childhood* (pp. 321–55). New York: Wiley.

Bayley, N. (1969). *Bayley scales of infant development.* New York: Psychological Corporation.

Beal, C.R., & Flavell, J.H. (1984). Development of the ability to distinguish communicative intention and literal message meaning. *Child Development, 55*, 60–70.

Beilin, H. (1978). Inducing conservation through training. In G. Steiner (ed.), *Psychology of the twentieth century* (Vol. 7, pp. 260–89). Munich: Kindler.

Beilin, H. (1992). Piaget's enduring contribution to developmental psychology. *Developmental Psychology, 28*, 191–204.

Belsky, J., Steinberg, L., & Draper, P. (1991). Childhood experience, interpersonal development, and reproductive strategy: An evolutionary theory of socialization. *Child Development, 62*, 647–70.

Berk, L.E. (1992). Children's private speech: An overview of theory and the status of research. In R.M. Diaz, & L.E. Berk (eds.), *Private speech: From social interaction to self-regulation* (pp. 17–53). Hillsdale, NJ: Erlbaum.

Berk, L.E., & Spuhl, S.T. (1995). Maternal interaction, private speech, and task performance in preschool children. *Early Childhood Research Quarterly, 10*, 145–69.

Berndt, T.J. (1981). Relations between social cognition, nonsocial cognition, and social behaviour: The case of friendship. In J.H. Flavell, & L. Ross (eds.), *Social cognitive development* (pp. 176–99). Cambridge: Cambridge University Press.

Berndt, T.J. (1988). The nature and significance of children's friendships. In R. Vasta (ed.), *Annals of child development* (Vol. 5, pp. 155–86). Greenwich, CT: JAI Press.

Berndt, T.J., Hawkins, J.A., & Hoyle, S.G. (1986). Changes in friendship during a school year: Effects on children's and adolescents' impression of friendship and sharing with friends. *Child Development, 57,* 1284–97.

Bertalanffy, L. von (1968). *General systems theory*. New York: Braziller.

Bertenthal B.I., & Campos, J.J. (1987). New directions in the study of early experience. *Child Development, 58,* 560–67.

Bertenthal, B.I., & Clifton, R.K. (1998). Perception and action. In W. Damon (Gen. ed.), D. Kuhn, & R. Siegler (Vol. eds.), *Handbook of child psychology: Vol. 2. Cognition, perception and language* (pp. 51–102). New York: Wiley.

Bertenthal, B.I., Campos, J.J., & Kermonian, R. (1994). An epigenetic perspective on the development of self-produced locomotion and its consequences. *Current Directions in Psychological Science, 3,* 140–45.

Bertenthal, B.I., Profitt, D.R., & Kramer S.J. (1987). The perception of biomechanical motions. Implementation of various processing constraints. *Journal of Experimental Psychology. Human Perception and Performance, 13,* 577–85.

Best, C.T. (1988). The emergence of cerebral asymmetries in early human development: A model. In D.L. Molfese, & S.J. Segalowitz (eds.) *Brain lateralization in children* (pp. 5–35). New York: Guilford Press.

Biben, M., & Suomi, S. (1993). Lessons from primate play. In K. MacDonald (ed.), *Parent–child play: Descriptions and implications* (pp. 185–196). Albany, NY: State University of New York Press.

Biederman, J., Milberger, S., Faraone, S., and Kiely, K. (1995). Family–environment risk factors for attention-deficit hyperactivity disorder. *Archives of General Psychiatry, 52,* 464–70.

Bijeljac-Babic, R., Bertoncini, J., & Mehler, J. (1993). How do 4-day-old infants categorize multisyllable utterances? *Developmental Psychology, 29,* 711–21.

Birch, E.E. (1993). Stereopsis in infants and its developmental relation to visual acuity. In K. Simons (ed.), *Early visual development: Normal and abnormal* (pp. 224–36). New York: Oxford University Press.

Blass, E.M., & Ciaramitaro, V. (1994). A new look at some old mechanisms in human newborns: Taste and tactile determinants of state, affect, and action. *Monographs of the Society for Research in Child Development, 59* (1, Serial No. 239).

Block, N. (1995). How heritability misleads about race. In A. Montagu (ed.), *Race & IQ: Expanded edition* (pp. 444–86). New York: Oxford University Press.

Bloom, L. (1998). Language acquisition in its developmental context. In W. Damon (Gen. ed.), D. Kuhn, & R. S. Siegler (Vol. eds.), *Handbook of child psychology: Vol. 2. Cognition, perception, and language* (5th ed., pp. 309–71). New York: Wiley.

Bohannon, J.N. III (1993). Theoretical approaches to language acquisition. In J. Berko Gleason (ed.), *The development of language* (pp. 239–97). New York: Macmillan.

Bohannon, J.N. III, & Stanowicz, L. (1988). The issue of negative evidence: Adult responses to children's language errors. *Developmental Psychology, 24,* 684–9.

Bonitatibus, G. (1988). Comprehension monitoring and the apprehension of literal meaning. *Child Development, 59,* 60–70.

Borke, H. (1971). Interpersonal perception of young children: Egocentrism or empathy? *Developmental Psychology, 5*, 263–9.

Borke, H. (1975). Piaget's mountains revisited: Changes in the egocentric landscape. *Developmental Psychology, 11*, 240–43.

Bornstein, M.H. (1989). Sensitive periods in development: Structural characteristics and causal interpretations. *Psychological Bulletin, 105*, 179–97.

Bornstein, M.H., & Arterberry, M.E. (1999). Perceptual development. In M.H. Bornstein, & M.E. Lamb (eds.), *Developmental psychology: An advanced textbook* (4th ed., pp. 231–74). Mahwah, NJ: Erlbaum.

Bouchard, C. (1994). *The genetics of obesity*. Boca Raton, FL: CRC Press.

Bouchard, T.J., Jr., & McGue, M. (1981). Familial studies of intelligence: A review. *Science, 212*, 1055–58.

Bower, T.G.R. (1982). *Development in infancy*. New York: W.H. Freeman.

Bowlby, J. (1958). The nature of the child's tie to his mother. *International Journal of Psychoanalysis, 39*, 350–73.

Bowlby, J. (1960). Grief and mourning in infancy and early childhood. *The Psychoanalytic Study of the Child, 15*.

Bowlby, J. (1969). *Attachment and loss: Vol. 1. Attachment.* New York: Basic Books.

Bowlby, J. (1973). *Separation and loss*. New York: Basic Books.

Brainerd, C.J. (1978). The stage question in cognitive developmental theory. *Behavioural and Brain Sciences, 1*, 173–213.

Bremner, J.G. (1994). *Infancy* (2nd ed.). Oxford: Blackwell.

Broadbent, D. (1984). The Maltese cross: A new simplistic model for memory. *Behavioural and Brain Sciences, 7*, 55–94.

Bronfenbrenner, U. (1972). The roots of alienation. In U. Bronfenbrenner (ed.) *Influences on human development.* Hinsdale, IL: Dryden.

Bronfenbrenner, U. (1974). Developmental research, public policy, and the ecology of childhood. *Child Development, 45*, 1–5.

Bronfenbrenner, U. (1979). *The ecology of human development: Experiments by nature and by design.* Cambridge, MA: Harvard University Press.

Bronfenbrenner, U. (1989). Ecological systems theory. In R. Vasta (ed.), *Annals of child development* (Vol. 6, pp. 187–251). Greenwich, CT: JAI Press.

Bronfenbrenner, U., & Crouter, A.C. (1983). The evolution of environmental models in developmental research. In P.H. Mussen (Series ed.), & W. Kessen (Vol. ed.), *Handbook of child psychology: Vol. 1 History, theory, and methods* (pp. 357–414). New York: Wiley.

Bronfenbrenner, U., & Morris, P. (1998). The ecology of developmental processes. In W. Damon (Gen. ed.), & R.M. Lerner (Vol. ed.), *Handbook of child psychology: Vol. 1. Theoretical models of human development* (5th ed., pp. 993–1028). New York: Wiley.

Brooks-Gunn, J. (1988a). The impact of puberty and sexual activity upon the health and education of adolescent girls and boys. *Peabody Journal of Education, 64*, 88–113.

Brooks-Gunn, J. (1988b). Antecedents and consequences of variations in girls' maturational timing. *Journal of Adolescent Health Care, 9*, 365–73.

Brown, A.L., & Palinscar, A.S. (1982). Inducing strategic learning from texts by means of informed, self-control training. *Topics in Learning and Learning Disabilities, 2*, 1–17.

Brown, R. (1973). *A first language: The early stages.* Cambridge, MA: Harvard University Press.

Brown, R., & Hanlon, C. (1970). Derivational complexity and order of acquisition in child speech. In J.R. Hayes (ed.), *Cognition and the development of language* (pp. 11–53). New York: Wiley.

Bruner, J. (1983). *Child's talk: Learning to use language.* Oxford: Oxford University Press.

Bryant, P.E., & Trabasso, T. (1971). Transitive inferences and memory in young children. *Nature, 232,* 456–8.

Bühler, C. (1930). *The first year of life.* (P. Greenberg & R. Riben, Trans.). New York: John Day.

Bühler, C. (1935). *From birth to maturity: An outline of the psychological development of the child.* London: Routledge & Kegan Paul.

Buhrmester, D. (1996). Need fulfillment, interpersonal competence, and the developmental contexts of friendship. In W.M. Bukowski, A.F. Newcomb, & W.W. Hartup (eds.), *The company they keep: Friendship during childhood and adolescence* (pp. 158–85). New York: Cambridge University Press.

Bushnell, E.W. (1985). The decline of visually guided reaching during infancy. *Infant Behaviour and Development, 8,* 139–55.

Buss, A.H., & Plomin, R. (1975). *A temperament theory of personality development.* New York: Wiley.

Buss, D.M. (1995). Evolutionary psychology: A new paradigm for psychological science. *Psychological Inquiry, 6,* 1–30.

Cairns, R.B., Elder, G.H., & Costello, E.J. (1996). *Developmental science.* Cambridge: Cambridge University Press.

Campbell, D.T., & Stanley, J.C. (1963). *Experimental and quasi-experimental designs for research.* Chicago: Rand McNally.

Campos, J.J., & Bertenthal, B.I. (1989). Locomotion and psychological development in infancy. In F. Morrisson, C. Lord, & D. Keating (eds.), *Applied developmental psychology* (Vol. 3, pp. 229–58). New York: Academic Press.

Campos, J.J., Barrett, K.C., Lamb, M.E., Goldsmith, H.A., & Stenberg, C. (1983). Socioemotional development. In P.H. Mussen (Series ed.), M.M. Haith, & J.J. Campos (Vol. eds.), *Handbook of child psychology: Infancy and developmental psychobiology* (4th ed., pp. 783–915). New York: Wiley.

Campos, J.J., Bertenthal, B., & Kermonian, R. (1992). Early experience and emotional development: The emergence of wariness of heights. *Psychological Science, 3,* 61–4.

Campos, J.J., Langer, A., & Krowitz, A. (1970). Cardiac responses on the visual cliff in prelocomotor human infants. *Science, 170,* 196–7.

Camras, L.A. (1994). Two aspects of emotional development: Expression and elicitation. In P. Ekman, & R.J. Davidson (eds.), *The nature of emotion: Fundamental questions* (pp. 347–51). New York: Oxford University Press.

Camras, L.A., Malatesta, C., & Izard, C. (1991). The development of facial expressions in infancy. In R. Feldman, & B. Rime (eds.), *Fundamentals of nonverbal behaviour.* New York: Cambridge University Press.

Camras, L.A., Oster, H., Campos, J.J., Miyake, K., & Bradshaw, D. (1992). Japanese and American infants' responses to arm restraint. *Developmental Psychology, 28,* 578–83.

Cantwell, D.P. (1996). Classification of child and adolescent psychopathology. *Journal of Child Psychology and Psychiatry and Allied Disciplines, 37,* 3–12.

Capage, L., & Watson, A.C. (in press). Individual differences in theory of mind, aggressive behaviour, and social skills in young children. *Early Education and Development.*

Carey, S. (1978). The child as word learner. In M. Halle, G. Miller, & J. Bresnan (eds.), *Linguistic theory and psychological reality* (pp. 264–93). Cambridge, MA: MIT Press.
Carey, S. (1985). *Conceptual change in childhood.* Cambridge, MA: Bradford/MIT Press.
Carey, S. (1996). Perceptual classification and expertise. In R, Gelman, & T. Kit-Fong Au (eds.), *Perceptual and cognitive development* (pp. 49–69). New York: Academic Press.
Carlson, V., Cicchetti, D., Barnett, D., & Braunwald, K. (1989). Disorganized/disoriented attachment relationships in maltreated infants. *Developmental Psychology, 25,* 525–31.
Caron, A.J., Caron, R.F., & MacLean, D.J. (1988). Infant discrimination of naturalistic emotional expressions: The role of face and voice. *Child Development, 59,* 603–16.
Carpendale, J., & Chandler, M. (1996). On the distinction between false belief understanding and subscribing to an interpretative theory of mind. *Child Development, 67,* 1686–706.
Case, R. (1985). *Intellectual development: A systematic reinterpretation.* New York: Academic Press.
Case, R. (1992a). Neo-Piagetian theories of child development. In R.J. Sternberg, & C.A. Berg (eds.), *Intellectual development* (pp. 161–96). New York: Cambridge University Press.
Case, R. (1992b). *The mind's staircase.* Hillsdale, NJ: Erlbaum.
Case, R. (1992c). The role of the frontal lobes in the regulation of cognitive development. *Brain and Cognition, 20,* 51–73.
Case, R., & Griffin, S. (1990). Child cognitive development: The role of central conceptual structures in the development of scientific and social thought. In C.A. Hauert (ed.), *Developmental psychology: Cognitive, perceptuo-motor and neuropsychological perspectives* (pp. 193–230). Amsterdam: North Holland.
Caspi, A., & Moffit, T.E. (1991). Individual differences are accentuated during periods of social change: The sample case of girls at puberty. *Journal of Personality and Social Psychology, 61,* 157–68.
Caspi, A., & Silva, P.A. (1995). Temperamental qualities at age three predict personality traits in young adulthood: Longitudinal evidence from a birth cohort. *Child Development, 66,* 486–98.
Cassidy, J. (1994). Emotion regulation: Influences of attachment relationships. *Monographs of the Society for Research in Child Development, 59* (Serial No. 2–3), 228–83.
Cassidy, J., & Berlin, L.J. (1994). The insecure/ambivalent pattern of attachment: Theory and research. *Child Development, 65,* 971–91.
Cernoch, J.M., & Porter, R.H. (1985). Recognition of maternal axillary odors by infants. *Child Development, 56,* 1593–98.
Chase-Lansdale, P.L., Mott, F.L., Brooks-Gunn, J., & Phillips, D.A. (1991). Children of the national longitudinal survey of youth: A unique research opportunity. *Developmental Psychology, 27,* pp. 918–31.
Chomsky, N. (1957). *Syntactic structures.* The Hague: Mouton.
Chomsky, N. (1959). Review of B.F. Skinner's *Verbal Behavior. Language, 35,* 26–129.
Chomsky, N. (1968). *Language and mind.* New York: Harcourt Brace & World.
Chorney, M.J., Chorney, K., Seese, N., Owen, M.J., Daniels, J., McGuffin, P., Thompson, L.A., Detterman, D.K., Benbow, C., Lubinski, D., Eley, T., & Plomin, R. (1998). A quantitative trait locus associated with cognitive ability in children. *Psychological Science, 9,* 159–66.
Cicchetti, D. (1990). An historical perspective on the discipline of developmental

psychopathology. In J. Rolf, A. Masten, D. Cicchetti, K. Nuechterlain, & S. Weintraub (eds.), *Risk and protective factors in the development of psychopathology* (pp. 2–28). New York: Cambridge University Press.

Cicchetti, D. (1993). Developmental psychopathology: Reactions, reflections, projections. *Developmental Review, 13*, 471–502.

Cicchetti, D., & Rogosch, F. (1996). Equifinality and multifinality in developmental psychopathology. *Development and Psychopathology, 8*, 597–600.

Cicchetti, D., & Toth, S.L. (1998). The development of depression in children and adolescents. *American Psychologist, 53*, 221–41.

Clifton, R.K., Perris, E., & Bullinger, A. (1991). Infants' perception of auditory space. *Developmental Psychology, 27*, 161–71.

Clifton, R.K., Rochat, P., Robin, D.J., & Berthier, N.E. (1994). Multimodal perception in the control of infant reaching. *Journal of Experimental Psychology: Human Perception and Performance, 20*, 876–86.

Cohen, L.B., & Salapatek, P. (1975). *Infant perception: From sensation to cognition*. New York: Academic Press.

Coie, J.D., & Dodge, K.A. (1983). Continuities and changes in children's social status: A five-year longitudinal study. *Merrill-Palmer Quarterly, 29*, 261–82.

Cole, M. (1985). The zone of proximal development: Where culture and cognition create each other. In J.V. Wertsch (ed.), *Culture, communication, and cognition: Vygotskian perspectives* (pp. 146–61). Cambridge: Cambridge University Press.

Conti, D., & Camras, L. (1984). Children's understanding of conversational principals. *Journal of Experimental Child Psychology, 38*, 456–63.

Cooper, R.P., & Aslin, R.N. (1990). Preference for infant-directed speech in the first month after birth. *Child Development, 61*, 1584–95.

Courage, M.L., & Adams, R.J. (1990). Visual acuity assessment from birth to three years using the acuity card procedures: Cross-longitudinal samples. *Optometry and Vision Science, 67*, 713–18.

Crain, W. (2000). *Theories of development: Concepts and applications*. Upper Saddle River, NJ: Prentice Hall.

Crockenberg, S. (1986). Are temperamental differences in babies associated with predictable differences in care-giving? In J.V. Lerner, & R.M. Lerner (eds.), *Temperament and social interaction in infants and children* (pp. 53–74). San Francisco: Jossey-Bass.

Crook, C. (1987). Taste and olfaction. In P. Salapatek & L. Cohen (eds.), *Handbook of infant perception. Vol. 1. From sensation to perception* (pp. 237–64). Orlando, FL: Academic Press.

Crook, C.K., & Lipsitt, L.P. (1976). Neonatal nutritive sucking: Effects of taste stimulation upon sucking rhythm and heart rate. *Child Development, 47*, 518–22.

Dadds, M.R. (1997). Conduct disorder. In R. Ammerman, & M. Hersen (eds.), *Handbook of prevention and treatment with children and adolescence* (pp. 521–50). New York: Wiley.

Damon, W. (1977). *The social world of the child*. San Francisco: Jossey-Bass.

Damon, W., & Hart, D. (1992). Self-understanding and its role in social and moral development. In M.H. Bornstein, & M.E. Lamb (eds.), *Developmental Psychology: An advanted textbook* (3rd ed., pp. 421–64). Hillsdale, NJ: Erlbaum.

Dannemiller, J.L., & Stephens, B.R. (1988). A critical test of infant pattern preference models. *Child Development, 59*, 210–16.

Davidson, R.J. (1994a). Asymmetric brain function, affective style, and psychopathology: The role of early experience and plasticity. *Development and Psychopathology*, *6*, 741–58.
Davidson, R.J. (1994b). Temperament, affective style, and frontal lobe asymmetry. In G. Dawson, & K.W. Fischer (eds.), *Human behaviour and the developing brain*. New York: Guilford Press.
DeCasper, A.J., & Spence, M.J. (1986). Prenatal maternal speech influences newborns' perception of speech sounds. *Infant Behaviour & Development*, *9*, 133–50.
DeFries, J.C., Plomin, R., & Fulker, D.W. (1994). *Nature and nurture during middle childhood*. Cambridge, MA: Blackwell.
Dellarosa Cummins, D., & Cummins, R. (1999). Biological preparedness and evolutionary explanation. *Cognition*, *73*, 37–53.
Demorest, A., Silberstein, L., Gardner, H., & Winner, E. (1983). Telling it as it isn't: Children's understanding of figurative language. *British Journal of Developmental Psychology*, *1*, 121–34.
deVilliers, P.A., & deVilliers, J.G. (1979). *Early language*. Cambridge, MA: Harvard University Press.
deVilliers, P.A., & deVilliers, J.G. (1992). Language development. In M. Bornstein, & M. Lamb (eds.), *Developmental psychology: An advanced textbook* (3rd ed., pp. 337–418). Hillsdale, NJ: Erlbaum.
Dixon, R.A., & Lerner, R.M. (1998). History and systems in developmental psychology. In M. Bornstein & M. Lamb (eds.), *Developmental psychology: An advanced textbook* (4th ed., pp. 3–46). Mahwah, NJ: Erlbaum.
Donaldson, M. (1978). *Children's minds*. New York. W.W. Norton.
Dubow, E. Roecker, C., & D'Imperio, R. (1997). Mental health. In R. Ammerman, & M. Hersen (eds.), *Handbook of prevention and treatment with children and adolescents: Interventions in the real world context* (pp. 259–86). New York: Wiley.
Dunn, J. (1988). *The beginnings of social understanding*. Cambridge, MA: Harvard University Press.
Dunn, J., Brown, J., Slomkowski, C., Tesla, C., & Youngblade, L. (1991). Young children's understanding of other people's feelings and beliefs: Individual differences and their antecedents. *Child Development*, *62*, 1352–66.
Dunphy, D.C. (1963). The social structure of urban adolescent peer groups. *Sociometry*, *26*, 230–46.
Durlak, J.A., Fuhrman, P., & Lampman, C. (1991). Effectiveness of cognitive-behaviour therapy for maladapting children: A meta-analysis. *Psychological Bulletin*, *110*, 204–14.
Eckerman, C.O. (1993). Imitation and toddlers' achievement of coordinated action with others. In J. Nadel, & L. Camaioni (eds.), *New perspectives in early communicative development* (pp. 116–56). New York: Routledge.
Eisenberg, N., Fabes, R.A., Guthrie, I.K., & Murphy, B.C. (1996). The relations of regulation and emotionality to problem behaviour in elementary school children. *Development & Psychopathology*, *8*, 141–62.
Eisenberg, N., & Fabes, R.A. (1998). Prosocial development. In W. Damon (Gen. ed.), & N. Eisenberg (Vol. ed.), *Handbook of Child Psychology. Vol. 3. Social, emotional and personality development* (5th ed., pp. 701–78). New York: Wiley.
Elder, G.H. (1974). *Children of the great depression*. Chicago: University of Chicago Press.
Elder, G.H. (1995). Human lives in changing societies: Life course and developmental

insights. In R.B. Cairns, G.H. Elder, & E.J. Costello (eds.), *Developmental science: Multidisciplinary perspectives*. New York: Cambridge University Press.

Elder, G.H. (1998). The life course and human development. In W. Damon (Gen. ed.), & R.M. Lerner (Vol. ed.), *Handbook of child psychology: Vol. 1. Theoretical models of human development* (5th ed., pp. 939–91). New York: Wiley.

Elkind, D. (1967). Egocentrism in adolescence. *Child Development, 38*, 1025–34.

Elkind, D., & Bowen, R. (1979). Imaginary audience behavior in children and adolescents. *Developmental Psychology, 15*, 33–44.

Ellis, B.J., McFayden-Ketchum, S., Dodge, K.A., Petit, G.S., & Bates, J.E. (1999). Quality of early family relationships and individual differences in the timing of pubertal maturation in girls: A longitudinal test of an evolutionary model. *Child Development, 77*, 387–401.

Ellis, S., Rogoff, B., & Cromer, C. (1981). Age segregation in children's social interactions. *Developmental Psychology, 17*, 399–407.

Ellsworth, C.P., Muir, D.W., & Hains, S.M.J. (1993). Social competence and person-object differentiation. An analysis of the still face effect. *Developmental Psychology, 29*, 63–73.

Elman, J.L., Bates, E.A., Johnson, M.J., Karmiloff-Smith, A., Parisi, D., & Plunkett, K. (1996). *Rethinking innateness: A connectionist perspective on development.* Cambridge, MA: Bradford/MIT Press.

Emde, R.N., Gaensbauer, T.J., & Harmon, R.J. (1976). Emotional expression in infancy: A biobehavioural study. *Psychological Issues* (Vol. 10, No. 37). New York: International University Press.

Emde, R.N., Plomin, R., Robinson, J., Corley, R., DeFries, J., Fulker, D.W., Reznick, J.S., Campos, J., Kagan, J., & Zahn-Waxler, C. (1992). Temperament, emotion, and cognition at fourteen months: The MacArthur longitudinal twin study. *Child Development, 63*, 1437–55.

Erikson, E.H. (1963). *Childhood and society* (2nd ed.). New York: W.W. Norton.

Ervin-Tripp, S. (1979). Children's verbal turn-taking. In E. Ochs, & B. Schieffelin (eds.), *Developmental pragmatics* (pp. 391–414). New York: Academic Press.

Fantz, R.L. (1961). The origin of form perception. *Scientific American, 204*, 66–72.

Fantz, R.L. (1966). Pattern discrimination and selective attention as determinants of perceptual development from birth. In A.H. Kidd, & J.L. Rivoire (eds.), *Perceptual development in children.* New York: International University Press.

Farrington, D.P. (1991). Childhood aggression and adult violence: Early precursors and later life outcomes. In D.J. Pepler, & K.H. Rubin (eds.), *The development and treatment of childhood aggression* (pp. 5–29). Hillsdale, NJ: Erlbaum.

Fenson, L., Dale, P.S., Reznick, J.S., Bates, E., Thal, D.J., & Pethick, S.J. (1994). Variability in early communicative development. *Monographs of the Society for Research in Child Development, 59* (5, Serial No. 242).

Fernald, A. (1985). Four-month-old infants prefer to listen to motherese. *Infant Behaviour and Development, 8*, 181–95.

Fernald. A., & Kuhl, P. (1987). Acoustical determinants of infant preference for motherese speech. *Infant Behaviour and Development, 10*, 279–93.

Field, T.M. (1990). *Infancy.* Cambridge, MA: Harvard University Press.

Fischer, K.W. & Rose, S.P. (1994). Dynamic development of coordination of components in brain and behaviour: A framework for theory and research. In G.

Dawson, & K.W. Fischer (eds.), *Human behaviour and the developing brain* (pp. 3–66). New York: Guilford.

Fischer, K.W., & Rose, S.P. (1995). Concurrent cycles in the dynamic development of brain and behaviour. *SRCD Newsletter*, pp. 3–4, 15–16.

Flavell, J.H. (1985). *Cognitive development* (2nd ed.). Englewood Cliffs, NJ: Prentice-Hall.

Flavell, J.H., & Miller, P.H. (1998) Social cognition. In D. Kuhn, & R.S. Siegler (eds.), *Handbook of Child Psychology: Vol. 2. Cognition, perception, and language* (5th ed., pp. 851–888). New York: Wiley.

Fogel, A. (1993). *Developing through relationships: Origins of communication, self, and culture.* Chicago: University of Chicago Press.

Fox, N.A., Calkins, S.D., & Bell, M.A. (1994). Neural plasticity and development in the first two years of life: Evidence from cognitive and socioemotional domains. *Development and Psychopathology*, *6*, 677–96.

French, D.C. (1988). Heterogeneity of peer rejected boys: Aggressive and nonaggressive subtypes. *Child Development*, *59*, 976–85.

French, D.C. (1990). Heterogeneity of peer rejected girls. *Child Development*, *61*, 2028–31.

Freud, S. (1917). *A general introduction to psychoanalysis.* New York: Washington Square Press.

Frith, U., & Happé, F. (1999). Theory of mind and self-consciousness: What is it like to be autistic? *Mind and Language*, *14*, 1–22.

Frodi, A.M., & Lamb, M. (1978). Sex differences in responsiveness to infants: A developmental study of psychophysiological and behavioural responses. *Child Development*, *49*, 1182–88.

Gallahue, D.L. (1989). *Understanding motor development* (2nd ed.). Carmel, IN: Benchmark.

Gardner, H. (1973). *The quest for mind: Piaget, Lévi-Strauss, and the structuralist movement.* Chicago: University of Chicago Press.

Garmezy, N. (1985). Stress-resistant children: the search for protective factors. In J.E. Stevenson (ed.), Recent research in developmental psychopathology: *Journal of Child Psychology and Psychiatry Book Supplement 4* (pp. 213–33). Oxford: Pergamon Press.

Garmezy, N., & Masten, A.S. (1994). Chronic adversities. In M. Rutter, E. Taylor, & L. Hersov (eds.), *Child and adolescent psychiatry: Modern approaches* (3rd ed., pp. 191–208). London: Blackwell.

Garvey, C. (1974). Requests and responses in children's speech. *Journal of Child Language*, *2*, 41–60.

Geary, D.C., & Bjorkland, D.F. (2000). Evolutionary developmental psychology. *Child Development*, *71*, 57–65.

Gesell, A.L. (1928). *Infancy and human growth.* New York: Macmillan.

Gesell, A., & Thompson, H. (1929). Learning and growth in identical infant twins: An experimental study by the method of co-twin control. *Genetic Psychology Monographs*, *6*, 1–24.

Gibson, E.J. (1969). *Principles of perceptual learning and development.* New York: Appleton.

Gibson, E.J., & Walk, R.D. (1960). The 'visual cliff'. *Scientific American*, *202*, 64–71.

Gibson, E.J., & Walker, A.S. (1984). Development of knowledge of visual-tactual affordances of substance. *Child Development*, *55*, 453–60.

Gibson, J.J. (1979). *The ecological approach to visual perception.* Boston: Houghton Mifflin.

Ginsburg, H.P., & Opper, S. (1988). *Piaget's theory of intellectual development* (3rd ed.). Englewood Cliffs, NJ: Prentice-Hall.

Gleitman, L.R. (1990). The structural sources of verb meanings. *Language Acquisition, 1*, 3–55.

Glucksberg, S. & Krauss, R.M. (1967). What do people say after they have learned to talk? Studies of the development of referential communication. *Merrill-Palmer Quarterly, 13*, 309–16.

Glucksberg, S., Krauss, R.M., & Weissberg, R. (1966). Referential communication in nursery school children: Method and some preliminary findings. *Journal of Experimental Child Psychology, 3*, 333–42.

Glueck, S., & Glueck, E. (1968). *Delinquents and nondelinquents in perspective.* Cambridge, MA: Harvard University Press.

Goldsmith, H.H. (1996). Studying temperament via construction of the Toddler Behaviour Assessment Questionnaire. *Child Development, 67*, 218–35.

Goldsmith, H.H., & Gottesman, I. (1981). Origins of variation in behavioural style: A longitudinal study of temperament in young twins. *Child Development, 52*, 91–103.

Goldsmith, H.H., Buss, A.H., Plomin, R., Rothbart, M.K., Thomas, A., Chess, S., Hinde, R.W., & McCall, R.B. (1987). Roundtable: What is temperament? Four approaches. *Child Development, 58*, 505–29.

Gomez, R., Harvey, J., Quick, C., Scharer, I., & Harris, G. (1999). DSM-IV AD/HD: Confirmatory factor models, prevalence, and gender and age differences based on parent and teacher ratings of Australian primary school children. *Journal of Child Psychology and Psychiatry and Allied Disciplines, 40*, 265–74.

Goodman, S., & Gotlib, I. (1999). Risk for psychopathology in the children of depressed mothers: A developmental model for understanding mechanisms of transmission. *Psychological Review, 106*, 458–90.

Gopnik, A. (1996). The post-Piaget era. *Psychological Science, 4*, 221–25.

Gopnik, A., & Meltzoff, A. N. (1987). The development of categorization in the second year and its relation to other cognitive and linguistic developments. *Child Development, 58*, 1523–31.

Gopnik, A., & Meltzoff, A. (1996). *Words, thoughts and theories.* Cambridge, MA: Bradford Book/MIT Press.

Gopnik, A., & Wellman, H.M. (1994). The theory theory. In L. A. Hirschfeld, & S.A. Gelman (eds.), *Mapping the mind: Domain specificity in cognition and culture* (pp. 257–93). New York: Cambridge University Press.

Gordon, S. (1989). The socialization of children's emotions: Emotional culture, competence, and exposure. In C. Saarni, & P. Harris (eds.), *Children's understanding of emotions* (pp. 319–49). New York: Cambridge University Press.

Gottesman, I.I. (1963). Genetic aspects of intelligent behaviour. In N. Ellis (ed.), *Handbook of mental deficiency: Psychological theory and research* (pp. 253–96). New York: McGraw-Hill.

Gottlieb, G. (1991). Experimental canalization of behavioural development: Theory. *Developmental Psychology, 27*, 4–13.

Gottlieb, G., Wahlsten, D., & Lickliter, R. (1998). The significance of biology for human development: A developmental psychobiological systems view. In W. Damon (Gen. ed.), & R.M. Lerner (Vol. ed.), *Handbook of child psychology: Vol. 1. Theoretical models of human development* (pp. 233–73). New York: Wiley.

Gottman, J.M. (1983). How children become friends. *Monographs for the Society for Research in Child Development, 48* (Serial No. 201).

Gottman, J.M., & Mettetal, G. (1986). Speculations on social and affective development:

Friendship and acquaintanceship through adolescence. In J.M. Gottman, & J.G. Parker (eds.), *The conversations of friends* (pp. 192–237). New York: Cambridge University Press.

Graber, J.A., Brooks-Gunn, J., & Warren, M.P. (1995). The antecedents of menarcheal age: Heredity, family environment, and stressful life events. *Child Development, 66*, 346–59.

Greenberg, M.T., Kusche, C., & Speltz, M. (1991). Emotion regulation, self-control and psychopathology: the role of relationships in early childhood. In D. Cicchetti, & S. Toth (eds.), *Internalizing and externalizing expressions of dysfunction* (pp. 21–55). Hillsdale, NJ: Erlbaum.

Greenough, W.T., Black, J.E., & Wallace, C.S. (1987). Experience and brain development. *Child Development, 58*, 539–59.

Grice, H.P. (1975). Logic and conversation. In P. Cole, & J.L. Morgan (eds.), *Syntax and semantics: Vol. 3. Speech acts* (pp. 41–58). New York: Academic Press.

Gross, D., & Harris, P.L. (1988). False beliefs about emotion: Children's understanding of misleading emotional displays. *International Journal of Behavioural Development, 11*, 368–98.

Gunnar, M.R., Malone, S.M., Vance, G., & Fisch, R.O. (1985). Coping with aversive stimulation in the neonatal period: Quiet sleep and plasma cortisol levels during recovery from circumsion. *Child Development, 56*, 824–34.

Haight, W., & Miller, P. (1993). *The ecology and development of pretend play*. Albany, NY: State University of New York Press.

Haith, M.M., & Benson, J. (1998). Infant cognition. In W. Damon (Gen. ed.), D. Kuhn, & R. Siegler (Vol. eds.), *Handbook of child psychology: Vol. 2. Cognition, perception and language* (5th ed., pp. 199–254). New York: Wiley.

Halliday, M.A.K. (1975). *Learning how to mean: Exploration in the development of language.* London: Arnold.

Halverson, H.M. (1931). An experimental study of prehension in infants by means of systematic cinema records. *Genetic Psychology Monographs, 10*, 107–286.

Harrington, R., Rutter, M., & Fombonne, E. (1996). Developmental pathways in depression: multiple meanings, antecedents, and endpoints. *Development and Psychopathology, 8*, 601–16.

Harris, P.L. (1989). *Children and emotion.* New York: Blackwell.

Harris, P.L., Johnson, C.N., Hutton, D., Andrews, G., & Cook, T. (1989). Young children's theory of mind and emotion. *Cognition and Emotion, 3*, 379–400.

Hart, E., Lahey, B., Loeber, R., & Applegate, B. (1995). Developmental change in attention-deficit hyperactivity disorder in boys: A four-year longitudinal study. *Journal of Abnormal Child Development, 23*, 729–49.

Harter, S., & Buddin, B.J. (1987). Children's understanding of the simultaneity of two emotions: A five-stage developmental acquisition sequence. *Developmental Psychology, 23*, 388–99.

Harter, S. (1998). The development of self-representations. In N. Eisenberg (ed.), *Handbook of Child Psychology: Vol. 3. Social, emotional, and personality development* (5th ed., pp. 553–618). New York: Wiley.

Hartmann, D.P., & George, T.P. (1999). *Design, measurement, and analysis in developmental research.* In M. Bornstein, & M. Lamb (eds.), *Developmental psychology: An advanced textbook* (4th ed., pp. 125–95). Mahwah, NJ: Erlbaum.

Hartup, W.W. (1983). Peer relations. In P.H. Mussen (Series ed.), & E.M. Hetherington (Vol. ed.), *Handbook of child psychology: Vol. 4. Socialization, personality, and social development* (4th ed., pp. 103–96). New York: Wiley.

Hartup, W.W. (1989). Social relationships and their developmental significance. *American Psychologist, 44*, 120–26.

Haslam, S.A., & McGarty, C. (1998). *Doing psychology: An introduction to research methods and statistics.* London: Sage Publications.

Hawkins, A.J., & Dollahite, D.E. (1997). *Generative fathering.* Thousand Oaks, CA: Sage.

Hecox, K. (1975). Electrophysiological correlates of human auditory development. In L.B. Cohen, & P. Salapatek (eds.), *Infant perception: From sensation to cognition: Vol. 2. Perception of space, speech and sound* (pp. 151–91). Orlando, FL: Academic Press.

Hoff-Ginsburg, E. (1997). *Language development.* Pacific Grove, CA: Brooks-Cole.

Hopkins, B., & Westra, T. (1988). Maternal handling and motor development: An intracultural study. *Genetic, Social and General Psychology Monographs, 14*, 377–420.

Horgan, D. (1978). The development of the full passive. *Journal of Child Language, 5*, 65–80.

Horobin, K., & Acredolo, L. (1986). The role of attentiveness, mobility history, and separation of hiding sites on Stage IV search behaviour. *Journal of Experimental Child Psychology, 41*, 114–27.

Howes, C. (1987). Social competence with peers in young children: Developmental sequences. *Developmental Review, 7*, 252–72.

Hoza, B., Molina, B., Bukowski, W.M., & Sippola, L.K. (1995). Aggression, withdrawal and measures of popularity and friendship as predictors of internalizing and externalizing problems during adolescence. *Development and Psychopathology, 7*, 787–802.

Humphrey, T. (1978). Function of the nervous system during prenatal life. In U. Stave (ed.), *Perinatal physiology* (pp. 651–83). New York: Plenum.

Humphreys, A.P., & Smith, P.K. (1987). Rough-and-tumble, friendship, and dominance in school children: Evidence for continuity and change with age. *Child Development, 58*, 210–12.

Huttenlocher, J., Haight, W., Bryk, A., Seltzer, M., & Lyons, T. (1991). Early vocabulary growth: Relation to language input and gender. *Developmental Psychology, 27*, 236–48.

Huttenlocher, P.R. (1990). Morphometric study of human cerebral cortex development. *Neuropsychologia, 28*, 517–27.

Huttenlocher, P.R. (1994a). Synaptogenesis in human cerebral cortex. In G. Dawson, & K.W. Fischer (eds.), *Human behaviour and the developing brain* (pp. 137–52). New York: Guilford.

Huttenlocher, P.R. (1994b). Synaptogenesis, synapse elimination, and neural plasticity in human cerebral cortex. In C.A. Nelson (ed.), *Threats to optimal development. The Minnesota symposia on child psychology* (Vol. 27, pp. 35–54). Hillsdale, NJ: Erlbaum.

Ingram, D. (1986). Phonological development: Production. In P. Fletcher, & M. Garman (eds.), *Language acquisition* (2nd ed., pp. 223–39). Cambridge: Cambridge University Press.

Inhelder, B., & Piaget, J. (1958). *The growth of logical thinking from childhood to adolescence: An essay on the construction of formal operational structures.* New York: Basic Books.

Izard, C.E. (1994). Innate and universal facial expressions: Evidence from developmental and cross-cultural research. *Psychological Bulletin, 115*, 288–99.

Izard, C.E., & Malatesta, C.Z. (1987). Perspectives on emotional development I.

Differential emotions theory of early emotional development. In J.D. Osofsky (ed.), *Handbook of infant development* (2nd ed., pp. 494–554). New York: Wiley.

Jackson, B. & Farrugia, D. (1997). Diagnosis and treatment of adults with ADHD. *Journal of Counseling and Development*, *75*, 312–19.

James, W. (1890). *The principles of psychology*. New York: Dover Publications.

Johnson, M.H., Posner, M.I., & Rothbart, M.K. (1991). Components of visual orienting in early infancy: Contingency learning, anticipatory looking and disengaging. *Journal of Cognitive Neuroscience*, *3*, 335–44.

Johnson, M.J. (1998). The neural basis of cognitive development. In W. Damon (Gen. ed.), D. Kuhn, & R. Siegler (Vol. eds.), *Handbook of child psychology* (5th ed., pp. 1–49). New York: Wiley.

Jones, M.C. (1965). Psychological correlates of somatic development. *Child Development*, *36*, 899–911.

Jones, M.C., & Bayley, N. (1950). Physical maturing among boys as related to behaviour. *Journal of Educational Psychology*, *41*, 129–48.

Jones, M.C., & Mussen, P.H. (1958). Self-conceptions, motivations, and interpersonal attitudes of early- and late-maturing girls. *Child Development*, *29*, 491–501.

Jusczyk, P.W., Friederic, A.D., Wessels, J., Svenkerund, V.Y., & Jusczyk, A.M. (1993). Infants' sensitivity to the sound patterns of native language words. *Journal of Memory and Language*, *32*, 402–20.

Kagan, J. (1998). Biology and the child. In W. Damon (Gen. ed.), & N. Eisenberg (Vol. ed.), *Handbook of child psychology: Vol. 3. Social, emotional, and personality development* (5th ed., pp. 177–235). New York: Wiley.

Kagan, J., & Zetner, M. (1996). Early childhood predictors of adult psychopathology. *Harvard Review of Psychiatry*, *3*, 341–50.

Kail, R., & Hall, L.K. (1994). Processing speed, naming speed, and reading. *Developmental Psychology*, *30*, 949–54.

Kaplan, J.A., Brownell, H.H., Jacobs, J.R., & Gardner, H. (1990). The effects of right hemisphere damage on the pragmatic interpretation of conversational remarks. *Brain and Language*, *38*, 315–33.

Kaye, K.L., & Bower, T.G.R. (1994). Learning and intermodal transfer of information in newborns. *Psychological Science*, *5*, 286–8.

Kazdin, A.E. (1990). Premature termination from treatment among children referred for antisocial behaviour. *Journal of Child Psychology and Psychiatry*, *31*, 415–25.

Kazdin, A.E. (1997). Conduct disorder across the life-span. In S. Luthar, J. Burack, D. Cicchetti, & J. Weisz (eds.), *Developmental Psychopathology: Perspectives on adjustment, risk and disorder* (pp. 248–72). Cambridge: Cambridge University Press.

Keating, D.P. (1979). Adolescent thinking. In J. Adelson (ed.), *Handbook of adolescent psychology* (pp. 211–46). New York: Wiley.

Keating, D.P. (1990). Adolescent thinking. In S.S. Feldman, & G. Elliott (eds.), *At the threshold: The developing adolescent* (pp. 54–89). Cambridge, MA: Harvard University Press.

Keenan, T., & Harvey, M. (1998). What's in that child's mind? *New Zealand Science Monthly*, *9*, 6–8.

Keenan, T., & Quigley, K. (1999). The role of echoic mention in young children's understanding of sarcasm. *British Journal of Developmental Psychology*, *17*, 83–96.

Keenan, T., Ruffman, T., & Olson, D.R. (1994). When do children begin to understand logical inference as a source of knowledge? *Cognitive Development, 9*, 331–53.
Kellman, P.J., & Banks, M.S. (1998). Infant visual perception. In W. Damon (Gen. ed.), D. Kuhn, & R. Siegler (Vol. eds.), *Handbook of child psychology: Vol. 2. Cognition, perception and language* (5th ed., pp. 103–46). New York: Wiley.
Klahr, D., & MacWhinney, B. (1998). Information processing. In W. Damon (Gen. ed.), D. Kuhn, & R. S. Siegler (Vol. eds.), *Handbook of child psychology: Vol. 2. Cognition, perception, and language* (5th ed., pp. 631–78). New York: Wiley.
Klin, A., & Volkmar, F.R. (1997). The pervasive developmental disorders: Nosology and profiles of development. In S. Luthar, J. Burack, D. Cicchetti, & J. Weisz (eds.), *Developmental Psychopathology: Perspectives on adjustment, risk and disorder* (pp. 208–26). Cambridge: Cambridge University Press.
Klinnert, M.D., Emde, R.N., Butterfield, P., & Campos, J.J. (1986). Social referencing: The infant's use of emotional signals from a friendly adult with mother present. *Developmental Psychology, 22*, 427–32.
Kochanska, G. (1995). Children's temperament, mother's discipline, and security of attachment: Multiple pathways to emerging internalization. *Child Development, 66*, 597–615.
Kuczaj, S.A. (1986). Thoughts on the intentional basis of early word description: Evidence from comprehension and production. In S.A. Kuczaj, & M.D. Barrett (eds.), *The development of word meaning* (pp. 99–120). New York: Springer-Verlag.
Kuhn, D. (1995). Microgenetic study of change: What has it told us? *Psychological Science, 6*, 133–9.
Kupersmidt, J.B., & Coie, J.D. (1990). Preadolescent peer group status, aggression, and social adjustment as predictors of externalizing problems in adolescence. *Child Development, 61*, 1350–62.
Kupersmidt, J.B., Burchinal, M., & Patterson, C.J. (1995). Developmental patterns of childhood peer relations as predictors of externalizing behaviour problems. *Development and Psychopathology, 7*, 649–68.
Lafreniere, P.J., & Sroufe, L.A. (1985). Profiles of peer competence in the preschool: Interrelations between measures, influence of social ecology, and relation to attachment history. *Developmental Psychology, 21*, 56–69.
LaLonde, C.E., & Chandler, M. (1995). False belief understanding goes to school: On the social-emotional consequences of coming early or late to a first theory of mind. *Cognition and Emotion, 9*, 167–85.
Lamb, M. (1981). Developing trust and perceived effectance in infancy. In L.P. Lipsitt (ed.), *Advances in Infancy Research: Volume 2* (pp. 101–27). Norwood, NJ: Ablex.
Landau, B., & Gleitman, L.R. (1985). *Language and experience: Evidence from the blind child.* Cambridge, MA: Harvard University Press.
Langlois, J.H. (1985). From the eye of the beholder to behaviour reality: The development of social behaviours and social relations as a function of physical attractiveness. In C. P. Herman (ed.), *Physical appearance, stigma, and social behaviour.* Hillsdale, NJ: Erlbaum.
Langlois, J.H., & Downs, C.A. (1979). Peer relations as a function of physical attractiveness: The eye of the beholder or behavioural reality? *Child Development, 50*, 409–18.
Last, C., Perrin, S., Hersen, M., & Kazdin, A. (1997). A prospective study of childhood

anxiety disorders. *Journal of the American Academy of Child and Adolescent Psychiatry, 35,* 1502–10.

Lennenberg, E. (1967). *Biological foundations of language.* New York: Wiley.

Lewis, C., Freeman, N.H., Kyuadidou, C., Maridaki-Kassotaki, K., & Berridge, D.M. (1996). Social influences on false belief access – specific sibling influences or general apprenticeship? *Child Development, 67,* 2930–47.

Lewis, M. (1987). Social development in infancy and early childhood. In J.D. Osofsky (ed.), *Handbook of infant development* (pp. 419–93). New York: Wiley.

Lewis, M. (1989). Cultural differences in children's knowledge of emotion scripts. In C. Saarni, & P.L. Harris (eds.), *Children's understanding of emotion.* New York: Cambridge University Press.

Lewis M., & Brooks, J. (1974). Self, other and fear: Infants' reactions to people. In M. Lewis, & L. Rosenblum (eds.), *The origins of fear.* New York: Wiley.

Lewis, M., & Brooks-Gunn, J. (1978). *Social cognition and the acquisition of self.* New York: Plenum.

Lewis, M., Sullivan, M.W., Stanger, C., & Weiss, M. (1989). Self development and self-conscious emotions. *Child development, 60,* 146–56.

Lewis, M., Alessandri, S., & Sullivan, M.W. (1992). Differences in shame and pride as a function of children's gender and task difficulty. *Child Development, 63,* 630–38.

Lie, N. (1993). Follow-ups of children with attention-deficit hyperactivity disorder (ADHD): review of literature. *Acta Psychiatrica Scandinavia, 85,* 40.

Livesley, W.J., & Bromley, D.B. (1973). *Person perception in childhood and adolescence.* London: Wiley.

Loehlin, J.C. (1992). *Genes and environment in personality development.* Newbury Park, CA: Sage.

Lorenz, K. (1963). *On aggression.* New York: Harcourt Brace Jovanovich.

Lotter, V. (1978). Follow-up studies. In M. Rutter, & E. Schopler (eds.), *Autism: A reappraisal of concepts and treatment.* New York: Plenum.

Luthar, S. (1991). Vulnerability and resilience: A study of high-risk adolescents. *Child Development, 62,* 600–16.

Lutz, D.J., & Sternberg, R.J. (1999). Cognitive development. In M. Bornstein, & M. Lamb (eds.), *Developmental psychology: An advanced textbook* (4th ed., pp. 275–311). Mahwah, NJ: Erlbaum.

Lyons-Ruth, K., Connell, D.B., Gruenbaum, H.U., & Botein, S. (1990). Infants at social risk: Maternal depression and family support services as mediators of infant development and security of attachment. *Child Development, 61,* 85–98.

Lyons-Ruth, K., Easterbrooks, M.A., & Cibelli, C.D. (1997). Infant attachment strategies, infant mental lag, and maternal depressive symptoms: Predictions of internalizing and externalizing problems at age 7. *Developmental Psychology, 33,* 681–92.

Maccoby, E.E. (1990). Gender and relationships: A developmental account. *American Psychologist, 45,* 513–21.

Maccoby, E.E., & Jacklin, C.N. (1987). Gender segregation in childhood. In H.W. Reese (ed.), *Advances in child development and behaviour* (Vol. 20, pp. 239–88). New York: Academic Press.

MacFarlane, A. (1975). Olfaction in the development of social preferences in the human neonate. *Ciba Foundation Symposium, 33,* 103–17.

Magnusson, D., & Cairns, R.B. (1996). Developmental science: Toward a unified framework. In R.B. Cairns, G.H. Elder, & E.J. Costello (eds.), *Developmental science* (pp. 7–30). Cambridge: Cambridge University Press.

Main, M., & Cassidy, J. (1988). Categories of response to reunion with the parent at age 6: Predictable from infant attachment classification and stable over a 1-month period. *Developmental Psychology, 24,* 415–26.

Main, M., & Solomon, J. (1990). Procedures for identifying infants as disorganized/disoriented during the Ainsworth strange situation. In M. Greenberg, D. Cicchetti, & E.M. Cummings (eds.), *Attachment in the preschool years: Theory, research and intervention* (pp. 121–60). Chicago: University of Chicago Press.

Malatesta, C.Z., & Haviland, J. (1982). Learning display rules: The socialization of emotional expression in infancy. *Child Development, 53,* 991–1003.

Malatesta, C.Z., & Haviland, J. (1985). Signals, symbols, and socialization. In M. Lewis & C. Saarni (eds.), *The socialization of emotions.* New York: Plenum.

Malina, R.M. (1975). *Growth and development: The first twenty years in man.* Minneapolis: Burgess Publishing.

Mannuzza, S., Klein, R., Bessler, A., & Malloy, P. (1993). Adult outcome of hyperactive boys: educational achievement, occupational rank, and psychiatric status. *Archives of General Psychiatry, 50,* 565–76.

Maratsos, M. (1998). The acquisition of grammar. In W. Damon (Gen. ed.), D. Kuhn, & R.S. Siegler (Vol. eds.), *Handbook of child psychology: Vol. 2. Cognition, perception, and language* (5th ed., pp. 421–66). New York: Wiley.

Markman, E.M. (1989). *Categorization and naming in children.* Cambridge, MA: MIT Press.

Markman, E.M. (1992). Constraints on word learning: Speculations about their nature, origins, and domain specificity. In M.R. Gunnar, & M.P. Maratsos (eds.), *Minnesota Symposia on Child Psychology* (Vol. 25, pp. 59–101). Hillsdale, NJ: Erlbaum.

Matas, L., Arend, R., & Sroufe, L.A. (1978). Continuity of adaptation in the second year. The relationship between quality of attachment and later competence. *Child Development, 49,* 547–56.

Maurer, D., & Barrera, M. (1981). Infants' perception of natural and distorted arrangements of a schematic face. *Child Development, 52,* 196–202.

Maurer, D., & Maurer, C. (1988). *The world of the newborn.* New York: Basic Books.

Maurer, D., & Salapatek, P. (1976). Developmental changes in the scanning of faces by young infants. *Child Development, 47,* 523–7.

McGhee, P.E. (1979). *Humor: Its origin and development.* San Francisco: Freeman.

McGraw, M.B. (1935). *Growth: A study of Johnny and Jimmy.* New York: Appelton-Century-Crofts.

Meins, E., Russell, J., Fernyhough, C., & Clark-Carter, D. (1998). Security of attachment as a predictor of mentalising abilities: A longitudinal study. *Social Development, 7,* 1–24.

Meltzoff, A.N., & Borton, R.W. (1979). Intermodal matching by human neonates. *Nature, 282,* 403–4.

Menella, J.A., & Beauchamp, G.K. (1996). The effects of repeated exposure to garlic-flavored milk on the nursling's behaviour. *Pediatric Research, 34,* 805–8.

Menyuk, P., Liebergott, J.W., & Schultz, M. (1995). *Early language development in full-term and premature infants.* Hillsdale, NJ: Erlbaum.

Meyer, A. (1957). *Psychopathology: A science of man.* Springfield: Thomas.

Miller, G.A. (1956). The magical number seven, plus or minus two: Some limits on our capacity for information processing. *Psychological Review, 63,* 81–97.

Millcr, P.H. (1993). *Theories of developmental psychology* (3rd ed.). New York: W.H. Freeman.

Miller, S.A. (1998). *Developmental research methods* (2nd ed.). Upper Saddle River, NJ: Prentice Hall.

Miller, S.M., & Green, M.L. (1985). Coping with stress and frustration: Origins, nature, and development. In M. Lewis, & C. Saarni (eds.), *The socialization of emotions* (pp. 263–314). Plenum: New York.

Moerk, E.L. (1992). *A first language taught and learned.* Baltimore, MD: Paul H. Brookes.

Moffit, T.E., Caspi, A., Belsky, J., & Silva, P.A. (1992). Childhood experience and the onset of menarche: A test of a sociobiological model. *Child Development, 63*, 47–58.

Molfese, D.L., & Molfese, V.J. (1979). Hemisphere and stimulus differences as reflected in the cortical responses of newborn infants to speech stimuli. *Developmental Psychology, 15*, 505–11.

Morrongiello, B.A., Hewitt, K.L., & Gotowiec, A. (1991). Infant discrimination of relative distance in the auditory modality: approaching versus receding sound sources. *Infant Behaviour Development, 14*, 187–208.

Moshman, D. (1998). Cognitive development beyond childhood. In W. Damon (Gen. ed.), D. Kuhn & R.S. Siegler (Vol. eds.), *Handbook of child psychology: Vol. 2. Cognition, perception, and language* (5th ed., pp. 947–78). New York: Wiley.

Mufson, L., & Moreau, D. (1997). Depressive disorders. In R. Ammerman, & M. Hersen (eds.), *Handbook of prevention and treatment with children and adolescence* (pp. 403–30). New York: Wiley.

Muir, D., & Clifton, R. (1985). Infants' orientation to the location of sound sources. In G. Gottlieb, & N. Krasnegor (eds.), *Measurement of audition and vision in the first year of postnatal life: A methodological overview* (pp. 171–94). Norwood, NJ: Ablex.

Muir, D., & Field, J. (1979). Newborn infants orient to sounds. *Child Development, 50*, 431–6.

Murray, L., & Trevanthen, C. (1985). Emotional regulation of interactions between two-month-olds and their mothers. In T. Field, & N. Fox (eds.), *Social perception in infants* (pp. 166–97). Norwood, NJ: Ablex.

Naigles, L.G., & Gelman, S.A. (1995). Overextensions in comprehension and production revisited: Preferential-looking in a study of dog, cat, and cow. *Journal of Child Language, 22*, 19–46.

Nánez, J., Sr. (1987). Perception of impending collision in 3- to 6-week-old infants. *Infant Behaviour and Development, 11*, 447–63.

Neimark, E.D. (1975). Intellectual development during adolescence. In F.D. Horowitz (ed.), *Review of child development research* (Vol. 4, pp. 543–94). Chicago: University of Chicago Press.

Neisser, U. (1976). *Cognition and reality: Principles and implications of cognitive psychology*. San Francisco: W.H. Freeman.

Nelson, K. (1973). Structure and strategy in learning to talk. *Monographs of the Society for Research in Child Development, 38* (1–2, Serial No. 149).

Nelson, K. (1988). Constraints on word learning? *Cognitive Development, 3*, 221–46.

Newcomb, A.F., & Bagwell, C.L. (1995). Children's friendship relations: A meta-analytic review. *Psychological Bulletin, 117*, 306–47.

Nilzon, K.R., & Palmerus, K. (1997). Anxiety in depressed school children. *Social Psychology International, 18*, 165–77.

Nolen-Hoeksema, S. (1994). An interactive model for the emergence of gender differences in depression in adolescence. *Journal of Research on Adolescence*, *4*, 519–34.

O'Neill, D. (1996). Pragmatics and the development of communicative ability. In D. Green et al. (eds.), *Cognitive science: An introduction* (pp. 244–75). Oxford: Blackwell.

Olson (1994). *The world on paper*. Cambridge: Cambridge University Press.

Olson, D.R. (1988). Or what's a metaphor for? *Metaphor and Symbolic Activity*, *3*, 215–22.

Osherson, D., & Markman, E. (1975). Language and the ability to evaluate contradictions and tautologies. *Cognition*, *3*, 213–26.

Palinscar, A.S., & Brown, A.L. (1984). Reciprocal teaching of comprehension–monitoring activities. *Cognition and Instruction*, *1*, 117–75.

Parker, J.G., & Asher, S.R. (1987). Peer acceptance and later personal adjustment: Are low accepted children at risk? *Psychological Bulletin*, *102*, 357–89.

Parker, J.G., & Asher, S.R. (1993). Friendship and friendship quality in middle childhood. *Developmental Psychology*, *29*, 611–21.

Parker, J.G., & Gottman, J.M. (1989). Social and emotional development in a relational context: Friendship interaction from early childhood to adolescence. In T.J. Berndt, & G.W. Ladd (eds.), *Peer relationships in child development* (pp. 95–131). New York: Wiley.

Parkhurst, J.T., & Asher, S.R. (1992). Peer rejection in middle school: Subgroup differences in behaviour, loneliness and interpersonal concerns. *Developmental Psychology*, *28*, 231–41.

Parten, M. (1932). Social participation among preschool children. *Journal of Abnormal and Social Psychology*, *27*, 243–69.

Patterson, G. (1996). Some characteristics of a developmental theory for early-onset delinquency. In M.F. Lenzenweger, & J.J. Haugaard (eds.), *Frontiers of developmental psychopathology* (pp. 81–124). New York: Oxford University Press.

Patterson, G.R., DeBaryshe, B., & Ramsey, R. (1989). A developmental perspective on antisocial behaviour. *American Psychologist*, *44*, 329–35.

Paul, R. (1987). Natural history. In D. Chen, A. Donnelan, & R. Paul (eds.), *Handbook of autism and pervasive developmental disorders* (pp. 121–30). New York: Wiley.

Pedlow, R., Sanson, A., Prior, M., & Oberklaid, F. (1993). Stability of maternally reported temperament from infancy to 8 years. *Developmental Psychology*, *29*, 998–1007.

Pegg, J.E., Werker, J.F., & McLeod, P.J. (1992). Preference for infant-directed over adult-directed speech: Evidence from 7–week-old infants. *Infant Behaviour and Development*, *15*, 325–45.

Perner, J. (1988). Higher-order beliefs and intentions in children's understanding of social interaction. In J.W. Astington, P.L. Harris, & D.R. Olson (eds.), *Developing theories of mind* (pp. 271–94). Cambridge: Cambridge University Press.

Perner, J. (1991). *Understanding the representational mind*. Cambridge, MA: Bradford Books/MIT Press.

Perner, J., & Leekam, S.R. (1986). Belief and quantity: Three-year-olds' adaptation to listener's knowledge. *Journal of Child Language*, *13*, 305–15.

Perner, J., Ruffman, T., & Leekam, S.R. (1994). Theory of mind is contagious: You catch it from your sibs. *Child Development*, *5*, 1228–38.

Piaget, J. (1926). *The language and thought of the child*. New York: Harcourt Brace & World.

Piaget, J. (1932). *The moral judgement of the child*. New York: Harcourt Brace & World.

Piaget, J. (1952). *The origins of intelligence in children*. New York: International Universities Press.

Piaget, J. (1954). *The construction of reality in the child.* New York: Basic Books.

Piaget, J. (1962). *Play, dreams and imitation in childhood.* New York: W.W. Norton.

Piaget, J. (1969). *The mechanisms of perception.* New York: Basic Books.

Piaget, J. (1971). *Biology and knowledge.* Chicago: University of Chicago Press.

Piaget, J. (1983). Piaget's theory. In P.H. Mussen (Series ed.), & W. Kessen (Vol. ed.), *Handbook of child psychology. Vol. 1. History, theory, and methods* (pp. 103–28). New York: Wiley.

Piaget, J., & Inhelder, B. (1956). *The child's conception of space.* London: Routledge & Kegan Paul.

Pinker, S. (1994). *The language instinct: How the mind creates language.* New York: William Morrow.

Plomin, R. (1987). Developmental behavioural genetics and infancy. In J.D. Osofsky (ed.), *Handbook of infant development* (pp. 363–414). New York: Wiley.

Plomin, R., DeFries, J.C., McClearn, G.E., & Rutter, M. (1997). *Behavioural genetics* (3rd edition). New York: W.H. Freeman and Co.

Plomin, R., Pedersen, N.L., Lichtenstein, P., & McClearn, G. E. (1994). Variability and stability in cognitive abilities are largely genetic later in life. *Behaviour Genetics, 24,* 207–15.

Pollitt, E. (1994). Poverty and child development: Relevance of research in developing countries to the United States. *Child Development, 65,* 283–95.

Porges, S. (1991). Vagal tone: An autonomic mediator of affect. In J. Garber, & K. Dodge (eds.), *The development of emotional regulation and dysregulation* (pp. 111–28). Cambridge: Cambridge University Press.

Porter, R.H., Makin, J.W., Davis, L.B., & Christensen, K.M. (1992). Breast-fed infants respond to olfactory cues from their own mother and unfamiliar lactating females. *Infant Behaviour and Development, 15,* 85–93.

Prinz, R.J., & Miller, G.E. (1991). Issues in understanding and treating childhood conduct problems in disadvantaged populations. *Journal of Clinical Child Psychology, 20,* 379–85.

Pulaski, M. (1980). *Understanding Piaget: An introduction to children's cognitive development.* New York: Harper & Row.

Quine, W. (1960). *Word and Object.* Cambridge, MA: MIT Press.

Radke-Yarrow, M., Zahn-Waxler, C., & Chapman, M. (1983). Children's prosocial dispositions and behaviour. In P.H. Mussen (Series ed.), & E.M. Hetherington (Vol. ed.), *Handbook of child psychology: Vol. 4. Socialization, personality and social development* (pp. 469–545). New York: Wiley.

Rakic, P. (1995). Corticogenesis in human and nonhuman primates. In M.S. Gazzaniga (ed.), *The cognitive neurosciences* (pp. 127–45). Cambridge, MA: MIT Press.

Ratner, N.B. (1993). Atypical language development. In J. Berko Gleason (ed.), *The development of language* (pp. 325–68). New York: Macmillan.

Reich, P.A. (1986). *Language development.* Englewood Cliffs, NJ: Prentice Hall.

Reisman, J.E. (1987). Touch, motion and proprioception. In P. Salapatek, & L. Cohen (eds.), *Handbook of infant perception. Vol. 1. From sensation to perception* (pp. 265–304). Orlando, FL: Academic Press.

Renshaw, P.D., & Brown, P.J. (1993). Loneliness in middle childhood: Concurrent and longitudinal predictors. *Child Development, 64,* 1271–84.

Restak, R.M. (1984). *The brain.* New York: Bantam.

Reznick, J.S., & Goldfield, B.A. (1992). Rapid change in lexical development in comprehension and production. *Developmental Psychology, 28*, 406–13.

Riegel, K.F. (1973). Dialectic operations: The final period of cognitive development. *Human Development, 16*, 346–70.

Rieser, J., Yonas, A., & Wilkner, K. (1976). Radial localization of odors by human neonates. *Child Development, 47*, 856–9.

Robinson, E., Goelman, H., & Olson, D.R. (1983). Children's understanding of the relation between expressions (what was said) and intentions (what was meant). *British Journal of Developmental Psychology, 1*, 75–86.

Rogoff, B. (1998). Cognition as a collaborative process. In W. Damon (Gen. ed.), D. Kuhn, & R.S. Siegler (Vol. eds.), *Handbook of child psychology: Vol. 5. Cognition, perception and language* (5th ed., pp. 679–744). New York: Wiley.

Rosenstein, D., & Oster, H. (1988). Differential facial response to four basic tastes in newborns. *Child Development, 59*, 1555–68.

Ross, H.S., & Conant, C.L. (1992). The social structure of early conflict: Interactions, relationships, and alliances. In C.U. Shantz, & W.W. Hartup (eds.), *Conflict in child and adolescent development* (pp. 153–85). Cambridge: Cambridge University Press.

Rothbart, M.K. (1986). Longitudinal observation of infant temperament. *Developmental Psychology, 22*, 356–65.

Rothbart, M.K. (1989). Temperament in childhood: A framework. In G.A. Kohnstamm, J.E. Bates, & M.K. Rothbart (eds.), *Temperament in childhood* (pp. 59–73). Chichester, England: Wiley.

Rothbart, M.K, & Bates, J. (1998). Temperament. In W. Damon (Gen. ed.), & N. Eisenberg (Vol. ed.), *Handbook of child psychology: Vol. 3. Social and emotional development* (5th ed., pp. 105–76). New York: Wiley.

Rothbart, M.K., Ahadi, S.A., & Hershey, K.L. (1994). Temperament and social behaviour in childhood. *Merrill-Palmer Quarterly, 40*, 21–39.

Rothbart, M.K., Derryberry, D., & Hershey, K. (1995). *Stability of infant temperament in childhood: Laboratory infant assessment to parent report at seven years.* Unpublished manuscript.

Rothbart, M.K., Ziaie, H., & O'Boyle, C.G. (1992). Self-regulation and emotion in infancy. In N. Eisenberg, & R. Fabes, (eds.), *Emotion and its regulation in early development* (pp. 7–23). *New Directions for Child Development, 55.* San Francisco: Jossey-Bass Inc.

Rovee-Collier, C. (1997). Dissociations in infant memory: Rethinking the development of implicit and explicit memory. *Psychological Review, 104*, 467–98.

Rubin, K.H. (1985). Socially withdrawn children: An 'at risk' population? In B. Schneider, K.H. Rubin, & J. Ledingham (eds.), *Children's peer relations: Issues in assessment and intervention* (pp. 125–39). New York: Springer-Verlag.

Rubin, K.H., & Coplan, R. (1992). Peer relationships in childhood. In M. Bornstein, & M. Lamb (eds.), *Developmental psychology: An advanced textbook* (pp. 519–78). Hillsdale, NJ: Erlbaum.

Rubin, K.H., Bukowski, W., & Parker, J.G. (1998). Peer interactions, relationships, and groups. In W. Damon (Gen. ed.), & N. Eisenberg (Vol. ed.), *Handbook of child psychology: Vol. 3. Social, emotional, and personality development* (5th ed., pp. 619–700). New York: Wiley.

Rubin, K.H., Coplan, R.J., Nelson, L.J., Cheah, C.S., & Lagace-Seguin, D.G. (1999). Peer relationships in childhood. In M. Bornstein, & M. Lamb, (eds.), *Developmental psychology: An advanced textbook* (4th ed., pp. 451–501). Mahwah, NJ: Erlbaum.

Rubin, K.H., Fein, G., & Vandenburg, B. (1983). Play. In P.H. Mussen (Series ed.), & E.M. Hetherington (Vol. ed.), *Handbook of child psychology: Vol. 4. Socialization, personality and social development* (pp. 693–774). New York: Wiley.

Ruff, H.A., Saltarelli, L.M., Capozzoli, M., & Dubiner, K. (1992). The differentiation of activity in infants' exploration of objects. *Developmental Psychology*, *28*, 851–61.

Ruffman, T. (2000). Nonverbal theory of mind: Is it important, is it implicit, is it simulation, is it relevant to autism? In J.W. Astington (ed.), *Minds in the making: Essays in honor of David Olson* (pp. 456–79). New York: Blackwell.

Ruffman, T.K., & Keenan, T.R. (1996). Children's understanding of surprise: The case for a lag in understanding relative to false belief. *Developmental Psychology*, *32*, 40–9.

Ruffman, T., Perner, J., Olson, D. R., & Doherty, M. (1993). Reflecting on scientific thinking: Children's understanding of the hypothesis–evidence relation. *Child Development*, *64*, 1617–36.

Ruffman, R., Perner, J., & Parkin, L. (1999). How parenting style affects false belief-understanding. *Social Development*, *8*, 395–411.

Rutter, M. (1979). Protective factors in children's responses to stress and disadvantage. In W. Kent, & J. Rolf (eds.), *Primary prevention in psychopathology: Social competence in children* (pp. 49–74). Hanover: University of New England Press.

Rutter, M. (1985). Resilience in the face of adversity: Protective factors and resistance to psychiatric disorder. *British Journal of Psychiatry*, *128*, 493–509.

Rutter, M. (1987). Psychosocial resilience and protective mechanisms. *American Journal of Orthopsychiatry*, *57*, 316–31.

Rutter, M. (1990). Psychosocial resilience and protective mechanisms. In J. Rolf, A.S. Masten, & D. Cicchetti (eds.), *Risk and protective factors in the development of psychopathology* (pp. 181–214). New York: Cambridge University Press.

Rutter, M., & Garmezy, N. (1983). Developmental psychopathology. In P.H. Mussen (Series ed.), & E.M. Hetherington (Vol. ed.), *Socialization, personality and social development* (4th ed., pp. 775–911). New York: Wiley.

Rutter, M., & Quinton, D. (1987). Parental mental illness as a risk factor for psychiatric disorders in childhood. In D. Magnusson, & A. Ohman (eds.), *Psychopathology: An interactional perspective* (pp. 199–219). Orlando, FL: Academic Press.

Rutter, M., & Rutter, M. (1993). *Developing minds: Challenge and continuity across the lifespan.* New York: Basic Books.

Rutter, M., and the English and Romanian Adoptees (ERA) Study Team (1998). Developmental catch-up and deficit, following adoption and severe global early privation. *Journal of Child Psychology and Psychiatry*, *39*, 465–76.

Saarni, C. (1990). Emotional competence: How emotions and relationships become integrated. In R.A. Thompson (ed.), *Socioemotional development* (Nebraska Symposium on Motivation, Vol. 36), Lincoln: University of Nebraska Press.

Saarni, C., Mumme, D.L., & Campos, J.J. (1998). Emotional development: Action, communication, and understanding. In W. Damon (Gen. ed.), & N. Eisenberg (Vol. ed.), *Handbook of child psychology: Vol. 3. Social, emotional, and personality development* (pp. 237–310). New York: Wiley.

Sameroff, A. (1983). Developmental systems: Contexts and evolution. In P.H. Mussen (Series ed.), & W. Kessen (Vol. ed.), *Handbook of Child Psychology: Vol. 1. History, theory, and methods* (pp. 237–94). New York: Wiley.

Saracho, O.N., & Spodek, B. (1998). A historical overview of theories of play. In O.N.

Saracho, & B. Spodek (eds.), *Multiple perspectives on play in early childhood education: Inquiries and insights* (pp. 1–10). Albany, NY: State University of New York Press.

Scarr, S. (1992). Developmental theories for the 1990s: Development and individual differences. *Child Development, 63*, 1–19.

Scarr, S. (1996). How people make their own environments: Implications for parents and policy makers. *Psychology, Public Policy & Law, 2*, 204–28.

Scarr, S., & McCartney, K. (1983). How people make their own environments: A theory of genotype environment effects. *Child Development, 54*, 424–35.

Schaffer, H.R. (1979). Acquiring the concept of the dialogue. In M.H. Bornstein, & W. Kessen (eds.), *Psychological development from infancy: Image to intention* (pp. 279–305). Hillsdale, NJ: Erlbaum.

Schaffer, H.R. (1996). *Social development.* Cambridge, MA: Blackwell.

Schaie, K.W. (1965). A general model for the study of developmental problems. *Psychological Bulletin, 64*, 92–107.

Searle, J. (1969). *Speech acts: An essay in the philosophy of language.* Cambridge: Cambridge University Press.

Segalowitz, S.J. (1983a). On the requirements of a developmental theory of lateralization. In S.J. Segalowitz (ed.), *Language functions and brain organization* (pp. 215–20). New York: Academic Press.

Segalowitz, S.J. (1983b). *Two sides of the brain.* Englewood Cliffs, NJ: Prentice-Hall.

Segalowitz, S.J. (1995). Brain growth and the child's mental development. In K. Covell (ed.), *Readings in child development: A Canadian perspective* (pp. 51–71). Toronto: Nelson Canada.

Selman, R.L. (1980). *The growth of interpersonal understanding.* New York: Academic Press.

Selman, R.L. (1981). The child as a friendship philosopher. In S.R. Asher, & J.M. Gottman (eds.), *The development of children's friendships* (pp. 242–72). New York: Cambridge University Press.

Shantz, C.V. (1983). Social cognitions. In P.H. Mussen (Series ed.), J.H. Flavell, & E.M. Markman (Vol. eds.), *Handbook of child psychology: Vol. 3. Cognitive development.* New York: Wiley.

Shapiro, D.A., & Shapiro, D. (1982). Meta-analysis of comparative therapy outcome studies: A replication and refinement. *Psychological Bulletin, 92*, 581–604.

Shatz, M., & Gelman, R. (1973). The development of communication skills: Modifications in the speech of young children as a function of the listener. *Monographs of the Society for Research in Child Development, 38* (5, Serial No. 152).

Shiffrin, R.M., & Schneider, W. (1977). Controlled and automatic human information processing: II. Perceptual learning, automatic attending, and a general theory. *Psychological Review, 84*, 155–71.

Shirley, M.M. (1933). *The first two years: A study of 25 babies.* Minneapolis: University of Minnesota Press.

Siegal, M. (1991). A clash of conversational worlds: Interpreting cognitive development through communication. In L. Resnick, J. Levine, & S. Teasley (eds.), *Perspectives on socially shared cognition* (pp. 23–40). Washington: American Psychological Association.

Siegal, M., Carrington, J., & Radel, M. (1996). Theory of mind and pragmatic understanding following right hemisphere damage. *Brain and Language, 53*, 40–50.

Siegler, R.S. (1996). *Emerging minds: The process of change in children's thinking.* New York: Oxford University Press.

Siegler, R.S. (1998). *Children's thinking* (3rd ed.). Upper Saddle River, NJ: Prentice-Hall.

Skinner, B.F. (1957). *Verbal behaviour.* New York: Appleton-Century-Crofts.

Slater, A.M., & Morrison, V. (1985). Shape constancy and slant perception at birth. *Perception, 14,* 337–44.

Slater, A., Mattock, A., & Brown, E. (1990). Size constancy at birth: Newborn infants' responses to retinal and real size. *Journal of Experimental Child Psychology, 49,* 314–22.

Smyth, R. (1995). Conceptual perspective-taking and children's interpretation of pronouns in reported speech. *Journal of Child Language, 22,* 171–87.

Sodian, B., Zaitchik, D., & Carey, S. (1991). Young children's differentiation of hypothetical belief from evidence. *Child Development, 62,* 753–66.

Sonnenschein, S. (1988). The development of referential communication: Speaking to different listeners. *Child Development, 59,* 694–702.

Sorce, J.F., Emde, R.N., Campos, J.J., & Klinnert, M.D. (1985). Maternal emotional signaling: Its effect on the visual cliff behaviour of 1-year-olds. *Developmental Psychology, 21,* 195–200.

Spangler, G., & Grossman, K.E. (1993). Biobehavioural organization in securely and insecurely attached infants. *Child Development, 64,* 1439–50.

Spelke, E.S. (1987). The development of intermodal perception. In P. Salapatek, & L. Cohen (eds.), *Handbook of infant perception. Vol. II. From sensation to perception* (pp. 233–74). Orlando, FL: Academic Press.

Spelke, E.S., Breinlinger, K., Macomber, J., & Jacobson, K. (1992). Origins of knowledge. *Psychological Review, 99,* 606–32.

Sperling, G. (1960). The information available in brief visual presentations. *Psychological Monographs, 74,* No. 11.

Springer, S.P., & Deutsch, G. (1993). *Left brain, right brain.* New York: W.H. Freeman.

Sroufe, L.A. (1979). Socioemotional development. In J.D. Osofsky (ed.), *Handbook of infant development* (pp. 462–516).

Sroufe, L.A. (1996). *Emotional development: The organization of emotional life in the early years.* New York: Wiley.

Sroufe, L.A., & Rutter, M. (1984). The domain of developmental psychopathology. *Child Development, 55,* 17–29.

Sroufe, L.A., Egeland, B., & Kreutzer, T. (1990). The fate of early experience following developmental change: Longitudinal approaches to individual adaptation in childhood. *Child Development, 61,* 1363–73.

Sroufe, L.A., Waters, E., & Matas, L. (1974). Contextual determinants of infant affectional response. In M. Lewis, & L. Rosenblum (eds.), *Origins of fear.* New York: Wiley.

Stattin, H., & Magnusson, D. (1990). *Pubertal maturation in female development* (Vol. 2). Hillsdale, NJ: Erlbaum.

Stein, B.E., & Meredith, M.A. (1993). *The merging of the senses.* Cambridge, MA: MIT Press.

Steinberg, L. (1987). Impact of puberty on family relations: Effects of pubertal status and pubertal timing. *Developmental Psychology, 22,* 451–60.

Steiner, J.E. (1979). Human facial expressions in response to taste and smell stimulation. In H. Reese, & L.P. Lipsitt (eds.), *Advances in child development and behaviour* (Vol. 13, pp. 257–93). New York: Academic Press.

Sternberg, R., & Okagaki, L. (1989) Continuity and discontinuity in intellectual development are not a matter of 'either-or'. *Human Development, 32*, 158–66.

Stevenson-Hinde, J., & Hinde, R.A. (1986). Changes in associations between characteristics and interactions. In R. Plomin, & J. Dunn (eds.), *The study of temperament: Changes, continuities, and challenges* (pp. 111–31). Hillsdale, NJ: Erlbaum.

Strayer, F.F., & Strayer, J. (1976). An ethological analysis of social agonism and dominance relations among preschool children. *Child Development, 47*, 980–89.

Streri, A., & Pecheux, M. (1986). Tactual habituation and discrimination of form in infancy: A comparison with vision. *Child Development, 57*, 100–104.

Sullivan, H.S. (1953). *The interpersonal theory of psychiatry*. New York: W.W. Norton.

Tanner, J. (1990). *Fetus into man: Physical growth from conception to maturity*. Cambridge, MA: Harvard University Press.

Teller, D.Y. (1997). First glances: The vision of infants. The Friedenwald Lecture. *Investigative Ophthalmology & Visual Science, 38*, 2183–203.

Thatcher, R.W. (1994). Cyclic cortical reorganization: Origins of human cognitive development. In G. Dawson, & K.W. Fischer (eds.), *Human behaviour and the developing brain* (pp. 232–66). New York: Guilford.

Thelen, E. (1995). Motor development: A new synthesis. *American Psychologist, 50*, 79–95.

Thelen, E., & Fisher, D.M. (1982). Newborn stepping: An explanation for a 'disappearing reflex'. *Developmental Psychology, 18*, 760–70.

Thelen, E., & Smith, L.B. (1994). *A dynamic systems approach to the development of cognition and action*. Cambridge, MA: MIT Press.

Thelen, E., & Smith, L.B. (1998). Dynamic systems theories. In W. Damon (Gen. ed.), & R.M. Lerner (Vol. ed.), *Handbook of child psychology: Vol. 1. Theoretical models of human development* (5th ed., pp. 563–634). New York: Wiley.

Thelen, E., & Ulrich, B.D. (1991). Hidden skills: A dynamic analysis of treadmill stepping during the first year. *Monographs of the Society for Research in Child Development, 58* (Serial No. 223).

Thelen, E., Corbetta, D., Kamm, K., Spencer, J.P., Schneider, K., & Zernicke, R.F. (1993). The transition to reaching: Mapping intention and intrinsic dynamics. *Child Development, 64*, 1058–98.

Thomas, A., & Chess, S. (1977). *Temperament and development*. New York: Bruner/Mazel.

Thomas, A., & Chess, S. (1986). The New York Longitudinal Study: From infancy to early adult life. In R. Plomin, & J. Dunn (eds.), *Changes, continuities and challenges*. Hillsdale, NJ: Erlbaum.

Thompson, R.A. (1990). Vulnerability in research: A developmental perspective on research risk. *Child Development, 61*, 1–16.

Thompson, R.A. (1991). *Emotional regulation and emotional development. Educational Psychology Review, 3*, 269–307.

Thompson, R.A. (1998). Early sociopersonality development. In W. Damon (Gen. ed.), & N. Eisenberg (Vol. ed.), *Handbook of child psychology: Vol. 3. Social, emotional, and personality development* (5th ed., pp. 25–104). New York: Wiley.

Thompson, R.A., Lamb, M.E., & Estes, D. (1982). Stability of infant–mother attachment and its relationship to changing life circumstances in an unselected middle-class sample. *Child Development, 53*, 144–8.

Tinbergen, N. (1951). *The study of instinct*. Oxford: Oxford University Press.

Torrance, N., & Olson, D.R. (1987). Development of the metalanguage and the acquisition of literacy. *Interchange, 18*, 136–46.

Trabasso, T., Stein, N., & Johnson, L.R. (1981). Children's knowledge of events: A causal analysis of story structure. In G. Bower (ed.), *Learning and motivation* (Vol. 15). New York: Academic Press.

Trehub, S.E., & Trainor, L.J. (1993). Listening strategies in infancy: The roots of music and language development. In S. McAdams, & E. Bigand (eds.), *Thinking in sound: The cognitive psychology of human audition* (pp. 278–327). New York: Oxford University Press.

Tschann, J.M., Kaiser, P., Chesney, M.A., & Alkon, A. (1996). Resilience and vulnerability among preschool children: Family functioning, temperament, and behaviour problems. *Journal of the American Academy of Child and Adolescent Psychiatry, 35*, 184–92.

Vasey, M., Crnic, K., & Carter, W. (1994). Worry in childhood: A developmental perspective. *Cognitive Therapy and Research, 18*, 529–49.

Vaughn, B.E., Egeland, B., Waters, E., & Sroufe, L.A. (1979). Individual differences in infant–mother attachment at 12 and 18 months: Stability and change in families under stress. *Child Development, 50*, 971–75.

Vaughn, B.E., & Langlois, J.H. (1983). Physical attractiveness as a correlate of peer status and social competence in preschool children. *Developmental Psychology, 19*, 561–67.

Vygotsky, L.S. (1978). *Mind in society: The development of higher mental processes*. Cambridge, MA: Harvard University Press.

Vygotsky, L.S. (1981). The genesis of higher mental functions. In J.V. Wertsch (ed.), *The concept of activity in Soviet psychology* (pp. 144–88). Armonk, NY: Sharpe.

Vygotsky, L.S. (1986). *Thought and language* (A. Kozulin, Trans.). Cambridge, MA: MIT Press.

Waddington, C.H. (1975). *The evolution of an evolutionist*. Ithaca, NY: Cornell University Press.

Waterman, A.S. (1985). Identity in the context of adolescent psychology. In A.S. Waterman (ed.), *Identity in adolescence: Processes and contents*. San Francisco: Jossey-Bass.

Waters, E. (1978). The stability of individual differences in infant–mother attachment. *Child Development, 49*, 484–94.

Waters, E., Matas, L., & Sroufe, L.A. (1975). Infants' reactions to an approaching stranger: Description, validation, and functional significance of wariness. *Child Development, 46*, 348–56.

Waters, E., Vaughn, B.E., Posada, G., & Kondo-Ikemura, K. (1995). Caregiving, cultural, and cognitive perspectives on secure-based behaviour and working models: New growing points of attachment theory and research. *Monographs of the Society for Research in Child Development, 60*, (2–3, Serial No. 244).

Waters, E., Wippman, J., & Sroufe, L.A. (1979). Attachment, positive affect, and competence in the peer group: Two studies in construct validation. *Child Development, 50*, 821–29.

Watkins, W.E., & Pollitt, E. (1997). 'Stupidity or worms': Do intestinal worms impair mental performance? *Psychological Bulletin, 121*, 171–91.

Watson, A.C., Nixon, C.L., Wilson, A., & Capage, L. (1999). Social interaction skills and theory of mind in young children. *Developmental Psychology, 35*, 386–91.

Watson, J.B. (1928). *Psychological care of infant and child.* New York: W.W. Norton.

Watson, J.B. (1930). *Behaviourism.* New York: W.W. Norton.

Watson, J.B., & Raynor, R. (1920). Conditioned emotional reactions. *Journal of Experimental Psychology, 3,* 1–14.

Wellman, H.M. (1990). *The child's theory of mind.* Cambridge, MA: MIT Press.

Wellman, H.M., & Lempers, J.D. (1977). The naturalistic communicative abilities of two-year-olds. *Child Development, 48,* 1052–57.

Wenar, C., & Kerig, P. (2000). *Developmental Psychopathology* (4th ed.). New York: McGraw-Hill.

Wentzel, K.R., & Asher, S.R. (1995). The academic lives of neglected, rejected, popular, and controversial children. *Child Development, 66,* 754–63.

Werner, H. (1957). The concept of development from a comparative and organismic point of view. In D.B. Harris (ed.), *The concept of development* (pp. 125–48). Minneapolis: University of Minnesota Press.

Wertsch, J.V. (1991). A sociocultural approach to socially shared cognition. In L.B. Resnick, J.M. Levine, & S.D. Teasley (eds.), *Perspectives on socially shared cognition* (pp. 85–100). Washington, DC: American Psychological Association.

Wertsch, J.V., & Tulviste, P. (1992). Vygotsky and contemporary developmental psychology. *Developmental Psychology, 28,* 548–57.

Williams, S., Anderson, J., McGee, R., & Silva, P.A. (1990). Risk factors for behavioural and emotional disorders in preadolescent children. *Journal of the American Academy of Child and Adolescent Psychiatry, 29,* 413–19.

Wilson, M.N. (1986). The black extended family: an analytical consideration. *Developmental Psychology, 22,* 246–58.

Wimmer, H., Landerl, K., & Schneider, W. (1994). The role of rhyme awareness in learning to read a regular orthography. *British Journal of Developmental Psychology, 12,* 469–84.

Wimmer, H., & Perner, J. (1983). Beliefs about beliefs: Representation and constraining function of wrong beliefs in young children's understanding of deception. *Cognition, 13,* 103–28.

Wing, L. (1993). The definition and prevalence of autism: a review. *European Child and Adolescent Psychiatry, 2,* 61–74.

Winner, E. (1988). *The point of words: Children's understanding of metaphor and irony.* Cambridge, MA: Harvard University Press.

Winner, E., & Leekam, S. (1991). Distinguishing irony from deception: Understanding the speaker's second-order intention. *British Journal of Developmental Psychology, 9,* 257–70.

Wintre, M.G., & Vallance, D.D. (1994). A developmental sequence in the comprehension of emotions: Intensity, multiple emotions and valence. *Developmental Psychology, 30,* 509–14.

Wood, D., & Middleton, D. (1975). A study of assisted problem-solving. *British Journal of Psychology, 66,* 181–91.

Wood, D., Bruner, J., & Ross, G. (1976). The role of tutoring in problem-solving. *Journal of Child Psychology and Psychiatry, 17,* 89–100.

Worobey, J., & Lewis, M. (1989). Individual differences in the activity of young infants. *Developmental Psychology, 25,* 663–7.

Yonas, A., & Owsley, C. (1987). Development of visual space perception. In P. Salapatek, & L. Cohen (eds.), *Handbook of infant perception. Vol. II. From sensation to perception* (pp. 80–122). Orlando, FL: Academic Press.

Younis, J. (1980). *Parents and peers in social development.* Chicago: University of Chicago Press.

Youniss, J., & Volpe, J. (1978). A relational analysis of children's friendships. In W. Damon (ed.), *New directions for child development* (No. 1, pp. 1–22). San Francisco: Jossey-Bass.

Zahn-Waxler, C., Cole, P.M., & Barrett, K.C. (1991). Guilt and empathy: sex differences and implications for the development of depression. In J. Garber, & K.A. Dodge (eds.), *The development of emotion regulation and dysregulation* (pp. 243–72). New York: Cambridge University Press.

Zelazo, P.R., Kearsley, R.B., & Ungerer, J.A. (1984). *Learning to speak: A manual for parents.* Hillsdale, NJ: Erlbaum.

Zelazo, P.R., Zelazo, N.A., & Kolb, S. (1972). 'Walking' in the newborn. *Science, 176,* 314–15.

Index

NOTE: page numbers in *italics* refer to figures or tables.